The English Martyr from Reformation to Revolution

ReFormations

MEDIEVAL AND EARLY MODERN

Series Editors:
David Aers, Sarah Beckwith, and James Simpson

ALICE DAILEY

The
English
Martyr

from Reformation to Revolution

University of Notre Dame Press
Notre Dame, Indiana

Manufactured in the United States of America

Library of Congress Cataloging-in-Publication Data

Dailey, Alice.
    The English martyr from reformation to revolution / Alice Dailey.
        p.   cm. — (ReFormations: Medieval and Early Modern)
    Includes bibliographical references and index.
    ISBN 978-0-268-02612-7 (pbk. : alk. paper) — ISBN 0-268-02612-2
(pbk. : alk. paper) — ISBN 978-0-268-07778-5 (ebook)
    1. Martyrs—England.   2. Martyrs in literature.   3. Martyrdom in literature.
4. Martyrdom—Christianity—History.   I. Title.
    BL626.5.D35   2012
    272.0942 — dc23
                                                                        2012030741

∞ *The paper in this book meets the guidelines for permanence and
durability of the Committee on Production Guidelines for
Book Longevity of the Council on Library Resources.*

For Josh

Contents

Acknowledgments
_____

Although the work of this book was largely done in solitude, I could not have written it alone. I owe thanks to several institutions and many special people. I am indebted to librarians and archivists across the western hemisphere, especially those of the Huntington Library, the Harry Ransom Center, the British Library, and the British National Archives. The final chapter of the book was written with the support of a fellowship from the Folger Shakespeare Library, where I spent several blissfully productive months. My research travel to London was funded by fellowships from my home institution, Villanova University.

Two extracts from this book have been published in article form: a section of chapter 2 appeared in *Prose Studies* 25.3 (2002) and is reprinted by permission of Taylor & Francis, and a section of chapter 3 appeared in *Religion and Literature* 38.3 (2006). Both chapters benefited from the advice of my referees and from the feedback of *Religion and Literature* special issue editors Graham Hammill and Julia Reinhard Lupton. I wish to thank Stephen Little at the University of Notre Dame Press for his warm professionalism; my copyeditor, Ann Delgehausen; my indexer, Meg Davies; and the production team at the press. I'm grateful for the incisive feedback I received from my two anonymous readers, who helped me to negotiate some of the book's stickier wickets. I am honored to be part of the ReFormations series and thank series editors David Aers, Sarah Beckwith, and James Simpson for their enthusiastic interest in the project.

This book began as a dissertation at UCLA, where I enjoyed the benefits of both fellowship and faculty support. Debora Shuger looked at many a half-baked draft with kindness and saintlike patience, and V. A. Kolve introduced me to a body of literature that continues to fascinate and excite me. My debt to Lowell Gallagher is inexpressible.

Lowell's mentorship at UCLA was only the beginning of his long and steady support of me and of this book. Without him, neither the book nor I would be what we have become. I am deeply grateful to Lowell for his gifts of time, passion, wisdom, and, above all, friendship.

I am fortunate to have a wonderful English department to call home. My colleagues at Villanova, especially Heather Hicks, Jean Lutes, and Lisa Sewell, have provided companionship, feedback, sympathy, and a collegial environment in which I have felt supported and appreciated. I am grateful to my chair, Evan Radcliffe, for the countless ways he helps me work better and for enabling me to explore many aspects of this project in the classroom. My thanks as well to the students who have peopled that classroom, greeting my quirks and enthusiasm with good humor, curiosity, and enthusiasm of their own, and to my graduate research assistant, Jessica Cortes, for her reliability and meticulousness. I could not have asked for a better colleague than my fellow early modernist at Villanova, Lauren Shohet. She is a model of personal and professional generosity, and I count myself exceptionally lucky to have her as a resource, mentor, and friend. It is thanks to Lauren that I came to join the Philadelphia Area Working Group in Early Modern Studies, an amazing group of scholars who have helped me to formulate important aspects of this project. They include Claire Busse, Jane Hedley, Matthew Kozusko, Zachary Lesser, Nichole Miller, Shannon Miller, Kristen Poole, Katherine Rowe, Eric Song, and Jamie Taylor. I am grateful to all for their reading and invaluable feedback.

No doubt everyone thinks they entered the profession with the brightest group of young scholars who ever blessed the academy, but I feel certain that such is the case with the early modernists who have enriched my thought and work as this book developed. My thanks to all the wonderful people who have offered ideas and feedback at conference panels, in Shakespeare Association seminars, and over postseminar cocktails. I especially want to thank Holly Crawford Pickett, who has been a valued friend and fellow religious lit scholar since early grad school. Regina Buccola and Jonathan Walker have read drafts, commiserated, and played hooky with me from Seattle to Stratford-upon-Avon, and their companionship has made my moments of doubt less daunting. Matt Kozusko is simply one of the best human beings I know, and I am grateful for his company at conferences and in Philadelphia, for his encouraging conversation over the years, and for his feedback on many chapters. I am thankful to Zack Lesser for his readings and rereadings of several sections of this book and for his level-headed advice at all turns. My life and work in Philadelphia would not be the same without Shawn Kairschner, my plucky companion to bad plays, my coconspirator in the classroom and out, my sounding board through many challenges of this project, and my dear friend.

I owe much to my parents, Steven and Margaret Leary, who filled our house with books and cultivated in us the independence to pursue our interests. I thank my mother especially for encouraging me as a writer and for her interest in this project. I am grateful for the unconditional love and friendship of my sister, Joyce Leary, who understands what it is to work long and work hard. And I thank my brother, Paul Leary, for his boundless energy, support, and love, which enrich immeasurably my life and my labors.

My son, Adam, ably supervised the final revisions to this book when he was but six weeks old. Although he can't yet read, write, walk, or talk, he has made my world anew.

Twenty years ago, after we had been dating only a few months, my husband, Josh, helped me pay my university tuition bill so that I could finish my bachelor's degree. In his infinite number of everyday gifts over our two decades together, he has made possible the life, the work, and the book I love.

Note on Spelling, Punctuation, and Editions

Although authoritative or scholarly editions have been cited when appropriate, many of the primary materials studied in this volume have not been reproduced in modern editions. In these cases, original editions or manuscripts are cited. The Corpus Christi plays are quoted in accordance with the Early English Text Society editions. For all other early texts, original punctuation, capitalization, and spelling are preserved with the exception of transposed i/j and u/v, the use of vv to signify w, and obsolete abbreviations, all of which have been modernized.

When a nation is powerful, it tells the world confident stories about the future. The stories can be enchanting or frightening, but they make sense of the world. But when that power begins to ebb, the stories fall apart. And all that are left are fragments that haunt you like half-forgotten dreams.

—Adam Curtis, *It Felt Like a Kiss*

Introduction

Being killed is an event. Martyrdom is a literary form, a genre.

—Daniel Boyarin, *Dying for God*

Father John Gerard was not a martyr, although the course of his life suggested he might be. Born in Derbyshire in 1564 and educated at Exeter College, Oxford, he left England to pursue the Catholic priesthood, taking Jesuit orders at the English College in Rome in 1588. He returned to England later that year in disguise and under an assumed name, serving the outlawed Catholic mission in secrecy until his arrest for high treason in 1594. In what might well look like incipient martyrdom, Gerard was imprisoned for more than three years under Elizabethan anti-Catholic statutes, during which time he was tortured repeatedly by rack and manacles. He would later write that he withstood the pain by recalling his desire for martyrdom, finding comfort in reminding himself, "you have often wanted to give your life for your Lord God." He was able to endure torture without betraying other Catholics, fortified as he was with "resignation" and "a desire to die."[1]

But Gerard did not die. On the night of October 4, 1597, he and a fellow Catholic prisoner escaped from the Tower to the safety of their confederates, who were waiting in a boat below. Why did Gerard choose to escape when he had already endured horrific torture and had only to await his inevitable execution? As his narrative attests, it

1

was not simply death he initially desired but martyrdom. And although death surely awaited him, martyrdom might not have. Writing in defense of English Catholics in 1582, Cardinal William Allen had complained that Elizabethan law, which made it treason to live in England as a priest or practicing Catholic, brought Catholics "into the sclaunderous suspition & obloquie of crimes never thought of" instead of condemning them for their faith and "ma[king] them away for religion without more a doe."[2] Allen's remarks point to the troublesome rhetorical disparity between an accusation of treason and an explicitly religious persecution. Like Allen's polemic, Gerard's paradoxical narration of both the desire for martyrdom and the unashamed escape from imprisonment and execution reveals a discrepancy between the treason proceeding and its potential for martyrological recuperation.

John Gerard intuited the foundational premise of this book: that martyrdom is not a death but a story that gets written about a death. Like Allen, he recognized the representational dissonance between the terms of his persecution and the structures of the martyrological genre. What awaited him if he remained in custody was a trial that would criminalize his allegiance to Rome and a popular press that would sensationalize his secret life. What awaited him was a barbarous execution that would inscribe on his body a heinous villain's story. In the rhetorical parameters of 1597, Gerard could not complete the martyrdom narrative he had begun. Unable to inhabit the story of a martyr, he evidently preferred to dislodge himself from the alternative narrative that was being composed for him: the story of a traitor.

The relationship between the paradigmatic martyr story and the unruly exigencies of history is the central interest of this book, which revisits an important body of literary-historical texts to ask new questions about the dialogue between history and literary form. The book posits martyrdom not merely as a narrowly drawn historical construction—a record of what people of the period thought, believed, and did—but as the enactment of a specific discursive protocol, a narrative construction whose potency persists only so far as its story can be told. This book argues that martyrdom is created through the interplay between blood and narrative, between the action of persecution and an always-mediating literary structure. Because the martyr is a retrospectively constructed figure created in and through literature, martyrology exposes the operations of form as much as the events of history or the imperatives of faith.

Traditionally, Christian martyrdom is a repetition of the story of Christ's suffering and death; the more closely the victim's narrative replicates the Christological model, the more legible the martyrdom.[3] But if the textual construction of martyrdom depends on the rehearsal of a paradigmatic story, how does the discourse reconcile the broad range of individuals, beliefs, and persecutions seeking legitimation in martyrology? Through close study of texts ranging from late-medieval passion drama and hagiography to John Foxe's *Acts and Monuments* and the martyrologies of the English Counter-Reformation to King Charles I's *Eikon Basilike* and John Milton's *Eikonoklastes*, this book considers the shifting religio-political rhetoric of Reformation and post-Reformation England, studying the effects of this shift on the capacity of individuals from rival factions to occupy the coveted position of martyrological victim. The book discovers early modern persecutions, like that of John Gerard, that conventional martyrological structures cannot successfully accommodate, describing the formal and circumstantial features that force this rupture and tracing its lasting effects on the discourse.

Much has been written on the topic of early modern martyrdom in recent years, an outcome of the "turn to religion" in literary studies.[4] This turn has generated a rich and nuanced account of early modern England's complex religious climate. For the past two decades, scholars have progressively refined our notions of what it meant to be Catholic and Protestant as the Reformation unfolded, limned the sites where those identities overlapped, and argued persuasively for religion's significance in political, social, and private spheres. The principal interest of this influential body of work has been the illumination of cultural history, and in this respect, the turn to religion has come to reflect the current dominance of historical and cultural criticism in literary studies. Under the sway of New Historicism, work on religious literature has often sought to elide the difference between literary artifacts and other forms of cultural expression, participating thereby in a broader erosion of the disciplinary distinctions between literary and nonliterary modes of inquiry.[5] The Jamesonian imperative "Always historicize!" has evolved into a literary criticism that is often diluted of the formalist investments that would distinguish it from the work of historians.[6]

The antiformalism embedded in much historicist practice limits what can be said about literature as literature, leaving scholars like Stephen Cohen, Heather Dubrow, Mark David Rasmussen, Richard Strier, and Douglas Bruster to call for a return to form.[7] Rather than proposing a break with historicist criticism in a reprised New Critical practice that would isolate and reify the literary text, historical formalism reads form as history and history as form. Cohen writes, "historical formalism neither imposes nor assumes any simple understanding of form, history, or the relationship between them, but instead explores the complexity of their mutual implication. If, generally speaking, form is the set of techniques and conventions that characterize literature and mark its difference from other social practices, those characteristics are neither unchanging, intrinsic, nor autonomous, but historically specific, historically determined, and historically efficacious."[8] In this model, the text is not reduced to a reflection of cultural values or a site where cultural pressures get expressed. Literary texts are not "anecdotes or synecdoches of the real," as Bruster has put it.[9] The literature is the thing itself. In ways that are specific to its forms, literature structures the world it describes and organizes the audience's engagement with that world. The literary form operates as a medium, Cohen argues—the "middle term," between author and audience and between text and context—and as such, literary forms function "not simply as containers for extrinsic ideological content, but as practices with an ideological significance of their own."[10] These practices are themselves constituted by history and constitutive of it.

The work of this book extends historical formalism beyond poetry and drama, where it gained its first footholds, to the enormously popular medieval and early modern genre of martyrology.[11] Martyrology presents a unique case study, a junction point between history and form. Its implicit claim to be the unmediated documentation of lived events has logically made it fruitful territory for historicist inquiry. Brad Gregory's magisterial *Salvation at Stake* usefully outlines the range of martyr experiences across early modern Europe, for example, but it likewise exposes the limitations of historicist readings of martyrology that elide the centrality of discursive form to both the performance and narration of martyrdom. Gregory's aim—to "plumb the living souls of early modern martyrs," thereby producing a reading that is "intelligible on the martyrs' own terms"—reads martyrology as a transparent record of early modern Christian belief.[12] In its inattention to the literary structures that order the reproduction of martyrdom, such conventional historiographic studies miss the constitutive pressure that form asserts over historical events.

Martyrology mediates historical events through literary form, a form that itself has a history, a history that the form everywhere self-consciously indexes. At the same time, that form gives shape to what transpires in private devotion, in the courtroom, on the scaffold, and in the close chambers of the Tower. Genre structures the history that the genre in turn narrativizes, and vice versa. To adequately address these relations, we must attend to genre, as Julia Reinhard Lupton reminds us, because genre "situates the work in the matrix of conventions that make up not the context, outside, or prehistory of the work, but the very being of the work in time."[13] This kind of critical practice introduces questions that conventional historicist inquiry cannot ask, let alone answer. How does the victim's anticipation of being narrativized—of being recuperated by devotional text and memory—structure the experience of persecution? Can martyrdom ever entirely precede martyrology?

Such questions enable us to think about what Barbara Fuchs calls "the political effectivity of genre—how it not only reflects but creates its ideological context."[14] The boundaries that have conventionally organized studies of religious literature disable these lines of inquiry, especially those that lead to the critical isolation of Catholic from Protestant and medieval from early modern.[15] By placing the genre of English martyrology on a longer, cross-confessional developmental continuum, this book offers a corrective to the field's tendency to periodize and confessionalize. Susannah Brietz Monta's *Martyrdom and Literature in Early Modern England* aims "to think about religion and religious habits of representation cross-confessionally," arguing that Catholic and Protestant martyrologists employ shared strategies to create and reinforce interpretive and confessional communities.[16] By extending Monta's claim both backward and forward chronologically, this book observes the continuities and ruptures in representational habits that arise when an old genre encounters the new challenges of radical historical change. *The English Martyr from Reformation to Revolution* traces the development of martyr discourse in England from its biblical roots and medieval paradigms through the roughly hundred years of intense religious controversy spanning from about 1550 to 1650. As such, it does not offer an exhaustive study of either the Catholic or Protestant martyrological traditions, nor does it attempt an account of the broader forms of Christian witnessing represented by figures like the confessor. Rather, it unfolds a dialectic between key martyrological texts and political, legal, and religious developments to argue that generic shifts have less to do with confessional identity than with the specific rhetorical and historical circumstances of discursive production. In this way, the book works to realize what Cohen has described as historical formalism's potential for "revealing literature to be not simply a site of ideological conformation or contradiction, but a model of a more multivalent social interaction, and an engine of social and political change."[17] Through this lens it becomes evident, for example, that even the seemingly fixed and timeless martyrological imperative of *imitatio Christi* means something different in 1606 than what it means in 1649, an observation that becomes possible only through attention to the interdynamics of history and form.

The book's opening chapter describes the model of martyrdom inherited by early modern England by tracing the conventional features of medieval martyr literature through Jacobus de Voragine's thirteenth-century *Golden Legend* and the Christ figure of the late-medieval vernacular passion plays. By examining the structures by which these texts are organized, the chapter describes the dominant performative and narrative topoi of Christian martyrological literature: how a martyr behaves, what the transaction between victim and persecutor consists of, and how the martyr's transcendent status is represented. Although Protestant martyrologist John Foxe vehemently rejected *The Golden Legend* as a model for his work, the second chapter in this book, on Foxe's *Acts and Monuments,* demonstrates that both the victims of the

Marian persecution and their martyrologist necessarily relied on the formulations of Christian suffering popularized by the medieval tradition. The production of early modern martyrdom hinges on the victim's ability to operate simultaneously in two seemingly incompatible frameworks: local and transcendent, or historical and typological. While Foxe's martyrology documents specific moments in history, its narrative and performative references to Christ's passion and the early martyrs ensure that those moments contain within them the whole of the Christian martyr tradition, effectively transfiguring the victim into a heroic soldier in the sacred struggle of the persecuted church. Indeed, Foxe's martyrological discourse is the textual site of this transfiguration.

But what happens when history and typology do not coincide — when, rather, historical circumstances produce an event that cannot be absorbed by martyrological paradigms? This is the question that occupies chapters 3 through 5, which study the martyr discourses of the Catholic Counter-Reformation in England. These chapters explore how the claims of martyrdom made by the Elizabethan and Jacobean Catholic community are frustrated by the rhetoric of treason, which comes to organize both government discourse and compensatory Catholic narratives. Chapter 3 focuses on the 1581 execution of Edmund Campion, the first Jesuit executed in England during the Elizabethan persecution, and the wave of polemical responses it generated, in particular William Allen's *A Briefe Historie of the Glorious martyrdom of XII Reverend Priests* and *Defense of English Catholics*, and *The Execution of Justice in England* by William Cecil, Lord Burghley. These texts disclose emerging fault lines in the construction of conventional martyrdom — faultlines produced by the discursive structures of the treason trial and execution ritual.

Chapter 4 explores the implications of the treason charge on the reproduction of the martyrological miracle — traditionally the incontrovertible, external evidence of the victim's sanctity and salvation — arguing that generic fracture becomes visible in this foundational narrative topos. The chapter studies two martyrologies: Father John Mush's *The Life and Martyrdom of Mistress Margaret Clitherow*, the story of a Catholic recusant pressed to death in 1586 for refusing to enter a plea in her treason trial; and John Gennings's *The Life and Death of M. Edmund Geninges Priest,* a martyrology of the author's brother, caught saying Mass and executed in London in 1591. Building on the discursive developments traced in chapter 3, this chapter demonstrates how the textual reproduction of martyrdom is compromised by an internal cleft in the structure of the miracle topos, a development that confessionally-bound and historiographic readings cannot see.

Chapter 5 thinks about these generic and representational fractures in relation to several primary texts connected with the Gunpowder Plot and the Jesuit mission in England, including the trial and execution accounts of Fr. Robert Southwell and Jesuit Superior Henry Garnet, who introduced the doctrine of equivocation into the discourse of Catholic recusancy; Garnet's *Treatise of Equivocation* and subsequent texts in the equivocation controversy; and *The Autobiography of a Hunted Priest,* Father Gerard's fascinating account of disguises, coded speech, and invisible handwriting from the period of his imprisonment and escape from the Tower. These texts describe a martyrological subject in hiding—a compromised figure caught in the paradoxical imperative to both "enclose and disclose."[18] Despite the texts' efforts to draw legible parallels to typological martyr models, the reproduction of the genre becomes compromised by the tactics of elusiveness and obscurity, which have no established provenance in the Christian martyrological tradition.

Having mapped the subtle unraveling of conventional martyr typology, the book then concludes with a chapter on the transformation of the martyr figure in two key texts from the execution of King Charles I: *Eikon Basilike* and Milton's *Eikonoklastes.* In *Eikon Basilike,* Charles relocates the sacred from exterior to interior—from God and the Word to his own conscience, which becomes sacralized through his death. Conscience thus functions as a formal solution to the discursive fracture traced by the preceding chapters. Reconstituting the site of martyrological truth, *Eikon Basilike* adopts a radical subjectivity, divorcing the martyr figure from history. In a text that has survived as the antagonistic double of *Eikon Basilike,* Milton's *Eikonoklastes* rejects Charles's claims to martyrdom by insisting on martyrdom as a visible, historical event, not the carefully crafted series of rhetorical gestures modeled by *Eikon Basilike*. Milton's text attests to both the representational limitations and the rhetorical potency of Charles's renovation of martyrdom.

By setting history and form in conversation with one another, *The English Martyr from Reformation to Revolution* describes not only the reformation of one of the oldest, most influential genres of the Christian West but a revolution in the very concept of martyrdom. The title's reference to Reformation and Revolution thus points to the interrelatedness of its historical and formal investments — to the events that shape and reshape the martyrological form and to literary form as it acts upon events. Rather than the static, embalmed genre produced by readings that bracket literary form, martyrology emerges in this study as deeply nuanced and subtly responsive to historical circumstance. This adaptability is evident in the resurgence of martyr discourse in contemporary representational contests between radical-Islamacist violence and secular-Western encomium, as the book's postscript suggests. From medieval notions of strict typological repetition, martyrdom develops through the late sixteenth and early seventeenth centuries into Charles I's defense of individual conscience — an abstracted, metaphorized form of martyrdom that survives into modernity.

Chapter 1

Medieval Models

The Golden Legend and the Corpus Christi Passion Plays

We are confronted with a wondrous play—an iniquitous judge,

a bloodthirsty torturer, a martyr unconquered, a contest between

cruelty and piety.

—Augustine

Augustine's summary of the principal elements of the drama of martyrdom illustrates a defining characteristic of martyr literature that will be revisited time and again through the course of this study: its narrative formula.[1] In order for an individual to be inscribed into the transcendent narrative of Christian martyrological suffering, his or her story must contain the legible markers of that suffering. These markers, as Augustine suggests, include not only the structural components of the narrative—judge, torturer, martyr, and contest—but a set of organizing behavioral attributes: iniquity, bloodthirstiness, invulnerability. A victim's death becomes a martyr's story only when the actors play their parts legibly and follow martyrdom's paradigmatic script.

This chapter explores the complexity of that script, disclosing the subtle multidimensionality of Augustine's "martyr unconquered," the discourse's complex representations of "cruelty," and the paradoxical—

even contradictory—modes of constructing martyrological "piety." The chapter studies two strands of the martyrological tradition: *The Golden Legend* of Jacobus de Voragine, a collection of stories about the martyrs and saints of the early church, and the late-medieval passion plays of the Corpus Christi drama cycle. Though scriptural accounts of Christ's suffering establish the *imitatio Christi* tradition, ostensibly providing the model for all Christian martyrdom to follow, comparison of medieval passion dramas and martyr legends reveals two distinct traditions, both of which will figure importantly in later martyrology. One is the truculent, belligerent, and seemingly unassailable martyr of the early church, who goads the persecutor and feels no pain. The other is the dramatized Christ—passive, suffering, and largely silent. Examining the structures that organize concepts of martyrdom, the chapter describes the dominant performative, narrative, and interpretive mechanisms of Christian martyrological literature, mapping at once the complexity and the rigidity of its representational forms.

The Golden Legend

The Golden Legend was written in the mid-thirteenth century by Jacobus de Voragine, a Dominican monk who held a number of important clerical offices, including the archbishopric of Genoa, before his death in 1298. The volume gained enormous popularity throughout Europe, especially later in the period, as William Granger Ryan notes: "The popularity of the *Legend* was such that some one thousand manuscripts have survived, and, with the advent of printing in the 1450s, editions both in the original Latin and in every Western European language multiplied into the hundreds. It has been said that in the late Middle Ages the only book more widely read was the Bible."[2] It was one of the first volumes translated by Caxton, whose English edition appeared in 1483, with another eight editions by 1527.[3] Publication figures suggest even greater popularity for other European vernacular translations.[4] In addition to its own widespread use as a devotional text, *The Golden Legend* engendered the production of other popular vernacular books of saints, such as Osbern Bokenham's *Legendys of*

Hooly Women and the *South English Legendary,* both of which borrow heavily from Jacobus.

Arranged according to the calendar of the church's feast days, *The Golden Legend* describes the history and theological foundations of celebrations such as the Birth of the Blessed Virgin and the Conversion of Saint Paul. But the bulk of the text is taken up with some 160 saints' legends, 93 of which are about martyrs. The martyr narratives are drawn from the Bible and from a range of patristic sources such as Augustine and Ambrose. The extent to which Jacobus exerted authorial liberty in shaping and arranging his source materials has been the subject of some critical discussion. Ryan, for example, calls the volume "basically the work of a compiler," while Sherry Reames argues for the singularity of Jacobus's vision and product.[5] The mere popularity of Jacobus's text ensured that its version of these legends, however idiosyncratic in the range of martyrological works composed throughout the church's history, became the definitive representation of martyrdom for late-medieval European Christianity.

The Maccabees Model

Christianity's earliest models of martyrdom originate from the Old Testament story of the persecution of the Jews under the pagan king Antiochus. In the second book of Maccabees, the Jews are forced to abandon the sabbath, to allow their synagogues to be used for pagan debauchery and sacrifices, and to give up adherence to the laws of Moses or suffer torture and execution. This persecution produces the Maccabees martyrs—the veteran scribe Eleazar and a family of seven brothers and their mother. Eleazar, an elderly and important member of the Jewish community, chooses to be executed rather than eat pork, publicly and consciously making an example of himself. Upon Eleazar's refusal of the pork, his fellow elders suggest that he merely pretend to eat it while actually consuming another meat, but he refuses this charade, claiming, "Such pretense is not worthy of our time of life" and that doing so would give younger generations the wrong impression: "By bravely giving up my life now, I will show myself worthy of my old age and leave to the young a noble example of how to die a good death willingly and nobly for the revered and holy laws."[6] Eleazar then submits to be tortured to death, saying that he is "glad to suffer" because he does so out of reverence for God.[7] The mother and her seven sons, whose story is told in the next chapter, are martyred for the same offense. Announcing their preference of violent death to the violation of Jewish law, one after another undergoes a series of horrific and ultimately fatal tortures: each has his tongue cut out, his scalp removed, and his hands and feet cut off, and then is finally thrown into a heated frying pan and cooked to death. Before dying, each brother defiantly makes a statement about his faith in eternal life or the punishment awaiting the Jews' persecutors, suggesting that it is the victim, not the tormentor, who triumphs through these executions.[8]

The Maccabees martyrs are the only Old Testament figures celebrated in the calendar of saints' feast days outlined by *The Golden Legend*.[9] Jacobus explains their inclusion by stating that it is because they were martyred and suffered great torture that they "are accorded the privilege of having their passion celebrated" (2.33). Furthermore, the brothers' mystical number of seven, "the number of universality," allows them to stand for all the deserving patriarchs of the Old Testament in the church calendar (2.33). Most importantly, they are included for the model they provide Christians in their patient suffering and their willingness to be tortured and killed for the laws by which they live, "just as Christians suffer in defense of the law of the Gospel" (2.33).

The Maccabees martyrs are more than mere examples for the Christian; their story illustrates several elements of martyrological storytelling that become the template for Christian martyrologists like Jacobus himself.[10] It describes elaborate tortures but does not image individuals in concomitant physical agony (or any sensation whatever, in the case of the seven brothers), instead depicting heroic resilience and imperturbability. By contrast, the figure of the persecutor is easily enraged, devising fantastic means of inflicting pain to satisfy his sadism and temper. The speeches of the martyrs announce their rejection of earthly concerns in favor of heavenly, and their words and behavior signal them as moral superiors whose serenity and courage in the face of violent death prove them victorious over the evil represented by their tormentor. These elements form the foundation of the martyr story as it is rendered by *The Golden Legend* and other medieval martyrology, where the dynamic between martyr and persecutor, the representations of torture and the individual being tortured, and the words spoken by the martyr draw on the patterns established by the stories in Maccabees.[11]

The Narrative of Saint Laurence

One of the lengthiest and richest of *The Golden Legend*'s martyr narratives, the legend of Saint Laurence offers a model of medieval martyrological structures and topoi. After describing the political circumstances surrounding the Christian persecution under Decius (c. 257 c.e.), Jacobus narrates the capture, torture, and death of Saint Laurence, whose passion "is seen to stand out above the passions of the other martyrs" (2.70). Believing that Laurence possesses a great store of the church's money, Decius's prefect demands that he produce the treasure, becoming very angry when he comes to understand that the "treasure" is the Christian people, not a hoard of cash. Laurence is then ordered to sacrifice to the pagan idols, the plot point that operates as the central site of friction between Christian martyrs and pagan persecutors throughout *The Golden Legend*. Already angered by the misunderstanding over the treasure, Decius becomes enraged when Laurence refuses to offer pagan sacrifice. Decius orders him to be whipped with scorpions and subjected to "all sorts of tortures," to which Laurence responds, "Unhappy man, this is the banquet I have always desired!" (2.66).[12] Laurence is then beaten with clubs and leaden whips and has heated blades pressed to his sides. None of this seems to faze the martyr, who hopes for death and asks God to receive his spirit. A voice from heaven tells him that he has "many trials" still to endure, which incenses Decius still further (2.66). He accuses Laurence of withstanding torture through witchcraft and orders him whipped once again with scorpions. During this second whipping, the smiling Laurence thanks God and prays for the bystanders.

Through the course of his torture, Laurence effects the conversion of several of Decius's men, including a soldier named Romanus who claims that he can see an angel offering the saint succor in his passion: "I see a beautiful young man standing in front of you and wiping your limbs with a towel!" (2.66). Romanus is later baptized by Laurence and, confessing himself a Christian before Decius, is beheaded. Threatened then with a night-long torture session unless he submits to pagan sacrifice, Laurence tells Decius, "My night has no darkness, and all things gleam in the light!" (2.66). This incites Decius to have Laurence thrown on an iron grill heated with burning coals while hot iron pitchforks are pressed into him. Laurence's response reflects both serenity and defiance: "'Learn, wretched man, that your coals are refreshing to me but will be an eternal punishment to you, because the Lord himself knows that being accused I have not denied him, being put to the question I have confessed Christ, and being roasted I give thanks!' And with a cheerful countenance he said to Decius: 'Look, wretch, you have me well done on one side, turn me over and eat!'" (2.67). Giving thanks to God, Laurence finally dies.

The legend goes on to clarify the date of Laurence's death and to narrate a number of miracles related to his relics and intercession, concluding with a lengthy discussion of the superiority of his passion to that of other martyrs. The first reason Jacobus gives that Laurence's martyrdom is remarkable is the singular "bitterness of his sufferings" (2.70). Forced to undergo multiple tortures heaped on one another, Laurence surpasses other martyrs who are merely beheaded or who suffer pain in only one part of their body. Jacobus further notes that while other martyrs are said to have suffered equal or even greater pain than Laurence, their stories are unsubstantiated: Laurence's "martyrdom is authenticated and approved, because, while greater torments are attributed to some others, their authenticity is uncertain and sometimes held to be doubtful" (2.70). Second, Laurence's martyrdom is superlative because of "its effectiveness or usefulness" (2.70). His defeat of the raging persecutor, his physical suffering to gain heavenly salvation, his holiness of living, and his example of faith and "fortitude of spirit" made the fire of his martyrdom a light that "warmed the hearts of all Christians" (2.71–72). The final reason for Laurence's special place among martyrs is "his wonderful fight and the mode of his victory," which Jacobus discusses in some detail, describing five external fires that threatened him and three "refrigerants" that cooled these fires and led to his blessed death (2.72–73).[13] Further, he burned with three internal fires—faith, love, and knowledge of God—that rivaled the external fires and, according to Jacobus's quote from Ambrose, "heated him inwardly" so that he did not feel the burning of the torturer's flames (2.74). It is these qualities that render Laurence's martyrdom remarkable and make the celebration of his feast a special event in the liturgical calendar.[14] With this, Jacobus concludes the legend of Saint Laurence, a narrative that articulates many of the basic elements of late-medieval martyrological story-telling.

"The Banquet I Have Always Desired"

G. W. H. Lampe remarks that postapostolic martyrs like Laurence held death in itself as "the goal and crown of discipleship and the supreme mode of union with Christ."[15] The original apostles, even those who were martyred, were primarily concerned with the proliferation of the gospel and the expansion of the Christian church. Although martyrdom was not an aim in itself, these earliest Christian martyrs nonetheless believed in the salvific and exemplary power of offering their lives for their beliefs. For example, Jacobus tells how the apostle Andrew, having been condemned for preaching Christianity, is handed over to be crucified, a punishment that the gathering crowd believes is unjust. Andrew urges them not to interfere with his martyrdom, however, embracing the cross as the object of his longing and the answer to his prayers: "O good cross, honored and beautified by the limbs of the Lord, long desired, constantly loved, ceaselessly sought, and now prepared for my wishful heart!" (1.17). Peter approaches his death on the cross with similar willingness; like Andrew, he begs a crowd angered by the brutal scene not to hinder his martyrdom (1.345).

The desire for death evidenced by Andrew and Peter grows into an active pursuit of martyrdom in Jacobus's stories of the Christian persecutions of the second and third centuries. As Lampe's observation suggests, martyrdom ceases to be a hazard of Christian witnessing and becomes an end in itself, a means of securing salvation and situating oneself at the top of an elaborate hierarchy of the saved. Comparison of Jacobus's narratives to one of his main sources, the *Ecclesiastical History* of Eusebius, reveals that the active longing for death was not necessarily a historical reality for those who died for the faith but, rather, is a feature of the genre of martyrological literature as it develops in the Middle Ages. The stories of martyrdom in Eusebius are darkened by the reality of the many Christians who recanted their faith and were thereby ignobly preserved from torture and execution at the cost of their souls.[16] On the contrary, *The Golden Legend* leaves one with the distinct impression that nothing of the kind ever happened and that Christians eagerly embraced death.[17] The notion—reinforced by literary representations of martyrdom—that the summit of Christian devotion was the active pursuit of a martyr's death held powerful sway through the Middle Ages, as evidenced by figures like Theresa of Avila, whose writings reflect an obsessive preoccupation with the desire for martyrdom.

The men and women who populate *The Golden Legend* express their hope for martyrdom in several ways, such as Laurence's description of torture as the "banquet I have always desired" (2.66). In other stories, the martyr signals his or her wish for death by simply appearing before the persecutor and announcing Christian beliefs, as with Laurence's convert Romanus. A particularly clear example is provided by the legend of Saint Ignatius, who presents himself to Trajan knowing he will be martyred. In the letters the saint wrote before his martyrdom, which Jacobus quotes from Eusebius, Ignatius expresses his great anticipation:

> O salutary beasts that are being readied for me! When will they come? When will they be turned loose? When will they be allowed to feast on my flesh? I shall invite them to devour me! I shall beg them to begin, lest they be afraid to touch my body as they have been with some others. I shall use force, I shall throw myself upon them! Pardon me, Romans, I beg of you! I know

what is best for me—fire, crosses, wild beasts, my bones scattered about, limb being torn from limb and flesh from bone, all the devil's tortures piled upon me, if only I may gain Christ! (1.141)

Ignatius imagines his gruesome death with particular relish, but nearly every martyr story in *The Golden Legend* makes use of this element, if more subtly. Jacobus's martyrs do everything in their power to call attention to themselves, enrage their persecutors, and incite violence, knowing that the pagans cannot help taking the bait. Saint Apollonia's zeal drives her to break free of her bonds and throw herself into the fire prepared for her, leaving her persecutors "shocked beyond measure at finding a woman even more eager to undergo death than they to inflict it" (1.269). Similarly, Saint Vincent eagerly places himself on the grill heated for his death, where he is cooked and stabbed with pikes (1.106). Indeed, there is a marked difference between the approach to death evidenced by the apostles Peter and Andrew and what is described in *The Golden Legend.* The attitude of the former, Lampe notes, is "primarily defensive," while the latter martyrs "really tak[e] the initiative."[18]

In their desire for martyrdom, Jacobus's saints clearly communicate what they understand their deaths to signify. Exhorting two young men to remain strong in the face of their parents' pleas that they spare themselves, Saint Sebastian delivers a sermon on the virtues of rejecting the earthly life for the heavenly: "Since the world began, life has betrayed those who placed their hopes in it, has deceived their expectations, has fooled those who took its goods for granted, and so it has left nothing certain and proves itself false to all" (1.98). Reminding the men of the relative insignificance of their temporary physical sufferings in the face of the promise of eternal bliss, he concludes, "Therefore let us stir up our desire, our love for martyrdom!" (1.98). The apostle Andrew prays for death as a liberation from his body, a "most burdensome garment" whose weaknesses and desires have waged unwelcome "assaults" on his spiritual repose (1.18). Here martyrdom is envisioned as a spiritually superior choice—the ultimate sacrifice of the earthly for the heavenly.[19] Further, as we learn in the story of Saint Maurice and his companions, who offer their heads to the executioner "with joyful hearts" because of the "fervor of their love," martyrdom comes to symbolize human beings' ultimate gesture of love for their creator (2.191). In turn, as we saw in the case of Laurence, the fire of this love helps to preserve the martyr from the fires and other tortures of the persecutor.

The emphasis in *The Golden Legend* on ardently desired martyrdom exposes a hierarchy of martyr experiences that is suggested in Jacobus's discussion of Laurence and is a pervasive theme of the work. Jacobus describes different levels of martyrdom based on the suffering and significance of the martyr's death, placing Laurence at the top.[20] In his legend of Saint Stephen, the first martyr after Christ, he further outlines this hierarchy, describing three kinds of martyrdom: "the first is willed and endured, the second willed but not endured, the third endured without being willed" (1.50). Both the desire to die for Christ and the good fortune of execution are necessary to achieving the highest level, where most of Jacobus's martyrs sit. But even those who both will and suffer death are hierarchized according to a set of values that structure the martyrs' procedure through their trials and tortures. It is based on sex, social standing, and suffering. In the story of Sebastian, a woman whom the saint has converted professes her faith, is tortured, and dies, leaving her husband to complain that the women are being crowned with martyrdom ahead of the men (1.100). The high-born martyr Euphemia, observing the torture of other Christians, complains to the judge, "I am of noble birth, and I want to know why you put these nobodies, these common folks, ahead of me, letting them reach Christ and attain the promised glory before I do!" (2.181). Repeatedly, the material wealth and social rank of martyrs is emphasized (especially with young women, where beauty is also a mark of superiority), and the sacrifice of this wealth and position is offered as evidence of their particular holiness. As Helen White observes, Jacobus "had a taste for the remarkable and the dramatic, and in view of the suffering ahead of the martyr and the bare, hard life in store for the saint, it is not surprising that, as a rule, he selected those who in choosing the straight and narrow path gave up most, and that he delighted in emphasizing the splendor of the sacrifice."[21]

This value system is evident as well in Eusebius, who includes education among wealth and class as one of the qualities of an eminent martyr.[22] The final hierarchical organizer, suffering, guides the martyr in the shaping of his or her story, as in the case of Saint Adrian, whose zealous wife encourages him to ask that in addition to his other tortures, his hand be amputated "so that he would be on a par with the other saints, who had suffered more than he had" (2.163). Adrian finds that there are plenty of torments to go around.

Martyrological Violence

In addition to the martyr's active desire for death, spectacular violence forms an essential component of Jacobus's martyr story. Threats of torture, the various tortures inflicted, and the martyr's responses to torture make up the bulk of any given martyr narrative in *The Golden Legend.* The tortures endured by Laurence only begin to scratch the surface of the variety of violence inflicted on Jacobus's martyrs. In other stories, martyrs are hung up by their hair, torn with rakes and hooks, flayed, boiled in a variety of liquids, fried in pans, burned alive, mutilated with specially designed torture devices, racked, crucified, pierced with arrows and other weapons, and subjected to a variety of amputations, to provide but an inexhaustive list. Amid this wide range of tortures, there is one element common to them all, illustrated by Laurence: the martyr's reaction to violence. The martyrs of *The Golden Legend* respond to physical violence with a mixture of defiance and joy, mocking their persecutors' futile attempts at making them recant and rejoicing in the opportunity to suffer for God.

In martyrological literature, violence is a vehicle by which the martyr—not the persecutor—gains and exhibits power over the human body and human nature. Violence operates as a cleansing purgative that gives the martyr power over the flesh, an aspect of the martyr experience that Vincent articulates. Having been racked and torn, the saint is asked if he is willing to sacrifice to the idols, to which he responds, "O happy me! The harder you try to frighten me, the more you begin to do me favors! Up, then, wretch, and indulge your malicious will to the full! You will see that by God's power I am stronger in being tortured than you are in torturing me" (1.106). Enraged, the emperor Dacian then proceeds with further tortures:

So he was taken down from the rack and carried to a gridiron with a fire under it. The saint reproached the torturers for being too slow and hastened ahead of them toward the suffering that awaited him. Willingly mounting the grill he was seared, singed, and roasted, and iron hooks and red-hot spikes were driven into his body. Wound was piled upon wound, and, as the flames spread, salt was thrown on the fire so that the hissing flames could make the wounds more painful. The weapons of torture tore past his joints and into his belly, so that the intestines spilled out from his body. Yet with all this he remained unmovable, and turning his eyes toward heaven, prayed to the Lord. (1.106)

According to Prudentius' account of the martyrdom, Vincent responds to his tortures by claiming, "Torments, dungeons, iron claws, fiery spikes, and death, the ultimate pain—all this is play to Christians."[23] Vincent's remark exposes Christian martyrs' underlying attitude toward torture: it is fundamentally a game they engage for their own benefit, one that makes them stronger while the persecutor believes it does harm. It is a staged event—an opportunity for the martyr to demonstrate the complete renunciation of the flesh by exhibiting unconcern with the violence inflicted on his or her body.

In the story of Vincent and throughout *The Golden Legend*, torture also functions as a means of making the saint more pliable to the will of God. Augustine describes how Vincent "was stretched and twisted to make him suppler, scourged to make him learn better, pummeled to make him more robust, burned to make him cleaner."[24] Saint Agatha believes that her spirit can be made pure enough for heaven only if her body is mortified: "These pains are my delight," she tells her tormentor; "my soul cannot enter paradise unless you make the headsman give my body harsh treatment" (1.155). For Dionysius, the torture of being burned alive brings him to greater understanding of the word of God and is cause for thanksgiving: "Thy word is refined by fire," he says, "and thy servant has loved it" (2.240).

Far from weakening the martyr, violence serves as a source of strength, increasing spiritual status as well as the power of his or her example to others. Ambrose observes in his story of Laurence: "We may compare the blessed martyr Laurence to the mustard seed, because, rubbed and crushed by many sufferings, he merited to spread throughout the whole earth the fragrance of his mystery. Previously he was unimpressive in body, unknown and unrecognized, a nobody: after he was tortured, torn apart, roasted, he infused all the churches throughout the world with the aroma of his nobility."[25] Like Bartholomew, who "purpled the earth with [his] gore," Laurence is imagined as undergoing an atomizing violence that acts as a means by which the message of his martyrdom and faith is dispersed throughout the Christian world, a phenomenon described in the pointedly sensory terms of the wafting smell of his roasting flesh (2.116). Violent persecution raises his spiritual status as it "infuse[s]" or rejuvenates the church. The story of Peter Martyr constructs a similar metaphor: "Thus the grain of wheat, falling into the ground and caught and killed by the hands of unbelievers, brings forth abundant fruit; thus the bunch of grapes, crushed in the winepress, gives out juice in plenty; thus spices, ground in the mortar, pour forth a richer perfume; thus mustard seed is all the stronger once it is pulverized" (1.259).[26] In its specific formulation of the saint's body as caught and killed, crushed, ground, and pulverized, the topos emphasizes the role of violence in the benefit the saint then provides as sustaining and regenerative food for the church.

The notion that violence inflicted on the martyr's body makes him or her a source of sustenance for Christ's people is also at the root of *The Golden Legend*'s images of the martyr's wounded body bleeding milk instead of blood. Most commonly, milk emanates from the wounds of female martyrs—particularly from severed breasts, as in the legend of Saint Christina (1.387).[27] But milk flows from a variety of wounds. The narrative of Saint Blaise includes the story of seven women whom the saint converted to the faith who were martyred after having their flesh torn with iron rakes. Instead of appearing gruesomely disfigured, "their flesh was seen to be white as driven snow, and from their torn bodies milk flowed instead of blood" (1.153). Milk flows from the decapitated body of Saint Catherine (2.339), while the head of Saint Paul, which has a number of adventures after being severed from his body, spurts both milk and blood (1.354). In all of these examples, the milky wound signals two phenomena: it transforms the wound—a violent rending of the body—into a life-giving spring, and it situates the martyr's body as a metaphorical food source for the church, a food source made available only through the violence of the persecutor.

The mutilated human-body-as-food echoes Laurence's provocative claim that violent death is the "banquet I have always desired" (2.66). Coupled with his taunt to his persecutor to "turn me over and eat" while being roasted alive, Laurence's description of martyrdom as a banquet suggests that he imagines himself offering his body to his tormentors as food: abandoning the flesh, he presents his body to the world to be eaten so that he may "through the torture . . . bec[o]me more powerful in fear of the Lord, more fervent in love, more joyous in ardor" (2.67, 2.72). Saint Ignatius imagines his body refined through violence into a Eucharist-like bread: "I am the wheat of Christ! May I be ground fine by the teeth of the beasts, that I may be made clean bread!" (1.142).

The Golden Legend's treatment of violence is fundamentally paradoxical, a feature these narratives share with the passion of Christ. Although martyrdom, by its very definition, relies on the violent persecution of one party by another, in both Christ's passion and those of Jacobus's martyrs, violent death serves an important purpose for the one who suffers and for the cause for which he or she is persecuted. In *The Golden Legend*, martyrdom is figured as useful not only to the individual, who gains salvation, but to the church, which relies on martyrs' blood. Though ignorant of it, the persecutor simultaneously inflicts suffering on his victim and enables that victim to conquer him by ensuring his own damnation and providing a forum for the promotion of the religion he despises.

In addition to sharing this paradox with Christological passions, *The Golden Legend*'s treatment of violence exposes a paradox of its own, one that articulates some of the central tensions of the late-medieval martyr figure. While these legends are relentless in their descriptions of the physical violence inflicted on the saint, they communicate very little sense that the martyr experiences pain. The verb "to suffer" (*patior*) is used liberally (as in the statement about Saint Fabian, "He suffered about the year of our lord 253" [1.97]), but the verb sits awkwardly within the narratives themselves, where there is a great deal of torture but no expression of pain, duress, or even discomfort. References to pain are so rare as to be remarkable. The only *Golden Legend* narrative that distinctly communicates human pain is the story of James the Dismembered, who dies having his fingers, toes, feet, legs, and arms amputated one at a time. Before finally being beheaded, "Blessed James, stricken with unspeakable pain, cried out, saying: 'Lord Jesus Christ, help me, because the groans of death have surrounded me!'" (2.346). The martyr's plea for aid, coupled with this rare reference to physical suffering, position this story not as the norm one would expect, but as the exception.

Given that suffering is a foundational element of martyrdom, why do these saints' legends depict so little of it? The answer lies in another imperative of the martyrological narrative, one that overrides the need for suffering. The saint's ability to withstand torture without recanting or displaying human weakness functions as a marker of sanctity. As Peter Brown has noted, "the exemplary courage of the martyrs and apostles had been lifted by God out of the domain of mere human physical endurance and mere human moral strength."[28] God intervenes to ameliorate the pain of torture; defiance, composure, and even joy in the midst of unfathomable violence is evidence of God's ratification of the martyr's cause. This is the central paradox of the medieval martyr legend's representation of suffering: while these narratives rely on the topos of suffering as evidence of the martyr's supreme love of God and rejection of the flesh, their simultaneous need to communicate God's participatory approval forecloses any expression of human pain.

The Miracle of Preservation

The tension between these two narrative necessities — suffering and miraculous protection from suffering — produces some rather odd stories, chief among them the legend of Saint Christina. Christina will not sacrifice to the pagan idols, so her father has her stripped and beaten, but the tormentors grow exhausted and quit. Her flesh is then torn off with hooks, but she picks up the pieces and throws them at her father.

She is then stretched on a wheel with a fire under her, but the fire kills others, not her. Her father then has her thrown in the sea with a weight around her neck, but angels bear her up and Christ descends from heaven to baptize her in the water. Her father orders her beheaded but then dies himself before it can be accomplished. A new judge orders her to be thrown in a cradle filled with boiling oil, pitch, and resin, but she is unharmed, God having willed that "she should be rocked in a cradle like a newborn babe" (1.387). Then her head is shaved and she is led naked through the city to be forced to worship the idols, which she refuses to do. She prays that the idol be turned to dust, and when it is, the second judge dies of fear. A third judge then puts her into a furnace; after five days of "walk[ing] about, singing with angels," she is unharmed (1.387). He then throws two asps, two vipers, and two cobras in with her, but they fawn on her. The snakes turn on their conjurer and kill him, and Christina brings him back to life. Her breasts are cut off, milk flowing from the wounds instead of blood. Her tongue is then cut out, but she retains the power of speech, throwing her severed tongue at the judge's eye and blinding him. She is finally killed by being shot in the heart with arrows.[29]

The narrative of Saint Christina demonstrates the *Golden Legend* martyr stories' most common manifestation of the miraculous: the preservation of the martyr from physical harm attempted by the persecutor. Though Christina's legend provides one of the more extreme examples, there is something of the tennis match in many of these narratives. As White remarks, "One does not know which to marvel at more, the dogged persistence of the pagan tyrants who in the face of indescribable frustrations still persisted in trying to kill these seemingly indestructible zealots or the toughness of the victims."[30] Those martyrs in *The Golden Legend* who successfully survive multiple tortures are most often finally killed by beheading. "Not the least curious thing in these accounts is this respect for a sharp edge," White observes. "Again and again what fire or boiling lead or wild beasts or hanging or starvation cannot compass, the sword brings off."[31]

In some instances, the attempt to torment the martyr ends up backfiring completely, resulting in the deaths of pagan torturers and bystanders, as in the case of the so-called Catherine Wheel, the elaborate torture contraption devised for putting Saint Catherine to death:

Now a certain prefect urged the furious ruler to have prepared, within three days, four wheels studded with iron saws and sharp-pointed nails, and to have the virgin torn to pieces with these horrible instruments, thus terrorizing the rest of the Christians with the example of so awful a death. It was further ordered that two of the wheels should revolve in one direction and the other two turn in the opposite direction, so that the maiden would be mangled and torn by the two wheels coming down on her, and chewed up by the other two coming against her from below. But the holy virgin prayed the Lord to destroy the machine for the glory of his name and the conversion of the people standing around; and instantly an angel of the Lord struck that engine such a blow that it was shattered and four thousand pagans were killed. (2.338)

The torture proposed here is particularly creative, but the saint's miraculous deliverance is a commonplace of *The Golden Legend.* Ironically, while she asks that the miracle be performed as a sign to others, most of the bystanders whom Catherine imagines being converted by God's miraculous intervention in her torture are killed by the machine.

Though the iconography of Saint Sebastian most commonly depicts him shot through with arrows, this was not—according to Jacobus's legend—the manner in which he died, for he too was preserved by miraculous intervention to later be beaten to death with cudgels (1.100). Sebastian explains his preservation by telling the tyrant Diocletian that he was revived so that he could scold him for the malicious persecution of Christians.[32] The notion that God's miraculous intervention provides a means by which persecutors are frustrated, rebuked, and made to look ridiculous is particularly evident in the story of Saint Anastasia. Harassed by an evil suitor, Anastasia and her three maids are locked in a kitchen chamber so that he may ravish them. God intervenes by making him senseless so that, "thinking that he was dealing with the three virgins, [he] caressed and kissed the stoves, kettles, pots and other utensils. Having satisfied himself in this manner he went out blackened with soot and his clothes in tatters" (1.44). Not only is the ladies' virginity spared but the man suffers a severe beating by his servants and by strangers on the road who mistake him for a madman.

The preservation of virginity is another form of the miraculous that pervades *The Golden Legend*. Without exception, the virgin martyr must undergo an unsuccessful attempt on her chastity.[33] God's protection of his consecrated virgins comes in many forms: for Anastasia, it is the episode with the pots and pans; for Lucy, it is the ravishers' inability to move her from the place in court where she stands, despite the aid of 1,000 yoke of oxen; for Agnes, it is the instantaneous growth of the hair on her head, which covers her body "better than any clothing" (1.103); and for the Virgin of Antioch, it is the sudden appearance of a knight who exchanges places with her, permitting her to escape from the brothel in his clothing. Before her rescue, the Virgin of Antioch comforts herself with the knowledge that she can only be an adulteress if her will submits, suggesting that virginity is a state of mind or spirit rather than body. The story itself, however, confirms the opposite, as do the other virgin martyr tales: she is miraculously protected from physical penetration and allowed to die a virgin. The effect of these stories' insistence on the preservation of virginity serves to naturalize the human preoccupation with female chastity into a divine preoccupation—or, if viewed in reverse, to provide evidence of the value God places on chastity so that humans may imitate this value. These stories describe a God who imagines virginity and chastity in the same physical terms as humans and who intercedes to protect the hymeneal integrity of his servants. Thus the topos of miraculous intervention can serve, as it does in these instances, to express not only divine values through the body of the martyr but also the social values of church and community.[34]

God's agency as miracle-worker in *The Golden Legend* is never in doubt for the text's Christian audience. Examples abound in which divine intervention is directly stated, as in the case of Saint Nazarius, who withstands torture because "the real agent of victory, Christ himself, fought for him" (2.21).[35] Ignatius is similarly enabled to endure torture "by the help of Christ" (1.142). But in most of the *Golden Legend*'s moments of miraculous preservation, the intervention of God is implied rather than stated directly. The ability to recognize the miracle as the work of the true God functions as one of the markers of an individual chosen for conversion. Such a moment occurs in the legend of Saint Laurence when the bystander Romanus sees a "beautiful young man," presumably Christ or an angel, "wiping [Laurence's] limbs with a towel" (2.66). For the hopeless pagans, the Christian martyrs' ability to withstand or thwart their carefully devised tortures is evidence of witchcraft. But for the late-medieval audience of these legends, there is never any doubt that it is God who protects his servants through such miracles.

The topos of divine intervention is connected to the martyr narratives' paradoxical representation of suffering. For if the martyrs are to be recognizable as sanctified, superhuman representatives of God's great power, their narratives must contain the markers of divinity. The miraculous thus becomes a sign of God's participation in the martyr's battle against the pagan persecutor and, ultimately, of the cosmic truth of the martyr's belief system.[36] While the narrative form depends on torture, it also depends on preservation from torture. Likewise, while a virgin's chastity must be threatened, that chastity must always remain intact. As Brown has shown in his discussion of the spread of saints' cults, through the miraculous, the body of the martyr comes to represent a junction of human and divine.[37]

Witness and Inspiration

Verbal witnessing and inspired speech function as the two other primary means by which divine intervention is indicated in these narratives. In contrast to Christ, who responds to his persecutors' questions with silence or evasive riddles, the martyrs of *The Golden Legend* are verbally confrontational, at times even abusive. Jacobus's legendary includes not one instance in which a martyr responds to a persecutor's interrogation with silence. Rather, the martyr takes advantage of these exchanges as an opportunity to publicly and unequivocally proclaim Christian beliefs, to insult the beliefs and practices of paganism, and to antagonize the persecutor.

According to Jacobus's discussion of the Feast of All Saints, verbal declaration of one's beliefs is a necessary part of being a Christian: "The heart's confession is insufficient unless it is expressed in speech" (2.277). He borrows at length from Chrysostom on the matter of verbal confession of faith:

The root of confession is faith in the heart, and confession is the
fruit of faith. As long as the root is alive in the ground, it must
produce branches and leaves; otherwise you may be sure that the
root has dried in the ground. So also as long as faith is whole in
the heart, it always sprouts in oral profession; if confession has
withered in the mouth, you may be sure that faith has already
dried up in the heart. . . . If faith in the heart were sufficient, God
would have created only a heart for you. Now, however, he has also
created a mouth for you, in order that you may believe in your heart
and confess with your mouth. (2.277–78)

Chrysostom's metaphor of the fruit tree reveals a symbiotic relationship between faith and confession: without the fruit of confession, the
tree of faith will eventually die. The fruit metaphor further suggests
that confession is necessary to the continuing growth of the church,
since the fruit contains the seeds that ensure the sprouting of new trees
or converts to the faith. In Chrysostom's formulation, both individual
faith and the continued flourishing of the church depend upon verbal
confession. The choice between claiming one's faith before persecutors
and remaining silent is essentially another version of the choice between the flesh and the spirit, "between *fidei Christo* and *fidei mundo*."[38]

It is not sufficient, then, for martyrs merely to die for their beliefs;
they must act as witnesses to the truth of Christ by confessing their
beliefs to their pagan persecutors. But the relationship between witnessing and martyrdom is more than situational. It is also linguistic,
as Lampe has shown in his brief history of the word "martyr," from
the Greek word μάρτυς, which originally denoted an individual who
offered verbal "witness," not someone who actually died.[39] For Laurence, the confession of faith is so central a component of martyrdom
that it is this element of his passion—not suffering or death—that he
believes will earn him salvation. Early in his tortures, he prays, "Lord
Jesus Christ, God from God, have mercy on me your servant, because,
being accused, I have not denied your holy name, and being put to the
question I have confessed you as my Lord!" (2.66). When he is later
placed on the grill to be cooked, Laurence assures his persecutor that
his confession of faith will be sufficient to ensure his freedom from
physical pain. In the legend of Saint Vincent, the saint's would-be

companion in martyrdom, the bishop Valerian, is deprived the glory of a martyr's death because he is a poor public speaker and is unable to perform a public confession of faith. Though an ardent Christian, he leaves the preaching to his deacon Vincent, who is "readier of speech" than he (1.105). At the moment when the two are questioned by the tyrant Dacian regarding their faith, Valerian cannot speak up, despite Vincent's encouragement, and asks the younger man to answer for both their faiths. As a result, Valerian is merely exiled, while Vincent earns the crown of martyrdom.

Lampe further illuminates the role of witnessing in acts of martyrdom by tracing the relationship between the martyr's verbal confession of Christ and the intervention of the Holy Spirit. "Certain passages in the Gospels constitute the foundation of the development of the Christian idea of witness and martyrdom as a primary operation of the Holy Spirit."[40] According to the gospel of Mark, Christ assured the apostles before beginning his own passion that they would not be left alone in the persecution that they too were to suffer at the hands of unbelievers. In what Lampe calls an "unambiguous promise of direct inspiration," Christ assures them, "when they bring you to trial and deliver you up, do not be anxious beforehand what you are to say; but say whatever is given you in that hour, for it is not you who speak, but the Holy Spirit."[41] The stories in the book of Acts about the spread of Christianity through the preaching of the apostles attribute their evangelizing success to the Holy Spirit, whose inspiration was promised by Christ at Pentecost.[42] Peter's learned and self-assured testimony before the Sanhedrin, for example—delivered while he is "filled with the Holy Spirit"—leaves his questioners amazed because they know that he is a man of no education.[43]

The inspiration of the Holy Spirit is everywhere at work in the acts of Christian witnessing related in *The Golden Legend*. The unfaltering resolve with which Jacobus's martyrs answer their persecutors and the ability of unlearned, sometimes extremely young, men and women to gracefully and forcefully expound the theological intricacies of Christian doctrine are two of the text's most prominent markers of sanctity.[44] In the stories of Peter, Sebastian, and Cecilia, for instance, the direct inspiration by the divine is signaled by the reading of the confession of faith from a book held by an angel.[45] Saint Lucy makes direct reference to Christ's promise of the Holy Spirit's inspiration to explain her bold answers to the tyrant Paschasius (1.28). The direction of the Holy Spirit in Saint Agnes's story is implied by the way she elaborates her devotion to Christ in a careful syllogistic argument, although she is only thirteen years old (1.102).[46] In the narrative of Saint Catherine, the saint's inspired witnessing becomes the main plot of the story as the young woman converts, by airtight theological argument, the group of esteemed orators assembled by her persecutor to defeat her. In these legends and the many others that employ this device, the act of verbal confession is a form of divine intervention no less miraculous than delivery from torture and pain. In the section on the Feast of All Saints, this is one of the reasons that Jacobus gives for the honor of relics: when the saints were alive, their bodies were "the organ[s] of the Holy Spirit" (2.275). He quotes Ambrose's *Hexaemeron*: "Here is something priceless—that a man could be the organ of the divine voice, and with the body's lips utter divine pronouncements" (2.275). The operation of the Holy Spirit in confessing faith is thus a cornerstone of the narrative's argument for the martyr's sanctity.

What is unusual about the manner of witnessing found in late-medieval martyrologies like *The Golden Legend* is the particular truculence with which the martyrs claim their faith and confront their tormentors, especially in comparison with earlier legends, where martyrs' confessions are more restrained.[47] The legend of Saint Cecilia demonstrates several important aspects of the role of confession in late-medieval martyrological narrative. In the early parts of the story, before she is captured, Cecilia converts her husband, Valerian, to Christianity. Upon his conversion, Valerian is granted one wish by the angel who guards Cecilia's chastity, and he wishes that his brother Tiburtius may also be converted. Thus, before Tiburtius is even introduced, his conversion is assured, such that Cecilia's instruction to him in the Christian faith is carried out in the spirit of merely filling him in on the details. But her approach to those who are not marked for conversion is decidedly antagonistic, as her conversation with Almachius, the pagan tyrant, demonstrates:

Almachius again summoned Saint Cecilia and asked her: "What is your status in life?" "I am freeborn and of noble descent," she said. Almachius: "I'm asking about your religion!" Cecilia: "Then your interrogation began badly, because the one question called for two answers." Almachius: "Where do your presumptuous answers come from?" "From a clear conscience and unfeigned faith!" she retorted. Almachius: "Don't you know where my power comes from?" Cecilia: "Your power is a balloon filled with wind! Prick it with a pin and it collapses, and what seemed rigid in it goes limp." Almachius: "You began with insults, and with insults you continue!" Cecilia: "You cannot speak of insults unless what is said is false! Show me the insult, if what I said was false. Otherwise blame yourself for uttering a calumny! We, who know the holy name of God, cannot deny it, and it is better to die happy than to live unhappy." (2.322–33)

When speaking to a hopeless pagan such as Almachius, Cecilia does not try to convert him by relating the story of Christ's sacrifice for human redemption, as she does with Tiburtius. Instead, her rhetoric is aimed at insulting the tyrant's misguided belief in his own human (and phallic) power as a way of professing her faith in the greater power of the Christian God. Cecilia's response is emblematic of the confessional mode of the *Golden Legend* martyrs in general. In Jacobus's rendering of these stories, Christian witnessing before unbelievers becomes belligerent invective. Though conversions are often effected by the martyr's words and actions, Christian witnessing in *The Golden Legend* is shaped less by its intended effects on others than by the individual's desire to demonstrate faith and sanctity.

The Pagan Persecutor

In addition to highlighting the particularly confrontational manner of Christian confession in *The Golden Legend*, the exchange between Cecilia and Almachius also illustrates late-medieval martyrology's characterization of the persecutor, a key figure in the drama of martyrdom. The main point of conflict between persecutor and martyr—the demand that the martyr sacrifice to the idols—provides an opportunity for the Christian confessor to expound on the illogic and stupidity of worshipping human-made objects and human power instead of revering the creator of everything, the all-powerful, true God. The martyrs' responses consistently characterize the persecutor as spiritually blind, intellectually crippled, and morally corrupt; inevitably, the martyr ends up looking a good deal smarter, wittier, more theologically astute, and more powerful than those who do the violence. When the tyrant Quintianus is insulted by Saint Agatha's comparison of him to Jupiter and his wife to Venus, the martyr retorts, "I marvel that a sensible man like you can fall into such stupidity as to call gods those whose lives neither you nor your wife would want to imitate! Indeed you consider it an insult if you are said to follow their example. If your gods are good, I've made a good wish for you: if you repudiate any association with them, then you agree with me!" (1.155). Though Agatha's remarks are logically sound, Quintianus disregards them and orders more torture for her. The function of such debates between martyr and persecutor is not to rationally evaluate the theological underpinnings of each other's position but to edify a Christian audience by presenting a martyr who boldly professes the faith in conflict with a pagan whose lack of reason and monomaniacal thirst for blood drives him to persecute innocent Christians.

The pagan persecutor of *The Golden Legend* is an individual who makes no sense—whose orientation toward the notion of divinity is fundamentally illogical or backward and who clings to the wrongness of his position even when doing so is no longer viable. Saint Catherine's divinely inspired theological argumentation convinces even the finest pagan orators in the land to convert to Christianity but only further enrages the emperor, who orders not only torture for Catherine but the execution of these new converts, including his own wife (2.336–37). Although it is the saint's theological astuteness that initially impresses him, and although he values learning enough to keep fifty gifted orators on hand, he cannot himself be swayed by reason and is finally revealed to be a brute. The *Golden Legend* tyrant is a one-dimensional character who is motivated by simple desires and who behaves predictably when these desires are not fulfilled. A figure of godless pagan excess, he is without logic, reason, or self-control, representing the fleshly passions and unhinged chaos that must reign for those who fail to grasp the universal order and logic provided by faith in Christ.

In some cases, the persecutors become so frustrated by either failed torture or failed debate that they are almost sympathetic figures. *Poor, dumb pagans,* Jacobus suggests—*if only they weren't so obtuse.* The tremendous frustration expressed by these men is again and again set in contrast to the cool self-possession of the martyrs, so that the martyrs' poise comes to act upon the persecutor as a catalyst for incredible outrage. Saint Vincent relishes the effect that his unflappability has on the tyrant Dacian, taunting, "the more wrathful I see you, the greater and fuller is my rejoicing" (1.106). Vincent's ability to respond to Dacian's taunts and tortures with dignity signals his identification with the divine, while Dacian's rage and lack of self-control identify him with the demonic, as Vincent suggests when he calls Dacian "venomous tongue of the devil" (1.106).

The relationship between the devil and the actions of the persecutors is less explicit in *The Golden Legend* than in Eusebius. An exception is Jacobus's legend of Dionysius, Rusticus, and Eleutherius, where the devil is the ultimate author of the Christian persecution: "The devil was alarmed to see that while the number of his own worshipers was decreasing day by day, converts to the faith were multiplying and the church was winning the fight. He therefore provoked Emperor Domitian to such a state of anger that the emperor issued a decree that anyone who found out that a given person was a Christian must either force that person to sacrifice to the idols or be put to all sorts of torture" (2.240). Such passages are unusual in *The Golden Legend* but abound in Eusebius, where the devil's jealousy and hunger for power are frequently cited as the root of a given tyrant's action against the Christians. The effect of this difference is striking: in Eusebius, agency is shifted away from the individual persecutor and assigned to a greater force, whereas in Jacobus's text, responsibility for the heinous violence done to innocent Christians rests squarely on the moral depravity of the persecutors themselves. Eusebius figures the devil as a being separate from the persecutor; for Jacobus, the persecutor is a figure of the devil.

The *Golden Legend* persecutors' relationship to the devil is most pronounced in their manner of death. These tyrants do not live to a ripe old age and die peacefully or naturally. Those responsible for the torment of Christians pass hideously from this world into an assured damnation, sometimes with the explicit assistance of demons.[48] In the legend of Saint Euphemia, the executioner is devoured by a lion (2.183). Earlier, the jailer who attempted to open Euphemia's cell so that the evil judge, Priscus, could rape her "was seized by a demon, screamed, tore his own flesh, and barely escaped with his life" (2.182). Priscus himself "chewed on his own flesh and was found dead" (2.183). Such scenes are the stuff of morality plays, suggesting the gaping hell-mouth, the scurrying devils, the hokey special effects. It is in these moments that the late-medieval martyr legend most clearly announces the cosmic significance of its actions and characters: as pointedly as in a morality play, the relationship between martyr and persecutor is figured as the battle between good and evil, between eternal life and eternal death.[49]

The Golden Legend represents an essentially heroic model of martyrdom. With no fear of physical pain, the martyr ardently desires death, treating the willing forfeiture of life as a bold statement of his or her rejection of all things earthly, including the flesh itself. Achieving this glory requires violent trial, which the martyr craves as an opportunity to display his or her willingness to suffer for love of God and for the assurance of perpetual heavenly bliss. In many ways, the *Golden Legend* martyr is a conundrum of both self-sacrifice and self-preservation: he or she gives up life in service of faith, but the emphasis placed on what is ultimately gained by this sacrifice suggests that the desire for eternal self-preservation motivates earthly self-immolation.

This is an important element of *The Golden Legend*'s paradoxical treatment of suffering. The text purports to represent sacrifice as it simultaneously accentuates gain, using the martyr's confession to articulate all that is won by losing life. And although the experience of suffering is central to this model of martyrdom—the greater the suffering, the greater the martyr—the late-medieval martyr narrative depicts no suffering. Even through unimaginable acts of violence, the martyr has no experience of the world- and self-dissolving agony Elaine Scarry, for example, describes as essential components of the structure of torture.[50] There is no humiliation here—no breaking down or crying out. Instead, the martyr endures torture in comfort, protected from the experience of pain by miraculous intervention that functions in the narrative as evidence of sanctity and justness. Thus several contradictory imperatives of the late-medieval martyr legend—the experience of suffering and the experience of not suffering, the sacrifice of everything and the sacrifice of nothing—operate at once and without apparent conflict.

The Corpus Christi Passion Plays

In contrast to *The Golden Legend,* which was composed in Latin by an important cleric, the Corpus Christi dramas represent popular literature that was performed in the vernacular by English laypeople. Dating of the four extant cycles—York, Wakefield, Chester, and N-Town—is inexact, but scholars believe the plays were written and performed between the mid-fifteenth and mid-sixteenth centuries, the latest performances of the Chester cycle not fully suppressed by Protestant pressures until 1575.[51] In their treatment of universal history from Creation to Judgment, these plays pay particular attention to the events of Christ's passion, central to medieval Christian soteriology. Not only does the passion complete the transaction for human redemption, it is also the first Christian martyrdom. The Corpus Christi passion sequences thus suggest how late-medieval Christian culture imagined the persecution and death of its originary martyr. Unlike *The Golden Legend,* which is essentially a mythic battle between figures who are largely emblematic, the Corpus Christi passion plays are insistently, relentlessly realistic. They dramatize Christ's capture, trial, and execution with a gritty violence that is shocking to a first-time reader. Christ's humanity is emphasized—even reified, as Peter Travis has suggested[52]—by the plays' unflinching attention to the details of his humiliation, torture, and execution. In their constructions of victim, persecutor, and audience response, these plays unfold a late-medieval vision of Christian martyrdom that far surpasses *The Golden Legend* in its pathos and complexity.

Tortores and *Mali Actori*

The persecutors who people these plays—Herod, Pontius Pilate, the Pharisees Caiaphas and Annas, and a cast of soldiers, torturers, and commoners—fall into two basic categories: those who actively seek Christ's death and those who harass him for entertainment or political self-protection. Rarely do they represent pure evil, instead suggesting a range of complex human responses to the threat posed by Christ. Their behavior is generally underwritten with real political and personal concerns, creating a nuanced portrait of Christ's antagonists. Those who actively set the wheels of his capture and condemnation in motion are not merely ranting madmen who lack self control, as in *The Golden Legend,* though these figures have their place in the drama as well. More often they are cool and calculating—manipulating juridical and penal procedures to achieve Christ's demise.

For the most part, the plays represent the Pharisees as the primary instigators of Christ's death. An exception is the Wakefield Pilate, who describes himself as "*mali actoris*" [*sic*]—"author of evil"—and who participates eagerly in the plot to capture and execute Christ.[53] But even in Wakefield, the Jewish characters provide the energy to carry the action forward. In the York, Chester, and N-Town plays, the Pharisees instigate Christ's capture and provide the pressure for his condemnation and death, which ultimately makes them the most morally culpable figures in the play.[54] The soldiers, or "*tortores*," as Wakefield calls them, are ignorant men following orders, proxies for the audience watching the play. In addition to its singular representation of Pilate, the Wakefield cycle is also remarkable in that it makes the commoners the primary accusers of Christ at key points in his trial, backgrounding the Pharisees, who are the dominant voices in the gospel accounts and in the other three Corpus Christi passion sequences.[55]

Christ's persecution is a response to what the Pharisees perceive as a real threat. Unlike the *Golden Legend* tyrants' irrational reaction to their victims, the Pharisees' animosity is based on concern about the power Christ's teachings have had over the masses. Their fear and hatred of Christ leads them to proceed against him with careful urgency, showing little regard for the restraints of law. When, in the three cycles aside from Wakefield, Pilate persists in maintaining Christ's innocence, the Pharisees suggest that if he does not rule in their favor, they will use the incident to turn Caesar against him and ensure his political demise. The success of Caiaphas's and Annas's machinations relies on their assurance of the corruptive nature of power. They trust that Pilate will turn against Christ in order to protect himself, and this is precisely what he does.

Though the Pharisees proceed with patience and skill, they do not act without emotion. Indeed, they detest Christ bitterly. In the York Conspiracy, Pilate repeatedly warns that the Pharisees' anger threatens to impede their aims, for they appear to seek Christ's life merely out of hatred. The Wakefield cycle depicts Caiaphas as nearly mad with rage and loathing, so eager to unleash violence on Christ that he would just as soon do without a trial and murder the captive himself. As David Bevington observes, "Caiaphas is the tyrant victimized by his own brutality, imprisoned in a nightmare of suspicion. Annas, on the other hand, is the smooth-tongued lawyer, the cleverer of the two by far. His hostility toward Jesus is more dangerous because he is so subtly adept at warping the law to his specious interests."[56] Though he shares Caiaphas's hatred and ultimate aims, Annas recognizes that if he is to maintain his position, he must behave in a manner that outwardly conforms to his role as a religious leader. "Sir, ye ar a prelate," he reminds the blood-thirsty Caiaphas with irritation.[57]

Herein lies a significant difference between Christ's persecutors in the Corpus Christi passions and the tyrants of *The Golden Legend*: the Pharisees are part of a dignified religious institution, and thus they must maintain the appearance of decorum, while the *Golden Legend* tyrants have nothing to keep their behavior in check. The latter are more openly vicious, while the former cover their wickedness in a veneer of civilized conduct and law. This difference in the representation of the persecutor marks a split in the Christian tradition of martyr construction between an irrational, openly sadistic *mali auctor* and a persecutor who is complexly motivated, politically calculating, and legally manipulative. Both constructions of the persecutor—the sadistic tyrant and the slippery, hypocritical Pharisee—will find their way into later representations of martyrdom.

The Romans are depicted as less interested than the Jewish Pharisees and commoners in Christ's destruction, but they are likewise Christ's antagonists. York's Pilate is a proud but generally fair man who at length resists putting Christ to death because it does not accord with the law he feels bound to uphold. His weakness is a love of power and position, which finally trumps his devotion to justice when he allows the crucifixion. York's Herod is presented in a less favorable light. Frustrated by Christ's complete silence during his hearing and disappointed that his captive will not entertain him with miracles, Herod spends a good deal of the play shouting insults. As biblical precedent dictates, however, he does not find legal fault with Christ and merely sends him back to Pilate dressed as a fool.[58] N-Town represents Herod less generously still, likening him to the Roman persecutors of the early church through his anachronistic self-description as an avid torturer of Christians.[59] Despite these embellishments, the biblical story is still fundamentally honored: when confronted with Christ himself, Herod orders a brutal scourging that is carried out by sadistic rank-and-file soldiers.

Threat and Containment

While the tyrants of *The Golden Legend* are simply outraged by the audacious insubordination of Christian martyrs who refuse to honor the power of human rulers and manufactured gods, the Pharisees who seek Christ's death in these plays are concerned that he poses a viable threat to the continuing survival of the religion and culture they represent. In the Corpus Christi plays, the friction between Christ and his persecutors arises from the binary conflict between two belief systems: the Old Law of the Jewish people, represented by Caiaphas and Annas, and the New Covenant, represented by Christ. This central conflict manifests itself in each of the cycles through direct reference to the contest between the two bodies of law, with the Jews seeking to maintain the dominance of their history, beliefs, and traditions. In York's Christ before Annas and Caiaphas, Caiaphas's primary accusation against Christ is that "Oure lawe he brekis with all his myght, / Þat is moste his desire."[60] The soldiers who bring Christ to trial claim that "with his lowde lesyngis he losis oure layes,"[61] words later echoed by Caiaphas in the message he sends to Pilate regarding the prisoner: "saie þis ladde with his lesyngis has oure lawes lorne; / And saie þis same day muste he be slayne."[62] A similar pattern of accusations is reflected in the Chester trial, where Annas and Caiaphas further voice their fear that lenient punishment of Christ will mean a threat to the Old Law and their way of life: "Therfore to dampne him we binne throo, / lest he us all destroye."[63] The Wakefield plays sketch Christ's threat still more clearly, indicating a direct conflict between Christ's teachings and the Old Law upheld by the priests. As representatives of the Jews' established religion, the Pharisees fear that Christ "wold fayn downe bryng / Oure lawes bi his steuen."[64] "If he reyne any more," they claim, "Oure lawes ar myscaryd."[65]

This conflict is most poignantly dramatized in the N-Town plays, where the very costuming conveys the conflict between the Old Law and the New. Annas and Caiaphas preen in fur-trimmed scarlet robes and mitres, both, according to the stage directions, *"after þe hoold lawe."*[66] Christ's lowly appearance offers a visual contrast between "The lawys of Moyses" they represent and the New Covenant he has come to make with his people. With this device in place, the N-Town plays refer with marked repetition to the threat Christ poses to the established church: "For oure lawys he dystroyt dayly with his dede"; "For yf he procede, oure lawys he wyl spyll!"; "Jesus ful nere oure lawys hath shent."[67] The sheer length of the extended buildup to the bargain with Judas serves to focus attention on the power they fear Christ wields; in the scenes leading up to the transaction, Christ is described as a formidable opponent with a host of supporters who threaten not only Jewish institutions but the judges and Pharisees themselves.[68] Further, the passion sequence of the N-Town play is inaugurated by prologues from Satan and John the Baptist, whose admonitions to the audience align them with the Old Law and the New, respectively. Through this framing device, the Old Law represented by the Pharisees takes on the moral equivalence of Satanic service, while the New Law figures its antithesis.

The Pharisees' response to Christ is focused on containment of this threat. They fashion his trial as an instrument for defining and condemning his actions and person. If he can be bound by colloquial labels and reductive categories, he is no real menace to them, for he is thereby proven to be not the son of God but a fellow human being— worse, a criminal. Toward this end, the antagonists in all four cycles resolve the catalog of miracles laid to Christ's credit into the realm of sorcery or witchcraft, particularly in York, where Christ is referred to throughout as "warlock." In N-Town, his deeds are determined not to be evidence of divinity but of "fals werkyng" and "wychecrafte and nygramansye," because if Christ were truly God's son, they argue, he would use his power to prove and free himself.[69] Like the miraculous events narrated in *The Golden Legend*, Christ's wonders must be rationalized as the frauds of a sinister magician if they are to be disarmed of their power to challenge the Old Law.

Another strategy for comprehending and containing Christ is labeling him a madman and fool. Consigning him to these categories means that everything he says and does can be discounted: if he is insane or senseless, then by definition he poses no threat. In Chester, Herod accounts for Christ's complete silence by suggesting that he is "dombe and deafe as a doted doo" and has him dressed in the white gown used "to cloth men that were wood / or madd, as nowe hee him mase, / as well seemes by his face."[70] In York, the white gown is described alternatively as a madman's dress or a fool's frock.[71] Frustrated by Christ's reticence, York's Herod assumes that he must be a "fonned ladde" if he has nothing to say for himself and has him dressed in white to formalize his status.[72] Herod's courtiers represent him as a witless country bumpkin who behaves so irregularly because he is struck with awe and fear by Herod's big voice, great power, and large sword. Herod agrees, speculating that Jesus, having never been at court, thinks that the king and his men are all angels because of their elaborate clothing.[73] As Richard Beadle and Pamela M. King note, the irony of these remarks, as well as the visual contrast presented between Herod's lavish finery and Christ's pure white garment, was certainly not lost on the play's audience,[74] and Clifford Davidson writes that "Herod, who assumes that Jesus is mad or a fool, illustrates the ultimate foolishness of those who reject salvation."[75]

Most important for the persecutors' purposes is the label of "traitoure," which serves to secularize Christ's threat, distancing him from the Jewish culture he endangers, and to criminalize that threat.[76] This becomes the most useful strategy for containment because it provides the avenue the persecutors need for summoning the agents of secular authority, Pilate and Herod. The list of inflammatory claims they attribute to Christ—that he is God's son and King of the Jews, that the Jews should not pay tribute to Caesar, and that he could destroy and rebuild the temple in three days—are rehearsed as evidence of his treason against Caesar, ultimately providing not only a label under which his teachings are contained but also a crime for which he is executed. In this representation of Christ as seditious, the Corpus Christi plays suggest the double valence of Christ's ministry as at once a religious and political message. This double construction of the threat posed by the martyr's belief system would later be invoked by both Catholic and Protestant discourses in the religious conflicts of the sixteenth and seventeenth centuries.

Christ's Silence

Christ's antagonists expect that he will assist them in their efforts to circumscribe him by answering their questions and reacting to their insults. Instead, he responds with silence. This silence is one of the most remarkable elements of these plays, for though Christ says almost nothing, he is unquestionably the dramatic focal point. It is easy to lose sight of the figure of Christ when merely reading the text, but when we imagine what a "potent presence" this silent, passive figure must have been in live performance, the effect is powerful.[77] The sheer number of the other characters' lines compared to those of Christ is staggering: for example, York's five trial and crucifixion plays in which Christ appears comprise a total of 2,151 lines, only 31 of which are spoken by him. The use of silence as Christ's primary response to persecution is a cornerstone of these plays' portrait of martyrdom.

Christ's silence serves several dramatic purposes. First, it contributes to the plays' figuration of him as the meek, humble, sacrificial Lamb. While those around him bustle in the ferocity of their hatred and vengeance, he is the still, quiet point at the center, the passive and willing victim of insult and injury. This figuration of Christ reflects the sensibilities of late-medieval affective piety, which encouraged the individual to ponder the gruesome details of Christ's passion in an effort to heighten sympathy for his suffering and to engender a sense of contrition for the crucifixion. Bevington relates N-Town's passion in particular to the broader trends in religious art encouraged by this devotional focus: "Unremittingly Christ must undergo indignities, torturings, and insults. He alone says little to his detractors. The emphasis on Christ's suffering is . . . a distinctive trait of late medieval or Gothic art, in marked contrast to the more stylized and liturgical renditions of the Passion during the twelfth-century Romanesque renaissance."[78] V. A. Kolve likewise draws a contrast between twelfth-century crucifixion iconography—which imaged Christ as Crucified King—and thirteenth- and fourteenth-century depictions of him as wounded and suffering, suggesting that this shift in sensibility shaped drama perhaps more than any other artistic genre.[79] Beadle and King observe that York's particular dramatic portrayal of Christ augments the meditative tradition's interest in his abjection, physical suffering, and humble passivity by emphasizing the festive pleasure his tormentors take in persecuting him.[80]

Christ's special suffering is highlighted by the plays' emphasis on the singularity of this crucifixion and on physical wounding, two other features of late-medieval passion devotion. Though crucifixion was a common Roman form of execution for thieves, murderers, and other felons, these plays represent Christ's punishment as an unusual task for which his persecutors are unprepared. Other late-medieval passion literature employs this same topos, which had become part of the popular tradition of stories that developed around the crucifixion. In the *Northern Passion,* the soldiers charged with Christ's crucifixion have to employ an ironsmith to have nails specially made, and since there is no prefabricated cross available, they must go in search of a "rode tre" on which to hang him.[81] All four of the Corpus Christi cycles include the popular legend of Christ being stretched to fit the holes bored incorrectly in the cross, an element that serves to further emphasize the singularity of Christ's execution and to provide the occasion for description of the horrific injury done to Christ's body. In York, "assoundir are bothe synnous and veynis" torn by the action of being pulled to fit the bores; in N-Town, the "*Judeus*" performing the crucifixion encourage each other to make Christ fit "Þow we brest both flesch and veyn."[82] Wakefield, whose executioners manage the crucifixion most like first-timers, makes use of a long lament from Mary at the cross to emphasize Christ's wounded body, which he himself calls "Blo and blody."[83]

In conjunction with this emphasis on bodily suffering, Christ's silence poses a distinct contrast to the martyrs of *The Golden Legend,* who are not only consistently verbose but aggressively—even abusively—so. It is in this response to persecution that we clearly see the most poignant divergence between these two late-medieval models of martyrdom. While in *The Golden Legend* the martyrs treat persecution as an opportunity to confess Christianity and insult pagans and paganism, the Christ figure of the Corpus Christi passion plays says and does nothing while his singularly horrible torture is carried out, using persecution instead to evidence the humility with which he offers himself for humankind. The trial is potentially a forum for repeating his teachings, as in the York appearance before Herod, where Christ's miracles and ministry are rehearsed in the hope that he will add more to the stories that circulate about him. Unlike the *Golden Legend* martyrs, however, Christ does not seize this chance to preach; his ministry has come to an end. N-Town highlights this with particular clarity. In the scenes leading up to his capture, Christ speaks at length to his apostles about his coming trials and the institution of the Eucharist, but when he is taken into custody he falls silent, speaking at length again only on the cross, where he addresses faithful followers such as Mary and James. Silence is a language particularly reserved for communicating with the persecutors. Christ has nothing to say to them; they are merely actors in the great cosmic transaction of his salvific death.

In addition to developing Christ's sacrificial function, his silence represents his complete rejection of the legal proceeding that seeks to bind him. The harassment and questioning to which he is subjected attempt to circumscribe him in a web of legally damning and socially debasing definitions. Christ's refusal to respond thwarts this effort, causing increased frustration for his persecutors. More than anything he might say in response to the accusations lodged against him, Christ's silence signals his position outside of and above human law. After all, as he himself remarks, any power exercised by human rulers or legal institutions is power granted by God. Silence thus becomes symbolic of Christ's divinity, for though his tormentors believe their condemnation, physical abuse, and crucifixion to be final and binding, Christ ultimately proves even death to have no power over him.

On the rare occasions when Christ does speak, the evasive and enigmatic quality of his words often reflects his essential rejection of this corrupted human trial, a feature that these plays borrow directly from their biblical sources.[84] In York, for example, when Annas and Caiaphas ask whether or not Christ is the Son of God, he replies, "Sir, þou says it þiselffe, and sothly I saye / Þat I schall go to my fadir þat I come froo, / And dwelle with hym wynly in welthe allway."[85] He does not directly answer the question of his patrilineage but responds with cryptic suggestions of his father's divinity. Pressed to explain himself, he tells them, "My reasouns are not to reherse," evading the query further.[86] When questioned about the substance of his teaching, Christ frankly refuses to repeat the contents of his ministry. He essentially equivocates, sidestepping the question as a means of thwarting his enemies and suggesting that anything about him that they have the right to know has already been publicly declared. This leads his persecutors to suspect that his silence is some kind of trick, a form of evasion employed to deflect their accusations. What it communicates to the audience, however, is his exemption from the human laws they try to enlist against him.[87] Thus even in what is an unusually lengthy utterance for Christ in these plays, speech is used as a form of resistance or rejection. In *The Golden Legend*'s representations of the trials of the early church martyrs, the ability to speak boldly and convincingly is a mark of sanctity and of the Holy Spirit's special intervention on behalf of the martyr's cause. By contrast, Christ never speaks during scenes of beating, scourging, or insult, and when he does respond to questioning, his answers are cryptic and otherworldly. In the trial scenes of *The Golden Legend*, bold, unequivocating speech is used as a sign of sanctity; in the passion plays, silence or riddling speech is a marker of Christ's divinity, indicating that the world of the trial is not his world.

Strategies of Violence

Although his antagonists hope that relegating Christ to the category of the marginal or criminal will go some distance toward containing the threat he represents, it is violence that they finally employ to eliminate him—cruel, publicly humiliating violence.[88] The specific tenor of this punishment grows out of the nature of the conflict between Christ and the Jews. The law upheld by Christ's persecutors is the Law of the Fathers—the patriarchal inheritance of "Moyses and Aaron / What þei weryn with þe Chylderyn of Israel in Egythp."[89] The conflict between Christ and his torturers is fundamentally a clash of masculine powers: the Old Law of the Fathers versus the New Law of the Son. Because Christ challenges the power of the patriarchal Pharisees, the violence done to his body becomes an effort not merely to subdue or silence him but to emasculate him through torture that is decidedly eroticized.

The persecutors' "almost libidinous pleasure in torment," as Claire Sponsler describes it,[90] is most evident in the Wakefield plays, where Caiaphas is characterized as nearly mad with longing to strip and beat Jesus: "Bot I gif hym a blaw / My hart will brist."[91] He fantasizes about the pain he will inflict on Christ, imagining that he will "out-thrist / Both his een on a raw" and "gyrd of his hede!"[92] The torturers of the Scourging echo these same desires, longing to penetrate the naked captive with their weapons so that they may watch him bleed: "War! lett me rub on the rust, / That the bloode downe glyde / As swythe."[93] In the York plays, much is made of stripping off Christ's clothes and of the soldiers' excitement over beating him. "I am cant in þis case," says one soldier; "I am prest for to pay hym" responds another.[94] As Kolve has shown, the dramatic action of torturing and crucifying Christ must be accompanied by dialogue that will extend these scenes to a realistic length.[95] As a result, his persecutors spend a good deal of time talking about the act of inflicting pain, which has the effect of coloring the soldiers as sadists who derive pleasure and entertainment from brutalizing their helpless victim.

The cumulative effect of each of the four cycles' scourging, buffeting, and crucifixion sequences is what Travis calls a "protracted mugging or gang rape" by male persecutors of a naked, passive subject.[96] Their primary aim is emasculation by means of opening, penetrating, and controlling the body of their victim.[97] Christ as man is humiliated and debased through a specifically masculine attack that leaves him, in the eyes of his torturers, redefined and reduced. The York antagonists further focus this dynamic by calling Christ "boy" or "lad" throughout the plays, as if he were not an adult male.[98] Frustrated and enraged by the independence and subversiveness of Christ's ministry and silence, his persecutors take this frustration out on that which can be affected and controlled. It is their aim that, through such violence, Christ's body can be made to speak the language of subjugation and humiliation— that his opened body can be made to function as a canvas upon which their threatened power writes its fury, its disgust, its fear, itself.

Several other elements of the drama reinforce this sense of debasement. All four cycles figure Christ's torture as a game, a theme based on biblical models but elaborated extensively by the Corpus Christi dramatists.[99] The persecutors of Christ in these plays refer throughout to their abusive actions as a form of sport and themselves and Christ as players, a dynamic, Kolve suggests, that strips Christ of any real identity by imposing on him a "game identity" that reduces him to a mere function within the game's structure.[100] In addition to its use of the game motif, Wakefield repeatedly figures Christ being driven like a work animal by his captors, who shout at him and whip him onward.[101] In Chester, the torturers insult Christ by suggesting that he may defecate in fear: "Though he him beshitt, / a buffet shall bite."[102] Caiaphas takes up this line of insult by later calling Christ "pewee-ars," another form of infantilizing attack.[103]

For Christ's antagonists, violence and insult function as means of revising his claims of divinity by transforming his body into a symbol of powerlessness and shame. The trial scenes serve not only to present the so-called evidence against Christ but to verbally construct a figure who will then be brutally and ritually torn down. After beating Christ bloody, the York soldiers carry out a mock worship of him during which they admire his lack of kingdom, his scanty followers, and his meaningless deeds, demonstrating for themselves how easily Christ's pretended power is reduced to buffoonery by a good beating.[104] The topos appears again as they watch Christ suffer on the cross, reiterating his deeds to him while he hangs, seemingly helpless, in the most ignoble form of execution.[105] Like Christ's persecutors in the gospels of Matthew and Mark, his antagonists in the passion plays revise his role as prophet into the demeaning "Play the Prophet" game. In Wakefield, where we see the most poignant use of the revision topos, the *tortores* carry out their scourging while they simultaneously rehearse stories of Christ's miracles—the changing of water into wine at Cana, the raising of Lazarus, the healing of a leper—in an effort to replace Christ's text with the message of their ominous power, thereby destroying the threat posed by his works.[106]

It is in their emphasis on a passive, debased victim that the Corpus Christi plays differ most markedly from *The Golden Legend*'s construction of martyrdom. While Christ faces death with steadfast resolve, his martyrdom bears the marks of human frailty and suffering, which we rarely observe in *The Golden Legend.* The passion plays insist on Christ's physical pain and humiliation through their unflinching depictions of his torture and crucifixion.[107] Further, the categories invoked by his antagonists to contain him—madman, boy, "pewee-ars"—emphasize his mortification and language his degradation. Nothing intervenes to deliver him from this agony—no voice from the clouds, no sudden deaths for his enemies, no shriveling up of the whips and clubs used to beat him. The scenes of violence themselves do little to mitigate the horror of Christ's pain. On the contrary, the audience's experience of his suffering is one of the drama's most effective didactic and devotional elements, engendering remorse for his brutal death at the hands of fellow humans.

Transcendence and Reversal

The layering of rehearsed Christian lore with revisionist violence has particular dramatic power, as we see in the Croxton *Play of the Sacrament,* a drama contemporary with the Corpus Christi plays that combines topoi from passion, martyr, and conversion literature in its depiction of the persecution of Christ's body-as-Eucharist. The

Croxton play dramatizes the exploits of five Jews whose hatred and curiosity incites them to commission the theft of a Eucharistic wafer, which they then proceed to harass in a scene that suggests the tortures of both Christ and the early church martyrs. They carry out their punishments—nailing to a post, boiling in oil, cooking in an oven—with the same sadistic relish we observe in the persecutors of the Corpus Christi passions—that is, until their efforts are thwarted by the Eucharist's indestructibility and the injuries they incur trying to "kill" it. They are completely unsuccessful; when Christ addresses them from the oven—now miraculously gushing blood—and asks them why they forsake him, they beg mercy and are converted. But before beginning their attempts to violently destroy "Christ in a cake," the Jews at length rehearse the theology of the Eucharist. This exposition of Christian beliefs is clearly intended as instruction and edification—with an explicit warning attached—for the play's Christian audience, but it also serves an important dramatic function. Like the torture of Christ in the passion plays, the insults inflicted on the Host are intended to prove the speciousness of Eucharistic theology by rendering the cake debased and powerless. In this version of the passion drama, as in the Corpus Christi plays, violence is imagined as a way of revising—and, ideally, obliterating—the victim's threatening narrative.

What the *tortores* of the passion plays fail to see is that their treatment of Christ fulfills rather than revises his ministry. This is a key aspect of the plays' complex figuration of the persecutor. Variously represented as jokesters, sadists, and even servants of the devil, the Jewish executioners are most consistently and insistently depicted as utterly ignorant of their role in the universe-shaping transaction in which they participate. In Chester, the progress to Calvary is interrupted by a lengthy, tedious dicing scene that slows the main action of the play to a halt. The drama of human salvation is suspended while four men—blinded by obstinate ignorance and short-sighted worldliness—decide who gets Christ's coat, a question more immediately relevant to them than their captive's fate. In N-Town, the Pharisees ironically suggest that Christ be made a scapegoat for the Jewish people. Imagining that killing him will protect them from the perdition in which his teaching is sure to bring them, they decide that one man should die so that all do not suffer, not realizing that this is in fact a version of Christ's plan.[108] Like N-Town's Satan, who understands too late that the plot he thought would ensure Christ's demise actually ensures his own, the Pharisees believe their humiliation and execution of Christ provides security for the Old Law they protect. Instead, they guarantee its ruin by enacting the prophesies in accordance with Christ's divine will. The violence of the Passion ultimately serves Christ by not only making human salvation possible but confirming his role as a passive, willing sacrifice for a brutal and undeserving humanity. Christ is ultimately in control of what happens to him, as Kolve reminds us: "He is in the game, by His own choice, to serve His larger purposes. And the game must go as God intends."[109]

The contrast between the persecutors' understanding of Christ and his actual identity is made especially vivid in the N-Town plays, where theatre-in-the-round staging effectively allows complementary scenes to take place simultaneously. While the Pharisees are in their council house discussing the threat posed by Christ's teaching, Christ is sharing the Passover meal with his disciples in a juxtaposition loaded with theological significance. Murray Roston has described this kind of device as "a hallmark of martyrological art" — the "medieval penchant for mingling expressionism with realism by superimposing the spiritual significance of a scene upon its physical representation."[110] At the same time that the Pharisees complain of the dangers of allowing Christ to proceed unchecked, Christ foretells the destruction that his ministry and death will bring to the Old Law. He explains to his disciples after finishing the Passover lamb,

> And as þe paschal lomb etyn haue we
> In þe eld lawe was vsyd for a sacryfyce,
> So þe newe lomb þat xal be sacryd be me
> Xal be vsyd for a sacryfyce most of price.[111]

Christ effectively proposes to replace the Old Law with himself, forming a New Covenant with his people. Specifically, it is his coming death that will ensure human salvation; the Pharisees' plot is revealed as Christ's plot. Through the institution of the Eucharist, which he discusses in great detail during N-Town's Last Supper, his persecutors' efforts to inscribe his body with a language of shame are superseded by his willing offer of his body as the spiritual food for his people. Made possible by the Pharisees' plot against Christ, the Eucharist represents the greatest of sacrifices, as Peter remarks: "For with more delycyous mete, Lord, þu may us not fede / Þan with þin owyn precyous body."[112] As Sarah Beckwith has observed, Christ's body "removes that most ordinary of objects, the human body, into a sacred sphere. Conversely, it takes that most extraordinary of objects, divinity, and transposes it to the banal domain of the human body."[113] Christ's ravaged body thus acts to ensure the continuation of his church in a transaction that the martyrs of *The Golden Legend* seek to replicate.

The torturers are completely ignorant of their role in this transaction. This is most evident in the crucifixion scenes, where they get so caught up in the practical matters of attaching Christ to the cross that they entirely lose sight of the gravity of the act of putting a man to death, let alone of putting to death the Son of God. In York's Crucifixion, the difficult process of stretching Christ to fit the incorrectly bored holes results in some humorous complaints about the job, including grumblings from the soldiers about how lifting the heavy cross makes their backs hurt.[114] The arrangement of this scene, with the cross and Christ lying flat on the stage and the soldiers bustling around, forces the audience's attention to these workmen, whose problems and attitudes intentionally echo those of the medieval tradesmen who performed the plays and watched from the audience. The men responsible for Christ's death resemble the audience members themselves, who would have recognized the actors as friends, neighbors, and community members. Beadle and King observe that the playwright exploits the audience's identification with these tradesmen-soldiers for moral purpose: "As the cross rises and drops upright into the mortice, the full force of the soldiers' workmanship becomes apparent, and the audience realize that in their laughter at the awkward efforts of four local workmen, they have been seduced into condoning the Crucifixion. The tenor of Christ's address to 'all men that walk by way or street,' combined with this visual impact, makes it plain that, for the playwright, the Crucifixion is an act in which all men at all times are necessarily implicated."[115]

In Beckwith's reading of this scene, the audience's alienation from Christ's tortured body produces a theatrical effect that exceeds remorse or complicity: "Christ's body is the sign that looks back, the real presence that exceeds the parameters of representational space and confronts the audience's detachment with the familiar, deeply reproachful spectacle of a suffering caused by that very detachment."[116] For Beckwith, the theatre's unique capacity to conjure "real presence" transforms mere spectacle into sacrament.[117]

While the Corpus Christi passions marshal a complex vocabulary of verbal and visual cues to generate audience culpability and devotionally profitable sacrament, correct reading of the drama relies upon the audience's knowledge of the big-picture Christian narrative. Christ will rise from the dead, reversing the violence done to him and the hierarchies that violence inscribed. In the broader story that these plays dramatize, humiliation, insult, and pain are emphatically resolved into a symbolic system that, crucially, always already includes the Resurrection.

The martyr tradition outlined by *The Golden Legend* communicates piety and transcendence through the victim's fearlessness, imperturbability, and near indestructibility. By contrast, the Corpus Christi Passions develop an alternative representational vocabulary in their complex negotiation of abjection and conquest. In their divergent constructions of the drama of martyrdom, theses two sets of texts at once present ready paradigms and pose discursive challenges to subsequent projects of martyr construction, performative and narrative. With neither the superhuman capacity to endure torture nor the benefit of immanent resurrection, sixteenth- and seventeenth-century martyrs faced the Marian fire and Elizabethan rack with a difference, adapting the inherited modes of enacting and inscribing Christian martyrdom to the contextual and metaphysical challenges of their own historical moment.

Chapter 2

New Actors in an Old Drama

The Martyrology of John Foxe

Even as a Lambe, paciently he aboade the extremitie therof,

neither moving forwardes, backwards, or to any side: but having

his nether partes burned, and his bowels fallen out, he died as

quietly as a childe in his bedde: and he now raigneth as a blessed

Martyr in the joyes of heaven.

—John Foxe, *Acts and Monuments*

From its first English publication in 1563 through the early twentieth century, John Foxe's magisterial Protestant martyrology, *Acts and Monuments*, was attacked as the work of a consummate propagandist prone to exaggeration and lies. Vitriolic character assaults on individual martyrs and a handful of misreported dates licensed the wholesale dismissal of "Foxe's Book of Martyrs" as a historical document. For Robert Persons and Nicholas Harpsfield, two of Foxe's earliest detractors, the undermining of individual character and pointing out of minor factual inaccuracies provided a platform from which to attack Reformed doctrine itself.[1] The rhetorical strategy of eroding the reputation of particular martyrs as a way of discrediting the cause for which they stood became the dominant mode of anti-Foxe criticism in the centuries following the book's publication. It was not until J. F. Mozley's

1940 defense of the text, *John Foxe and His Book*, that Foxe's credibility was restored. By comparing Foxe's accounts to extant civic papers and reports, Mozley argued that the facts recounted in Foxe's book show a remarkable fidelity to other contemporary records, the author's Protestant, reformist zeal notwithstanding. Mozley's work was a turning point in Foxe scholarship. The book's documentary reliability has since continued to be upheld and is no longer a subject of much discussion.

Great critical interest in *Acts and Monuments* has followed in the wake of Foxe's new-found credibility, but the acceptance of his book into the ranks of respectable historiography has created problems of its own. If we acknowledge Foxe as an accurate historian, we are suggesting that his text meets our modern standards for history—that his book reflects at least some of the values that shape current historiographic practice. What, then, are we to do with those aspects of *Acts and Monuments* that do not satisfy these standards? Most often, recent criticism has tended to ignore, discount, or problematize these elements; they are either eradicated or absorbed into a language of ruptures and tensions that suggest Foxe's vision was not altogether coherent and the book's execution not fully controlled. In the Latin preface "To the Learned Reader" (*Ad Doctum Lectorem*), Foxe had driven an indignant wedge between his martyrology and the medieval tradition that preceded him, arguing that his work had nothing in common with the "unnatural monostrosities of lies and most empty inventions" that characterized texts like Jacobus de Voragine's enormously popular thirteenth-century collection of saints' tales, *The Golden Legend*.[2] "I would like it to be made manifest to all," he says, "that I have taken pains to ensure that there should not be anything legendary in the work, or of such a kind as either could have been invented by me, or could not be everywhere very unlike that *Golden* (I should rather say Leaden) *Legend*."[3] Modern scholarship has assumed that in discarding the exaggerations of *The Golden Legend*, Foxe made a clean break from the medieval tradition. As a consequence, those elements of *Acts and Monuments* that accord with medieval hagiography have largely been marginalized.

Why have we been so ready to assimilate Foxe, who writes in one of the oldest popular genres of western Christendom, into a narrative of the early modern? For scholars of the period there is something disconcerting—perhaps even slightly embarrassing—in medieval hagiography, something we do not know how to approach critically. We have created a model of forward progress and modernization in which medieval Catholicism, with its superstitions and naïve preoccupations, represents what is left behind. As a primer for the thousands of English majors who pack our survey courses each year, *The Norton Anthology of English Literature* is a testament to this discomfort: medieval hagiography and martyrology, the most popular literary genres of the late Middle Ages, are not represented. Foxe has been excerpted in several editions, but only a brief paragraph relating the sensational death of Anne Askew is included, bringing the selections from Foxe to total less than a page.[4] The headnote to the eighth edition rehearses William Haller's long-dismissed thesis describing *Acts and Monuments* as a cornerstone text in the shaping of English nationhood, implying that the importance of Foxe's book for students of the period lies mainly in its political implications, real or imagined.[5]

To dismiss that which seems unmodern in Foxe or to treat the text as a document of protonationalism is to disregard constitutive elements of *Acts and Monuments*. This chapter argues that those elements in Foxe that seem incongruous, medieval, and Catholic—those elements that echo the tradition from which Foxe consciously seeks to distance himself in the preface—are essential to his martyrology. Identifying this generic residue does not undermine Foxe as a reliable historiographer. Rather, the text's interplay of traditional martyrological formulations and local moments of persecution comprises one of its most important contributions to the developing structure of the martyrological genre, a structure that later martyrologists will be challenged to replicate.

Formal Continuities

The representation of resistance and persecution in *Acts and Monuments* is largely dependent on a body of topoi that originate from a long history of Christian martyr literature including the Bible, patristic martyrology, and medieval Catholic texts. Despite Foxe's outward rejection of medieval martyrology and his claim to the unsullied purity of primitive, or early-church, authors like Eusebius, whose *Ecclesiastical History* he treats as his primary model,[6] there is no escaping the influence of the tradition represented by a text like *The Golden Legend*. It was neither feasible nor entirely desirable for Foxe to ignore this tradition or exclude everything that might create an echo. The echo is necessary. It lends his stories transcendent, typological significance, and it makes his subjects legible as martyrs for a sixteenth-century Protestant audience.

In its assertions of Foxe's normative Protestantism, criticism of *Acts and Monuments* generally fails to acknowledge a crucial fact of the book's martyr accounts: for the most part, Foxe is not their principal author.[7] He compiles, he edits, he shapes, he contextualizes—but he does not author in the sense of having controlling power over what happens in his stories. Instead, it is the martyrs themselves and the observers who report to Foxe who fashion these narratives, and thus many aspects of Foxe's book expose a connection to popular martyr traditions. A good deal of residual feeling that Foxe would have labeled "Catholic" still circulated among the "gospellers" he depicts with such fervor and assurance. In fact, the text occasionally exposes an overt disjuncture between Foxe's ideal portrait of the godly English faithful and the reality of religion in transition. For example, Foxe reports without commentary that many witnessing the execution of Nicholas Ridley were eager to gather up clothing, bones, and any unburned body parts to preserve as relics: "Happy was he that might get any rag of hym" (1,769). Miles Hogarde, in his 1556 anti-Protestant tract, *The Displaying of the Protestantes,* claimed that these incidents were not uncommon.[8] Relics had been condemned by Protestant theologians as superstitious and idolatrous, but evidently their veneration had not been thoroughly expelled.

This kind of popular Christianity shapes the behavior of not only the audience but the martyrs themselves. Sixteenth-century English Christians would have derived many of their ideas of martyrdom from medieval legendaries and from the sermons and stories they inspired. It is highly unlikely that Foxe's lay martyrs would have been familiar with a text like Eusebius's *Ecclesiastical History,* which was not published in English until 1577.[9] If they were to inscribe themselves into the tradition of primitive martyrdom, their models would likely be medieval and biblical. Foxe's martyrs operate within a circulating body of topoi that have filtered up to the sixteenth century through a variety of channels, not all of which Foxe's vehemently anti-Catholic, anti–*Golden Legend* perspective would approve. These topoi are rehearsed and recirculated through the martyrs' actions and through Foxe's narrative of those actions. Each martyr account in *Acts and Monuments* records a carefully crafted performance, one that is both consciously and unconsciously shaped like earlier martyr legends in order to ensure that its audience will interpret it correctly as the death of a true martyr for Christ. In order for the martyr's message to be clearly communicated to his or her audience, the two have to share a language of martyrdom — a set of gestures, words, and behaviors that signal the creation of a martyr.

A useful illustration of this common martyrological language is the martyr's expression of joy and merriment in anticipation of execution, an event he or she often describes as a wedding. The night before his death, Nicholas Ridley proposes a toast "to his mariage: for (saith he) to morrowe I must be maried: and so shewed hymselfe to bee as mery as ever he was at any time before" (1,769). Rowland Taylor goes to the stake "joyfull and mery, as one that accounted himselfe goyng to a most pleasant banquet or bridall" (1,525). John Knott remarks that the martyr's joy or talk of weddings "is the language of the martyrologist, celebrating a new kind of Protestant saint who seems beyond human weakness at the approach of death" and that "[p]rofessing that one was merry, even demonstrating this, was part of the unwritten script" of a specifically Protestant martyrdom.[10] But this topos is not an invention of Foxe or of his martyrs. It is a rehearsal of earlier models, ones that are neither new nor Protestant and that do in fact constitute something of a written script for sixteenth-century martyrdom. The demonstration of invulnerability is a hallmark of *The Golden Legend*, where martyrs employ similar gestures to indicate a desire for death, described as a banquet or wedding. Recall the story of Saint Laurence, when the martyr refers to torture as "the banquet I have always desired"; and the martyrs Valerian and Tiburtius, converted to Christianity by Saint Cecilia, "hasten to [their] deaths as to a banquet."[11] Eusebius's text employs a related topos: he reports that those who confessed Christ "wore even their fetters as a becoming ornament, like a bride adorned with golden lace of many patterns."[12]

Readings of Foxe that describe his martyrs as developing a distinctly Protestant brand of martyrdom often fail to acknowledge the unmistakable relationship between their behavior and the traditions of primitive and medieval martyrology.[13] Janel Mueller's conclusions about the construction of Protestant subjectivity in Foxe are largely undermined by their failure to admit these traditions. Citing a passage from Foxe's account of the martyr John Hooper, Mueller argues that the martyr's vision of himself being eaten, ground up, and processed to be made ready to join God's heavenly body is a Protestant reconception of transubstantiation.[14] Mueller identifies the "prototype" for Hooper's language as a first-century letter of Ignatius of Antioch written about his own impending martyrdom in which Ignatius says, "I am the wheat of God, and am ground by the wild beasts' teeth, so that I may be found to be the pure bread of Christ."[15]

This formulation of the martyr's body underlies not only Hooper's Protestant writings but the Catholic tradition that precedes him. The passage from Ignatius that Mueller traces through primitive authors such as Eusebius also appears in *The Golden Legend,* and it echoes the text's many transubstantiative images of the martyr's body being eaten or processed.[16] For example, as he is roasted alive on a gridiron, Saint Laurence tells his persecutor, "Look, wretch, you have me well done on one side, turn me over and eat!"[17] Jacobus borrows from Augustine's account of Saint Vincent to describe how the martyr "was stretched and twisted to make him suppler, scourged to make him learn better, pummeled to make him more robust, burned to make him cleaner."[18] Mueller argues that the notions of being burned or digested in a process of spiritual refinement are "coined by Marian Protestants . . . as historically specific compensations for their rejection of a Catholic ontology of presence."[19] But although these topoi may be especially attractive to Protestant martyrs seeking to articulate a reformed Eucharistic theology, they are not Marian coinages. Rather, they are part of the basic material of the martyrological narrative inherited by Foxe and his subjects, a narrative evident in the source Foxe claims and Protestantizes, Eusebius's *Ecclesiastical History,* as well as in the one he ostensibly rejects, Jacobus's *The Golden Legend.*[20]

The misattribution of long-circulating Christian martyr topoi to a specifically Protestant origin is the result of an overly localized reading of the martyr's historical moment, one that focuses on the Reformation's immediate tension between Catholic and Protestant, missing the broader religious and cultural context that produces and interprets the martyr narrative. In the case of Foxe scholarship, the interest in locating the text within the cultural moment of production has often meant that in our looking back, we don't look back far enough. The structures through which narratives of Christian martyrdom were generated in late-medieval literature remain viable and evocative in the sixteenth century, their afterlives forming the building blocks of Foxe's martyrology. The convenient but largely artificial periodization of the text makes it difficult for us to see that the moment of martyrological production is perhaps as much a medieval moment as an early modern one, attuned to the equal pressures of past, present, and future.

Morphology and *Habitus*

The genius of *Acts and Monuments* is not the invention of Protestant martyrdom but the text's successful positioning of the martyr figure within the double frameworks of local specificity and transcendent religious typology. This double frame serves an important function in Foxe's overall project: the production of "monuments" from stories of human life and death.[21] Coupled with the documentary aspects of the text, the narrative and iconographic impulse toward monument-making produces a martyrological subject who operates simultaneously in two registers: actual and typological. Modern scholarship often identifies this an element of Foxe's book as a textual rupture. Knott suggests that the realities of death by burning sometimes interfere with Foxe's attempt to create a narrative of archetypes.[22] Thomas Betteridge cites a "dialectical tension running through the English editions of *Acts and Monuments* between the universal, ahistorical act of martyrdom and the particular, historical record of persecution."[23] And Warren Wooden calls Foxe's fidelity to both realism and moral symbolism a "double commitment" that produces a "strain on the narrative."[24] This tension or strain exists only for modern readers, who find it difficult to reconcile history and typology. But for Foxe, his subjects, and his sixteenth-century audience, symbolic and typological truths were legibly revealed through contemporary events. The overlay of monumentalism onto local history is an expression of Foxe's vision of the world as a place in which eschatology is enacted by individual human beings.

In *Acts and Monuments*, the details of an individual case are important for establishing a sense of historical specificity. At the same time, these details operate to inscribe the martyr into a preexisting economy of folkloric and mythic structures that organize the martyr's experience as a moral narrative. Critical assumptions about the incompatibility of folklore/mythology and history have often led us to ignore the structural relationship between Protestant martyr narratives and the religious folk traditions of primitive and medieval hagiography. If Foxe is a respectable historian, what do we do with structures, characters, and gestures that smack of religious legend? The imperatives of documentary and of folkloric typology that are equally at work in Foxe do not create the kind of tension critics might expect. The text manifests two apparently contradictory impulses, because what Foxe records is a kind of performed folklore—a rehearsed, culturally resonant formula that signals both the emulation of earlier models and the spontaneous expression of individual faith. This folklore is comprised of a ready-made store of gestures, roles, and actions that pre-determine narrative shape. The documentary does not compete with the typological because what is often documented is typology itself, an enacted religious form that is recorded and redispersed by the martyrologist.

Vladimir Propp's *Morphology of the Folktale* provides a useful paradigm for conceptualizing the formulaic aspects of Foxe's book. For Propp, any given folktale breaks down into a cast of standard dramatis personae who perform a closed set of possible plot "functions"—the "stable, constant elements" that "constitute the fundamental components of the tale."[25] The dramatis personae carry out explicit roles (for Propp, the hero, the villain, and the seeker; for Foxe, the martyr and the persecutor) while the functions designate plot points shared, in some form or other, by all folktales. Like the martyr narratives of *The Golden Legend*, Foxe's stories have three structural segments: the martyr's transgression and capture, the trial or confrontation between the martyr and persecutor(s), and the execution.[26] Each of these structural segments also follows an established model. For example, the trial scene of a martyr narrative in Foxe's book has several static elements, or functions: the question and answer between martyr and persecutor, the persecutor's attempt to persuade the martyr to recant, the martyr's final statement of intractability, and condemnation. Propp's model provides that these functions can be repeated again and again while still retaining the essential characteristics that define them, as in the case of martyr John Philpot, whose prison letters record eleven discrete confrontations with his persecutors before he was finally condemned and executed. Propp's paradigm brings into focus the relationship between the structure of Foxe's narratives and of medieval martyrology. In *The Golden Legend*, the effort to persuade the martyr usually takes the form of physical torture, but aside from this surface variation the trial scenes in both texts share the same basic four-function structure.

What is important about Propp's paradigm is not so much the formal relationships that it reveals between Foxe and *The Golden Legend* but the underlying, sedimented structures it evidences—structures that constitute all Christian martyr-making. The circulation of martyr narratives over many centuries creates an accrued cultural knowledge of the narrative paradigm that informs the martyr's actions as well as subsequent iterations of the genre. Pierre Bourdieu calls this knowledge "the *habitus*," a body of accumulated structures that operate beneath conscious agency to inform human behavior. Bourdieu writes: "The *habitus*, a product of history, produces individual and collective practices—more history—in accordance with the schemes generated by history. It ensures the active presence of past experiences, which, deposited in each organism in the form of schemes of perception, thought and action, tend to guarantee the 'correctness' of practices and their constancy over time, more reliably than all formal rules and explicit norms."[27] The *habitus* is formed through a process of naturalization whereby structures are assimilated into culture so thoroughly that they become the filter through which people view their world. The *habitus* that underlies martyrdom does not appear as a set of formal narrative paradigms but has come to constitute the only way to conceive, enact, interpret, and narrate martyrdom. In short, it is not possible for Foxe's martyrs to look like martyrs, act like martyrs, talk like martyrs, or even think like martyrs without relying on the structures already in place.

New Historicist practice has often taught us to suspect the rehearsal of cultural models as inauthentic—as a kind of conscious, strategic, and political self-fashioning. Spontaneity and performativity are treated as directly exclusive of one another in a paradigm of containment and subversion that oversimplifies the complex relationship between individual expression and cultural patterns, one that leaves us without a language for describing authenticity. Louis Montrose has warned that this reductive impulse "threaten[s] to dissolve history into . . . an antinomy of objectivist determinism and subjectivist freeplay, an antinomy which allows no possibility for historical agency on the part of individual or collective human subjects."[28] In his critique of the problematic binarisms that oppose agency and cultural structures, Montrose proposes that while these structures curtail agency, they equally act to promote it. Certainly this is the case in a text like *Acts and Monuments,* which demands that we find a way to reconcile authentic expression with the rehearsal of long-established, culturally validated models.

Bourdieu's notion of the *habitus* extricates us from these binarisms. If the nature of the *habitus* is to be fully naturalized into the fabric of culture so that it no longer appears external, it distinctly does not function as a constraint to authentic expression. Yes, it determines the range of possible responses to a given stimulus, Bourdieu explains, but within this range authenticity is fully possible:

> Through the *habitus,* the structure of which it is the product governs practice, not along the paths of a mechanical determinism, but within the constraints and limits initially set on its inventions. This infinite yet strictly limited generative capacity is difficult to understand only so long as one remains locked in the usual antinomies— which the concept of the *habitus* seeks to transcend—of determinism and freedom, conditioning and creativity, consciousness and the unconscious, or the individual and society. Because the *habitus* is an infinite capacity for generating products—thoughts, perceptions, expressions and actions—whose limits are set by the his-

torically and socially situated conditions of its production, the con-
ditioned and conditional freedom it provides is as remote from
creation of unpredictable novelty as it is from mechanical reproduction of the original conditioning.[29]

The "usual antinomies" to which Bourdieu refers constitute an impedi-
ment to reading Foxe, forcing his narratives into either a cynical model
of strict performativity or a narrowly recuperative model of original
expression. As Bourdieu observes, authenticity and originality are not
synonymous, nor does the former depend on the latter, as Foxe's book
demonstrates in its representation of martyrdom as both a performative reference to earlier models and an authentic marker of religious
commitment.

The Foxean Miracle

Unlike medieval texts such as *The Golden Legend,* which recorded primarily legends of a distant, mythologized past, *Acts and
Monuments* is an insistently current representation of a recent and still
palpable history. But that history is understood and articulated in ways
that have little in common with secular, post-Enlightenment metaphysical models. The interpretive overlay of providence and miracle is
an essential component of Foxe's belief in the world as a place where
God perceptibly operates for the benefit of his elect. While this world
view does not fundamentally taint the reporting of historical events or
allow the wholesale invention of legends that would conveniently reinforce Foxe's argument, it operates as the primary interpretive lens
through which events are absorbed and communicated. Here, history
and miracle coexist without tension, because for Foxe and his audience,
God's active intervention through his elect was as much a historical fact
as the heretic burnings themselves. Foxe's greatest complaint about
medieval martyrology is its corrupted reporting of history, the proliferation of "Monkish miracles and grosse fables, wherewith these Abbey
Monkes were wont in time past to deceave the church of God, and to
beguile the whole world for their own advantage" (89).[30] As chapter 1

demonstrated, fantastic miracles and divine intervention are part of the foundational narrative fabric of vernacular and Latin hagiography, functioning as markers of sanctification. In these texts, miracles play an essential role in the construction of martyrdom by providing evidence of the martyr's righteousness in the eyes of God. The majority of the martyr stories in *The Golden Legend* include some kind of miracle, either in the form of the wondrous protection from harm or by the miraculous amelioration of suffering through healing or insensitivity to pain. Miracles performed by the martyr or issuing from the martyr's remains—as in Jacobus's legend of Saint Thomas à Becket, whose tomb produces countless cures—likewise demonstrate his or her sanctity.[31]

Our zeal to legitimize Foxe for the early modern canon has often entailed marginalizing his dependence on the miraculous. Thomas Freeman reminds us that scholars' juxtaposition of a "good Foxe" who verifies all his sources and a "bad Foxe" who reports fantastical stories of divine wrath is erroneous—that it is our modern notion of appropriate historiographic skepticism that has produced this inconsistent Foxe figure.[32] We have habitually drawn a distinction between Protestant providentialism and medieval miracle-mongering that is not borne out by the text itself. In her study of providence in the period, Alexandra Walsham remarks that despite Calvinist efforts to distinguish true providence from popish superstition, "in practice, application, and above all collective perception, the line of demarcation between miracles, providences, and prodigious but entirely natural events was very hazy indeed."[33] As Walsham's research shows, both church sermons and popular literature relied on patristic, medieval, and Catholic formulations—often at best only thinly Protestantized—to describe incidents of God's intervention.

Like earlier martyrologists, Foxe recognized the value of the miraculous for signaling God's favor. *Acts and Monuments* adapts the topos for sixteenth-century martyrology, exploiting the signifying qualities of the miraculous while maintaining documentary fidelity. In his text he relies on four main categories of miracles: he cites the regular working of divine providence as the protector and benefactor of the faithful;[34] he reports several incidents of prophesy; he depicts martyrs strengthened by God's intervention to withstand the difficulty of trial and the agony of fire; and he makes liberal use of the persecutors' hideous, unnatural deaths as evidence of divine punishment.[35] These four manifestations of the miraculous all have strong analogues in the primitive and medieval hagiographic traditions, where martyrs like Saint Cecilia and Saint Laurence are guided and strengthened by the hand of God and persecutors like Dacian and Lucretius suffer hideous, unnatural deaths.[36] The difference between Foxe and his predecessors is that these are the only kinds of miracles he relates. There are no martyrs who survive the fire, no scaffolds that fall apart and kill the executioner, no healings effected by the ashes. The traditions represented by Eusebius and *The Golden Legend* both make claims to spectacular miracles—to fantastic things happening. Polycarp is preserved from the fire when it leaps from his body to form an arch over his head. Saint Paul's head spurts milk; Saint Alban's head speaks after being severed from his body; Saint Cecilia lives three days with her head nearly off.[37] These are spectacular, objective miracles—empirically observable events that either happened or did not happen.

Foxe relies on no such miracles. Every miracle he reports is fundamentally interpretive—an inference of the miraculous applied to an undisputedly historical, empirically provable event.[38] Yes, there was an earthquake on the day John Wycliffe was to be tried, but whether it was miraculous preservation or coincidence is in the eye of the beholder. Roger Holland correctly predicted that his execution would be the last carried out by the "bloody" bishop Edmund Bonner; was it prophesy or might he simply have known that Queen Mary was on her deathbed? Could the amazing stamina of the burning martyrs be the product of sheer will, or did it come from divine protection? For Foxe, the answer always lies in God's miraculous power. But these same questions cannot be asked of many of Eusebius's and Jacobus's miraculous events, which are either history or fiction. By contrast, Foxe's claims to the miraculous are not based on objective observation. They are merely inferences made from corroborated reports.

Foxe's use of the miraculous demonstrates the continuing persuasiveness of an essentially religious metaphysics in which the operations of the world are understood as the direct and purposive operations of the divine. Foxe redefines what kind of information is admissible in martyrology by re-envisioning the genre as a mode of polemical historiography. At the same time, his stories retain the signifying value of divine intervention that is so central to the project of medieval martyr-making. Foxe is not opposed to any specific category of miracles, like speaking heads or marvelous preservation; he merely requires a higher level of proof than his medieval counterparts. For Foxe, a speaking head is not an invalid miracle per se, but it is not likely to be valid if it has not been corroborated by a group of reliable witnesses, as his accounts of the first ten persecutions of the early church demonstrate. He borrows most of this material from patristic sources, distinguishing between the earlier authors such as Eusebius and Origen, whom he deems trustworthy for their proximity to the events described and for their chronological distance from the abuses of medieval Catholicism, and later hagiographers such as Isidore and Bede, whose tales he dismisses. His criteria for skepticism have little to do with the nature of the miracles themselves but instead with the question of historiographic reliability. The absence of fantastical, objective miracles in *Acts and Monuments* is less the result of a budding early-modern rationalism as it is of Foxe's commitment to historical document.

Scaffold Scenes

It is in Foxe's execution accounts that we see his commitment to documentary detail most clearly. Characterized by the realistic portrayal of physical abuse and corporeal ruin, Foxe's unflinching portraits of death by burning force his reader to confront the reality of what was done to the victims he describes. The account of John Huss's burning exposes the particular cruelty of his executioners and the indignity of a heretic's death: "When all the wood was burned and consumed, the upper parte of the body was left hanging in the chaine, the which they threwe downe stake and all, and making a newe fire burned it, the heade being first cut in small gobbets, that it might the sooner be consumed unto ashes. The heart, which was founde amongst the bowels, being well beaten with staves and clubs, was at last pricked upon a sharpe sticke, and roasted at a fire a parte untill it was consumed" (625). While this description of Huss's execution focuses on the violence done to the victim's body, other reports emphasize suffering. Foxe's oft-quoted account of John Hooper's martyrdom describes the prolonged agony caused by the difficulties of keeping the fire going, the prayers uttered until Hooper's lips shriveled back to his gums, the first arm falling off and the second melting down to the bone, all while he was apparently still conscious (1,511). Problems with the fire were not uncommon, causing even more profound suffering for the victim. Hooper finally cries out, "For Gods love (good people) let me have more fire" (1,511). Unlike his companion Hugh Latimer, who dies quickly, Nicholas Ridley suffers a lengthy execution "by reason of the evill makyng of the fire unto hym" and at one point complains, "I cannot burne" (1,770). Only his lower half is burnt, and the explosion of the gunpowder worn in a pouch around his neck does little to speed his death. He finally dies only when his legs are so weakened that he collapses into the fire.

Foxe narrates these scenes in a relatively detached tone with few editorial interjections, allowing the hideous facts to speak for themselves.[39] His use of physical detail serves several purposes. As the Huss narrative suggests, the minutiae of the executions expose the cruelty of the men who carry them out, drawing a contrast between the patient martyr of God and the bloodthirstiness of the persecutor that has analogues in the *Golden Legend* tradition. However, in contrast to *The Golden Legend*'s depiction of martyrs who are completely insulated from pain by divine intervention, *Acts and Monuments* admits—even emphasizes—suffering in order to highlight the humanity of its subjects. Foxe's execution accounts individualize suffering by representing particular people and their tormented bodies.

The realism of the execution narratives underscores the martyr's identity as innocent victim, but it also signals his or her resistance to full absorption into representational topoi. For a moment, the reader's attention is shifted away from the confrontation between Catholic and Protestant theologies and toward the horror of a human being cruelly destroyed. Foxe's execution accounts confront the vulnerability of human flesh with an immediacy that shocks. The text does not fully resolve the martyr into an archetype, because the martyr's body is too radically physical to be merely symbolic, spilling beyond the boundaries of typology and ideology.

This unrelenting insistence on physicality combines with typological formulas to comprise one of Foxe's most important contributions to the genre of martyrology: the simultaneous representation of the martyr as a specific human being and as an archetypal soldier and sufferer for Christ. This representation produces a complex martyrological subject who is at once a historical fact—individuated by some combination of biographical particulars, unmediated speech,[40] and circumstances of trial and death—and a figure of the timeless Christian martyr—of Christ, the apostles, and the martyrs of the primitive church. From the torment of the stake, the faithful join the ranks of Christ's sanctified martyrs, the crowned procession stretching beyond the moment of physical death across all time. Many of Foxe's execution accounts, even those that are otherwise graphically violent, conclude with a string of stock phrases that signal the transition from bodily death to eternal glory. The climax of Hooper's horrific ordeal shifts between the stark reality of burning and the language of archetypal martyrdom, finally culminating in heavenly victory: "Even as a Lambe, paciently he aboade the extremitie therof [of the fire], neither moving forwardes, backwards, or to any side: but having his nether partes burned, and his bowels fallen out, he died as quietly as a childe in his bedde: and hee nowe raigneth as a blessed Martyr in the joyes of heaven" (1,511). Hooper is the lamb, the burned and disemboweled man, the peaceful child, and the triumphant martyr in a single sentence that exposes the text's impulses toward both documentary fidelity and religious typology.

The woodcut of Hooper's execution shows these same two semiotic codes at work (Figure 2.1). It illustrates some of the most grisly details of human incineration in Foxe's book. One of Hooper's arms has burnt off, its bones visible in the fire below. The other hand has fused to the chains around his middle, and the flesh of his legs is gone below the knees, revealing bare bones. In contrast to these details, the image's overall composition is highly formalized. It is not a scene of human suffering, but rather, of composure, ceremony, and transcen-

The burning of M. Iohn Hooper, Bifhop at Glocefter. An. 1 5 5 5. Februarie 9.

Lord Iefu receiue my foule.

Figure 2.1. The Burning of John Hooper. John Foxe, *Actes and Monumentes* (London, 1583). Reproduced by permission of The Huntington Library, San Marino, California. RB 59843.

dence. The martyr's body stands magnificently erect and robust, his face betraying no pain, and the carefully arranged flames conceal what would be the gruesome remaining stump of his arm. The woodcut of Hooper relies on both realistic and formalized elements to posit the martyr as simultaneously historical and typological.

In contrast to the Hooper woodcut, most of the illustrations in *Acts and Monuments* emphasize typological significance over physical deterioration. The account of John Badby's execution directly refers to the accompanying woodcut as a "manifestation of which torment" Badby suffered (523).[41] But the illustration depicts nothing resembling torment, instead representing Badby as serene and unscathed though surrounded by flames, his head and hands in a conventional saintly pose (Figure 2.2). The narrative of Badby emphasizes his role as human

Figure 2.2. The Burning of John Badby. John Foxe, *Actes and Monumentes* (London, 1583). Reproduced by permission of The Huntington Library, San Marino, California. RB 59843.

sufferer while the woodcut represents him as religious icon.[42] Similarly, the woodcut of John Rogers's burning depicts the martyr, despite his many months in Newgate, as a commanding, muscular figure who appears to take no notice of the enormous fire roiling around him (Figure 2.3).

Other woodcuts suggest hagiographic iconography through their overall composition. Large groups of martyrs are usually organized around three stakes, no matter how many individuals are being executed. Foxe's narratives suggest that this is in fact historically accurate, not an instance of artistic license, but there is no question that the image makes for compelling art in its overt allusion to the Crucifixion. The illustration of thirteen martyrs burned at Stratford-Le-Bow (Figure 2.4)

The burning of M. Iohn Rogers, Vicar of S.Pulchers,
and Reader of Paules in London.

Lorde receiue my fpirite.

Figure 2.3. The Burning of John Rogers. John Foxe, *Actes and Monumentes* (London, 1583). Reproduced by permission of The Huntington Library, San Marino, California. RB 59843.

depicts eleven of the martyrs tied to three stakes with two women "loose in the midst without any stake" (1916). What is most interesting about this woodcut is the arrangement of the bundles of faggots and wood into a backdrop for the execution. There is no evidence that such a structure was ever made at a Marian heretic burning. The text makes no reference to it, either in its account of the thirteen martyrs or in any other account; it would make little sense given that the audience was generally situated a full 360 degrees around the stake or scaffold; and it has no practical function in the execution and no visible structural support. Most likely, it is an artistic invention meant to set the martyrs

Figure 2.4. Thirteen Martyrs Burned at Stratford-Le-Bow. John Foxe, *Actes and Monumentes* (London, 1583). Reproduced by permission of The Huntington Library, San Marino, California. RB 59843.

apart from the surrounding crowd and suggest the architectural struc-tures common to religious iconography.

A smaller woodcut (Figure 2.5), one generic enough that it appears several times throughout the course of the book, makes use of a differ-ent kind of compositional device in which the flames and smoke make a frame for the martyr.[43] This formalized representation of the impervi-ous martyr, whose robelike clothing is untouched by the careful flames lapping around him, adapts a nonspecific figure into a constructed, symbolic representation of timeless, universal Christian martyrdom.

In addition to situating the martyr figure within a typological framework, the woodcuts of *Acts and Monuments* articulate a martyro-logical imperative shared with the exemplary figures of Christ and the

Figure 2.5. Generic martyr woodcut. John Foxe, *Actes and Monumentes* (London, 1583). Reproduced by permission of The Huntington Library, San Marino, California. RB 59843.

early church martyrs. Without exception, the pictured martyrs are engaged in some act of speech, indicated by either a banderole (Figures 2.1 and 2.2), a gesture of address (Figures 2.4 and 2.5), or both (Figure 2.3). In large groupings of martyrs like those of Stratford-le-Bow, every martyr whose hands are visible is represented in some motion of prayer or address to the crowd. The overwhelming predominance of speech and gestures of address points to the crucial relationship between verbal and physical witness in the text's portrait of martyrdom.

As chapter 1 demonstrates, the confession of Christ is an integral element of primitive martyrdom and its medieval representations, the mouth ideally functioning as a direct conduit for the word of Christ inscribed on the heart. Like their predecessors, Foxe's martyrs hold confession to be an imperative for salvation. They frequently echo scriptural admonitions that those who verbally forsake Christ will themselves be forsaken, in particular citing Christ's warning in the gospel of Luke, "whosoever shall be ashamed of me and of my words, of him shall the Son of man be ashamed, when he shall come in his own glory."[44] John Philpot recalls Paul's advice in Romans that "the beliefe of the hert justifieth, and the knowledge with the mouth maketh a man safe" (1,706).[45] Describing apostasy as a form of dissimulation, John Hullier quotes the warnings of Revelation, "where it is wrytten: 'That the fearefull shall have theyr parte wyth the unbeleeving and abhominable, in the lake that burneth with fire and brimstone, which is the seconde death'" (1,907).[46] Scripture organizes the martyr's approach to persecution and provides a means of envisioning the self within biblically prescribed modes of resistance.

The role of verbal confession was especially crucial during the Marian persecution, when the survival of the fledgling Protestant church in England depended on the faith and support of individual believers. With no way to foresee how long Mary's reign would last or what kind of church would succeed Marian Catholicism, Reformers could keep their cause viable only if Mary's Protestant subjects continued to voice dissent. It was an uncertain time for the bodies and souls of English Protestants. Even if they remained steadfast through their trials, ecclesiastical authorities might seek to demoralize the Reformed cause by reporting that they had recanted. Foxe's book describes martyrs' attempts to preempt such slanders in this perilous climate. For example, Robert Samuel decides that it is best to be armed with a clear, written proclamation of his beliefs: "Considering with my selfe these pearillous times, pearishing daies and the unconstante and miserable state of man, the decay of our faith, the sinister reporte and false sclaunder of Gods most holy word, these urgent causes in conscience do constraine me to confesse and acknowledge my faith and meaning in Christes holy Religion" (1,706). Perhaps fearing that he might die without the opportunity to confes his faith, Simon Miller draws up a statement of his beliefs that he carries around in his shoe (2,005).

The most influential members of the imprisoned Protestant resistance—men like Ridley, Latimer, and Philpot—spent great energy exhorting the Christian flock not to bow under the yoke of Catholicism or passively submit to the Catholic church to spare themselves. A major theme of Philpot's departing letter to the faithful is the evil of conveniently remaining silent on matters of faith: "let no man deceive you with vayn words, saying, that you may keepe your faith to your selves, and dissemble with Antichrist, and to live at rest and quietnes in the world, as most men doe, yielding to necessitie" (1,831). Latimer is even more vehement on the subject, warning that someone who knows the truth and fails to speak it is a "traytour to the truth . . . a Traytor and a Judas unto Christe" (1,752). Protestants who decide to remain in England should prepare themselves to die, Ridley writes, or else suffer eternal damnation by recanting. The choice is one between earthly death and "deny[ing] thy mayster Christ, which is the losse at the last, both of body and soule unto everlasting death" (1,781).[47]

As in Eusebius and in *The Golden Legend,* verbal confession emerges in Foxe's book as a cornerstone of Christian duty. In their supplication to Queen Mary for tolerance, the men of Norfolk argue that all true Christians must "embrace . . . in heart" the religion taught in King Edward VI's day and must "confesse it with mouth, & (if need require) loose and forsake, not onely house, land, & possessions, riches, wife, children, and friends: but also (if God will so call them) gladly to suffer all manner of persecution, and to loose their lives in the defense of GODS worde and trueth" (1,902). Their statement exposes a logical relationship between faith, speech, and death, articulating a view at the heart of Foxe's accounts. In Foxe, confession becomes the central act of martyrdom. Whereas the medieval tradition emphasized death as the martyr's final goal, Foxe's martyrs treat death as a form of confession, making Christian witness the defining martyr enterprise. Death operates as a demonstrative ratification of the word of God, a way to "confirme and seale Christes Gospell" (1,572).

The men and women of Foxe's book resurrect and literalize the root meaning of the word "martyr" as "witness" by describing their deaths as the "confirmation," "seal," and "testimony" of their confession of faith. Hullier describes his death as the concluding flourish of his written text of faith, a textual extension of hortatory letter to the faithful: "I do not only write this, but I will also (with the assistance of God's grace) ratify and confirm and seal the same with the effusion of my blood" (1,908). For other martyrs, such as William Tyms, Ralph Allerton, and Richard Roth, the intimacy of writing and violent death is signaled by composing letters in blood "for lacke of other inke" in a gesture that renders the text itself a metaphor for impending martyrdom and a metonym for the persecuted body (2,017).

The demonstration of confession by death is particularly vivid in cases where a parish priest is returned to his home town to be executed in front of the congregation he once led. Hooper declares himself happy to be brought back to Gloucester to die "amongest the people, over whom he was pastor, there to confirme with his death the truth which he had before taught them" (1,508). Returning to the town of Hadley, which Foxe presents as a kind of Christian utopia, Taylor tells his parishioners, "I have preached to you Gods word & truth, and am come this day to seale it with my bloud" (1,526). Conversely, a bad death could signify the negation of the martyr's confession, as Robert Ferrar suggests when he tells one of his parishioners "that if he saw hym once to stirre in the paynes of his burnyng, he should then geve no credite to his doctrine" (1,555). This portrait of the martyr as an orator whose death functions as a final, consummating speech act is reinforced by the woodcuts, where the martyr's death and speech are regularly figured as one.

This connection between death and speech reveals the necessity of memorializing the acts of the Protestant martyrs; through the creation of a text of Christian witness, the testimony sealed by blood is never silenced. The writing and circulation of their stories ensures that the message of the martyrs' deaths continues to be rehearsed, retaining potency and immediacy long after the ashes have blown away. As Mark Breitenberg has observed, "The final, visible victory of the Word is precisely in the *Acts and Monuments* itself."[48] Like the martyrologists who came before him, Foxe produces a lasting witness to the glory of Christ by telling the story of his faithful people.

"A Vice in a Play"

By the time the narrative reaches the climactic execution scenes depicted in the woodcuts, much has already been done to establish the martyrs' necessary connection to typological models. Following the pattern established by earlier martyrology and passion literature like *The Golden Legend* and the Corpus Christi dramas, the trial provides a forum for both martyr and martyrologist to declare and demonstrate the moral superiority of the victim and the depravity of the persecutor. Because the Marian persecutions pitted one group of self-proclaimed Christians against another, the Protestant on trial must convincingly represent his or her beliefs as true Christianity and Catholic belief as a false doctrine leading souls to eternal damnation. These claims are aided by a pattern of persecutor and victim metaphors through which the martyrs cast themselves as helpless innocents in the clutches of bloodthirsty monsters. Much of their language is derived from the book of Revelation, where they find not only ready-made images of persecutors but a divine narrative that describes the religious turmoil of their own day. John Bale's *The Image of bothe churches*, published in 1545, had painstakingly described the history of the corruption of the Catholic church through the narrative of Revelation. This book, Leslie Fairfield has noted, "underlay all of Bale's writing from the 1540s onward," including his martyrological work, which was a powerful model for Foxe.[49] The charge that the Roman church was like Babylon and the pope like the Antichrist had been circulating in Reformed culture for at least several decades and had become part of the standard polemical language of English Reformers.[50]

This language is everywhere present in the verbal combat Foxe's martyrs wage against their Catholic persecutors. In one of his disputes, Ridley argues that when the bishop of Rome began to seek power over temporal rulers he became "the very true antichrist, whereof saynct John speaketh by the name of the whore of Babilon, and say with the sayd sainct Gregory: he that maketh himselfe a Byshop over all the worlde, is worse then Antichrist" (1,758). Later at the ceremony of his degradation, "Doctor Ridley did vehemently invey against the Romysh Byshyp and all that foolysh apparell, callyng hym Antichrist, and the ap-parell foolysh and abominable, yea to fond for a Vice in a play" (1,767). Ridley appears almost reserved in these exchanges when we compare them to the passionate condemnation of Catholicism that runs through his writings. In a farewell letter written from prison, he addresses the Roman church as not only Antichristian but heathenishly idolatrous: "harken thou Whoorishe Baude of Babylon, thou wicked lymme of Antichrist, thou bloudy Woolfe, why slayest thou downe, and makest havocke of the Prophetes of GOD? Why murtherest thou so cruelly Christes poore seely sheep. . . . Thy GOD which is the worke of thy handes, and whom thou sayest thou hast power to make, that thy deafe and dumbe God (I say) will not in deede, nor cannot (although thou art not ashamed to call him thy maker) make thee to escape the re-venging hand of the high and almighty God" (1,774). Cranmer echoes the accusation that the pope's assumption of power "above all Emper-ours and kinges of the world" identifies him with the Antichrist, and he charges that the pope is "more insolent then Lucifer" (1,804). Ex-plaining why he cannot submit to the authority of Rome, Cranmer says the pope "is like the Devill in his doinges" and that his behavior matches Christ's description of the Antichrist (1,874). Although lack-ing Cranmer's biblical learning, nonclerical martyrs nonetheless make some of these same accusations. Six martyrs of Colchester, all trades-men, call the Roman Catholic Mass "Babylonicall" and full of "all other of antichristes marchaundise" (1,909). Though he does not specifically identify the Catholic church as Antichristian, admitting himself "un-learned," the London merchant-tailor Roger Holland launches a full-scale attack on Catholic doctrine and the church's claim to primitive descent, skillfully associating Catholicism with the idolatrous worship of heathen gods: "I trust there be vii. C.M. [seven hundred thou-sand] . . . that have not bowed their knees to that idol your masse, and your god Maozim" (2,040).[51]

Stephen Gratwick's criticism of the Catholic judges who examine him employs another powerful paradigm for describing martyr and persecutor, one that relies on a culturally resonant language of Christian oppression. When Gratwick repeatedly insists that he is being unlawfully examined and is answered with laughter from the panel of clergy, he responds, "Why do ye laugh? are ye confederate together for my bloud, and therein triumph? you have more cause to looke waightely upon the matter: For I stand here before you upon life and death. But you declare yourselves what you are, for you are lapped in Lambes apparell, but I would to God ye had coates according to your assemblye here, which are scarlet gownes; for I do here perceive you are bent to have my bloud" (1,977). Gratwick's response reveals several connections to earlier formulations of martyrdom. He characterizes his judges as interested not in trying him fairly or in objectively determining his guilt but in seeing him dead. He accuses them of cloaking themselves in "Lambes apparel," a reference both to feigned meekness and innocence as well as to the garment they make of Christ, the *Agnus Dei*. His assessment of the true characters—the "scarlet gownes"— that lurk beneath this deceptive outer garment links them with the blood they seek and with the Pharisees responsible for Christ's death, often depicted in red robes.[52] By echoing these biblical topoi, Gratwick implicitly recasts the present in a framework of the past and the transcendent, situating himself in relation to Christ's death and the universal struggle between godly and ungodly. Foxe picks up some of this same language, criticizing the restoration of Catholicism by calling it the "sheepe skinnes, under the which (as Christ saith) ravening Wolves cover themselves" (1,903).[53] "[A]mongest all the Wolfes," Foxe warns, "they are most cruellest which are clothed in lambes skinnes."[54]

A few of Foxe's Catholic villains earned the reputation for particular cruelty. Edmund Bonner, bishop of London, who came to be known as "bloody Bonner" for his brutal treatment of Protestants, occupies the position of arch persecutor in Foxe's accounts of the Marian martyrs. Admitting that such stories are somewhat off-topic and "touch no matter of religion," Foxe nonetheless narrates several incidents of Bonner's behavior because, as he explains, they "toucheth some thyng the nature and disposition of that man" (2,062). Apparently Bonner had a fondness for beating Protestant captives in his garden, a practice Foxe sarcastically refers to as Bonner's "accustomed devotion" or "the bishops blessing" (2,062).[55] Writing from prison, John Bradford hints that Bonner's cruelty is cannibalistic: the bishop is "almost glutted with suppyng so much bloud," and his chaplains feast on "meat roasted in Smithfield at the fire of the stake" (1,842). Foxe reports that another particularly vilified persecutor, bishop Stephen Gardiner, was afflicted with a hideous deformity that expressed the demonic inner character of the man: "I will not heare speake of that which hath bene constantly reported to me, touching the monstrous making & mishaped fashion of hys feete and toes, the nayles wherof were sayd not to bee like to other mens, but to crooke downeward, and to be sharpe lyke the clawes of ravening beastes" (1,785).[56]

The figure of the persecutor is of central importance to Foxe's martyrology. He functions much like the pagan persecutors of *The Golden Legend* and the villainous Pilates, Herods, and devils of the medieval morality and mystery plays. These traditions have an unquestionable influence on both Foxe and his martyrs. For the martyrologist's purposes, this caricatured representation of consummate evil reinforces the text's argument that the Catholic church is anti-Christian and dramatizes the universal import of defeating this enemy. The martyrs themselves participate in shaping this interpretation of the persecutor by describing him variously as bloody wolf, Antichrist, and Pharisee. These labels justify the martyr's cause and provide assurance for both the martyr and the audience of whose side God is on.

"Symple Lambes"

The counterpart to these images of evil Catholic persecutors is the representation of their victims as innocent lambs. In his preface "To the Persecutors of God's Truth," Foxe demands that Catholics "consider the number almost out of nomber of so many, silly & symple lambes of Christ, whose bloud you have sought and suckt."[57] This language figures the martyrs as harmless, unsophisticated, guileless, and morally pure victims of the heinous atrocities Foxe then goes on to list. In his introduction to the account of seven martyrs of Canterbury, he describes the Catholic church as feeding on the blood of its victims, Christ's lambs, to sustain its church: the clergy, "being never satisfied with bloud to maintaine their carnall kingdome, presume so highly to violate the precise law of Gods commandments in slaying the simple pore Lambes of the glorious congregation of Jesus Christ" (1,980). Foxe's account of John Lambert, a preacher executed for heresy during Henry VIII's reign, describes the martyr as "the humble lamb of Christ" who is "devoured . . . amonge so many wolves and vultures" (1,122, 1,124).

The many variations of the wolf/lamb dyad expose an important element of Foxe's production of the persecution narrative: an insistence on the innocence of the martyrological subject. The profusion of metaphors describing martyrs as lambs, particularly in contrast to their wolfish persecutors, presents a consistent argument for the martyr as a helpless, artless, and above all, innocent, victim. This characterization is further refined by a range of adjectives modifying "lamb," such as "meek," "poor," "silly," "simple," and "little." Foxe's diverse martyrs are gathered wholesale under a banner of spotless, virtuous innocence, as in his charge that the Catholic clergy murder alike "the chiidren [*sic*] and servaunts of God, bothe men and women, wives and maydes, old & young, blinde and lame, madde and unmadde, discreete and simple innocentes, learned with the unlearned, and that of all degrees from the high Archbishop to the Clark and Sexten of the church, and that most wrongfully and wilfully; with such effusion of innocent Christian bloud, as cryeth up dayly to God for vengeance" (1,949). Patrick Collinson notes that this passage subsumes every stratum of English life in "a representative cross-section of the entire nation."[58] It shows the ready elasticity of Foxe's martyr text to absorb into a language of guileless spiritual purity nearly anyone who opposes Catholicism.

One of the text's strategies for cultivating martyred innocence is the attention and honor awarded nonaristocratic, nonclerical, and unlearned people who gave their lives in defense of the gospel. Foxe remarks that this is one of the ways his text differs from the corrupted Catholic tradition: "What poore lay man or lay woman, were their lives never so Christian, their faith and confession never so pure, their death never so agonising for the witnes of Christ, and truth of his word, shall finde any place or favour . . . in the Popes Calendar" (582).

Instead of high-born aristocrats, Foxe's text focuses on parsons like Rowland Taylor and the tradesmen and families who formed his parish. The longest of Foxe's narratives are devoted to clerical martyrs, no doubt due to the notoriety of their cases and the bulk of surviving documents surrounding them. But the ranks of unlettered common folk executed for their religion outnumber the priests. Foxe's account of the Welsh martyr William Nichol indicates how the uneducated lay martyr becomes a polemical asset by functioning as a foil for the cruelty of the Catholic clergy, whose vast theological knowledge leads only to spiritual blindness and moral depravity. Their treatment of Nichol seems particularly egregious given that he may have had a mental disability. If Nichol were truly impaired, he would have had diminished legal responsibility for his actions, which would catch his persecutors in yet greater cruelty: "the more simplicitie of feeblenes of wit appeared in him, the more beastly and wretched dothe it declare their cruell & tyrannicall acte therein" (2,034–35).

The text pays careful attention to those who are weakest and meekest. In his portrait of Latimer, a man of respect and formidable learning, Foxe regularly emphasizes Latimer's age and infirmity and capitalizes on the pitiful impression his shrunken figure and fortunes must have made. Like Nichol, whom many thought "half foolish," Hugh Laverock and John Apprice are noted for their afflictions and weakness, the former "an olde lame man" of sixty-eight and the latter a blind man. Foxe remarks that even these humble creatures can be the vessels of God, whose "unsearchable mercies" lead him to choose "as well the poore, lame, and blinde, as the rich, mighty, and healthful, to sette foorth hys glory" (2,034, 1,909). The qualities of nonthreatening innocence represented by Laverock and Apprice are set in contrast to the cruelty of their persecutors, "in whome was so little favour or mercye to all sortes and kindes of men, that they also spared neither impotente age, neither lame, nor blinde, as may well appeare by these two poore creatures" (1,803). Without the polish, education, or savvy of their enemies, these men stand for the simple virtue of the gospel and illustrate an indispensable type in Foxe's argument against the Romish religion. Women too (here with husbands and children—not the exquisite virgins of old) are candidates for the crown of martyrdom. Foxe relates the deaths of Anne Potten and Joan Trunchfield, "[i]n whose sufferyng their constancie worthily was to be wondered at, who beyng so simple women, so manfully stoode to the confession and testimony of Gods worde and veritie" and "ended their lives with great triumph: the Lord graunt we may do the like" (1,893–94). These narratives demonstrate to their audience the great power of God, through whom "simple women" are made into "manfully" triumphant Christian models and the "poore, lame, and blinde" become the mouthpieces of "glory."[59] The narrative itself participates in effecting this transformation, turning a quintessential figure of weakness into an archetype of conquering power and making an ordinary person into a legend—a monument.

The emphasis on simplicity occasionally tends toward infantilization, particularly when applied to women, whose challenge to established authority is often neutralized by the commonplaces of childish ignorance used to describe them.[60] Foxe calls the four female martyrs of Canterbury "seely pore women, whose weake imbecilitie the more strength it lacketh by natural imperfection, the more it ought to be helped, or at least pitied" (1,980). The words "silly" and "seely" are liberally used not only by Foxe but by the martyrs themselves, who purposely employ the words to characterize themselves as simple and innocent.[61] The *Oxford English Dictionary* gives several suggestive sixteenth-century usages of "silly," including "plain," "simple," "humble," "poor," "weak," "feeble," "helpless," "foolish," and "unlearned," and indicates that it may be applied particularly in reference to women, children, and animals. When Ridley calls the martyrs "Christ's poore seely sheep," he carries the suggestion of weakness and simplicity beyond the category of women and children to create a polemical contrast between the innocence of the martyrs and the cruel machinations of the Romish clergy (1,774).[62]

Innocent Conquerors

Foxe's representation of the martyr as an innocent victim works, somewhat paradoxically, in concert with his other dominant martyr metaphor, which figures the martyr as a victorious soldier for Christ. At the same time that the language of both Foxe and his martyrs insists on naïve innocence, it posits its subjects as valiant warriors "buckling with two mighty enemies, Antichrist and death," and defeating both through martyrdom (1,496). Although Foxe's martyrs do not bait their persecutors with verbal abuse to the same degree as their forbears in *The Golden Legend,* they are plenty combative, and the text's martial metaphors highlight this aspect of their character. Rowland Taylor addresses Cranmer, Ridley, and Latimer as three "captaines in the foreward under Christs crosse, banner or standerd in such a cause and skirmish, when, not onely one or two of our deare redemers strongholds are besieged, but all his chiefe castles ordeyned for our safeguard, are traiterously impugned" (1,893). Ridley describes the Reformers as in a state of "chivalrie and warfare, wherein I doubt not but we be set to fight under Christes banner, and his crosse agaynst our ghostly enemy the devill and the old serpent Satan," and extends the metaphor to include the engines, artillery, army, and seige that will make up the war (1,725). Such military metaphors emphasize a heroic brand of martyrdom in which the martyr acts as an armed combatant in triumphant battle.

This martial metaphor is apparent in the epistles of Paul and pervades texts like *The Golden Legend.*[63] But the marriage of soldier and victim metaphors to describe the figure of the martyr is not a direct rehearsal of *The Golden Legend* tradition. As chapter 1 observed, the martyrs of *The Golden Legend* do not experience any real suffering because of God's miraculous intervention, and their verbal ferocity positions them not as victims or innocents but as heroes and fearless instigators of the battle against Satan. Metaphors such as "lamb" and "silly sheep" that would figure them as weak or simple are few; rather, they are "athletes" and "soldiers" in Christ's army. By contrast, in *Acts and Monuments*, innocence is a fundamental component of the claim to martyrdom. In the bitter battle with the evils of Catholicism, innocence emerges as one of the primary distinctions between the true Christian and the conniving, conspiring, Catholic enemy. At the same time, the construction of martyrdom depends on the victim's ultimate conquest of that enemy in a heroic subversion of the power of earthly death.

While the representation of the martyr as a triumphant warrior is certainly shared with the medieval martyr legend, the paradoxical coupling of triumph and innocence has its primary source in the figure of

Christ. Christ is "that most mild Lamb, that invincible Lion of the tribe of Judah," who, "once conquered of the world . . . yet conquer[s] the world after the same manner he was conquered" (vi^r). This formulation of Christ as lion and lamb, conquered and conquering, is nowhere more evident than in the late-medieval Corpus Christi drama. The Corpus Christi passions insist on the silence, passivity, and humility of Christ by detailing his spectacular torture and physical suffering. At the same time, his death on the cross is self-willed and serves his own ends. Through the drama's culmination in resurrection, ascension, and judgment, Christ achieves ultimate victory over the powers that bound him in humiliation and death. This is precisely the transaction effected in Foxe's narratives, where the martyrs successfully communicate meekness and innocence through metaphoric and performative references to Christ, the innocent Lamb. Further, they imitate Christ's victory by claiming one of their own. Like the Pharisees of the Corpus Christi dramas, the Catholic persecutors in Foxe are allowed to harm the faithful only "by Gods sufferance and good will, to his praise and honour, and to our eternall joye and felicitie" (1,705). The martyr's execution produces a reversal of power whereby the persecutor becomes an instrument of God and a creator of his own destruction, while the martyr, like Christ, conquers through death. Like the weapons of Christ's passion or *arma Cristi,* the stake is transformed from an instrument used against the martyr to an instrument used in service of the martyr's own ends.[64] Thus late-medieval passion traditions provide a model for Protestant martyrdom not only through Christ's sacrificial death but in his paradoxical role as innocent conqueror.

As Stephen Gratwick's reference to "scarlet robes" has already suggested, the comparison between the martyrs and Christ logically carries with it the suggestion that the Catholic inquisitors are the moral and typological equivalent of those who put Christ to death. A scathing letter to Bishop Bonner from an anonymous friend of the martyr John Philpot shows this equation in action. She writes: "Now my Lord I perceivyng your lordship to be a more cruell tyraunt than ever was Herode, and more desirous to destroy Christ in hys poore members then ever was he, which to destroy Christ killed hys owne sonne, I thought good to take the Angels counsaile, and to come no more at you, for I see that you are set all in a rage lyke a ravenyng wolfe agaynst the poore lambs of Christ appoynted to the slaughter for the testi-monye of the truth" (1,842). Here the author invokes the images of wolf and lamb while drawing a relationship between the Catholic clergy and the biblical persecutors of Christ. This representation of the persecutor is a consistent theme of Foxe's trial scenes. In an account borrowed largely from Bale of the Lollard martyr John Oldcastle, the martyr is reported to have said to his examiners, "[Y]e are very An-tichristes. . . . No ground have ye in all the Scripture so Lordly to take it uppon you, but in Annas and Cayphas, which sat thus upon Christ, and uppon his Apostles after hys ascension" (562). Roger Holland refers to these villains in his accusation that his judges "have the same zeal that Annas and Caiaphas had, trusting to their authoritie, tradi-tions, and ceremonies, more then to the worde of God" (2,041). Be-yond providing a paradigm through which the martyr becomes a figure of Christ persecuted by Jews, the Pharisee metaphor is a vehicle for communicating one of the cornerstones of Reformed polemic: the true Christian is armed with the simplicity of scripture while the enemies of Christ rely on pomp, sophistry, and misdirected learning, or what Holland calls "authoritie, traditions, and ceremonies." Oldcastle tells his examiners, "your Lordly order esteemeth not greatly the lowly be-haviour of poore Peter," and Foxe describes the project of Wycliffe's followers as "defend[ing] the lowlynesse of the Gospell against the exceeding pryde, ambition, symony, avarice, Hypocrisie, whoredome, sacrilege, tyranny, ydolatrouse worshippinges, and other fylthy fruts of those stifnecked Phariseis," the Roman clergy.[65] Knott has observed that "Foxe makes simplicity an index of the 'spiritual' religion that he opposes to 'corporal' religion preoccupied with 'external matters and ceremonial observations.'"[66] Comparing the Catholic clergy to the persecutors of Christ acts as a shorthand for comparing the fleshly/worldly to the spiritual/heavenly.

Performing Typology

Foxe's martyrs also do their part to draw a resemblance be-tween themselves and the crowned saints of religious literature and iconography. As they imagine and experience death, their behavior echoes the whole of the Christian martyr tradition, from Christ's passion to the early church martyrs to the hagiography of the Middle Ages. One of the central arguments of the English Reformation was that the Protestant church was not invented by Martin Luther and John Calvin but claims a continuous history all the way back to the apostles. And one of the most effective ways of solidifying this argument was by consciously connecting Reformers' executions with established notions of what constitutes a legible martyr's death. If Protestant victims were to be interpreted as martyrs, they had to demonstrate their kinship to the martyrs of the early church by behaving similarly.

At its most basic level, all Christian martyrdom is an imitation of the death of Christ and an expression of faith in the salvific power of that death. In their enactment of martyrdom, the men and women of Foxe's book often draw direct parallels between themselves and Christ. Turning himself in to the Catholic authorities, George Marsh declares, "I take my selfe . . . for a sheepe appaynted to be slaine, paciently to suffer what crosse so ever it shal please my merciful Father to lay on me" (1,563).[67] Marsh's remarks call up both Christ's suffering on the cross and Paul's letter to the Romans: "For thy sake we are killed all day long; we are accounted as sheep for the slaughter."[68] Foxe reinforces the idea of Marsh's Christological death by describing his appointed execution day as the day "he should suffer" (1,567). When the Lollard martyr John Huss is made to wear a white robe at his degradation, Foxe reports that he "called to his remembraunce the white vesture which Herode put upon Jesus Christ to mock him withall. So likewise in al other things he did comfort himselfe by the example of Christ" (623). In this contemporary reiteration of Christ's trial before Herod, Huss's judges make him wear a paper cap with devils drawn on it, but the gesture fails to achieve its intended humiliation: "My Lord Jesus Christ for my sake did weare a crowne of thorne," Huss says; "why should not I then for his sake againe weare thys light crowne, be it never so ignominious? Truly I will do it, and that willingly" (624). Huss's follower, Jerome of Prague, is also given the paper cap to wear at his degrading. In a response clearly modeled on Huss's, Jerome proclaims, "Our Lorde Jesu Christ, when as he shoulde suffer death for me most wretched sinner, did weare a crowne of thorne upon his head: and I for his sake in stede of that crowne, will willingly weare this miter and cappe" (637). With this speech, Jerome announces his conscious imitation of both the humiliation of Christ and the successfully performed martyrdom of his teacher and predecessor, Huss. He is imitating Christ as well as imitating Huss imitating Christ. Breitenberg describes this relationship between martyr models as dependent and reciprocal: "A martyr's death . . . could only be understood in its relation to Christ's original martyrdom; at the same time, the meaning of Christ's suffering was revealed to those who witnessed the martyr's suffering, or who read about it in the *Acts and Monuments.* This kind of self-legitimating circularity is frequently a part of an apocalyptic tradition in which biblical prophecy and history are entwined in a relationship of mutual fulfillment."[69]

As Knott has demonstrated, many of the notions of Christian martyrdom reflected in Foxe have their roots in scripture, which prophesies the persecution of Christ's people and promises the crown of a martyr's salvation to those who wager their lives in defense of the gospel.[70] With the biblical promise of the rewards of martyrdom as a constant backdrop to their actions, Foxe's martyrs explicitly invoke scriptural paradigms as a way of guiding their actions and framing them for their audience. The death of Stephen, the first apostolic martyr, is often echoed in condemnation or death scenes in which martyrs beg God to have mercy on their persecutors.[71] Another commonly borrowed gesture is the martyr consigning his or her spirit to God, usually effected through the Latin intonation "*in manus tuas*" ("into your hands"), an imitation of Stephen, of Christ, or of Stephen imitating Christ.[72] Because the words and behavior of Foxe's martyrs are so filled with this kind of mimesis, it is difficult to identify with certainty their specific sources. Are they following the example of Christ, of an apostolic or primitive martyr, or of someone they saw executed a few months back? When a martyred laborer refers to himself as "gold tried in the fire," a popular topos in Foxe, is he consciously echoing the epistles of Peter or the book of Wisdom?[73] Is he following the example of Polycarp? Is he rehearsing models he learned from medieval martyrology? Or is he imitating what took place at another heretic burning? There is no way to arrive at a definitive answer, because the source is a composite, a Bour-dieuian *habitus* that includes the example of contemporary martyrs.

Foxe himself does not acknowledge the mimetic nature of the deaths he records. His remarks on the martyrs' behavior suggest instead that a true martyr simply responds to the moment with spontaneous expressions of his or her faith and election by God. In his account of John Hooper, he reports that the martyr asked not to be bound to the stake because he believed that God would "give him strength sufficient to abide the extremity of the fire, without bands" (1,510). Hooper surely knew his gesture to be an imitation of the second-century martyr Polycarp. In the story reported of Polycarp, the martyr refuses to be bound: "Leave me thus," he says, "for He who gives me power to endure the fire, will grant me to remain in the flames unmoved even without the security you will give me by the nails."[74] Foxe's description of Hooper's action ignores its mimesis; his "[c]omparison between Hooper and Polycarp" suggests that the similarity is a manifestation of Hooper's godliness and Christian spirit and that these qualities prove him to be on a par with this exalted martyr of the early church: "[I]t is wrytten of Polycarpus, when hee should have bene tied to the stake, he required to stand untied. . . . So likewise Hooper, *with the like spirite,* when hee shoulde have been tied with three chaines to the stake, requiring them to have so [*sic*] such mistrust of him, was tied but with one, who and if he had not bene tied at all, yet (no doubte) woulde have no lesse aunswered to that great patience of Polycarpus" (1,512, emphasis added). This representation suits Foxe's polemical agenda: to demonstrate the righteousness of the Reformed church by demonstrating the holiness of his subjects. The continued rehearsal of martyr models—of Christ, of the early martyrs, and of one's own fellow sufferers—gives each an ongoing efficacy that is circulated and confirmed through Foxe's text.

Earlier martyr literature provides a language through which the martyr spontaneously expresses his or her faith. It forms the structure within which sixteenth-century martyrdom is conceived and enacted. Imitation of Christ, the apostles, or Polycarp provides the martyr with a language for understanding and declaring faith and furnishes the audience with a means of reading that declaration. Foxe's martyrs show themselves aware of not only the textual tradition that informs their actions but their position in the future of that tradition.

On occasion, their actions appear to be organized with conscious attention to their stories' circulation as literary texts. In the self-authored accounts of his eleven trials before the ecclesiastical authorities, Philpot numbers each trial according to a sequence of what he calls "tragedies": "Thus endeth the fift Tragedy," he says, to mark the end of his fifth examination (1,805). In doing so, Philpot casts himself as the tragic hero in a drama that he records for the benefit of a larger reading community. Hullier's departing prayer, written in the last days of his imprisonment, shows awareness of the prayer's future as a textual artifact. Hullier's prayer is a public one, a text written for the benefit of others who will be encouraged by the steadfastness of one who has suffered for Christ. Coupled with the conventional gestures and speeches Hullier performs at his execution, the prayer serves to shape public interpretation of his confession and death. Unlike Eusebius's martyrs, who "neither proclaimed themselves as martyrs, nor allowed [others] to address them by this title," Hullier ensures by the authoring and circulation of his prayer that his identity as a sufferer for Christ is secure. Like many other martyrs, Hooper is not allowed to address the crowd gathered at his execution. By what appears to be some prior arrangement, however, a friend situated close to the stake is on hand to transcribe his final prayer, which then becomes circulated through the community. Cynthia Wittman Zollinger has remarked that "the example of poor Hooper illustrates the actions that Protestant martyrs take to construct as well as respond to the textuality of the faith. Other martyrs as well set down accounts of their sufferings and interrogations, creating an autobiographical textual tradition that models for its readers the 'true' witness of the faith in the crucible of interrogation."[75]

Foxe's martyrs are aware of the pressure of the impending narrative they will become. While imprisoned, they hear reports of other martyrs' behavior, which not only comforts them but provides models for their own. Stories are in constant circulation through the prisons. Foxe includes a great number of letters written by the captive John Bradford that show him regularly corresponding with other prisoners, including Cranmer, Ridley, and Latimer, as well as with faithful supporters at large. In these letters, Bradford exhorts others to remain steadfast in the faith while representing himself, his sufferings, and his hopes through traditional martyr topoi.[76] Ridley's letters map the circulation of martyr narratives from one prison to the next. He reports hearing news of Rowland Taylor's confession of faith and passes this on in a letter to Bradford. Bolstered by word he's received of John Rogers' burning and "stout confession of Christe and his truth even unto the death," Ridley excitedly writes to Bradford about his own impending execution (1,726). He invites Bradford to share his letters with fellow prisoners and perhaps anticipates their survival and circulation in the community at large, which is eventually achieved through Foxe. In a letter he receives from his exiled friend Edmund Grindal, Ridley gets news that the citizens of Frankfurt approve and admire the English Reformers' constancy and imprisonment for the faith. He reports back that this "greatly comfort[ed]" him and "warmed [his] heart" (1,729). Such exchanges position Ridley as an audience to other martyrs' acts and deaths even while he is behind bars. Further, they put him in touch with his own audience, a citizenry across the sea alert to see what he will do.

Acts and Interpretations

Foxe's narratives are largely the product of audiences and martyrs creating meaning together based on a shared symbolics of language and gesture. This transaction ultimately ensures that the heretic's burning will be interpreted as a martyr's death. The audience's act of interpretation is therefore crucial to the narrative produced. Minute gestures become translated into a conclusive reading of the martyr's death first by the audience witnessing the execution and again by the audience of Foxe's text.[77] The narrative of William Flower suggests one way this transaction might work. After having his right hand cut off because he assaulted a priest, Flower is burnt as a heretic:

And thus fire was set unto hym, who burning therein, cried with a loud voyce: Oh the sonne of God have mercye upon me, Oh the sonne of God receyve my soule, three tymes, and so his spech beyng taken from hym, he spake no more, liftyng up notwith-standyng his stumpe with hys other arme, as long as he could.

And thus endured this constant witnes and faythfull servaunt of God, the extremitie of the fire, beyng therein cruelly handled, by reason that to his burning little wood was brought, so that for lacke of fagots there not sufficient to burne hym, they were fayne to strike hym downe into the fire. Where he lying along (which was dolefull to behold) upon the ground, hys nether part was consumed in the fire, whilest hys upper part was cleane without the fire, hys tongue in all mens sight still moovyng in hys mouth. (1,577)[78]

Despite his crime against the priest, the constellation of Flower's actions at the stake convince enough of the audience that Flower was a "constant witnes and faythfull servaunt of God" to ensure his inclusion in Foxe's collection. He was condemned for heresy and refused to recant; he prayed loudly enough that his words were heard and approved; he lifted his mangled arm heavenward; and he showed no signs of unseemly struggle or resistance. His audience interprets these actions, and report goes out that he died a martyr.

Flower's conduct is interpreted a second time by the audience of Foxe's text, who are to read the account of his death and arrive at the same conclusion. How does this readerly audience interpret the narrative's most remarkable detail, Flower's moving tongue? What does the tongue say? Modern physiology might account for it as a reflexive action of the nerves, but here it is resolved into the realm of metonym, signifying the martyr's miraculous ability to continue purposive functioning in an extremity of torment. More specifically, the moving tongue represents the continuation of one of the martyr's most important acts: verbal confession of Christ. After the narration of Flower's prayer, then the prayer's repetition, and then Foxe's description of him as a "constant witness," the reader understands the moving tongue as the martyr continuing to confess Christ even beyond when it would seem humanly possible to do so. To call Flower a "constant witnes" in the midst of this account is to carefully shape how the reader translates the information about his moving tongue. The reader supplies the correct conclusion based on the interpretation of actions within a closed semiotic system, where *moving tongue + prayer + burning = confessor of Christ,* and not *moving tongue = demonic possession* or *moving tongue = evil man cursing his persecutors.* Further, the tongue detail is one in a string of bald facts about the destruction of Flower's body by fire and violence. It operates as what Roland Barthes might call "the real," a signifier referring to "what really happened," standing in to authenticate the scene with unflinching truth.[79] Thus the moving tongue speaks much, operating simultaneously in the registers of the purely incidental and the pregnantly symbolic, both a synecdoche for the real human body experiencing the contortions of death and a metonym of the Christian spirit conquering that death.

In Foxe's text, details of physical actions like that of Flower's moving tongue are seamlessly resolved into a language of Christian martyrdom. Praying and looking heavenward represent the martyr's earnestness in an interpretive move that happens almost invisibly. Thomas Bilney, for example, "made his private prayer with such earnest elevation of his eyes and handes to heaven, and in so good and quiet behaviour, that he seemed not to consider the terror of his death" (1,013).[80] The conclusion that Bilney had no fear of death is less subtly drawn than the assumption on which it is based—that the raising of the eyes and hands is a transparent gesture of earnestness. How does the reporter know he was earnest? The reader is to assume, as the reporter does, that: (a) the truth is in the behavior, (b) behavior is a transparent window to the soul, and (c) the sum of behavior adds up to martyrdom. When Ridley enters the place of execution, we are similarly told that he "marvelous earnestly holding up both his hands, loked towards heaven" (1,769). Though Foxe "can learne of no man" what was said between Ridley and Latimer before they died, the narrative assures us that Ridley "most effectuously prayed," a conclusion drawn from his posture of kneeling and kissing the stake (1,769). The narrative of two French martyrs, Nicholas Cene and Peter Gabart, reports that "these blessed sayntes ceased not in all these torments, to turne up theyr eyes to heaven, and to shewe forth infinite testimonyes of theyr fayth & constancy," although their tongues had been removed (920).[81] The "infinite testimonyes" themselves are elided; whatever specifically may have happened at the stake has been effortlessly adopted into the topoi of martyrdom, probably long before the story reached Foxe.[82]

On one rare occasion, Foxe exposes the underlying interpretive act at the heart of martyrdom, a construction otherwise represented as unmediated or natural. The case of a Spanish friar who attended Cranmer's execution suggests the possibility that even the careful rehearsal of martyrological behavior may lead to misinterpretation. Foxe recounts the great "constancy and steadfastness" with which Cranmer suffered death, then remarks: "This fortitude of mynd which perchaunce is rare and not found among the Spaniards, when Frier Joh. saw, thinkyng it came not of fortitude, but of desperation (although such maner of examples which are of the like constancy, have bene common here in England) ranne to the L. Williams of Tame, crying that the Archb. was vexed in mind, and died in great desperation. But he which was not ignorant of the Archbishoppes constancy, beyng unknowen to the Spaniards, smiled only, and (as it were) by silence rebuked the Friers folly" (1,888). The incident, with its attendant jabs at the Spanish, suggests that Friar John is outside the interpretive community and therefore does not understand what he has seen. Though this audience member lacks the language to read Cranmer's death, both Foxe and Lord Williams approve it as an unmistakable example of Christian martyrdom. But what Foxe unwittingly reports here is a moment of semiotic slippage, a breakdown between signifier and signified that results in an interpretation of Cranmer's death as bad, desperate, and faithless—in short, as not a martyr's death. The moment exposes the mechanism behind the luminous figure with the heavenly crown. It discloses how this act of spiritual transcendence works on a discursive level—how martyrdom is made. A person may be burned to death for religious conviction, but without an audience that can correctly interpret the codes, there is no martyrdom, for martyrdom is a semantic distinction—an interpretive construction negotiated by victim and viewer, by historiographer and reader. As Miri Rubin puts it:

> [T]he act of martyrdom is twofold: it is a choice taken in testing circumstances by an individual, or a group; but it is also a social-collective act, that of martyr-making, of martyr-naming. Thus a double-edged perspective is necessary in order to contain the variety of contexts in which martyrdom is practiced: in the intention

of the martyr/victim, and in the interpretations of those who will declare a given demise to be the crowned death of a martyr. As we enter the area of interpretation we must perforce step into fields of authority and dissent, of perspective and subjectivity; of meaning, as one man's cult of a martyr is another woman's superstition.[83]

"Disturbances Around the Scaffold"

The Marian persecutors in Foxe's book do everything they can to disrupt the successful rehearsal of martyr models and to create the kind of semiotic slippage we see in the example of Friar John. The scene of public execution, Michel Foucault has suggested, is designed to demonstrate how criminality, contagion, and otherness are successfully eliminated by the power of the state.[84] The performance of martyr topoi and achievement of a martyr's death undermine the display of punitive power described by Foucault, instead turning the execution into a display of the power of the martyr's faith and cause. Thus the scene at the stake operates as the victims' central defining moment, when they have their final and most powerful opportunity to confirm themselves as martyrs. Executioners walked a fine line on these occasions: overly strict management could miscarry if the audience perceived that the executioners were trying to prevent a victim from praying or having a good death, but if victims were given carte blanche, they could more easily turn the scene to their benefit and the crowd to their side. Foxe reports that at the execution of Joyce Lewes, "the Papistes had appoynted some to rayle uppon her openly, and to revile her, both as she went to the place of Execution, and also when she came to the stake" as a countermeasure to any sympathy she might stir up (2,013).[85] In this case, the atmosphere surrounding the execution is carefully orchestrated to ensure that the law—not the martyr—shapes the proceedings and the way those proceedings are interpreted.

Often authorities could do little more than prevent the victim from making a public address to the crowd. John Hooper and Rowland Taylor, both executed in their home parishes in front of sympathetic audiences, were altogether forbidden from speaking, and Foxe suggests that Taylor and other martyrs were threatened with having their tongues cut out if they did not keep quiet (1,526). Such measures were apparently common in France. In the narrative of the execution of Peter Serre, a priest who became a cobbler after rejecting Catholicism, the martyr appeals to the king not to have his tongue cut off because he needs it to pray before he dies. His appeal is denied and his tongue removed "so that he would say nothing agaynst theyr religion" (909). Sometimes an iron ball was placed in the victim's mouth after the tongue was removed to ensure that nothing intelligible could be spoken. In cases where the tongue was left intact, the execution was accompanied by very loud trumpet blasts that prevented victims from being heard by the crowd. But even without speech, their gestures and behavior could provide sufficient evidence of a martyr's death and undermine the penal mechanisms brought to bear against them. It is said of Serre: "being put to the fire, he stood so quiet, looking up to heaven all the time of his burning, as though he had felt nothing, bringing such admiration to the people, that one of the Parliament said, that way not to be best, to bring the Lutherans to the fire, for that would do more hurt then good" (909).

The most overt strategy for countering the claim to martyrdom was through the assertion of a rival text, usually a sermon describing the victim's heresy and assured place in hell. In the case of Ridley and Latimer, a sermon is delivered while they are at the stake, providing a narrative of the victims' damnation in order to challenge whatever narrative may be constructed from their manner of death. The sermon, given by Dr. Richard Smith of Oxford, directly confronts the erroneous conclusions that might be drawn from a good death, positing an Augustinian formulation of martyrdom (*non poena sed causa*, "it is the cause, not the death") to challenge the victims' efforts at self-representation: "[H]e alledged, that the goodnesse of the cause, and not the order of death: maketh the holyness of the person: Which he confirmed by the examples of Judas, and of a woman in Oxford that of late hanged her selfe, for that they and such lyke as he recited, might then be adjudged righteous, which desperately sundered their lyves from their bodies, as he feared that those men that stood before hym would do" (1,769). While Ridley and Latimer aim to inscribe themselves into biblical or martyrological narratives in which they resemble Christ, the apostles, or primitive martyrs, Smith chooses different exemplars for them. In comparing the martyrs to Judas and a local woman who recently committed suicide, Smith shows the representational importance of drawing legible parallels to familiar figures. He provides a preemptive reading of the deaths of Ridley and Latimer that seeks to strip them of the claim to martyrdom and to label them as suicides, men of faithless desperation whose eternal damnation is certain. Predictably, Ridley and Latimer are afforded no opportunity to respond unless they wish to recant.

Although Smith asserts a dissenting model for interpreting this execution scene, the popularity and influence of *Acts and Monuments* testify to the persuasiveness of the martyrological claims made by Ridley, Latimer, and Foxe. As the succeeding chapters argue, the judicial terms by which English Catholics were prosecuted in the decades following Queen Mary's death challenged the Counter-Reformation's capacity to reproduce the Foxean martyrological paradigm, creating representational crises on the scaffold and in polemical texts and martyrology. Tried and executed for treason against the Queen, English Catholic martyrs—along with the apologists who documented their ordeal—struggled to recuperate the topoi of transparency, religious suffering, and heroic innocence that would make them legible participants in the Christian martyrological tradition.

Chapter 3

Secular Law and Catholic Dissidence

The Case of Edmund Campion

M. Ford being set up in the carte, he blessed him self with the

signe of the Crosse, being so weake as he fel downe in the carte,

& after he was up, he said: I am a Catholike, and do dye in the

catholike religion. [A]nd therewith he was interrupted by Sherife

Martine, saying, you come not hither to confesse your religion,

but as a traitor and malefactor to the Queenes Majestie and

the whole Realme, moving and sturing of sedition.

—William Allen, *A Briefe Historie of*

the Glorious Martyrdom of XII Reverend Priests

For all intents and purposes, England discontinued the punishment of heresy after Queen Mary I's death, sidestepping the ethical implications of open religious persecution and putting an end to the particular spectacles chronicled by Foxe. The widespread popularity of *Acts and Monuments* and the backlash against the Marian persecutions that the book provoked made heresy executions dangerous and distasteful to Queen Elizabeth I and King James I.[1] Though this brought with it a small degree of religious toleration and allowed recusant Catholics to absent themselves from Anglican services if they were willing to suffer harassment and heavy fines, friction between the English government and its Catholic subjects was merely reconfigured into another discourse, one dominated not by accusations of heresy but of treason. In place of the legible performance of sacred typology initiated by the heresy trial, the treason trial produced a story of a secular criminal—a traitor. Within this alternative legal discourse, the narrative and behavioral reproduction of martyrological exemplarity became radically compromised.

This compromise is the subject of the next three chapters, which turn to the conflict between English Catholics and their sovereign during the reigns of Elizabeth I and James I. Studying the political and narrative developments that complicate the Counter-Reformation's construction of the acts and texts of conventional martyrdom, these chapters argue that the government's strategic relocation of religious dissidence within a discourse of secular crime truncated both victims' and martyrologists' access to the typology of sacred suffering. Rather than documenting the continuity between human acts and narrative monuments as Foxe's book does, Counter-Reformation martyrology discloses the form's diffusion and fracture.

The interest of this chapter is the 1581 conviction and execution of Father Edmund Campion, the first Jesuit prosecuted for treason under Elizabethan anti-Catholic policy. Campion's trial and the body of polemical, apologetic, and martyological texts that developed around it illustrate a rupture between the practical exigencies of the English mission and typologically legible suffering. The statutes against English Catholics trapped recusants in an inescapably circular argument that reproduced its own signs of treason while simultaneously alienating the Catholic subject from the discursive mechanisms of martyrdom. The rhetorical substitution of treason for martyrdom is made possible by their structural similarities: the figure of religious exceptionalism is structurally analogous to the figure of consummate political crime, and thus the construction of both martyrdom and treason depends on what is fundamentally the same set of discursive operations. By reading the texts surrounding the Campion case with attention to his efforts to inscribe himself into the martyrological tradition, we can see the structural fissures that the charge of treason produces for martyrological discourse. Ultimately, it is a formal rather than merely a confessional or a political disruption that renders the charge of treason such an effective measure for containing the Catholic mission to England.

As chapter 2 showed, the construction of a martyr depends on transposing the historical events of an individual's life and death into a suprahistorical narrative that connects Christ, the martyrs of the early church, and the contemporary victim through typological reiteration. Martyrology's stories of witnessing, torment, and constancy in death convert its subjects from discrete religious dissidents into transcendent Christian exemplars. The construction of martyrdom is made possible only through strict narrative repetition. Although Augustine wrote that it is the cause, not the death, that makes a martyr, martyrdom is neither merely cause nor death; it is a set of retrospective, narrative operations that depend on the legible rehearsal of martyr models. In his study of medieval hagiography, James Earl describes the genre as "literary iconography" in which "the individual, by conforming the patterns of his moral behavior to the larger patterns of history, enters into a typological relationship with that history."[2] The legibility of the martyr icon is key: if an individual's actions are inconsistent with established martyr formulas or cannot easily be read as reiterations of apostolic or Christological suffering, the individual cannot transcend the death event. The victim must fit the conventions if he or she is to be interpreted or reproduced as a martyr. Moreover, the mold is inflexible: the victims must be persecuted for their faith; they must openly confess that faith and readily defend it against the adversary, who represents heretical belief; they must die in defense of the faith and cannot appear to will their own deaths; in their manner of death, they must exhibit constancy and piety; and ideally, death is attended by miraculous or providential evidence of God's favor.

The treason trial radically disrupts this paradigm, in large part because it restructures the relationship between victim and persecutor into a conflict between the would-be martyr and his or her own sovereign. The consolidation of religious and temporal power under Queen

Elizabeth posed a problem, at least philosophically, for the Catholic recusant, whose allegiances became divided between monarch and pope. This problem was exacerbated in 1570 when Pope Pius V issued the bull excommunicating Elizabeth, deposing her from power, and absolving her subjects from obedience to her (Appendix A). Through this action, the pope essentially positioned the entire body of English Catholics as enemies to the Crown, threatening that any who continued in obedience to her would be "innodate[d] with the like sentence of Anathema."[3] Spurred by the very real fears of domestic rebellion, foreign invasion, and assassination that grew out of the bull, the Elizabethan government developed several strategies designed to rid the realm of those Catholics who held with the pope over their sovereign and to protect the state from the internal threat they might pose. By 1585, Parliament had passed a series of laws naming any Catholic priest in England a traitor. The immediate targets of these policies were Jesuit and seminary priests, who, it was believed, were being sent to England from the Continent to stir up rebellion and prepare English Catholics to take up arms against their queen in support of a pope-sponsored invasion. A 1571 act of Parliament reminded subjects that not only direct actions against the state but also "imagining" or "intending" the queen's death, dethronement, or defeat by foreign power were points of treason.[4] A 1582 royal proclamation, followed up by a 1585 act of Parliament, made it illegal for Catholic priests to remain in or come to England on penalty of death for treason, on the stated presumption that any who did so were acting secretly against the queen.[5] Aiding, maintaining, hiding, and failing to turn in a known priest were also declared acts of treason, punishable by death. Two proclamations of 1591, citing the insidiously secretive nature of Catholic priests as particular cause for alarm, erected panels of inquiry to question suspected priests and abettors and established a series of questions intended to probe suspects' allegiance to the queen (Appendix B).[6]

James came to the throne with plans for greater religious toleration that were quickly set aside in the wake of the Gunpowder Plot of 1605 (discussed at length in chapter 5). In response to the plot and the perceived threat posed by secret Catholics, James's administration passed an act in 1606 that included the Oath of Allegiance, which suspected Catholics would be required to take (Appendix C). The contents of the oath reveal many of the anxieties that arose from Elizabeth's excommunication and subsequent Catholic plots, real or imagined. It required one to state that James was the true and legitimate king of England; that no pope or foreign power could rightfully depose him or release his subjects from obedience to him; that "notwithstanding any declaration or sentence of Excommunication," his subjects must maintain faithful allegiance to him and defend his person and throne; and that, regardless of any statement issued by the pope to the contrary, it is "impious and Hereticall" to believe that subjects may depose and murder their sovereign.[7]

The Catholic church responded to these mechanisms by claiming religious persecution on the grounds that the questions being asked of Catholics, characterized in government literature (like James's own defense of the oath) as touching only secular allegiance, were fundamentally questions of religious conscience. But their argument for martyrdom was undermined by the charge of treason, a problem even Catholic apologists admitted. The relocation of Catholic dissidence into a discourse of secular crime had far-reaching effects on the production of Catholic martyrdom, making it very difficult for Catholic victims and their martyrologists to establish the typological connections that would enable them to transcend trial and execution and situate themselves within the sacred narrative of God's persecuted church on earth.

The Trial of Edmund Campion

Edmund Campion was one of the first two Jesuits, along with Father Robert Persons, to be sent on the mission to England. After training for the priesthood in France, he re-entered England in 1580 in disguise and under an assumed name. Once his activities there were detected by the elaborate spy network—managed by Elizabeth's Lord High Treasurer, William Cecil, Lord Burghley—Campion's capture was made a priority. The impetus to arrest him was sharpened by the publication of a private document that he had composed to defend

his missionary activities in the event of his capture. Campion had en-
trusted the treatise to a Catholic friend whose zeal led him to share it
with others. When it eventually caught the attention of authorities,
the audacity of the document, which came to be known as Campion's
"Challenge" or "Brag," incited the government all the more vehemently
against him.[8] His capture in July 1581 was regarded as a major victory
by the state. He was paraded through London on horseback with a sign
on his head proclaiming, "Campion, the Seditious Jesuit," then taken to
the Tower of London, where he was tortured on the rack in an effort to
extract information that would lead to the arrests of other Catholics.
Six months after capture, he and the other priests apprehended with
him were tried and convicted of treason. They were hanged, drawn, and
quartered at Tyburn on December 1, 1581.

Campion's conviction hinged on two primary problems: the alleged
meetings he had conducted with other Catholics in which Elizabeth's
death and overthrow were plotted, and his opinions regarding the
queen's supremacy. As the sixteenth century neared its end and the state
became more experienced at prosecuting Catholic recusants, these concerns would become streamlined to produce treason convictions that
invited steadily decreasing public dissent. Witnesses such as Anthony
Munday, who was brought in to provide testimony about Campion's
supposed meetings and plots, might easily be discredited, and questions
about the rights of the queen were challenged as unlawful by Catholic
apologists such as Cardinal William Allen.[9] But Campion's case is illustrative of the overarching rhetoric that would dominate Catholic
treason trials for decades to follow.

In his opening arguments to the court, the queen's council laid out
the relationship between Catholicism and treason that provided a template for subsequent trials. Catholic priests, he claimed, "must come
secretly into the realm, they must change their habit and names; they
must dissemble their vocations, they must wander unknown — to what
end? To dissuade the people from their Allegiance to their prince, to
reconcile them to the pope, to plant the Romish Religion, to supplant
both prince and province — by what means? By saying of Mass, by ad-
ministering the Sacrament, by hearing Confessions."[10] This argument
equates the secrecy and duplicity necessitated by the laws enacted

against Catholics with treasonous plots to overthrow the state by arguing that secrecy is a symptom of treason. Situating Catholic doctrine and practice within this discourse of treason, the state made the argument that Catholicism was a category of political sedition and not a matter of religious conscience, preemptively challenging Catholic claims of religious persecution. The facts presented in the trial—Munday's dubious testimony and the priests' ambiguous statements regarding the queen's supremacy—were then normalized into this broader rhetorical scheme of Catholic treason.

The state's case against Campion and his fellow priests was founded on the premise that the pope was above all a political enemy of England, a point driven home by the prosecution's rehearsal of the bull of excommunication and its implications. The pope was posited as the author of all treasonous plots against the queen, and Catholic priests were posited as the pope's agents in England, ministers commissioned "to execute the Bull sent from Pius Quintus against her majesty" (1,053). Witnesses were brought forth to testify to meetings with papal emissaries in Rheims and Rome, where the defendants "conspired the death of the queen's majesty, the overthrow of the religion now professed in England, the subversion of the state" (1,049). They were accused of hatching plots to ambush and stab Elizabeth while she was out on a walk, or set her barge on fire as it floated down the Thames (1,067–68).

Campion, the most notorious as well as eloquent and outspoken of the defendants, denied the charges and accused the state of persecuting Catholics merely for religion. The fact that he and his fellow priests had been offered clemency in exchange for attending Anglican sermons was proof, he argued, that "Religion was cause of our Imprisonment and the consequence of our condemnation" (1,055). This argument, to which Catholic apologists would return, insists on religious affiliation as a strictly spiritual category that has no relationship to questions of political sedition. Thus while the prosecution insisted on Catholicism as a purely political category—a means "to supplant both prince and province"—the defendants insisted on it as exclusively spiritual, obfuscating any link between ecclesiastical power and secular rule (1,053). This link was firmly established in the long history of the Catholic church and had been made current by the papal bull, as

Ronald Corthell observes in regard to Allen, whose *Defense of English Catholics* "upholds a division of loyalties while eliding the undeniable historical relationship between the spiritual and temporal orders."[11]

In response to the claim that he and his fellow priests were sent into England for seditious purposes, Campion stated, "We are dead men to the world, we only traveled for souls; we touched neither state nor policy, we had no such commission" (1,054). His remarks were immediately seized upon by the prosecution in an effort to discredit his claims of ascetic religiosity and political innocence:

> Were it not that your dealing afterwards [after Campion came into the realm] had fully bewrayed you, your present Speech perhaps had been more credible; but all afterclaps make those excuses but shadows, and your deeds and actions prove your words but forged; for what meaning had that changing of your name, whereto belonged your disguising in apparel, can these alterations be wrought without suspicion? Your name being Campion, why were you called Hastings? You a priest and dead to the world, what pleasure had you to royst that? A velvet hat and a feather, a buff leather jerkin, velvet venetians, are they weeds for dead men? Can that beseem a professed man of religion which hardly becometh a layman of gravity? No; there was a further matter intended; your lurking and lying hid in secret places, concludeth with the rest, a mischievous meaning: had you come hither for love of your country, you would never have wrought in _____; or had your intent been to have done well, you would never have hated the light, and therefore this beginning decyphereth your Treason. (1,059)[12]

Under the prosecutor's management, Campion's attempts to hide himself are treated as manifest evidence of treason, which is intended to undermine anything he may say in his own defense. The luxurious clothing that he donned to avoid capture is used to challenge his religious commitment, likewise suggesting that his purposes for being in England were secular rather than spiritual.

Campion acknowledged his attire but contested the conclusion that it in any way proved treason. Rather, he said, his disguise was necessitated by the persecution of Catholics and was consistent with the model of apostolic behavior: "I wished earnestly the planting of the gospel. I knew a contrary religion professed. I saw if I were known I should be apprehended. I changed my name: I kept secretly. I imitated Paul. Was I therein a traitor? But the wearing of a buff jerkin, a velvet hat, and such like is much forced against me, as though the wearing of any apparel were treason, or that I in so doing were ever the more a traitor. I am not indicted upon the statute of Apparel, neither is it any part of this present arraignment" (1,060). Campion confronts the logic imposed by the prosecution by arguing that wearing a disguise and plotting treason are not the same thing. The parallel he draws between his own behavior and that of the apostolic missionaries was reiterated by another priest tried with him, Ralph Sherwin, who described his secret ministry as a model of "the apostles and fathers in the primitive church" (1,064). Such comparisons were rejected by the court: "your case differeth from theirs in the primitive church, for that those apostles and preachers never conspired the death of the emperors and rulers in whose dominions they so taught and preached" (1,064). According to the prosecution's logic of political crime, secrecy proves the treason, and treason invalidates the secrecy.

Campion and his fellow priests were caught in a circular argument from which there was no viable exit. The English statutes against Catholics forced missionaries into hiding and disguise; in turn, hiding and disguise provided the state with proof of the very treason it feared. Although designed to protect the state against crime, the law produced a set of behaviors that it then seized upon as evidence of that crime. In response to this double bind, Campion attempted to legitimize Catholics' condemned actions by linking them to the uncontested sanctity of the originary Christian church: "At what time the primitive church was persecuted and that Paul laboured in the propagation and increase of the Gospel, it is not unknown, to what straits and pinches he and his fellows were diversely driven" (1,059). The legitimizing religious narrative Campion provides—that secrecy is evidence of the true, persecuted church—has no efficacy within the context of the secular treason trial. There, what might be offered as evidence of persecution is construed as evidence of crime, ultimately undermining one of the foundational assumptions of martyrology: that persecution itself witnesses to the truth of the victim's cause.

The priests' attempts to justify their position were further complicated by the vexed relationship to secular and ecclesiastical authority that the treason trial exposed. The martyrological imperative of witnessing to one's faith, in conjunction with the papal bull, placed the Catholic defendant in a difficult position: his or her allegiance to the Crown had been directly prohibited by papal authority, which Catholics were bound to obey. The competing demands of sovereign and pope left the English Catholic caught between two equally dismal and damnable categories: the traitor and the excommunicate heretic. The accounts of the trial of Campion and his companions reveal the priests' fraught attempts to avoid both categories by situating themselves in a delicate medial space. As a consequence of this tension, however, they become alienated from the discourses of both secular loyalty and Catholic orthodoxy.

Before his formal trial, each defendant was interrogated regarding his allegiance to the queen and to the pope. The crown had carefully developed a series of questions meant to probe recusants' beliefs regarding the pope's right to depose temporal monarchs, the lawfulness of violent rebellion against the queen, and the part the recusant would take in the event that a papal army invaded the realm. The questions were put to the defendants and their answers recorded for use in the prosecution's case against them. For the most part, however, the defendants' answers were vague and noncommittal. Two of Campion's fellow priests, Ralph Sherwin and Alexander Brian, refused to offer opinions on the pope's right to depose on the grounds that doing so would imperil their own lives.[13] Brian remarked that the question was "too high, and dangerous for him to answer," and Sherwin "prayeth to be asked no such question, as may touch his life" (1,078). Two others, Thomas Cottam and John Shert, affirmed that they "swerveth in no point from the Catholic Faith" but refused to elaborate their understanding of what Catholic doctrine demanded in present political circumstances (1,080). William Filbee went so far as to confirm the pope's power to depose but would not be pushed to apply this doctrine to the case of Elizabeth, claiming that "touching the Bull of Pius Quintus, he can say nothing" (1,081). Campion himself made a bolder break with Catholic orthodoxy, testifying that he thought it unlikely that the papal bull was lawful: "the divines of the catholic church do distinguish of the pope's authority, attributing unto him ordination and inordination, *potestatem, ordinatem,* whereby he proceedeth in matters merely spiritual and pertinent to the church, and by that he cannot excommunicate any prince or potentate" (1,062).

In all of their answers, the Catholic defendants sought to avoid positioning themselves as traitors—as men who challenged or rejected the queen's authority over her subjects. But in their careful efforts to sidestep incriminating statements, they failed to affirm the rights of the pope, a cornerstone of Catholic orthodoxy.[14] Their claims of religious persecution were therefore confounded by their own reticence to boldly confess the faith. This is the ingenious effect of the treason proceeding: it placed the defendant in an impossible situation. If he affirmed the righteousness of Catholic doctrine—that is, the pope's right to dethrone Elizabeth and absolve her subjects from allegiance to her—the defendant fell into a discourse of treason that substantiated anti-Catholic sentiment. But if he did not uphold papal prerogative, he failed in one of the necessary acts of Christian martyrdom, the confession of the tenets of faith. In either case, the reproduction of exemplary martyrdom was jeopardized.

This crisis is produced through the repositioning of religious dissidence within the structure of secular law. The treason trial rendered it extremely perilous for the Catholic defendants to confess their religion—not because they would die, which is essential to martyrdom, but because they would die as criminals.[15] For the English Counter-Reformation, two fundamental imperatives of Christian martyrdom—persecution for religion and confession of religion—became radically fractured from one another. In consequence, defendants like Campion were trapped in a position of claiming that they were persecuted for religion while they were actively working to dissociate themselves from perilous Catholic doctrine. Probed once more at the trial about his opinion of the pope's supremacy, Campion finally stated, "I say generally that these matters be merely spiritual points of doctrine and disputable in schools, no part of mine Indictment, not to be given in evidence, and unfit to be discussed at the King's Bench" (1,063). Although Campion insisted that the trial was a religious persecution, he simultaneously had to argue that religion could have no place in the trial, illustrating how the charge of treason cut the defendant off from access to the legitimizing testimony of orthodoxy.

Taken as a whole, these elements create a prosecution scene whose overall structure is markedly different from that of patristic and medieval martyrology or Foxe's *Acts and Monuments.* Rather than a theological or doctrinal dispute between one religious faction and another, we are presented with a secularized debate in which the established church and its theology have no visible role. Instead of being carried out by rival theologians, the prosecution is managed by the representatives of secular law, and the justice handed down is authorized by secular rather than ecclesiastical power. Throughout these trials, the prosecution insists on Catholicism as a fundamentally political category by concentrating attention on the antagonistic relationship the pope's bull created for Catholic subjects regarding the queen's supremacy. Government propaganda, legal prosecution, and execution scenes focus on the Catholic as a political enemy of the state, so that the individual's belief—central to a heresy case—is shifted away from view. As such, priests' trial scenes concentrate not on questions of religious doctrine such as transubstantiation but on the issues of supremacy and seditious behavior: how defendants regard their duty to the queen in light of the papal bull, what coreligionists they met with or helped, where they secretly attended Mass. Within this structure, there is little opportunity for acts of religious confession or for the elaboration of doctrine. In the case of Campion, the defendant was granted a theological disputation while imprisoned in the Tower, but neither he nor his prosecutors ever mentioned that interview during the course of his trial; it had no place in the proceeding. Although Campion and his codefendants often openly state that they are Catholics, the mechanisms of the treason trial transform this into a political—not religious—confession. The confrontation between disparate belief systems provided by a heresy trial sets up precisely the narrative paradigm required for martyrological transcendence, but the treason trial forces the victim into an alternative paradigm from which he or she cannot easily escape. As a result, instead of being assigned an identity defined by faith, the condemned Catholic subject is assigned an identity defined by political allegiance.

Most importantly, the treason charge situated Catholic subjects in a fraught relationship to both secular and papal authority. If they were to demonstrate innocence of treason, they could not readily challenge the moral authority of the court but had to present themselves as appropriately respectful of and subdued by the sovereign. The movement away from the Catholic-Protestant debate central to Queen Mary's heresy trials toward a debate between Catholic subjects and their own temporal government foreclosed the victim-persecutor dyad so central to the martyrological paradigm. The position of persecutor became occupied not by a clear enemy but by a representative of the secular authority to which Catholics must continually demonstrate obedience. Further, the open confession of Catholic doctrine came to function in the trial as proof of treason. If defendants proclaimed their belief in papal supremacy—the only point of religious orthodoxy raised in the trials—this proved their rejection of Elizabeth's legitimacy and, thereby, their treason. If, on the other hand, they denied or suppressed their belief in the rights of the pope, Catholics were themselves in danger of excommunication. Their failure to fully confess the tenets of their faith further separated them from the rigid demands of exemplary martyrdom. Unless they were willing to give up their faith, which the government offered as the only way out of the conundrum, Catholic defendants found their relationships to both secular loyalty and Catholic orthodoxy compromised. They became what Julia Reinhard Lupton describes as vexed "citizen-saints," "figures caught between two competing, mutually exclusive, social, political, and religious structures."[16] Circumscribed within the treason discourse, they could not successfully represent themselves as at once true Catholics and true subjects of the queen.

Post-Mortem Polemics

The stakes were high for the government and for the English Catholic cause, both sides showing an acute awareness of the need to successfully disseminate their respective narratives. The Elizabeth government was faced with issues of national security and concerns about the regime's public image. The polemics of the period repeatedly play out the question of whether the state is justly defending itself against political threat or is engaged in the same cruel persecution that made Mary so notoriously "Bloody."[17] Such matters had bearing on English public opinion as well as on a larger European audience and on the country's engagement in international affairs. For Catholics, the question of whether their priests and faithful lay men and women would go down in history as arch criminals or as glorious martyrs presented alternative ramifications for the continuing viability and growth of the Catholic religion, especially in England. If Catholic apologists were unsuccessful—if the victims could not be recuperated into the ranks of faithful Christian martyrs—executed Catholics could become a liability rather than an asset for the Catholic cause. Failing to assuage public suspicion of Catholics' activities might compromise the English mission as well as potentially undermine Catholic authority in other countries. Moreover, if a priest executed for treason could not successfully be represented as a martyr, the victim's salvation might have come into question. The rival discourses of secular justice and Christian martyrology posit divergent outcomes for the victim: in the penal narrative unrepentant victims are damned, while in the martyrological narrative they are saved. How the victim was recorded for posterity—traitor or martyr—ultimately determined his or her eternal fate insofar as the Christian community could read and disseminate that fate.

Given the stakes, it is no surprise that Campion's case produced a heated controversy, one that gradually escalated from rumor to popular pamphlets to official tracts by the most prominent figures on both sides. A short, anonymous octavo titled *An advertisement and defence for Trueth against her Backbiters, and specially against the whispring Favourers, and Colourers of Campions, and the rest of his confederats treasons* (1581) is one of the earliest texts in the debate. Only five pages in length, it was published within the month of Campion's execution. The title points to the Campion case as contested territory and announces the text as a response to the effort of pro-Campion gossip to recast his death as religious persecution. The author writes, "it is maliciously, falsly, and traiterously by some of the secret favourers of the said Campion, and other the said condemned Traitours, whispered in corners,

that the offences of these traitours, were but for their secret attempt-
ings as jesuites by exhorting and teaching, with Shriving, Massing, and
such like actes, to move people to change their Religion."[18] Like the
trial itself, the pamphlet formulates these Catholic practices as political
acts—as "high Treasons committed against her Majesties most Royall
person, and against the ancient Lawes and statutes of this Realme"
(A3r). The text thus acts to circulate the principal arguments of the trial
in the effort to duplicate in the court of public opinion the conclusions
advanced in the court of law—that the claim of religious persecution
holds no weight since religious rites have been adapted by Catholic
missionaries into vehicles for treason. The aim of the text is thus to organize popular debate over the Campion case by secularizing the discussion in accordance with the same precepts that governed the trial.

The most interesting element of the pamphlet is its representation
of the defendants' attitudes toward papal supremacy. According to the
author, their refusal to condemn the pope's bull against Elizabeth is
tantamount to their agreeing with it and can thereby be understood as
evidence of treason: "none of them all . . . coulde be perswaded by any
their answeres to shewe in any part their mislikings eyther of the former Bull . . . or of the Pope that nowe is, if he shoulde nowe publish
the like Bull against her Majestie, so as they did apparantly shew their
traiterous hearts stil fixed to persist in their devilish mindes against
their naturall allegeance (A4r). In this formulation, the hearts of the
priests are laid bare not by what they say but what they fail to say. The
verbal lacuna operates as a signifier of treason and "apparantly shew[s]"
their "devilish mindes" as conclusively as any other form of testimony.
The rhetoric of treason resolves the priests' silence into an inflexible
semiotic code: *Silence = treason. Silence ≠ absence of opinion; silence ≠
ignorance; silence ≠ indecisiveness.* The discourses of secular law and public opinion operate according to a language in which silence is necessarily a signifier of guilt. By rehearsing and circulating this language,
the author of the pamphlet attempts to ensure that the codes of legal
discourse—rather than of a religious or conscientious discourse, for
example—penetrate popular renderings of the Campion narrative.

A Jesuit who was present at the priests' execution, Thomas Alfield,
soon responded with a pamphlet of his own, *A true reporte of the death*

& martyrdome of M. Campion Jesuite and preiste (1582).[19] He positioned his text as a rejoinder to *An advertisement against Backbiters* as well as to the "many slaunders" circulating to "diminish the honour of their [the priests'] resolute departure and Martirdome" (A1r). *A true reporte* operates on the assumptions of *ars moriendi,* the "art of dying"—namely, that comportment at death provides a transparent indication of the state of the victim's soul and clearly demonstrates whether he or she is saved. But in this account of Campion's execution, even the death scene is made problematic by the intrusion of secular authority, evidencing the impingement of the treason charge on martyrological narrative. For the most part, the account of Campion's death is devoid of the overt verbal and behavioral topoi that permeate patristic martyrological models: there are few displays of piety—like kneeling, prayer, or kissing instruments of persecution—and little or no echo of traditional martyr language like lamb-to-the-slaughter metaphors, forgiveness of persecutors, or phrases repeated from Christ's crucifixion. What we find instead is an execution that is closely focused on the question of whether or not Campion is guilty of treason.

At the scaffold, Campion's attention is repeatedly turned away from prayer and religious confession and back to the treason charge. Being brought into the cart from which he would be hanged, Campion proceeds to quote Paul, announcing himself "a spectacle, or a sight, unto God, unto his Angels, and unto men" (B4v–C1r). Those charged with overseeing his execution soon interrupt him, "earnestly urging him to confesse his treason against her majestie, and to acknowledge himself gilty" (C1r). He begs to be allowed to "speake a worde or too for discharge of [his] conscience" but is again prevented from prayer, and "being not suffered to go forward, gave answere to that point they always urged" (C1r). Campion proclaims that he is "giltless & innocent of all treason and conspiracie, craving credit to be geven to his answere, as to his last answere made upon his death & soule," and he forgives the jury who condemned him (C1r). The conversation then turns to his clarification of evidence presented in court, followed by the reading of his sentence, during which Campion is observed to be "devoutlye praying" (C2r). Still unsatisfied with Campion's failure to admit his treason, the officials next question him of his position on the bull of excommunication and his allegiance to the pope. He maintains himself a devout Catholic and resumes praying, again being interrupted and ordered to pray in English rather than Latin and to pray specifically for the queen. He defends his use of Latin but wishes Elizabeth "a long quiet raigne, with all prosperity," and then he is executed (C2v).

What we see in this account of Campion's death is how the trial's endeavor to establish his identity as traitor spills onto the scaffold, where the rival discourses of treason and martyrdom play themselves out in a final, all-important effort to secure the event for posterity. The continual shifting of attention back to the question of treason disrupts the victim's attempt to control the terms of his own death. Just as in the trial, the two sides are at odds about the nature of the discourse in which they are participating, each attempting to perform a discourse that is interrupted by the other. Campion's death becomes a drama whose genre is under contention. The state seeks to perform the script of a treason trial and execution, while Campion insists that the operative script is that of a religious persecution—a martyrdom.

As martyrologist, then, Alfield is presented with a challenge. From this fractured performance of competing scripts, Alfield is charged with fashioning a typologically legible, unproblematic story of exemplary, holy death. To manage this, he can either falsify the historical events, eliminating the disruptive treason cues, or situate those events within a larger framework of familiar typological formulas. Using the latter strategy, Alfield essentially bookends the narrative of Campion's death with the conventional language of Christian martyrdom. He introduces his account by saying that Campion "after many conflictes and agonies, joyfully [came] to receive his reward and crowne, the kingdome of heaven," and the conclusion of Campion's story rings with familiar martyrological topoi: "he meekely and sweetly yelded his soule unto his Saviour, protesting that he dyed a perfect Catholike"; he "triumfed on the world, the flesh, the divell, and received his long desired crown" (B4v, C2v).

This representation of Campion is compromised not only by the circumstances of the execution but by the account of Campion reported in Alfield's text. In his effort to prove once and for all that he is

not a traitor, Campion ends his life praying for the queen with no ac-
knowledgement of her as a heretic excommunicated by the Catholic
church. Alfield describes the executed priests as "paternes of piety,
vertue, and innocencie," but what the narrative reveals is a problemati-
cally heterodox figure, one who bears important differences from the
martryological paradigm modeled by patristic and medieval narratives
(A3r). While Alfield attempts to close these fissures by declaring that
"all men are perswaded that those innocentes suffered only for religion
for our fathers faith," the circumstances that he describes as prompting
his text—the "most infamous libel," *An advertisement against Backbiters*,
and the rumors that Campion had suffered a bad death—indicate that
the public's interpretation of the execution was far less homogeneously
sympathetic than he would wish (B1r, A3v). This is not to suggest that
Campion's death failed to persuade witnesses and readers. Rather, what
Alfield's text demonstrates is the inadequacy of martyrology's formal
conventions to inscribe the contingencies of recusant life. Like the ruptures of a Shakespearean problem play, the unconventional, heterodox,
and disruptive elements of Campion's execution sit uneasily alongside
the generic claims implicit in Alfield's martyrology.

The close structural relationship between the discourses of martyr
and traitor is what initiates these representational glitches. Martyrdom
is produced by transforming historical events (utterances, gestures, actions, death) into typological markers that allow for the positioning of
the victim in a narrative of spiritual transcendence. Because the victim's conscience is always finally a cipher, and what is written on the
heart—true faith or hypocrisy—is never fully legible to any but God,
the construction of martyrdom is necessarily an act of interpretive narration. If the martyr cannot be produced as a coherent literary figure,
the epistemological category of martyrdom is likewise imperiled. The
same is true for the traitor. As Rebecca Lemon reminds us, treason is
likewise a "conceptual category," a "political and legal construction" constituted in language. Just as martyrdom is not a death but a textual construction, treason is "not a violent action but a verbal phenomenon,"
one produced, Lemon demonstrates, through "interpretive work."[20] Although the execution victim's insides are exposed for all to see, the
executioner's traditional invitation to "behold the heart of a traitor" is

essentially an invitation to the same kind of interpretive act that constructs martyrdom, one that demands that the body and soul be read as part of a broader story of treason that has already been composed from the victim's words and behavior. This story, like the martyr's story, is equally transcendent, situating the victim as the anticitizen, the arch criminal, the exemplar of the damned. The narrative structure of treason is far more flexible than of martyrdom, which is always bound up with the rigid typological imperatives of Christological and hagiographic suffering. Thus Elizabeth's discursive substitution of treason for martyrdom—her reinscription of the cipher of the heart—is essentially the substitution of one narrative for another. In place of martyrological exemplarity, treason provides a rival story of transcendence that is easier to tell.

William Allen's XII *Reverend Priests*

The structural fracture between Campion's case and the narrative imperatives of typological martyrdom surfaces in a range of texts published in the wake of his execution. The account in *A true reporte* formed the foundation of an important martyrological text published later that year, *A Briefe Historie of the Glorious Martyrdom of XII Reverend Priests, executed within these twelvemonthes for confession and defence of the Catholic faith. But under the false pretense of Treason.* The book was written by Cardinal William Allen, the English expatriate who founded the seminary at Douai, France, where many of the missionary priests, including Campion, were trained. Allen's role as an apologist for the English mission was a complicated one. Beyond training priests, he was actively involved in precisely the kind of invasion plan that Elizabethan anti-Catholic statutes were intended to prevent. Robert Kingdon writes,

> [I]n 1585, Allen presented to Pope Sixtus V a memorial only recently reprinted and attributed to him, in which he reported that "we have now (although many have been recently deported) almost 300 priests in the households of noblemen and men of sub-

stance, and we are daily sending others, who will direct the consciences and actions of the Catholics in this affair when the time comes." The "time" coming was quite clearly the one of invasion. It would consequently appear that, no matter what the missionary priests were themselves informed, their leaders intended to use them for a subversive political purpose at the appropriate time. In a way, then, the Catholic Mission to England was engaged in treason, potentially if not actually, in intention if not in deed.[21]

Kingdon's remarks point to the ambiguous nature of the Catholic mission and, more broadly, of the English Catholic subject, whose divided political and religious allegiances created a fundamental division between intent and deed, between interior and exterior.

This divided subjectivity is articulated in the very structure of Counter-Reformation martyrology. As Allen's *XII Reverend Priests* lucidly demonstrates, representational fracture becomes the genre's central defining feature. In response to the criminal identity assigned to Campion and his compatriots by the trial, Allen's text, like Alfield's, reclaims the priests for Catholic martyrology by locating them within a discourse of religious persecution. In order to do this, however, Allen must carefully craft a rhetorical structure that separates the priests' martyrologies from his commentary on the political questions that surround them. His lengthy preface aggressively engages the problems presented by Elizabethan policy against Catholics, providing an interpretive framework for the martyrologies themselves. The martyrologies generally avoid these hot-button polemical issues, instead adhering to the narratives of godly living and exemplary death that traditionally comprise the genre. Through this structure, however, Allen ends up replicating the central problem set up by the treason trial—the incompatibility of typological martyrdom with the current political debate.

Unlike Alfield's account, Allen's *XII Reverend Priests* is framed by a preface that directly confronts the prosecution of recusant Catholics as political traitors. In it, he argues that the treason charge is itself a disingenuous political strategy, a "shamful sutteltie and too foule and brode deceipt" devised to taint public opinion.[22] He complains that instead of stirring up the kind of sympathy engendered by the Marian persecutions, the charge of treason fosters hatred of the condemned by representing them as guilty of the most heinous of crimes, in turn fomenting animosity toward Catholics, especially priests. The lesson of the Marian heretic burnings, emblazoned on the English imagination by Foxe, lies at the heart of Elizabethan anti-Catholic policy, Allen says. By charging Catholics with treason instead of heresy, the Elizabethan government hopes that "they would be counted both at home and abrode in such cases meeke and clement, and not blouddy as they say the Papists were towardes them, when the staffe was in their handes" (4). The purpose of Allen's preface is to recover the events of Campion's trial and execution from manipulative government propaganda by exposing the unsavory political machinations that attempt to undercut the claim to martyrdom. For Allen, it is the persecuting regime—not the innocent Catholic priests—who disguise base political motives under cover of justice and who further the destruction of their own nation. The Catholics are not the duplicitous traitors.

But Allen is an Englishman, and like Campion, he must take care not to undermine his own argument by making himself a traitor to the Crown. He cannot reinforce the charge of treason by including the queen herself among the Machiavels he maligns, so he is careful to delineate categories of culpability, insisting that Elizabeth is not the agent of persecution. Responsibility for the injustice lies "not so much at her M. handes, or her gravest Counsellers" but with the false witnesses brought against the victims and with the Protestant ministers vilified throughout the text (42). Putting men to death is against the queen's nature, which is marked by "a certaine pitie and natural clemencie" (30). By stating that the country at large "have not consented to this iniquitie," Allen also takes pains not to impugn a potential audience of English subjects for the injustice carried out by a small coterie of men in power (3).

This is a subtle rhetorical move. In the martyr narratives themselves, the audience often appears hostile to the victim and fully supportive of the executions. Allen's narrative of John Shert depicts the crowd urging the hangman to get on with the task because Shert has lived too long already, suggesting that the tactics of criminalizing the victim through the charge of treason had been entirely successful (107). Allen's preface frames these events by arguing that justice has been ignored. The issue at hand, then, is not whether one agrees or disagrees with acts of treason, which hardly need be answered, but whether the judicial body that declared the victim a traitor has reached that conclusion through a just process. Allen goes to great lengths to argue that it has not—that the procedures, witnesses, and charges brought to bear against the victim are not the mechanisms of justice but of iniquity. And injustice, Allen argues, is abhorred by the English people, even those who are misled into cheering these executions.

To make this claim, however, Allen cannot merely rely on martyrological structures for representing innocence. He must engage the trial on its own terms, the terms of law. The martyrological form cannot accommodate the legal debate that the treason charge forces, and so Allen must confront the issue of treason in the discursive space of a polemical preface. There, Allen addresses the legality of the six questions put to Campion and the other priests, particularly the one that came to be known as the "Bloody Question": whose side priests would take if the pope invaded the realm. Allen argues that by asking priests this hypothetical question, Elizabeth's ministers molded treason into a "crime of their hart and cogitation" instead of a crime of action (36). He contends that such thought crimes are not punishable by law. To punish "the future faults which we may commit in time to come . . . far passeth al Antichristian tyrrany" (35).[23] Further, it functions as a form of entrapment. Requiring subjects to state whether they agree with the papal bull declaring Elizabeth a heretic forces them to conceive of her in relation to heresy, which they may never have done without prompting. "This is to make traitors and not to punish treasons," he says; "[it] is not to execute laws, but to make men offend the laws. So to drink their blode" (38).

This line of argument points back to one of the primary problems raised by the secular prosecution of Catholic dissidents: to escape the category of treason, Catholics sought immunity by declaring that they had no opinion on the topic of Elizabeth's excommunication. But the papal bull had provided them with far more than an opinion. It had issued a clear command that Elizabeth's subjects were to abandon all allegiance to the queen. While it is a practical possibility that the judicial interrogation would present the first instance in which a priest might consider and form a position on such matters, that would be inconsistent with the demands of orthodoxy. In positing such a defense for the executed priests, Allen replicates precisely the fracture we see in Campion's trial, a fracture between Catholic orthodoxy and Catholic exemplarity.

To recenter the debate away from the problematic category of secular loyalty, Allen must situate his martyrs within a familiar paradigm of religious persecution. He does this by locating the Anglican church at the root of the treason trial. His painstaking demonstration of the injustice of the treason charge ultimately provides a platform from which he can attack Protestant belief, which he describes as heresy and atheism. The Protestant ministers whom he believes to be orchestrating the persecution are "Ministers of Satan" who model themselves on the heathen persecutors who tyrannized the early Christians with sadistic pleasure (2). This figuration of the persecutor as a satanic, heathenish, bloodthirsty murderer sets up the central conflict of Christian martyrology: the battle between guilty persecutor and innocent victim.

The victim's innocence is key: in order to be absorbed into the paradigm that underlies all Christian martyrdom—the spotless Lamb viciously slaughtered—the victim cannot carry the taint of crime, especially a crime so heinous as treason. The central project of Allen's preface is to wash the Catholic martyr clean of what he calls the "contagion" of treason and to soil the persecuting government with religiously motivated murder and injustice. The preface thereby aims to clear away the charge of treason in order to set up the discursive conditions for the martyrology that follows. Having reclaimed and reconfigured the terms of the argument, Allen constructs the martyr narratives to reiterate the priests' innocence, most often in a marginal gloss that simply proclaims "INNOCENCIE" alongside those moments in the narrative when a martyr proclaims his duty to the queen, prays for her health, or denies the charge of treason.

In Allen's narratives, the transformation from condemned traitor to blessed martyr is achieved through both the victims' and the martyrologist's legible repetition of conventional topoi. For example, Ralph

Sherwin's ascetic approach to imprisonment—"his spare diet, his continual praier and meditation, his long watching with ofte and sharpe discipline used upon his body"—persuades his jailer that he is "the best and devoutest Priest that ever he saw in his life" (82). The scene of Alexander Brian's torture contrasts the familiar, placid martyr figure with the furious persecutor: while Brian faces having needles thrust under his fingernails "with a constant mind and pleasant countenance," his tormentor becomes enraged, "as a man half beside him self" (87). Brian describes his racking as fulfillment of the "wicked lust" of his antagonists but says that he "was without sense and feeling well nigh of all greefe, and paine," suggesting that prayer provided "a kinde of supernaturall sweetnesse of spirit" and left him "comforted, eased and refreshed of the greeves of the torture by past" (90).

Events at the scaffold likewise echo martyr typology. For the victim, the performance of martyrdom includes announcing himself eager for death, kissing or embracing the instruments of persecution, forgiving the persecutor, and passively accepting physical torture. Allen's account of Campion's execution is borrowed almost word-for-word from *A true reporte,* and therefore it rehearses Alfield's problematic martyr narrative. But Allen's other narratives show a closer likeness to martyrological formulas. Thomas Cottam and Lawrence Richardson watch the execution of a third priest, Luke Kirby, "with cheerefull countenances," and Cottam further signals his intrepid attitude toward death by his "jeaste" with an Anglican minister while Richardson is "in cutting up," or being dismembered (121). The martyr John Paine expresses his desire to die for the faith by kneeling and praying for half an hour and kissing the gallows with a smile before the rope is placed around his neck and he "lifted upe up his eies and handes towardes heaven a pretie while" (135). Sherwin is said to have died "paciently, constantly, and mildely, crying Jesus, Jesus, Jesus," and William Filbee is "hanged knocking his breast several times," much like Foxe's John Hooper or Thomas Bilney (77, 113).[24]

To reinforce the martyrological paradigm, Allen draws explicit comparisons between the priest's antagonizers and the persecutors of the early church. Allen's marginalia liken the cheering crowd at Shert's execution to "the Jewes [who] cried against christ & S. Steven, at the instigation of the Pharisies" (107). When Allen recounts how Brian is brutally racked for the second time, a note in his marginalia reads, "So was Christ, and S. Paul used, by the like men" (88). Drawing out the comparison further, the main text says, "These torments and the mans constancie are comparable truly to the old strange sufferings of the renommed Martyrs of the primitive Church in the daies of Nero, Decius and Diocletian, which he could never have borne by humane strength, if God had not geven his singular and supernatural grace" (89). In this one sentence, Allen replicates several components of traditional martyrdom: the physical torment of the martyr is highlighted; the victim is legitimized through the claim that both his suffering and his "constancy" in suffering are equal to the undisputed early church martyrs; the persecutor is the equivalent of Nero; and the martyr's comportment shows evidence of divine protection and godly ratification of his cause.

As in Foxe's book, martyrs and martyrologist alike explicitly describe death as the recapitulation of typological suffering. About Paine's arraignment "with about 13. witches, other murderers and theves," Allen remarks, "As our Saviour, *Cum iniquis reputasus est &c*" (131).[25] Sherwin describes his anticipated martyrdom as "following [Christ's] fotesteps" (84). In a peculiar, hallucinatory moment as he prepares for his next session on the rack, Brian goes so far as to imagine stigmata on his injured hand: "I did muse and meditate upon the moste bitter passion of oure Savioure, and how full of innumerable paines it was. And whiles I was thus occupied: me thought, that my left hand was wounded in the palme, and that I felt the blood runne out, but in very deede there was no such thing, nor any other paine then that, which seemed to be in my hand" (90). Brian's hallucinated stigmata indicate how powerfully he understood his own suffering to be a repetition of Christ's. His meditation on Christ's passion slips into a meditation on his own physical pain, Christ's wounded body standing in for his own. Even though the image turns out to be not a miracle but a fantasy, the narrative leaves open the question of this fantasy's origin—whether it was the delusion of a man in physical agony or a sensation authorized by divine intervention. The inclusion of this incident in the narrative would suggest that both Brian and the martyrologist viewed it as a significant event in which God communicates with his martyr. The narration of this event functions for the reader as an unambiguous interpretation of Brian's suffering.

For the most part, Allen's martyr accounts are sanitized of the polemic that constitutes his preface; the narratives construct innocence not through confrontation with the treason charge but through the typological representation of saintly suffering. With little overt comment on the political context of the trials and executions, Allen's martyr narratives reflect the long-established tradition of Christian sacred biography: through performative reference to Christ's passion and the martyrs of the early church, Campion and his fellow sufferers are inscribed into the ranks of saints. The charge of treason is dismissed by the verbal and behavioral cues that Allen normalizes into the narrative of persecuted Christian "INNOCENCIE." His assertion in the preface that "God knoweth and now al England and a great part of Europe seeth, the innocencie of these saints, that our lord is glorified by their deaths, and his Church enriched with new Martyrs of most excellent vertue and constancie" is carried through in the martyrological narratives, where false accusations and ignominious death are transformed into edifying spiritual triumph that serves the very church under attack (33). These martyrological echoes are the primary mode by which Allen's argument is deployed in the narratives. The clear resemblance between the innocent martyrs of the past and the priests put to death under Elizabeth proves, he suggests, that they are indeed martyrs, not the traitors they are pretended to be. The preface establishes the terms of the text's debate by openly confronting the charge of treason to argue that it is simply masquerading as religious persecution and that those who are put to death are Christian martyrs. The martyrology narrates enacted Christian martyrdom (and, thereby, political innocence) through reference to models of religious persecution.

While the division of *XII Reverend Priests* into two complementary texts serves as one of Allen's most effective polemical devices, this structural feature likewise articulates the emerging polemical limitations of Counter-Reformation martyrology. The priests' apolitical identity is foundational to Allen's argument, as an anecdote about Campion demonstrates. When asked by a gentleman whose house he wants to preach in if he intends to try to turn the queen's subjects against her, Campion assures him that "he had neither other commission of his superiors, nor intention of him self, then to minister the holy Sacraments, preach, and teach the people to salvation: and that he neither could nor would medle with matter of state" (53). In fact, Allen adds, while Campion was a wonderful preacher, he did not have a head for politics and "was no man for worldly matters, but only for the schole, Church and pulpit" (53). This claim, reiterated by the very structure of Allen's text, functions to exculpate Campion from political conspiracy. At the same time, however, it attenuates his political potency and imposes distinct limitations on the potential polemical resonance of Campion's death.

The Execution of Justice

Elizabeth's government responded to the Catholic claims of martyrdom with *The Execution of Justice in England* (1583), a brief defense of Campion's execution and of the legal proceedings against him, especially the treason charge. The book, expanded in 1584 to include a justification of Campion's torture, was published anonymously but is believed to have been written by William Cecil, Lord Burghley.[26] As Kingdon has observed, it was "of great importance. It was widely circulated and possessed an official character," and it was translated into several languages.[27] The book is an effort to engage the traitor–martyr argument circulating in public conversation by reasserting secular law as a structure for organizing the problem of recusancy. In this way, *The Execution of Justice* attempts both to counter the Catholic claims of martyrdom in order to persuade its audience against Campion and to preemptively construct the discourse around future recusant arrests.

Cecil's central strategy is to rejoin what Allen's text puts asunder: the political and religious nature of English Catholicism. To this end, he insists on the pope's role as a political rival to the queen, "a foreign potentate and open enemy" who is "the principal author of the invasions of Her Majesty's dominions."[28] By ignoring the pope's identity as head of the Catholic church and focusing instead on his identity as political adversary, Cecil suggests that Catholics' allegiance to the pope is not a matter of religious conscience but of treason. The 1570 bull of excommunication, "provoking also and authorizing" rebellion, thus plays an important role in Cecil's argument (5). He states that the excommunication of the queen and release of her subjects from all obedience to her created a community of "secret traitors," Catholic men and women who would defend the right of the pope—a foreign prince—against that of their own sovereign (7). The germ of rebellion planted by the papal bull needs only the right occasion to grow into armed conflict. For those inclined to treason, "there should have wanted nothing but opportunity to feel their strength and to assemble themselves in such numbers with armor and weapons as they might have presumed to have been the greater part and so by open civil war to have come to their wicked purposes" (7). One does not have to actively plot the queen's demise or take up arms against her to be guilty of treason, he argues.

Cecil follows the model set by Campion's prosecutors for subtly recasting religious doctrine as secular crime. To merely agree with the contents of the papal bull is to be a latent traitor, he says; those who were executed were guilty because they "did obstinately maintain the contents of the Pope's bull" (13). In fact, however, this is a misrepresentation of the priests' position, which was marked by reticence and ambivalence, not obstinate maintenance. The author of *An advertisement against Backbiters* had stated that the priests' failure to deny the papal bull was the equivalent of agreement; Cecil goes one step further by claiming that they actually agreed. This development in anti-Catholic rhetoric demonstrates the filling in over time of the trial narrative's lacunae in order to eliminate ambiguity.

At the same time that he positions loyalty to the pope as inherently treasonous, Cecil attempts to draw distinctions between Elizabethan law and religious persecution. He offers the example of many retired Marian priests who may believe Elizabeth should not have authority over the church but do not meddle in politics and are left unharassed. He states that Elizabeth is tolerant of religious difference—that those who disagree with the Anglican church are not "for their contrary opinions in religion prosecuted or charged with any crimes or pains of treason, nor yet willingly searched in their consciences for their contrary opinions that savor not of treason" (9-10). Cecil claims that it is entirely possible for a religious dissident to "also profess loyalty and obedience to Her Majesty and offer readily in Her Majesty's defense to impugn and resist any foreign force, though it should come or be procured from the Pope himself" (9).

But according to Cecil, Campion and his fellow priests, and others who may enter the realm in service of the Catholic mission, are of a different sort altogether. The language Cecil uses to describe the men in question characterizes them as duplicitous sowers of discord rather than persecuted religious innocents. Cecil exploits the etymology of the word "seminary" to describe the missionaries as "seedmen in their tillage of sedition" who are sent into the realm "under secret masks" and take up residence "in divers corners" to carry out their "wicked and dangerous, traitorous and crafty course" (6–7). They are not martyrs but a "kind of vermin" who "creep by stealth into the realm . . . to spread their poison within the same" (9). Cecil reiterates the trial's contention that disguise and intrigue are evidence of treason and suggests that if they were not traitors they would have no reason to sneak around. In short, their behavior proves them to be "vagrant, disguised, unarmed spies" (37). Drawing on biblical representations of evil, he claims that "They speak lies, they are as venomous as the poison of a serpent, even like the deaf adder that stoppeth his ears" (40).[29] Cecil asks his audience to broaden its notion of treason to compass these "secret traitors" (7). The fact that the priests do not form an armed militia in open rebellion is not a defense against the charge of treason, as Catholics claim. Instead, their secrecy makes them all the more insidious. "[I]f they will deny that none are traitors that are not armed," Cecil says, "they will make Judas no traitor that came to Christ without armor, coloring his treason with a kiss" (36).

The Judas comparison illustrates one reason why both sides of the debate slip back and forth so effortlessly between secular and religious discourses. Christ's passion is a story of martyrdom as well as political persecution, and these two categories are therefore necessarily linked in the Christian tradition. In both Matthew and Mark, the crime for which Christ is ostensibly put to death is blasphemy, a religious infraction: "Again the high priest asked him, and said unto him, Art thou the

Christ, the Son of the Blessed? And Jesus said: I am: and ye shall see the Son of man sitting on the right hand of power, and coming in the clouds of Heaven. Then the high priest rent his clothes, and saith, What need we any further witnesses? ye have heard the blasphemy, what think ye? And they all condemned him to be guilty of death."[30] The gospels of Luke and John add to this religious crime the suggestion of treason or sedition. Luke writes that Christ is accused of "perverting the nation, and forbidding to give tribute to Caesar, saying that he himself is Christ a King."[31] The Jews claim that Christ "stirreth up" and "perverteth the people."[32] In John's account, the Jews threaten that Pilate's leniency toward Christ will be construed as disloyalty to Caesar: "If thou let this man go, thou art not Caesar's friend: whosoever maketh himself a king speaketh against Caesar."[33]

Popular passion literature like the Corpus Christi dramas expands these suggestions of political crime to represent Christ as both heretic and traitor, invoking the charge of "treasoun" far more directly than the gospel accounts do. In the N-Town passion play, Christ is figured as a threat to both civil and ecclesiastical authority. The Pharisees claim,

> He is an eretyk and a tretour bolde
> To Sesare and to oure lawe, sertayn,
> Bothe in word and in werke; and, ȝe beholde,
> He is worthy to dey with mekyl peyn![34]

The suggestion that Christ's actions render him at once guilty of heresy and treason points to the close proximity of civil and ecclesiastical authority. The same set of actions can be interpreted as religious and political defiance, so much so that it is difficult to distinguish where one ends and the other begins. The Corpus Christi plays dramatize this point, using the terms "heretic" and "traitor" interchangeably to compass Christ's crimes.

Given Christ's status as a multivalent signifier, it is no surprise that both sides in the debate over English Catholics claim Christological authority for their respective positions. In the midst of bitterly condemning Catholic propaganda for its representation of Campion and the others as martyrs, Cecil appropriates the narrative of Judas's betrayal of Christ to substantiate his contention that treason comes in forms other than armed rebellion and with equally catastrophic effect. Few Catholics would be likely to disagree with the characterization of Judas as a traitor. But Catholic apologists like Allen likewise invoke the model of the Passion to legitimize the suffering of Catholic victims and condemn the authors of persecution. Thus the question exposed by these texts is not whether one side or the other has a more rightful case for Christian moral authority but which side can make the most convincing discursive claim to that authority.

Toward this end, Cecil invokes the memory of the Marian martyrs, whose legitimacy he asserts over the "forged catalogue" of martyrs described by men like Allen (29). He enumerates the catalog of tortures endured by the wide range of men, women, and children "lamentably destroyed" under the Marian persecution to suggest that the superiority of these martyrs to the "pseudomartyrs" claimed by the Catholic community lies in the extreme suffering of a broad population of innocents (20). Their identity as martyrs is assured because "most of the youth that then suffered cruel death, both men, women and children," died in testimony of the faith in which they had been either baptized or confirmed, unlike the Catholic recusants who were baptized Protestant and apostatized (20). The model of martyrdom outlined by Cecil is consistent with his broader polemical purpose: martyrdom requires horrible suffering combined with religious constancy and political innocence. The element of political innocence is critical: Cecil insists that the Marian martyrs "never at their death denied their lawful queen, nor maintained any of her open and foreign enemies, nor procured any rebellion or civil war" (21).

If Catholics are martyrs, they are martyrs for a fundamentally traitorous cause. He writes that Catholic martyrologists "do falsely allege that a number of persons, whom they term as martyrs, have died for defense of the Catholic religion, the same in very truth may manifestly appear to have died (if they so will have it) as martyrs for the Pope but yet as traitors against their sovereign and queen in adhering to him, being the notable and only hostile open enemy in all actions of war against Her Majesty, her kingdoms, and people" (15). In a text whose overarching project is to convincingly situate Campion and his fellow priests in a discourse of secular crime, Cecil repurposes the claim to martyrdom itself to make the state's case. He concedes the term "martyr" but desacralizes the martyr's cause by situating the papal "enemy" in the place of God, claiming that their deaths are therefore evacuated of what makes true martyrdom holy. In this way, *The Execution of Justice* continues the representational work of Campion's executioners, again and again shifting the terms of the discourse back to the charge of treason.

A Defense of English Catholics

In 1584, Allen published a response to Cecil's book, titled *A True, Sincere, and Modest Defense of English Catholics That Suffer for their Faith both at Home and Abroad.* In it, Allen repeats much of what he argued in the preface to *XII Reverend Priests,* but he also presents a lengthy, wide-ranging argument for the rights of the pope and the innocence of Catholics executed for treason. In his introductory remarks, Allen acknowledges the important polemical role played by retrospection. Whether someone is remembered and represented as persecutor or martyr depends on the story that is circulated about his or her death. In the struggle over who controls the victim's story, the state has greater resources at hand than the individual: "They have the name of authority, the shadow of laws, the pens and tongues of infinite at their commandment," he says.[35] "They may print or publish what they like, suppress what they list. Whereof private men, be they never so wicked or good, have not so great commodity" (59). Allen's text is meant to remedy this imbalance by providing a learned defense of English Catholics — an alternative interpretation of the events Cecil characterized as treason.

But Allen's argument in *Defense* is caught once again in the crux produced by the treason charge. In constructing Catholic victims as true subjects innocent of political crime, Allen, like Campion, becomes trapped between the opposing demands of Catholic orthodoxy and secular allegiance. He condemns the persecution of Catholics, but he is careful to direct blame away from Elizabeth's "temporal sovereignty"

(258). He remarks that "there is a great difference" between denying the queen's religious authority and saying that "she is not queen or governor over the clergy, or that priests or ecclesiastical persons be not her subjects" (114). This statement is directly contrary to the papal bull, from which Allen tries to distance his argument. In an effort to dismiss the treason charge, Allen argues that the pope's power to depose temporal monarchs is not even discussed in the training of English missionaries. Although the church has every right to touch on this aspect of papal discretion, the seminaries "pass over all with silence" because they fear such discussion "might be interpreted by the suspicious" to pertain specifically to Elizabeth (122). Statements such as this, which Allen had made in *XII Reverend Priests,* construct the Catholic missionary as an apolitical individual, someone who could not meddle in the affairs of state if he tried because he has so little knowledge of or training in the subject. But alongside this claim, Allen spends three of the book's eleven chapters describing and defending the pope's power to depose. The sheer volume of his insistence on papal prerogative causes problems for his argument that Catholic priests are completely apolitical. Without acknowledging it, Allen seems to be suggesting that if Catholic priests were actually working with the pope to depose the monarch, it would be just and right for them to do so. By attempting to make the case that Catholics are innocent of the charges against them and are maligned for merely religious matters, Allen ends up justifying the very ideas that have been labeled treason: the pope's claim to supremacy over secular powers and the projected scenario of papal invasion.

If Elizabeth's secular supremacy is off limits for attack, then Allen must again locate an alternative author of Catholic suffering. Here he is more aggressive than he had been in the earlier text, where he identified Anglican divines as the ultimate source of persecution. He carefully divides Elizabethan authority into two discrete categories, secular and religious, genuflecting to the former and attacking the latter. Allen contends that "Her Majesty hath no charge, authority, or power over the Church or ecclesiastical affairs, no more than the poorest soul in her realm," and that until she reconciles with the Catholic church and pope, she has even less spiritual authority than a Catholic commoner

(258–59). He hints that the established hierarchy is tainted with the suggestion of royalist idolatry. Contrary to what Protestant apologists claim, Elizabeth's authority over the church

> is not to make her next to God in her realm (as the libeler [Cecil] saith) but to make her the god of her people. From which cogitation, though of herself having so many means to put her in mind of her mortality, we doubt not but she is very far; yet truly this abominable and blasphemous adulation of some about Her Highness may breed great temptations. As we see in certain of the old heathen emperors, who never rested till they were adored with divine honor. The next step unto which is (doubtless) to say and believe that a temporal king is above the priest in causes ecclesiastical; or that in a Christian commonwealth the next dignity to Christ or God is not the priest but the prince; and so arrogate the regiment of the Church to a queen. (249)

Allen stops just short of comparing Elizabeth to a heathen emperor, no doubt having in mind those who populate texts like *The Golden Legend.* But he has certainly said enough; his suggestion that the Protestant church is one step shy of heathen idolatry quite ably insinuates the parallel.

Set in contrast to this image of the persecutor is that of the Catholic martyr, whom Allen asserts above the Marian martyrs Cecil justified in his text. Cecil highlighted the number executed under Mary and the magnitude of their sufferings as proof of their martyr status. Allen responds with the familiar Augustinian precept that it is the cause, not the death, that makes a martyr. In the case of the recent Catholic martyrdoms, he asserts, the cause is defense of the faith, whereas he classifies the Marian executions as the "worthy punishment of heretics" who died by "shedding their blood obstinately in testimony of falsehood against the truth of Christ and His holy Spouse, and out of the unity of the same" (114–15).[36] Allen argues that the Marian victims were essentially suicides, "damnable murderers of themselves" (115).[37]

Like Foxe, who legitimizes reformed theology by drawing direct parallels between his martyrs and those of the primitive church, Allen makes an argument for martyrdom by comparing the priests' circumstances and behavior to that of Christ, the apostles, and the early church martyrs. In particular, he cites the similarity between the wrongful accusations against Christ and the charges brought against Campion. But Allen draws a relationship between his martyrs and Christ that goes a step beyond typology in a move that attempts to further compensate for the damaging effects of the treason charge. Foxe had made much of the spiritual efficacy of the Protestant martyrs' trials and suffering, repeatedly echoing Tertullian's precept that "the blood of the martyrs is the seed of the church."[38] As Foxe conceived it, the martyrs' constancy and faith in the face of torment and death provide a model for Christians, one that emphasizes witnessing to Christ, remaining steadfast in his teachings, and focusing on heavenly, not earthly, rewards. But for Allen, the death of Campion and his fellow Catholics is more than a moral model; it is a redemptive exchange much like Christ's death on the cross. He describes the English nation as being redeemed by the martyrs' deaths—not in the Foxean sense of finding redemption through renewed Christian devotion but in a much more literal transaction in which the martyrs "avert God's ire" from England by "offer[ing] themselves in sacrifice for the salvation of their best beloved country" (259–60). It is "far more to [God's] honor and glory, and the briefer way to salvation of our whole nation and of more souls in particular," Allen says, "that we should pass through this persecution and win our own and our brethren's salvation by our blood" (266). In this way, Allen counters the treason charge by figuring the martyrs not only as powerful Christlike redeemers but as the ultimate patriotic exemplars.

Under Allen's hand, Catholics' similarity to Christ and the apostles extends to the adoption of secrecy to avoid harassment and persecution. "How often do we read in the Evangelists that our Savior fled, that He did hide Himself, that He walked not openly, that He went up to Jerusalem on the feast day not openly but in covert?" he demands. "Who knoweth not that the apostles, as well before as after the coming of the Holy Ghost, kept themselves often secret in private parlors and chambers, as the first holy Bishops of Rome (for fear of their persecutors) kept their meetings, mysteries, and councils in caves and grottoes under the ground?" (263–64). Although Allen takes Gospel models to argue that craft is sometimes required for the survival of the true church, the martyr figure he constructs through these parallels is nonparadigmatic. The martyrs of *The Golden Legend* are distinctly open, frank, and confrontational. Christ's resistance in the Corpus Christi dramas is not crafty or subtle. His evasiveness is not strategic but, rather, a sign of his resignation to the fate that awaits him. Foxe's martyrs are insistently depicted as guileless innocents who willingly confess Christ in spite of the consequences, and Foxe's regard for the unlearned lay men and women who died in the Marian persecution highlights the Protestant martyr's simple and ready faith.

Although Allen's argument that many key martyrs in the Christian tradition—Christ himself, the martyred apostles, and the leaders of the early Christian church—used secrecy and disguise just as Catholic missionaries do cannot be undermined on the basis of historical record, his claim nonetheless creates ruptures in the text's project of inscribing Campion and others into the martyrological tradition. Secrecy and disguise are not common threads in primitive, late-medieval, or earlier sixteenth-century martyrology, a problem that chapter 5 will explore in greater depth. On the contrary, the Christian martyr narrative relies on precisely the opposite elements: a willingness to die and an open confession of Christ. Although fear of physical torture and death led many people through the ages to conceal their faith, as patristic writers like Eusebius attest, the genre of martyrology emphatically declares otherwise, and it is the demands of martyrology that Allen must meet. The secret nature of the Catholic mission in England is incoherent with the well-established conventions of Christian martyr-making.

Ultimately, Allen's attempt to draw familiar martyrological paradigms is compromised by the discrepancy between his martyrs and established models, as well as by his overtly aggressive engagement with the charge of treason. In narrative rehearsals of Campion's trial and execution and in the polemical debates over how to interpret those events, his struggle to achieve exemplarity is replicated in the equally troubled Catholic apologetics of the period. In the aftermath of the Campion case, both the Elizabethan government and its Catholic subjects sought ways to refine their approach to the conflict so that the

next wave of executions might be made to express their respective ideological positions with less ambiguity, less room for dissenting interpretations. The polemical and martyrological literature studied in the
next two chapters discloses a chasm between Catholics and the state
that widened with each successive treason trial, widening also the gap
between Catholic victims and the typologial sources of martyrological
legitimacy.

Chapter 4

"The Finger of God Is Heere"

Counter-Reformation Martyrs and Miracles

*[T]he glory of his martyrdom was declared and confirmed by
an evident sign, showed by the hand of Almighty God, who
by divine testimony manifested to the world the truth of his cause,
and the greatness of his reward.*

—John Gennings, *The Life and Death of
Mr. Edmund Geninges Priest*

The rupture between typological martyrdom and the secularized persecution of English Catholics mapped in chapter 3 is evident well beyond the literature surrounding Edmund Campion's death. In one way or another, every English Counter-Reformation martyrology of the period is coded with this representational crisis. In an effort to reduce ambiguity and reclaim typological legitimacy, Catholic victims and their apologists developed a set of behavioral and discursive strategies for offsetting the treason trial's disruption of traditional martyr paradigms. However, these compensatory strategies themselves inscribe a fracture in martyrological discourse, a discourse whose foundational organizing principle is typological repetition. Like the Campion narratives, the stories of subsequent Catholic victims are compromised by semiotic ambiguities that become embedded in the very structure of Counter-Reformation martyrology.

This chapter explores the implications of these developments for the reproduction of the martyrological miracle — traditionally the legible proof text of the victim's sanctity and salvation — arguing that generic fracture becomes evident in the topos of the miraculous. The chapter focuses on two martyrologies: Father John Mush's *The Life and Martyrdom of Mistress Margaret Clitherow*, the 1586 narrative of a York recusant pressed to death for refusing to submit to trial; and John Gennings's *The Life and Death of M. Edmund Geninges Priest*, a martyrology of the author's brother, executed in London in 1591 for illegally performing the Mass. Clitherow's refusal of trial raises questions for her audience about the extent to which she wills her own death. While she is able to sidestep the treason trial and traitor identity, the circumstances of her death leave her open to accusations of suicide. The miraculous, which could rescue her from this ambiguity by providing objective evidence of sanctity, is itself becoming an increasingly problematic discourse. Abounding with marvels and wonders, the Gennings text illustrates how the topos of miraculous intervention becomes relegated by the forensic mechanisms of the treason proceeding to an exclusively devotional function. In its study of Clitherow and Gennings, along with Anglican polemicist Richard Sheldon's critique of Catholic claims to the miraculous, this chapter argues that the narrative reproduction of martyrdom is compromised by the discursive separation between the circumstances of persecution and miraculous validation of the victim.

"If She Might Have Had Her Own Will"

Margaret Clitherow was the wife of a prosperous York butcher. She was a fervent Catholic who regularly hosted secret Masses at her home and had a special section of the property fitted up for harboring priests. One in particular, the seminary priest John Mush, maintained a steady residence with her and acted as her confessor and spiritual director.[1] Mush escaped capture when on March 10, 1586, Clitherow's house was ransacked by pursuivants. Convinced that Clitherow was treasonously sheltering priests, the men seized a child of her household, stripped him naked, and threatened to beat him if he did not reveal their hiding places. The frightened boy gave up a stash of contraband Mass paraphernalia. No priests were found, but Clitherow and her household were sent to prison. At her arraignment she refused to submit to trial by the state, even though refusal carried the penalty of pressing to death. Clitherow obstinately maintained her position, arguing, "Having made no offence, I need no trial," and on March 25 she was executed.[2]

Clitherow proclaimed herself a martyr throughout her trial, a position Mush took up in the account of her he wrote later that year.[3] *The Life and Martyrdom of Mistress Margaret Clitherow* is part polemic, part hagiographic life story, and part martyrology. Circulated but never printed, the manuscript begins and ends with lengthy vitriolic attacks on Protestant doctrine and government, specifically the persecution of priests and the charge of treason. As in Allen's *XII Reverend Priests,* however, the narrative sections on Clitherow's life and death are largely devoid of polemical commentary, attempting instead to construct a conventionally legible hagiography.[4] A large proportion of the text describes Clitherow's virtues—her humility, charity, obedience, and religious fervor—and represents her as saintly notwithstanding her martyrdom. This portrait of Clitherow is carried through the account of her apprehension, court interviews, imprisonment, and execution, where both author and martyr rely heavily on traditional martyrological formulations.

Mush presents Clitherow as eager for martyrdom; she looks to persecution as "a precious gift and benefit of God" (398). In a chapter titled "Of Her Marvellous Desire to Suffer for Christ and His Truth," Mush relates how Clitherow sought out suffering as a matter of course: "she would not let escape almost one day, if she might have had her own will, without something voluntarily taken whereby she might suffer pain either of body or of mind" (397). Mush reports that Clitherow's life was so rife with edifying trials that she suffered "double martyrdom," once in her life and again in her death (409).[5] For Clitherow, actual martyrdom represents the pinnacle of God's blessings. Even long before her arrest and execution, she ponders her "worthiness of martyr-dom" (398). She does not see how she could be chosen for such a calling but concludes, "if it be His will, I pray Him that I may be constant and persevere to the end" (398). Once she is arrested on the charge of trea-son, the prospect of execution brings particular delight to her. Accord-ing to Mush, "when the cross came indeed, as she was not often with-out one or other, she rejoiced so much in it that she would say that she feared to offend God with too much gladness" (397).

Clitherow regards her death as an act of God's will, but this as-sumption is compromised by the extent to which she seeks to care-fully control the terms of her suffering. One of the central tensions of Mush's text is its double claim to "her own will" and divine will, which Mush describes metonymically as "the finger of God" (375, 397). Mush's lengthy account of Clitherow's virtues indicates that she had long possessed the will to suffer. The figure who emerges from the narrative of her life is a woman who appears to have internalized a great deal of hagiography and is consciously working toward creating situations for herself that will provide an opportunity to exercise saint-like rectitude. Clitherow's management of her domestic duties sug-gests both her ability and desire to consciously manipulate her life into a typologically legible catalog of pious suffering. For example, Mush remarks that "in the time of her receiving the Blessed Sacrament of Christ His Body, she ever coveted to have the lowest place, so far as she could do it without trouble and noisomeness to others, for she would not seem to any to desire it" (393). As mistress of her prosper-ous husband's household, Clitherow must artificially reorganize its social hierarchy to create an image and experience of lowliness that is entirely self-willed, at the same time erasing any evidence of will. For example, the distribution of housework, none of which she would have needed to do of necessity, is arranged into an opportunity for humility: "there was nothing to be done in the house so base that she would not be most ready to do or take in hand herself, and the baser the office should be, the more unwilling would she be the maidens should do it, but rather keep it as a necessary exercise in store for herself of her own humility. . . . [S]he would not disdain . . . to make the fire, to sweep the house, to wash the dishes, and more gross matters also, choosing rather to do them herself, and to set her maids about sweeter business" (374–75). Clitherow's maids must have found this a curious arrangement indeed. But for her, this division of household affairs presents occasions for piety that would not have presented themselves otherwise. Mush also participates in the orchestration of such daily martyrdoms. "[D]esirous to make some especial proof of her charity to God, and obedience to her ghostly father" (Mush himself), he chastises her for committing offenses against God that he has invented out of whole cloth. As he anticipates, she responds with "perfect love and obedience" (380).[6] Working together in this manner, Mush and Clitherow fashion the life of a saint, first through the conscious administration of her day-to-day living and later through the careful management of death and narrative.

The Clitherow Case

By refusing a trial, Clitherow effectively short-circuited the treason accusation that proved so problematic for other Catholic victims. The events that structured Campion's case—the probing of secular allegiance, the presentation of evidence, the accusations and condemnation, the traitor's death—never come to pass. Rather, Clitherow's case becomes something of an anomalous event, divorced from the structures of either heresy or treason. Her liberal employment of martyr topoi in the conduct of this event, memorialized in turn by Mush's narrative confirmation of her as martyr, functions to inscribe specific meaning onto the strange tableau that replaces the treason proceeding.

According to Mush's account, Clitherow was arraigned on March 14 under the charge that she "had harboured and maintained Jesuit and Seminary priests, traitors to the Queen's Majesty and her laws, and that she had [heard] Mass, and such like" (413). Clitherow declared herself innocent of having harbored "any such persons . . . which are not the Queen's friends" (413). When asked how she would be tried, she answered that she would "be tried by none but by God and your own consciences," refusing repeatedly to be tried by the law of the country (413).[7] The council attempted to persuade her that a trial would likely lead to clemency—that she could not easily be convicted "upon this slender evidence of a child"—but she would not budge (414). She gave no public explanation for this refusal other than that she was guiltless of the charges against her.

After the first day's session in which no progress was made toward inducing Clitherow to reconsider, she was brought in for a second appearance in court. Seeing that she was still obstinate in her unwillingness to be tried, the judge reluctantly read the sentence of death: "You must return from whence you came, and there, in the lowest part of the prison, be stripped naked, laid down, your back upon the ground, and as much weight laid upon you as you are able to bear, and so to continue three days without meat or drink, except a little barley bread and puddle water, and the third day to be pressed to death, your hands and feet tied to posts, a sharp stone under your back" (417). Death by pressing was the standard penalty, evolved from a statute of Edward III, for refusing trial.[8] By the sixteenth century, it mercifully lasted only about fifteen minutes.

For two weeks following her arraignment and sentencing, the council attempted to convince Clitherow to change her mind about submitting to trial. Inquiries were made into whether she was pregnant, the results of which were inconclusive.[9] Steadfastly maintaining her position and refusing to claim the benefit of her possible pregnant condition, Clitherow was executed fifteen days after her arrest. On the day appointed for her execution, she was taken to a building on York's Ouse Bridge, stripped down to a linen habit, and made to lie on the ground. She was tied "to two posts, so that her body and her arms made a perfect cross," Mush writes: "A sharp stone, as much as a man's fist, [was] put under her back; upon her was laid to the quantity of seven or eight hundredweight at the least, which, breaking her ribs, caused them to burst forth of the skin" (432).

By drawing parallels like the one between the cross and the position of Clitherow's body during pressing, Mush presents her death according to a familiar martyrological formula.[10] Such behavioral and narrative gestures are foundational to the text's claim that her death is a typologically legible religious persecution. Clitherow appears merry at the sentence of death, she demonstrates happiness at being "bound for

Christ's sake," and she jokes about death by making "a pair of gallows on her fingers" to amuse others imprisoned for the faith (418, 412). Mush emphasizes these typological echoes in his role of martyrologist, ending her story with a formulaic declaration that might as well have appeared in Foxe's *Acts and Monuments*: "Thus most victoriously this gracious martyr overcame all her enemies, passing [from] this mortal life with marvellous triumph into the peaceable city of God, there to receive a worthy crown of endless immortality and joy" (432).

Mush offers a fascinating explanation of Clitherow's decision not to be tried, one he claims to have gathered from a conversation she had with a friend while imprisoned. Clitherow said that she knew the only evidence against her would be extracted from the children and servants of her own household, and she could not bear to have them testify against her. "[I]t would have been more grievous to me than a thousand deaths, if I should have seen any of them brought forth before me to give evidence against me," she said (436). Her second reason for refusing trial was to spare the jury from committing the sin of condemning her unjustly: "I knew well the country must needs have found me guilty to please the Council, which earnestly seek my blood; and then all they had been accessory to my death, and damnably offended God. I thought it therefore in the way of charity on [my] part to hinder the country from such a sin; and since it must needs be done, to cause as few to do it as might be; and that was the judge himself" (436). Mush holds these explanations up as "reasons which sufficiently defend and clear her from all slanders of obstinacy, desperation, or other crime at all"; rather, he says, they "convince a rare and marvellous charity in her" (436). Anne Dillon describes this explanation for Clitherow's actions as "tagged on by Mush" in his efforts at "preempting or rebutting already current criticism."[11] What Mush's remarks expose are the dissenting interpretations of Clitherow's actions by members of her community, for whom the motivation—and therefore meaning—of her death remained opaque.

In the explanation of her motives provided by Mush, Clitherow successfully sidesteps the treason charge by constructing herself as a scapegoat for the projected sins of her community. Far from a traitor, she instead positions herself as patriot par excellence, a woman willing to give up her own life to preserve the moral integrity of England—to "hinder the country from such a sin." She suggests that she has consciously chosen to take control of the terms of her own death, molding what it means and why it happens. This project of framing her death begins in the arraignment scenes, where she repeatedly rejects the authority of secular law over her case, referring her judgment to God and to the consciences of the council and fashioning her condemnation as an ethical rather than a legal decision. Her response to the death sentence exposes the distance between the way the court interprets its decision and the way she understands and represents that decision: "If this judgment be according to your own conscience," she says, "I pray God send you better judgment before Him." The judge corrects her interpretation of events: "'Nay,' said the judge, 'I do it according to law'" (417). Clitherow likewise argues with her accusers about the reason for her death, repeatedly insisting, "My cause is God's, and it is a great comfort for me to die in His quarrel" (422). The state sees it otherwise, as the sheriff at her execution declares: "'Mrs. Clitherow, you must remember and confess that you die for treason.' The martyr answered, 'No, no, Mr. Sheriff, I die for the love of my Lord Jesu;' which last words she spake with a loud voice" (431). As in Campion's execution scene, the terms of Clitherow's death continue to be debated in the final moments, the two parties operating from discrepant scripts.

An Enigmatic Death

The avoidance of trial severs Clitherow's death from the structures of the treason discourse. With the exception of moments like those noted above, the narrative of Margaret Clitherow does not consistently expose the tension between traitor and martyr that organizes texts like Alfield's account of Campion's death. But despite her insistence on religious persecution and her steady invocation of martyrological topoi, Clitherow's management of her arraignment and execution presents an equally insidious problem for her narrative: it opens up the suggestion of suicide, an act as damnable as treason. As John Donne would later argue, the discursive proximity between martyrdom and suicide can be traced as far back as Eusebius's account of the Roman persecutions. In his defense of suicide, *Biathanatos* (c. 1608), Donne argues that many martyrs of the early church sought their own deaths in order to gain martyrdom. In the centuries of the early church, martyrdom was so revered that the Christian population became "affected with a disease of this naturall desire of such a death."[12] Donne turns this comparison to condemnation in his later critique of the Counter-Reformation's claims to martyrdom, *Pseudo-Martyr* (1610), in which he posits martyrdom as God's answer to the human urge toward suicide.[13] As we saw in chapter 3, the accusation of suicide as a rhetorical strategy for discounting rival claims to martyrdom is not confined to Protestant polemics. In *The Defense of English Catholics,* Allen condemns the victims of the Marian persecution as "damnable murderers of themselves."[14]

Clitherow's death shares similarities with those critiqued by Donne and Allen as dubious martyrdoms. In place of the martyr–traitor ambiguity, her execution creates a figure who is either a martyr or a suicide, a problem sharpened by the role of Clitherow's self-conscious will in shaping both her daily suffering and her death. When she leaves the court after her sentencing with a joyful, smiling face, some remark that "It must needs be that she received comfort from the Holy Ghost," while others say that she is "possessed with a merry devil, and that she sought her own death" (418). For the witnesses to Clitherow's behavior, she is either a benefactor of divine intervention or a suicidal victim of demonic possession. In their attempts to persuade her away from the course she has chosen, the judges and ministers who visit her in prison repeatedly warn her, "you show yourself wilful in seeking your own death contrary to God's law, and damnable to your own soul" (420).

Clitherow's strategy for eluding the treason charge ultimately leads to a death that is equally vexed. Her silence—her refusal either to be tried or to explain her rejection of trial—acts as an open-ended signifier that can be interpreted in multiple, competing ways. In place of a clear subject—martyr or traitor, madwoman or suicide—the text inscribes a cipher, a subject who simultaneously occupies all and none of these positions. In both her silence and her positioning of herself as a scapegoat, Clitherow appears to model herself after Christ. She attempts to gain Christ by imitating his suffering, but her adoption of silence appropriates a feature of Christ's Passion that leads to illegibility. In the heated political climate of the late sixteenth century, recusant Catholics could not run the risk of leaving their deaths open to divergent interpretations, lest they finally be construed as nonmartyrs, guilty of either suicide or treason.

The Passion of Christ is marked by properties unique and irreproducible among Christian martyr stories. The gospel accounts describe Christ as a largely silent figure through the course of his trials and torments. In turn, popular representations of the Passion like the Corpus Christi plays accentuate precisely this feature of the story, making Christ's silence itself dramatic. His reticence is variously interpreted by his persecutors as madness, stupidity, shame, and awe, but the audience of the drama has the advantage of viewing the events retrospectively, from a moment in time after Christ's miraculous rising from the dead. As audience, we understand, as his tormentors cannot, what his silence means. Rather than a sign of weakness or guilt, it signifies both his willing sacrifice for human redemption and the superior nature of his being, above and removed from the trial that seeks to subdue and eliminate him. It is only Christ's defeat of death on the third day, however, that affords this understanding. We read back from after the resurrection to interpret Christ's silence as evidence of his divinity. Moreover, the resurrection tells us that he cannot be guilty of the blasphemy and treason of which he is accused because he himself is God. In this way, retrospection translates the trial of a criminal into the persecution of Christianity's originary martyr.

The English Corpus Christi plays emphasize the relationship between past and present by dramatizing all of earthly time, from Creation to the Last Judgment. As the Passion is acted out, Christ has always already risen, such that his identity as innocent, martyr, and divinity is never in question. The meaning of Christ's death is further elaborated by its relationship to the Last Judgment, where he appears again in order to separate the saved from the damned. It is in that moment that the significance of the Passion is made fully evident, for it is only the transaction of Christ's death and resurrection that snatches souls from the pains of hell. For the plays' audience, the significance of the Passion is thus linked inextricably to both past and future; it is interpreted through the lens of what did happen on the third day and what will happen on the day of Judgment.

Although the accusations brought against Christ and the ignoble nature of his execution would seem to provide legitimizing analogies for persecuted early modern Catholics like Clitherow, the temporal properties of Christ's Passion effectively foreclose the prospect of any phenomenological repetition. Christ's resurrection provides a way of reading his Passion that secures his identity as divine redeemer and human martyr, but the executions of Catholic recusants are not succeeded by any such event, leaving these deaths vulnerable to dissenting interpretations. Counter-Reformation martyrologists were challenged with retrospectively trying to interpret a death that had been carefully shaped into a criminal's just execution—or, in the case of Clitherow, a death that had no clear shape at all.

In the simplest terms, what prevents the figure of the persecuted Christ from being an ambiguous signifier is miraculous intervention. Christ becomes legible as God because he rises from the dead—because his nature is revealed by an extraordinary thaumaturgic event. While subsequent Christian martyrs do not have the benefit of this fate, the genre of martyrology substitutes the topos of the miraculous to create the same retrointerpretive effects. This is the purpose of miracles in the Christian martyrological and hagiographic traditions: to demonstrate that the subject is sanctified and that his or her cause is marked by God's favor. What Margaret Clitherow needed in order to translate her enigmatic death into an unmistakable example of Christian martyrdom was a good miracle.

Mush's text does not provide one, although a miracle story about Clitherow appears in other contemporaneous accounts of her. A manuscript account possibly also by Mush—titled *A Yorkshire Recusant's Relation* by its nineteenth-century editor, John Morris—relates a story in which Clitherow's body was retrieved six weeks after her death and found to have undergone no decomposition. It takes another six days to locate the required herbs to preserve the body, "all which time it remained without corruption or evil savour."[15] In the same manuscript is a text that Morris titles *An Ancient Editor's Note Book*, in which the story is related in greater detail and the miraculous incorruptibility extended for seven additional weeks: "The body of Mrs. Clitherow being by her tormentors buried in a filthy place the same night she was martyred, six weeks after a Catholic by diligent search found it, and taking it up he found it whole without any putrefaction, and so carried it a great journey where he buried it again more decently eight weeks after her martyrdom, leaving then her body so pure and uncorrupted as though the blessed soul had departed from the body the day before, albeit it was so pressed and bruised, as in the order of her death is set down."[16] Given the manner of Clitherow's death—her ribs having "burst forth of the skin," as Mush tells us—it is wondrous not only that her body is preserved but that it betrays so few signs of the horrific violence done to it. In this account, the phenomenon of Clitherow's incorruptible body is extracted from the gruesome forensic details of her death and situated instead within the hagiographic conventions for conceptualizing and narrating the sacred body of a saint. As Susannah Brietz Monta observes, "Through these miracles the martyr's desecrated body resists its traitor's punishment."[17]

The Life and Martyrdom of Mistress Margaret Clitherow circulated independently from these accounts of the miraculous preservation of her body, never finding their way into a unified text. This separation between the miracle and the troublesome death the miracle justifies is a key feature of Counter-Reformation martyrology. Whatever the provenance of their separate circulation in Clitherow's case, the absence of a disambiguating miracle in Mush's account of her death is consistent with developing generic patterns. *The Life and Martyrdom* itself was originally read among the recusant community in its two parts, *The Virtuous Life* and *The Virtuous Death*. Within months of Clitherow's execution, however, a composite text that included the polemical introductory and concluding material was in circulation. As Dillon notes, this polemical material functions to "plead the Catholic position in relation to the law," implying a broadly imagined audience of both Catholic and Protestant—sympathetic and antagonistic—readers.[18] Structured similarly, with a polemical preface and a devotional-hagiographic body, Allen's *XII Reverend Priests* had likewise aimed at a mixed audience. In addition to providing edifying material for Catholic devotion, both martyrologies include protracted polemics arguing for Catholics as martyrs in an effort to shape public opinion against governmental policy. Neither includes miracle stories.

Another kind of text, the periodic report sent from a missionary to his superior, is also usually devoid of miracles. When Father James Young writes to the Rector of the English College at Rome, Robert Persons, about the executions of Edmund Gennings and Oliver Plasden, he has no miracles to relate.[19] In a letter to Jesuit Superior Henry Garnet on the progress of the mission, Father Richard Holtby does not include any miracles,[20] although in another text more clearly intended for circulation among the faithful, *Account of Three Martyrs,* Holtby includes two miracles related to the Northumberland martyr Edward Waterson.[21]

These examples suggest that polemically inflected martyrologies aimed at a mixed audience and private correspondence between missionary priests and their superiors were not apt repositories for the miracle narrative. Other martyrologies, however—those intended exclusively for the devotion or instruction of faithful Catholics—incorporate a broad range of marvels and wonders, far broader than those represented in Foxe. Miracles could not function as polemical tools in the legalistic debate initiated by the treason trial. Stories of marvelous healings or claims of God's divine retribution were not regarded by either side as viable arguments against the charge of treason. As a result, Counter-Reformation martyrology becomes a fractured genre, loosely divided into two attenuated subgenres: the polemical and the devotional. Each makes a case for the sanctity and typological legibility of Catholic victims, but there are certain domains that they do not share. Polemical martyrology, like Allen's *XII Reverend Priests,* does not use miracles as part of its argument for Catholics as martyrs, and conversely, devotional martyrology, like Holtby's *Account of Three Martyrs,* distances itself from the forensic problems raised by the treason charge, justifying Catholic practice through reference to miraculous wonders. Because of this fracture, figures like Clitherow and Campion, whose stories are circulated within polemical texts condemning Elizabethan policy, have no legitimizing access to the miraculous.

Devotional Martyrology

The remainder of the texts studied in this chapter fall into the emerging subgenre of devotional martyrology. Although their location outside of the politicized treason debate allows them greater liberty in their engagement with miracle stories, their disconnection from the historical circumstances of Catholic suffering narrows the scope of their proselytizing influence. The disjuncture between the paradigmatic martyr and the Catholic defendant produced by the treason proceeding compromised martyrology's ability to transpose the victim from an historical into a sacred narrative. As Foxe's book demonstrates, the ideal relationship between the historical and the sacred is a perfect intersection: the historical event of death is fully legible as a sacred event and can be narratively reproduced without the kinds of fissures that show up in the Clitherow and Campion martyrologies. By relying on miracles as their primary method of demonstrating sanctity, Catholic devotional martyrologies situate their subjects, a priori, in God's sacred narrative, thereby de-emphasizing the martyr's relationship to the problematic events of the treason proceeding. This strategy abstracts the victim from the criminal discourse that threatens martyr production, but in so doing, it produces a martyr story with no currency or polemical potency—a story that can only justify the Catholic cause to other Catholics.

John Wilson's *English Martyrologe* (1608) provides a lucid illustration of this development. Explicitly addressing itself to Catholic readers, the book is a calendar of martyrs written to guide each person's "private and particular devotion."[22] In Wilson's text, as in martyrological literature more broadly, the miracle functions to ratify the victim's cause and announce his or her status as a true martyr. Wilson makes this point legible by the repetition of formulaic taglines after each martyr's catalog of miracles. God performs miracles for Saint Cowyne to "manifest his innocency," for Saint Dympna "in signe of her innocency," for Saint Ethelbert "to shew the innocency of his cause," for King Henry VI "in wittnesse of his innocent life," and, more specifically for Saint Brigit, "in testimony of her virginity" and "in signe of her sanctimony."[23] No narratives of the contemporary martyrs appear. Most of the calendar is comprised of the stories of primitive and pre-Reformation martyrs, with the martyrs of the Elizabethan and Jacobean persecutions appearing in a list at the end of the book. The individuals executed in recent history are inscribed into the ranks of faithful martyrs merely by their textual proximity to the stories of earlier holiness and divine justification. *English Martyrologe* is thus rather peculiar: it is written on the heels of the heated anti-Catholic persecution of King James I's early reign and includes the victims of contemporary persecution, but it has little to do with its own time. Instead, it constitutes a decidedly anachronistic addition to the period's Catholic martyrology in its style, structure, and content.

In other devotional martyrologies, miracles are presented to provide moral lessons that gesture toward contemporary debates but make no attempt to engage them polemically. The manuscript segment referred to as *An Ancient Editor's Note Book,* consisting of relatively spare narratives of contemporary men and women persecuted for the faith, reports many miracles meant to reinforce the righteousness of Catholic martyrs, doctrine, and practice. In a story that demonstrates the virtue of suffering for Catholic belief, the author writes of Stephen Rowsome, a priest "of singular perfection, [who] had in his lifetime many heavenly visions, as great lights in windows and places where he was alone and sometimes with others" (41). Once Rowsome is imprisoned for the faith, he begins to receive visitations from "God the Father, Christ our Saviour, our Blessed Lady, glorious souls of saints, [who] full often appeared unto him, leaving behind them such odoriferous smells" (42). The narrative also includes a felon arraigned in York with the martyrs John Amias and Robert Dalby, who "saw hanging over [the martyrs'] heads a great round light, which every time they spake, would as it were move itself, and at the end of their speeches vanished away" (51). The felon is converted to Catholicism with the aid of these miracles, and he too is executed for the faith.

The text abounds in miracle stories that confirm the godliness of Catholic practice, especially those ceremonies that had come under attack by Reformers. In a section titled "The Power of Priests," the author tells of a prison chamber inhabited by evil spirits that are expelled by a priest with holy water and the sign of the cross (52–53).

A chapter called "Devotion of Catholics" includes the story of a woman on her deathbed who is healed by the sacrament of extreme unction and another whose huge facial fistula is healed by receiving Catholic communion and promising to clothe three poor men (54–57). In the same chapter we learn of a fire in Staffordshire that forces all the residents to empty their houses of furniture. "[O]ne man only omitted to remove anything out of his house, whereat his neighbours marvelling, he said, 'I have fasted this day, as all my forefathers have done, let God work His will.' In sequel," the author writes, "not one house in all that town escaped unburnt besides that, and that remained untouched" (55). In all these stories, divine intervention serves to indicate to Catholic readers—some of whom may have been reconsidering their faith and devotional customs in a time of persecution—that the teachings of the church are ratified by God himself.

A final catalog cites both lax Catholics and heretics as objects of divine restitution. A man cooks meat on Maundy Thursday, and the cooking fire burns down his house (56). "[A]n apostata [*sic*] priest, twice married, a common drunkard," falls into a fevered frenzy, rolls out of bed, and breaks his neck (58). In a series of stories that have much in common with Foxe's tales of divine judgment, the author describes a Walsingham man who died suddenly and stank so badly that the stench of his corpse killed one of the men who buried him (59). Another man, Huddletone, "a great persecutor in the north," also died suddenly and "did stink so abominably that nobody could endure to come nigh him" (59). And in an ironic incident of martyrological comeuppance, the author reports that "One Robert Aston, parson, of Mucklaston in Staffordshire, the first married priest that ever was in that diocese, one of Fox his confessors in his *Book of Monuments*, . . . was suddenly with a just punishment from God deprived of both his tongue and his wit" and lived several years a mute idiot before meeting his death (57).

The Story of Edmund Gennings

The Life and Death of M. Edmund Geninges Priest (1614) is a much longer devotional martyrology focused on a single martyr. The book was written by Gennings's brother, John, who converted to

Catholicism after the death of Edmund in 1591. Having lived as a profligate until his conversion only days after Edmund's execution, John describes himself as having found Catholicism through the intercession of his heavenly sibling.[24] As a result of his conversion, John leaves England to take orders at the college in Douai and later joins the English mission himself. In the preface to his brother's martyrology, he writes that after long deliberation he has been persuaded to set down Edmund's story by the urging of friends and of God: "some secret motives have often assaulted my mind, and invited me to this enterprize, which in mature consideration seeme to me to have proceeded from God himself, who would not have the memory of his Saints so long obscured & forgotten" (9). The book, he suggests, is not only divinely inspired but offers a lesson about the value God places on the reverence of saints.

A verse preface titled "The Booke to his Reader" announces that the story is intended for the spiritual direction and comfort of the audience, who should "learne to suffer by [Edmund's] constancy" (4).[25] In addition to sharing this devotional purpose with medieval martyrology, the book has many features in common with texts like *The Golden Legend*: it posits Edmund as destined for martyrdom from birth; it frequently references a likeness between Edmund and the apostles or Christ; it draws parallels between the persecutors and biblical figures of evil; and it represents Edmund's trial and execution in the martial language of heroic combat. The text has very little to say about the historical or political circumstances of Edmund's death. Rather, the most dominant feature of the Gennings martyrology is its use of miracles to demonstrate the constant hand of God in the orchestration of Edmund's life. John organizes the major incidents of his narrative according to providential and miraculous interventions that span from birth to death, so that the narrative of Edmund's life relates the story of "offspring, birth, and education, to the end, that as well the secret and hidden decrees of God Almighty . . . might be made manifest" (14). According to the text, what God decrees through the miracles of Edmund's life is "the glory of his martyrdome" (90).

"[W]ithin an houre or two" of Edmund's birth, God signifies the destiny of his martyr by presenting "a signe of the magnanimity and great courage which he was afterward to let forth to the view of the whole world" (14–15). This sign is the "faire white tooth" with which Edmund is born (15). John reports that this "strange spectacle worthily put them all into admiration" (15). The family consults a minister who determines that the tooth "doth foretell, that he shall travayle further, then the Queene hath any land, & at the length retourne agayne to the unspeakeable joy and comfort of all that love him" (16). John describes this omen as "propheticall," suggesting that Edmund's "glorious Martyrdome, and great courage in the same, was foreshewed by his tooth" (16, 17).

Another wonder occurs a few years into Edmund's youth, when his habit of foregoing the company of other children in order to "behold the heavens" leads him to see a "strange spectacle" in the sky above the Gennings house: "He saw, as it were, armed men with weapons killing and murthering others that were disarmed, and altogeather destitute of like furniture, and great store of bloud running everywhere about them" (17–18). Edmund is frightened by the vision and calls his mother; she in turn gathers together several neighbors who "were all eye-witnesses of the same spectacle" (18). John, present as well but so young that he does not remember the event, claims that the sight was a vision of contemporary Catholic suffering: it "happened in the beginning of our chiefest persecution, not long before the glorious death of B. Father Campian, and the rest, about the yeare 1581" (18).

Although Mrs. Gennings would later claim that the minister who deciphered Edmund's portentous tooth was a Catholic priest, the family was in fact Protestant. John reports that his brother is brought to the "true fayth and religion" by "the providence of Almighty God, who by his secret and unexpected meanes bringeth ever that to passe which he hath preordayned" (21). At about the age of sixteen, he is taken into service as a page to a Catholic gentleman. Under this man's influence, Edmund converts to Catholicism and eventually leaves England to follow his master in training for the priesthood at Douai. There he falls ill, becoming so sickly that his superiors prepare to send him back to England before he has had time to be ordained. While reluctantly awaiting his passage, however, Edmund is "instantly greatly amended, and almost as well as ever he was" (36). His cure is hailed by his superiors as an example of divine intervention; they proclaim, "*Digitus Dei hic: haec mutatio dextra Excelsi.* The finger of God is heere: this change comes from the right hand of the Highest" (36). John confirms this interpretation of events: "Who ever saw, or heard of a disease so incurable as was his, being that he was farre spent with a long consumption, recovered naturally without a miracle in so short a time . . . ? But, *Opera Dei admiratio nostra,* Gods workes are our wonders" (37). By virtue of his cure, Edmund is able to continue his training. His zeal for the priesthood, combined with an exemplary piety "noted . . . throughout the whole Colledge," persuade his superiors to ordain him priest when he is "but 23. yeares of age" (45, 41). Soon after, he is sent to join the English mission, "like a sheep to the slaughter, and like a lambe to be sacrificed" (47). John notes that Edmund's fellows at the college weep at his leave-taking, "even as those good Christians did for the departure of S. Paul" (47-48).

Edmund's return to England and his desire to see his one living relative, the younger brother he no longer knows, proceed from divine guidance: "Almighty God the authour of all good motions, by his holy spirit, first directed this our blessed Priests will & purpose to draw neare to his owne proper Countrey, that he might profit and take some care of his owne particuler friendes, & kinsfolkes" (53). God's plan to bring about John's conversion by reuniting the brothers is enacted "*digito,* with his finger," which "directly point[s]" Edmund to the person he seeks (54). While walking the streets of London, Edmund unknowingly passes near John and is suddenly overcome with "a great distemperature in his body, in so much as his face glowed, and as he thought his hair stared, and all his joints trembling for feare" (55). The strange experience repeats itself when on a second occasion he comes into close proximity with his brother. Edmund turns to see who is following him, and when he asks the youth his name he discovers "his brother so long looked for" (57). Edmund knows that he will be charged with treason if he is found to have returned to England as a priest, so he does not admit to John that he has been ordained. After some discussion, from which Edmund concludes that John is "wilfully given to persist in his Protestancy, without any hope of a present recovery," the brothers part company forever, "the one to do his function, in converting of soules, the other to meditate how to corrupt his owne" (60).

Edmund is captured within a year of returning to England. He is arrested while saying Mass on the feast day of All Saints, a fitting occasion for the taking of "such mortal men as Almighty God in his secret wisedome had chosen as Saynts" (65). The arrest comes during Communion, "even at the Consecration of the holy body and bloud of our Saviour," and is managed by the queen's notorious priest-hunter and rackmaster, Richard Topcliffe (66). Without being given the opportunity to change clothes, Edmund is paraded to Newgate in his vestments "for greater shew of this theyr insulting triumph, and the more to make him a laughing stocke to all the beholders," an apparently unsympathetic crowd "who are commonly ready (as they well knew) exceedingly to scoffe at such an unwonted spectacle" (67). Little of the actual content of his trial is related in John's narrative. In fact, the treason charge is barely mentioned, the account focusing instead on Edmund's saintly utterances and typologically conventional behavior. As in much of the book, John relates here the inner thoughts and feelings of his brother without reference to a source for this information, though he announces in his preface that his text is composed in "truth and sincerity" and relies solely on what he himself observed, what the martyr said to him, and that which was passed on to him "from very honest, vertuous, and sufficient" Catholics (9, 10). According to one of these three categories of sources, John gleans that Edmund imagined the sufferings of his month-long trial and imprisonment as "lively representations" of Christ's own (74).

Edmund's execution at Gray's Inn Fields on December 10, 1591, is marked by what is perhaps the most extraordinary miracle of his short life. Among the "many Protestants who came rather to behould the spectacle then to pitty the innocent," Catholics too were present for the event, hoping "by the sight therof to confirme theyr fayth, & increase theyr charity, and to get courage to imbrace all like assaults and combats" (90–91). One of these was "a Virgin who had wholy dedicated her self to the service of God" and who desired "some little part or parcell of his sacred flesh, or guiltlesse bloud, powred on the ground, to keepe as a perpetuall relique for her private devotion" (91). Secretly, so that she might not arouse the suspicions of the crowd, she "used all diligence to drawe neere to the Gibbet, that she might ob-

taine her desire" (93). After his hanging, drawing, and dismember-
ment, Edmund's quarters were thrown into a basket in preparation to
be boiled. Spying an unguarded upper quarter, the Virgin took hold of
one of the martyr's thumbs, and "by the instinct of Almighty God,
she gave it a little pull, only to shew her love and desire of having it"
(93). "The sequele," John reports, "was miraculous":

> [B]y the divine power, the thumbe was instantly loosed from his
> hand, and being separated she carried it away safely both flesh,
> skinne, and bone without sight of any, to her great joy and admi-
> ration. O strange and miraculous separation! O benefit past all re-
> quitall! The thumbe of a man newly dead and quartered, to de-
> part from the hand, as it were, *sponte sua,* of its owne accord, to
> pleasure a friend, that loved him so entirely, and that in the mid-
> dest of so many hundreds of people, of a different Religion, yet
> not espyed by any. But the strangnes therof I leave to your pious
> consideration, confessing my selfe altogeather unworthy, and not
> any wayes able to explicate the worthines of the same. (93–94)

The Virgin retreated with her "miraculous purchase" and left the country to become an Augustinian nun (94). Upon learning that Edmund's
brother was in the seminary at Douai, she later sent him, "for a token, a
little peece of the same thumbe, inclosed in a letter written with her
owne hand, protesting the verity of all the aforesayd narration" (94).

The miracle of Edmund Gennings's thumb marks a fitting end to
an extraordinarily wondrous life, and it is central to the claims made by
the Gennings narrative. It functions as visible proof of Edmund's martyrdom and salvation. John writes, "the glory of his martyrdome was
declared and confirmed by an evident sign, shewed by the hand of
Almighty God, who by divine testimony manifested to the world the
truth of his cause, and the greatness of his reward" (90). The miraculous
thumb thus stands in as a digital testimony to the will of God. What's
more, the miracle "mak[es] knowne also how acceptable a thing it is in
his sight to esteem highly and reverence the sacred reliques of his chosen saynts," a practice that was attacked by Reformers as superstition
and idolatry (90). This miracle also retrospectively justifies Edmund's

audible prayer to Saint Gregory after the executioner had cut out his heart and bowels—a marvel in itself. Like the veneration of relics, the belief in saintly intercession was a Catholic behavior derogated by Protestants, including Edmund's executioner, who swears, "God's woundes, See his hart is in my hand, and yet *Gregory* in his mouth; o egregious Papist!" (86, italics original). The post-mortem miracle of Edmund's detached thumb thus accomplishes a great deal for John's narrative. Through it, not only Edmund's hand but "the hand of Almighty God" visibly confirm the virtues of Catholicism.

The Anti-Catholic Response

As might be expected, Anglican polemicists took issue with Catholic claims to divine intervention. In *A Survey of the miracles of the Church of Rome, proving them to be Antichristian* (1616), Richard Sheldon responds both to the Catholic church's general claim of miraculous justification and the claims of John Gennings in particular. Sheldon was a former priest who had left Catholicism to take up the work of Anglican apologetics. His response to Gennings draws on his experience as a fellow seminarian at Douai in order to refute the stories of Edmund's particular sanctity. Sheldon's discussion of the Gennings text is concerned with more than just miracles: it aims to refute the Catholic claim to martyrdom altogether. After contending that neither Edmund nor John was "ever reputed to be of any note of Sanctity" among their fellows at the college, Sheldon asserts that Edmund was ordained young and sent on the English mission because he was ill and likely to die anyway.[26] His "daily sicknesse and continuall infirmities, hastened him to the grave in a strange Countrey, if he had stayed at Rhemes any longer" (324).

Sheldon suggests that in fact Edmund was merely one of the pope's pawns in an elaborate device to regain authority in England. "[I]t mattereth not with the Pope and his Assecles [followers], of what life and conversation their Saints be," says Sheldon, "so it can be prooved that they die stoutly and obstinately, for the testimonie of his unlimited supremacie" (325). In the scenario Sheldon describes, those at the center of Catholic power see the generation of martyrs as the key to over-throwing Anglicanism. In this, he echoes Cecil's claim in *The Execution of Justice* that the Catholic martyr's cause is papal politics, not religious truth. Young men like Edmund Gennings are brought into the college, hastily ordained, and sent back to England "to suffer death for the glory of their Vice-Christ," having been carefully prepared for martyrdom by exercises that "make obstinate their mindes for the constant suffering of death" (326-27). Sheldon undermines the precepts of *ars moriendi* ("the art of dying") that form a cornerstone of martyrology by suggesting that the victims' constancy in the face of persecution arises not from "the spirit of God, which speaketh in them, and enableth them to beare patiently and joyfully those immane Torments, and deaths most cruell and shamefull" but from "politike or humane set exercises for such an end" (327). Anyone who puts his or her mind to it can face death calmly, he says; constancy through preparation is evident "even in the phrophanest and vilest Malefactours that come to die bravely, (as the phrase is) at Tiburne" (327).

Sheldon then looks specifically at the miracle stories meant to support what he regards as Edmund's spurious claim to martyrdom. He finds the story of the portentous tooth particularly amusing: "many there have been borne with a tooth or teeth in their head, and yet no omen made thereof" (329). By way of refuting the noteworthiness of Edmund's tooth, Sheldon relates a mocking tale of a woman from his neighborhood born with two teeth: "There was in my Parish of Ebbenye in Kent, a woman borne with two teeth in her mouth, yet shee never travailed beyond one or two Seas, neither fell it out, that shee was any great comfort to her Parents; shee is dead and hath left behinde her, children to her husband, for whose teeth he is put care-fully to provide; and this was the Omen of hir two teeth" (329). Shel-don's response to the tooth story does not simply refute its claims to the miraculous but resituates it within the realm of the banal, thereby extracting it entirely from the transcendent space John claims for it. On a more serious note, he suggests that instead of bolstering the Catho-lic church, ridiculous marvels like Edmund's tooth are "a moste cleare argument of the badnesse of their cause, that they do so hunt after prodigies and miracles for the stilting up of the same" (329-30).

Next Sheldon addresses the manner of Edmund's dying, during which the alleged martyr prayed to Saint Gregory while the executioner held his heart aloft. The Gennings text never overtly refers to this incident as a miracle or even as marvelous or wondrous. Sheldon, who admits not having the text in front of him, interprets this as another claim to divine intervention. Indeed, John is careful to support the story by referring it to the "credit" of "hundreds of People standing by, and to the Hangman himselfe," all of whom apparently heard what must have been a rather loud utterance.[27] John's concern with the credibility of the story suggests that he regards the act of speaking after one's heart has been removed to be *in*credible, even if he does not go so far as to claim it as miraculous. Sheldon is far more pragmatic, arguing that the incident proves nothing but that Edmund wasn't quite dead yet (330–31).

Sheldon lambastes the Gennings tale of the virgin and the thumb. This miracle he attacks namely on the basis of the quality of the evidence presented to support it, which he deems outrageously insufficient:

> I cannot without a kind of detestation thinke of the levitie and pronenesse which is in Papists, to admit of a miracle grounded upon so weake a testimonie of a maid, a simple maid, a nameless maid, a maid concealing, till she were beyond the seas; and there so covertly setting her miracle to sale, that for ought I could ever heare there were none made acquainted with it untill now when this idle narration was to be made publicke. . . .
>
> I doe assure my self that if the virgin maide had spoke of the miracle before the quarters of their martyr had been either rotten, taken, or consumed away, that the whole narration would have been found a lewd tale of a lewd lasses: it is wel for the credit of your narration master Gennings that you now come out with the thumbe, when the whole arme and hand from which it miraculously came are rotten or consumed, for ought I could ever heare. (332–33)

Sheldon speculates on the myriad "lewd" and profane sources from which the thumb segment mailed to Gennings may have originated and numbers it among the Catholic church's long history of forged relics. As in his response to the tooth, Sheldon implicitly denies the miracle claim by entirely refusing to enter into the logic of the relic, instead insisting on the thumb as the remnant of a long-rotten corpse, perversely and necrophilically preserved. Further, his criticism of this miracle opens up a broader critique of the nature of the miracles claimed by the Catholic community. His question about why the woman did not make the miracle public at a time when it could have been confirmed leads to the question of why such Catholic miracles are never performed "*toto inspectante populo,* the eyes of all the people beholding it" (333). This is the generally flimsy nature of the Catholic church's miracles, he suggests: "pitty it is that the claritie of your miracles is not more perspicuous, they are done by your selves, upon your selves, and your selves always, or for most part witnesses" (333). In regard to the Gennings text, this accusation is well founded. Indeed, as Monta has remarked, "an integral part of the [thumb] miracle is its secrecy," a feature that Sheldon sees as incoherent with the text's simultaneous assertions of visible truth.[28] John's claim that the "evident sign" of the thumb miracle "manifested to the world" his brother's righteousness and martyrdom is difficult to reconcile with the fact that no one saw or knew about it during the twenty-three years between Edmund's death and the publication of John's narrative. All of the miracles that mark the life of Edmund Gennings are performed without witness or to a sympathetic audience of family or co-religionists. Since Edmund and John's entire family is deceased by the time Edmund returns to England, the fantastic vision in the sky—the only semipublic miracle in the book—cannot be substantiated by anyone living.

The problem of credibility does not appear to trouble John Gennings, whose "honest, vertuous, and sufficient" sources are satisfactory for his purposes (10). Sheldon, on the other hand, regards the Gennings miracles as hallmarks of "a simple work" written by a "childish" and "ignorant" man of "slender" learning (323–24). The distance between Gennings's version of what is true and Sheldon's pragmatic approach to questions of evidence is based on more than just confessional difference. Gennings takes pains in his preface to establish himself as a trustworthy storyteller, protesting, "What then will it profit me to seeke to honour a Martyr, by faygning and forging a lye?" (10). And interestingly, Sheldon never attacks him as a liar but insinuates only that he is a naïve and credulous simpleton whose misguided religious zeal has allowed him to be swindled by a wily maiden out to make a buck. (It is not clear how Sheldon imagines the maiden to profit financially from the transaction, but he insists that she is driven by financial motives.)

The two authors are operating in conflicting discourses. Gennings's narrative presupposes Edmund's sanctity, and the logic of his miracle stories depends on this baseline assumption. Gennings presituates his brother in the sacred narrative, where miracle stories are inherently consistent and true. For Gennings, the technical details of how the virgin made off with the thumb and why she waited so long to reveal it are all but irrelevant; her story speaks to the metaphysical truth of Edmund's sanctity and the sanctity of Catholic belief. From the Gennings perspective, queries like Sheldon's simply miss the point. It is not for human beings to probe "the secret and hidden decrees of God Almighty" (14).

By contrast, Sheldon is interested in questions of forensic fact—the who, what, when, where, and why of Gennings's miracle stories. He applies an empirical approach to questions that Gennings treats as religious. Sheldon operates from the historical realm, interrogating Gennings's text from the legalistic perspective of reliable witnesses and evidence. In this way, Sheldon's argument reproduces the essential conflict of the treason trial, which situates the recusant Catholic within a politicized, legalistic discourse that denies the victim access to religious empirical or discursive modes. Sheldon's broader critique of Catholic claims to martyrdom operates by this same mechanism, flattening Gennings's sacred narrative into a rehearsal of historical inconsistencies and necrophilic perversity.

Scott Dudley's study of necrophilia and nostalgia helps us to see the deeper ideological and discursive tensions represented by the Gennings-Sheldon dialogue. According to Dudley, the necrophilic impulse marks a culture in descent, a nostalgia, a waning ideology: "Necrophilia is the displaced, uncanny desire to dig up the past and make it live again—to recover a trace of the lost other in order to fill the cultural and institutional gaps created by new ideologies. . . . It is the reactionary compulsion of a culture that feels cut off from the sacred past that once gave life meaning, and from the institutions, traditions and laws that once established order."[29] The insistent physicality that underlies Gennings's démodé celebration of the relic, which Protestant theology marked as the idolatrous veneration of dead objects, is likewise representative of an ideology whose grasp is slipping—an ideology whose tenuous hold on the cultural imagination forces the search for bodily analogues.

> Elaine Scarry has demonstrated that "when some central idea or ideology" ceases "to elicit a population's belief either because it is manifestly fictitious or because it has for some reason been divested of ordinary forms of substantiation," a society will then borrow "the sheer material factualness of the human body" in order "to lend that cultural construct the aura of 'realness' and 'certainty.'" This process, which Scarry calls "analogical verification," is clearly at work in [the Gennings text]. In the face of a culture that continued to marginalize it, in the midst of its disappointment that James failed to reestablish the Church of Rome in England, and in an attempt to counter the emerging discourses of Protestantism as well as of science that challenged its devotional rites both in England and on the continent, Roman Catholicism, ever more residual, sought during the Counter Reformation to substantiate itself physically within the faithful.[30]

The miraculous relic that crowns the Gennings claim to martyrdom is thus deaf to the context of treason and empirical evidence that Sheldon represents. However, as Dudley suggests and as this chapter's study of the miracle has argued more broadly, that very deafness to context is symptomatic of emerging crises of Catholic self-representation within a polemical environment increasingly governed by legalistic epistemologies. It is this crisis to which the preserved, dismembered, nostalgic finger points.

Sheldon is not the intended audience of Gennings's text, nor is anyone other than the Catholic faithful. It is highly unlikely that the proof Gennings offers for his miracle stories would convince a reader who did not share with him a belief in Catholic righteousness.[31] Devotional martyrologies like Gennings's elide the treason charge altogether, locating their subjects within a transcendent metaphysical space that all but ignores the historical circumstances of persecution. Conversely, without reference to the miraculous, martyrologies like Mush's *The Life and Martyrdom of Mistress Margaret Clitherow* are ultimately left with no way to irrefutably recuperate their subjects from ambiguous death. The Clitherow text implicitly makes the same claim as the Gennings narrative—that the finger of God everywhere declares her martyrdom. But the absence of explicit miracles in the text means that some readers might not see it. And by giving voice to a dissenting audience that interprets her death as a suicide, the Clitherow text opens up the possibility that the invisible finger may very well belong to the devil.

Neither the Clitherow nor the Gennings martyrology is able to accomplish the double framing that makes Foxe's martyr stories so effective a reiteration of the form. The production of a martyrological discourse that is at once typologically legible and engaged in the specific context of persecution is compromised by the marginalization of the miracle. For Catholic victims caught in the representational crux between martyr and traitor or martyr and suicide, the only available proof of sanctity is miraculous intervention. But the secular prosecution of Catholic dissidence, along with the skepticism of wonders and miracles ushered in by the Reformation, combine to hold miracles like Gennings's virgin–thumb anecdote up to ridicule. Miracles become relegated to the devotional domain. Only a miracle can ratify the victim's contested death as a martyrdom, but only an audience already convinced of a martyrdom is likely to believe in the miracle.

Chapter 5

"This Deceitfull Arte"

Catholic Martyrdom in the Age of the Jesuits

But this day shall witness to the world, that all is false, and yourself

condemned not by any but yourself, your own confessions and actions.

—Robert Cecil, *Trial of Henry Garnet*

The martyrologies of Margaret Clitherow and Edmund Gennings manifest two strategies that Catholics adopted in order to position their subjects outside of the English state's rhetoric of treason. The Clitherow martyrology rejects and thereby circumvents the treason trial, and the Gennings text inscribes the victim into a traditionally constructed martyr narrative that ignores the historical context of his execution. Both martyrologies reveal the representational ruptures created by these compensatory strategies, ruptures that hinder the victims from achieving the balance between history and typology required by rigid generic paradigms. Ultimately, both texts suggest that the strategies they outline are inadequate means of recuperating Catholic victims into legible narratives of Christian exemplarity. As a consequence, the martyrological project is left with few ways to avoid the snares presented by the charge of treason.

As the last years of the sixteenth century unfolded, Catholics' approach to this problem began to take shape and solidify. The only sure way not to get caught up in the crisis of allegiance, orthodoxy, and representation was to avoid apprehension altogether or, if caught, to try to prevent others from the same fate. The recusant Catholic community came to rely on elaborate methods of protecting itself through aliases, disguise, secret hiding places, coded messages, and equivocal speech. The aim of these strategies was not to avoid suffering and death but to avoid being situated within the ruinous discourse of treason. Allen had complained in *XII Reverend Priests* that it is not persecution to which Catholics object but the vilifying effects of the treason charge: "Trewly for us that through Christs grace be Catholike, if they had not used this matter in such an odde sort, to bring not onely these men of God, but the whole Catholike flocke of Christs afflicted Church in our countrey, into the sclaunderous suspition & obloquie of crimes never thought of: but onely executed their new lawes against them, and made them away for religion without more a doe, we should never have complained of any farther iniquitie or violence done against us."[1] Catholics have no complaint about being made into martyrs, Allen claims; it is to being made traitors that they object.

The strategies developed by the Catholic community for evading capture were not intended to help them dodge martyrdom. On the contrary, they were intended to protect Catholics from the threat of *not* achieving martyrdom—from being represented in a way that could not be recovered by martyrological paradigms. Like the compensatory strategies described by the narratives of Clitherow and Gennings, however, the means of escape themselves create a rupture between the circumstances of the recusant experience and the topoi of typological martyrdom. This chapter argues that not only secrecy and equivocation but the polemical defenses of these strategies impeded the production of Catholic martyrdom. The chapter studies a body of texts connected with the Jesuit mission and its martyrs: accounts of Robert Southwell's 1595 trial and execution, which introduced the doctrine of equivocation into the controversy around treason and Catholic recusancy; narratives of the Gunpowder Plot, which found Jesuit Superior Henry Garnet caught in a fatal constellation of treason, Catholic sacrament, and equivocation; key texts in the equivocation debate, including Garnet's *Treatise of Equivocation,* King James I's Oath of Allegiance, the polemics of Catholic apologist Robert Persons, and Henry Mason's *The New Art of Lying*; and *The Autobiography of a Hunted Priest*, Father John Gerard's narrative of underground ministry, imprisonment, and escape. What these texts describe is a compromised martyrological subject whose elusive strategies do not translate comfortably into the martyrological model to which Catholic victims aspire. The strategies to which recusants and their apologists were driven expose a widening disjunction between Catholic secrecy and Catholic exemplarity. In their struggle to make legible an indecipherable martyrological subject, these texts document the receding capacity of typological structures to describe the specific contingencies of recusant Catholic life and death.

Robert Southwell, S.J.

The state's claim that Catholics posed an internal threat to the security of the realm was bolstered by several thwarted plots against the crown in the late sixteenth and early seventeenth centuries. Chief among these were the Babington Plot to place Mary Stuart on the throne in 1586, Spain's failed attempt to invade England in 1588, and the Gunpowder Plot of 1605, in connection with which two Jesuit priests were executed. The anti-Jesuit sentiment that informed Edmund Campion's trial grew over this period as Jesuits came to represent an insidious foreign influence over the English Catholic community.[2] The widely publicized trial and execution of Father Robert Southwell in 1595 exacerbated matters by bringing the controversial doctrine of equivocation to public attention. In the years following Southwell's death, accusations of equivocation—the use of mental reservation—gradually supplanted the Bloody Question in the trials of Catholic priests charged with treason. Equivocation came to represent a body of duplicitous practices that were summoned in the state's moral and legal condemnation of the Catholic community. As the most vocal proponents of the doctrine, Jesuits in particular were maligned by the skillfully managed government propaganda that posited them as lying traitors with no claim to political innocence, let alone martyrdom.

Southwell was an especially gifted individual who faced persecution with remarkable fortitude and humility and whose martyrdom should have been a real boon for the Catholic cause in England. He was the author of some of the sixteenth century's most eloquent and passionate religious verse—poetry that affected Queen Elizabeth herself, it was reported[3]—and he seems to have impressed even his enemies with his singular grace and bearing. Following his Continental education and Jesuit ordination, Southwell returned to England with Father Henry Garnet in 1586 to join the English mission. He worked in secret for nearly six years before being caught. During that time he formed a close and perilous association with the Bellamys, a wealthy Catholic family that was suspected of involvement with the Babington Plot. Anne Bellamy was arrested for recusancy in early 1592 and imprisoned in the Gatehouse at Westminster, where she fell under the corrupting influence of Richard Topcliffe.[4] Agreeing to help him capture Southwell, she arranged for the priest to visit the family estate at Uxendon at a specific time when he would be met by Topcliffe and his men. The plan worked, and Southwell was arrested in June 1592. While imprisoned, he was subjected to Topcliffe's newly devised torture, the manacles, or gauntlets, whereby the victim was made to hang from metal rings secured around the wrists, sometimes for many hours at a stretch.[5] Southwell reported that he was tortured ten times by this method and was often revived from unconsciousness for brief periods so that he could be tortured further.[6] Questioned throughout about the activities of his Catholic friends, Southwell would reveal nothing. After about two months of custody and incessant interrogation, he was moved from his filthy cell at the Gatehouse to better accommodations in the Tower, where he was kept prisoner but harassed very little. He had been in custody nearly three years when he was moved to Newgate to be tried for treason.

Unlike the trial of Campion, in which the government had worked to prove the priest's active involvement in plans to overthrow the queen, Southwell's case hinged on his return to the country after having been ordained a Catholic priest, itself an act of treason according to Elizabethan law. No witnesses were brought against him to charge that he had spoken to them of sedition; the Bloody Question was not put to him at trial. Instead, it was confirmed by Southwell himself, speaking plainly and with great poise and dignity, that he was a priest and had entered the realm after the statute had been issued. The real interest of his trial was the doctrine of equivocation, which prosecutors were certain would taint the reputation of this otherwise impressive man and justify his death to the public. Anne Bellamy appeared in court to testify that while living with the family before he was captured, Southwell had introduced her to equivocation: "Her deposition was that father S. tould them, that if in case anie should inquire for him and propose to them an othe whether they had sene him, that they might deny it by oth; although they had seene him that same day; reserving this intention: — 'Not with a purpose to tell you.'"[7] When pressed to confirm whether he had advised Bellamy as such, Southwell "answeared that his words weir not altogether as she reported" but eventually conceded, "That which I then taught, I will defend by the law of God, by the common law civill and the law of all nations. No civill societie can be menteyned, if the contrarie be admitted."[8]

Southwell was condemned for treason and executed at Tyburn the following day, February 21, 1595. But Anne Bellamy's revelation did not die with him. In the hands of skillful government propagandists and in the popular imagination, the defense of equivocation came to compete with Southwell's claim to martyrdom and to cast even greater suspicion on English Catholics. The steadfast denial of wrongdoing that Allen had offered as proof of Catholic martyrs' innocence of treason in *XII Reverend Priests* was undermined by equivocation. Anti-Catholic pamphlet literature took the doctrine as proof that Catholics were stealthy destroyers of civil society, and suspicions about the Jesuit missionaries grew. As Cecil's *Execution of Justice* attests, criticism of the secrecy and stealth of the Catholic mission was a cornerstone of anti-Catholic rhetoric long before Southwell's case brought equivocation to the fore. The doctrine of equivocation added fuel to this polemical fire: Catholics were not only prepared to use aliases, hide in secret holes, and wear disguises; their very speech was a hiding hole and a disguise, and the Catholic church authorized their dishonesty through the amoral and unchristian doctrine of equivocation.

Henry Garnet and the Gunpowder Plot

Matters worsened for the Catholic cause with the discovery of the Gunpowder Plot in November 1605. The Gunpowder Plot has important implications for the Catholic project of martyr construction. In Southwell's trial, the state relied on two undisputed facts in order to secure a treason conviction: he had returned to the country illegally, and he had taught and upheld the doctrine of equivocation. The rhetoric of the trial had done little to draw a relationship between these two facts, relying on the public's moral outrage at Southwell's instructions to Bellamy to do the work of linking treason, equivocation, and the Jesuit priest. In the Gunpowder Plot, all of the elements of anti-Catholic sentiment that had been in circulation since Campion's trial converged in a manifest attempt to overthrow the government. The plot depended on secrecy for its development and deployment; Jesuit priests could be linked directly to it; these priests relied on equivocal statements under interrogation; and Catholic doctrine itself—in this case, the seal of confession—shielded those involved against public exposure. A more perfect rhetorical opportunity could not have been created for the state to advance its case against the Catholic cause.[9] In the climactic scene of the Gunpowder drama, the trial of Jesuit Superior Henry Garnet, the arbiters of secular law use these threads to weave together one continuous yarn of Catholic treason, continuing the work of retrospectively interpreting the deaths of Campion and Southwell while justifying Garnet's execution and the future persecution of English Catholics. As Lord Salisbury, Robert Cecil, put it, the trial was an "opportunity [that] was put into his hands, whereby there might be made so visible an anatomy of popish doctrine, from whence these treasons have their source and support."[10]

According to Garnet's written statements, he knew something was afoot more than six months before the plot was discovered and foiled.[11] A series of conversations with Robert Catesby, one of the principal authors of the plot, had revealed to him that a group of disaffected Catholics was planning violent action against James's newly installed government. Garnet claims that at this point he knew nothing specific about the plan; by his account, Catesby tried more than once to fill him in on the details but he did not care to hear them. Garnet had received instructions from the pope that all such actions were strictly prohibited, and he says that he tried to dissuade Catesby from his course. Catesby was undaunted and shared his plans with another Jesuit, Father Oswald Tesimond. Distraught by what he had heard and unsure of how sufficiently he had worked to dissuade Catesby, Tesimond sought out the council of his Superior. Under the seal of confession, Tesimond revealed the whole of the plan to Garnet, who was bound by the sacramental practice not to reveal it to anyone. Recognizing the potential implications of such information, however, Testimond left Garnet with this important caveat: he was not bound to keep the confession secret if he was put to torture. If he were tortured, Garnet had license from Tesimond to reveal what he had told him of the plot.

After a cache of gunpowder was discovered beneath the House of Lords on the morning of November 5, 1605, news of the plot traveled quickly. According to the contemporary account written by his fellow Jesuit, John Gerard, Garnet was in Coughton at the time and fled soon after to the safety of Hinlip, near Worcester. He did not yet know that he was suspected, but the circumstances of the plot meant that all Catholics, especially those closest to the conspirators, would be hunted with urgency. While in hiding at Hinlip, Garnet wrote an open letter to the Privy Council declaring his innocence.[12] In it, he falsely states that he was not made aware of the plot and would never have given consent to it, arguing that the conspirators knew of the pope's prohibition against such acts and would therefore not have been likely to share their plans with him. His involvement with such "bloody matters" would only bring odium on the Jesuits, he remarks. Further, he reminds them that he had proven himself a loyal subject in the past by helping to disclose a plot against the king's life.[13] He ends by reiterating his innocence and loyalty and offering to appear before them to clear himself. The government's response to this letter was to issue a warrant for the arrest of Garnet, Tesimond, and Gerard. Five days later Sir Henry Bromley, the sheriff of Worcestershire, arrived at Hinlip with a party of searchers. Having been tipped off that priests were hiding in the house, Bromley and his men searched for seven days before finding Garnet and another Jesuit, Edward Oldcorne, in a hiding place concealed by a false chimney.[14] They were taken in custody to London.[15]

Garnet was questioned countless times in an effort to implicate him in treason or, barring that, to gather evidence of the sort of unsavory doctrine that had successfully turned public opinion against Southwell. Garnet readily defended the practice of equivocation but provided little else that might be useful to the prosecution. Desperate to prove Garnet's collusion in the plot, the chief justice, Sir John Popham, devised a strategy for facilitating and eavesdropping on Garnet's private conversations. Garnet's jailer was made to pretend sympathy toward him, and by showing an interest in converting to Catholicism he managed to gain Garnet's trust. This accomplished, he then revealed to Garnet a hole in the wall through which he could carry on occasional conversations with Oldcorne, who had been strategically placed in the adjacent cell. Two eavesdroppers were posted in a third location from which they could hear and see what passed between the priests.

Contrary to Gerard's account, which claims that the eavesdroppers overheard Garnet tell Oldcorne that "no man living could touch him in that matter [the Gunpowder Plot], but one," no substantive information about either priest's foreknowledge of the plot was revealed by these conversations (see Appendix D).[16] What is interesting about them, however, is the extent to which the treason investigation organized their interactions, which consisted almost entirely of conferring on points of interrogation and making sure their testimony would be in agreement. If the eavesdroppers' transcripts are to be believed, the conversations are nearly devoid of religious discussion, prayer, or spiritual matters: "Wee againe observed that night at their first meeting, nor at parting, nor in anie part of their conference they used noe one word of Godliness or Religion, or recommending themselves or their cause to God, but all hathe bin how to continue safe answeres and to concur in so muche as may concern those matters they are examined of."[17] In the eavesdroppers' account, the discourse of treason extends beyond the bounds of the juridical scene to dominate and organize even the private conversation between two priests.

Garnet was tortured soon after these conversations. After torture, and presumably because the torture released him from the seal of confession, he revealed that he had had specific knowledge of the plot in advance from Tesimond. This was the smoking gun his adversaries had been looking for. Armed with his written statement, Popham and Attorney General Edward Coke brought Garnet at last to trial. Coke's presentation of the state's case consisted first of a lengthy rehearsal of all the Catholic-led plots that had been attempted since Garnet's return to England in 1586. His aim was to represent the Jesuits as "the proprietaries, plotters, and procurers" of treason and Garnet, arch-Jesuit, as the arch-traitor.[18] Garnet was not only the Jesuit Superior, said Coke, but "superior to all his predecessors in devilish Treason; a doctor of Jesuits, that is, a doctor of five DD's, as dissimulation, deposing of princes, disposing of kingdoms, daunting and deterring of subjects, and destruction" (234). Coke's argument provides little in the way of evidence that might connect Garnet to the various plots he chronicled, relying instead on a series of broadly sketched associations that placed the Jesuit at the center of Catholic treason.

The doctrine of equivocation played a pivotal role in the trial, operating as the foundation for other forms of Catholic duplicity, as Coke suggested: "Their dissimulation appeareth out of their doctrine of equivocation" (234). In response, Garnet upheld the use of equivocation but insisted that it was never lawful to equivocate in matters of faith. Lord Salisbury, Robert Cecil, accused him of equivocating when in an earlier examination he had denied having had conversations with Oldcorne through the prison wall; Garnet admitted the equivocation, claiming that it was lawful because the questioning was unjust. Coke then introduced two documents written by Garnet's Catholic friends, one by Francis Tresham, who had sworn that he had not seen Garnet in sixteen years, and another by Anne Vaux, who swore that Tresham and Garnet had met often. Garnet could not explain the discrepancy, but Coke presented it as proof that Catholics "will swear and forswear anything" (235). None of the points on which acts of equivocation could be attached to Garnet were inherently treasonous, but the presentation of the doctrine within the treason trial served to undermine his overall credibility. Proving Garnet and his fellow Catholics as equivocators, the prosecution was able to cripple his defense by representing him as fundamentally dishonest and untrustworthy. Equivocation was transformed into metaphor by the mechanisms of Garnet's treason trial, standing in as the parent of all Catholic treason, as Coke remarks: "note the heavy and woeful fruit of this doctrine of equivocation" (235).

Just as Campion's trial had construed his sacramental functions as a cloaking device, the trial of Garnet represented Catholic doctrine as a means by which treason was carried out and obscured from view. In particular, the prosecution accused Garnet of trying to use the seal of confession as an excuse for not disclosing what he knew of the "Powder Treason." Coke suggested that Garnet and Tesimond (who had by this time escaped from custody) plotted together against the king and invented a "disguised confession" to cover it up (231).[19] Confronted with these arguments, Garnet repeatedly fell back on the sacredness of the confessional, saying "he was bound to keep the secrets of Confession, and to disclose nothing that he heard in Sacramental Confession" (255). The prosecution proposed to him a hypothetical case that highlighted the impasse between what common law and Catholic ecclesiastical law demanded: "if one confessed this day to him, that tomorrow morning he meant to kill the king with a dagger, if he must conceal it. Whereunto Garnet answered that he must conceal it" (255). Though Garnet did not know the specifics of the plot except from his conversation with Tesimond, the prosecution argued that the seal of confession did not extend to his conversations with Catesby, which Garnet should have reported in accordance with common law (246).[20] Garnet justified his decision not to inform on Catesby by announcing that he modeled himself "after the example of Christ, who commands us, when our brother offends, to reprove him, for if he do amend, we have gained him" (240). In response, Salisbury described Garnet as "the man in whom it appeareth best what horrible treasons have been covered under the mantle of religion" (243).

The question of papal authority, which played such an important role in Campion's trial, arose again in the trial of Garnet to expose the Catholic subject's impossible relationship to religious orthodoxy and secular allegiance. By way of highlighting the Jesuits' obedience to a rival foreign power, the prosecution insisted on the pope's role "as a temporal prince" (231). Coke situated Garnet in relation to "Campion the Jesuit," who returned to his native country "purposely to make a Party in England for the Catholick cause, to the end that the Bull of

Pius Quintus might be put in execution" (223). This remark continued the polemical project of inscribing Campion into a narrative of treason by connecting his aims with those of the Gunpowder Plotters. Further, it situated Garnet within a paradigm of treasonous behavior that was already familiar to the English public, one in which the missionary priests functioned as emissaries of the pope to dethrone the rightful monarch. Of course, Elizabeth was no longer living, so the bull of excommunication had no official bearing on the attempt to blow up James's parliament. But the doctrine of papal supremacy nonetheless continued to be a sore spot for the English Catholic cause, as Garnet's trial demonstrates. Garnet was asked whether he believed that the pope had the power to depose temporal princes, and he said that he did, "yet for his own part, he always made a difference in the matter of excommunicating and deposing of princes, betwixt the condition and state of our king and of others, who having sometimes been Catholicks, did or shall afterwards fall back" (239). In his attempt to position himself as both a true Catholic and a true subject, Garnet resorted to an idiosyncratic interpretation of Catholic doctrine in which the pope's prerogative was upheld but had no relevance to the English kingdom. Pressed to give his opinion on whether the king's subjects "were bound to continue their obedience" to him if the current pope should excommunicate James, Garnet would give no answer (244).

Garnet's position outside the two legitimizing institutions of religious orthodoxy and secular obedience was exacerbated by his role as Jesuit Superior. The larger argument of his trial—Coke's sweeping narrative of Jesuit-led plots against the throne of England—relied on Catholicism's own top-down model of ecclesiastical government to trap not only the Catholic laymen who carried out the dirty work but those who were their spiritual directors. The logic of Coke's argument claims that Catholic laymen like Catesby do not carry out such actions without the authorization of their priests, and rank-and-file Jesuits like Tesimond do not direct their penitents without first learning the wishes of their Superior. This logic placed Garnet in a position of responsibility for the plot that was second only to the pope's. And by this logic, Garnet could have prevented the plot from ever being conceived, Coke argues: "Garnet, you are Superior of the Jesuits; and if you forbid it, must not the rest obey?" (256). While Garnet was cut off from the doctrinal dispute that could help to inscribe him into martyrological legitimacy, Catholicism's own doctrinally rooted hierarchy was co-opted by his adversaries as evidence of his crime. In a delicate manipulation of Catholic orthodoxy, the state effectively relocated the tenets of the Catholic church into a discourse of attempted regicide.

Garnet's Execution

The jury deliberated for only fifteen minutes before returning with a guilty verdict, and the sentence of death was pronounced. Garnet was executed in St. Paul's churchyard on May 3, 1606, the feast of the Finding of the Holy Cross. The two opposing sides published radically different accounts of Garnet's execution. The phrasing of many sections is identical, particularly in the reporting of words Garnet spoke, but the accounts disagree on the most salient points. The official version, published in 1606, represents Garnet as unquestionably guilty of treason, sorry for his crimes, and afraid of death.[21] He comes to the scaffold with "fear and guiltiness appearing in his face." Asked to admit his treason, he admits that he "had offended" the king by not reporting what he knew of the plot. When Garnet continues, however, saying that he had only specific knowledge of the plot under the seal of confession, he is reminded that he had signed a document stating his collusion in the plot.[22] According to this account of events, "Garnet answered, Whatsoever was under his hand was true. And for that he disclosed not to his majesty the things he knew, he confessed himself justly condemned; and for this did ask forgiveness of his majesty." He begins to pray in preparation for death but seems to be agitated: "fear of death, or hope of pardon, even then so distracted him." Garnet is told that there will be no pardon—that he has "come to die, and must die." He is admonished "not to equivocate with his last breath," to which he responds, "It is no time now to equivocate." Commending himself to the king and his fellow Catholics, he offers his soul "*In manus tuas, Domine*" ("Into your hands, Lord"), is turned off the ladder, and hangs until dead (356–58).

The Catholic version of events written by Father John Gerard represents Garnet as an innocent martyr. Gerard's lengthier account, derived principally from a fellow priest who paid twelvepence for a spot from which to view the proceedings, contains many familiar martyrological topoi: before he is taken to execution, Garnet jokes that the Tower cook will not need to make his dinner; while being dragged on the hurdle, "he [holds] his hands together, lifted up somewhat towards Heaven"; he treats everyone at the execution "kindly and cheerfully"; and he helps to remove his own clothes, a gesture that shows his willingness to die.[23] In contrast to the official version, Garnet continues to advocate his innocence, arguing that he justly concealed what he learned in confession and had no knowledge of the plot except from this source. When he is reminded of the signed document suggesting otherwise, Garnet denies that such a document exists.[24] Gerard's account includes a confession of faith in which Garnet proclaims that he dies "a true and perfect Catholic" and admonishes his coreligionists not to be stirred to violence against the king, because God will reward their suffering. He prays and is turned off the ladder. Gerard claims that it was the urging of the crowd, "so much moved with his modesty, and so altered from their former hard conceits of him by the sight of his constancy, and by his protestation of innocency at his death," that persuaded the executioner to let Garnet hang until dead, rather than disemboweling him while he was still conscious, as law and custom prescribed (295–96). No one cheered when Garnet's heart was cut out; no one uttered, "God save the King." Gerard writes that this kind of sympathy was "nothing usual when the people do presume men die for treason" (296). Indeed, even "the very heretics themselves" said that "without doubt he was in Heaven; others said, 'He died like a Saint'; others, that he looked not like a contriver of treason," and many in the crowd gathered beneath the scaffold to dip their handkerchiefs in his blood and gather any other relics that might be found (296).

Why are these accounts so contradictory? It is not merely that the facts of Garnet's execution are framed or interpreted differently; the facts themselves do not agree. Both accounts make reference to a remark made by Garnet that "his voice was low, his strength gone, the people could not hear him," yet it is in Garnet's speeches to the crowd that the accounts most concur.[25] These discrepancies suggest that the circumstances of Garnet's trial and conviction produced a narrative that could not easily be interpreted as both treason and martyrdom, forcing one or both sides to manipulate the facts in order to solidify their arguments. Garnet's case is unique: in contrast to the trials of Campion and Southwell, for example, the plot of which Garnet was accused was clear, concrete, and undisputed, the only question being the extent to which he had knowledge or was involved. This set the stakes higher for both sides. Given Garnet's admission of at least some foreknowledge and his intimate relationships with the guilty parties, the project of recovering him for martyrology was challenging. Conversely, with the facts of the attempted coup so publicly known—including the statements of Garnet's innocence made by Catesby and others at their trial—the government's case against Garnet required more than mere conjecture and speculation. These circumstances produce a death scene that is highly contested, the quietness of Garnet's voice providing a perfect pretext for both sides to shape the scene to their purposes.

According to the Gerard account, God himself was concerned about how badly the case against Garnet had damaged the martyr's reputation. Gerard writes that the trials of the Catholic martyrs in Elizabeth's time were so obviously trumped-up, the victims so evidently innocent, that it was not necessary for God to intervene with miracles to "manifest their innocent cause." In the case of Garnet, however, Gerard admits that

> it was very true, there was a real ground upon which the adversaries might raise a pretence of seeming truth in their accusation. There was a great and dangerous conspiracy intended and plotted and proceeded in by those gentlemen of whom I have before discoursed. Divers of these gentlemen were known to Father Garnett, and some of them had often used his help and the help of others of the Society in their spiritual affairs. And this matter also they had at length opened a little before it should have been executed unto two of the Society in the secret of confession, as I have before declared. Therefore in this case Almighty God did think it

more needful in His divine providence to give testimony of His servant's innocency than in former times, when the cause itself was so plain, that it could not be contradicted. (301)

To support the miracles he reports and to explain why other Catholic martyrs have no miracles, Gerard takes it upon himself to speculate about the logic of the mind of God, what he "did think" and how he put those thoughts into action. Gerard recognizes—as he assumes God does—that the gravity of the charges against Garnet require a particularly clear "testimony of His servant's innocency" to contradict the particularly clear case against him. God's evidence consists of several "miraculous events" that "manifest the truth, and set forth His own glory and the innocency of His servants with most apparent signs" (298, 300). Among these miracles are Garnet's straw, a shaft of hay on which a drop of his blood landed during his execution, producing a fantastically detailed portrait-in-miniature of Garnet's face. The report of this miracle gained some notoriety in England and abroad and was contradicted by Protestant and government skeptics, who regarded it as a forgery.[26] Another significant miracle was the "visible and apparent circle of red" that appeared around Garnet's severed head, posted in public view for the weeks following his execution (305). Rather than turning black and beginning the regular process of decomposition, Garnet's "face did continue so comely and with so pleasing a countenance, as it seemed rather the head of a man alive than separated from the body; and his quarters also so purely white, that it was much admired by all that did behold them" (305). The straw portrait and the incorruptible, red-crowned head make for a peculiar pair of miracles. The more famous of the two, the nearly microscopic straw, was held in private and shown to only a select group of people, its reputation growing largely by word-of-mouth. The miracle that would have been seen by many thousands of people over the course of time went comparatively unremarked. The issue of visibility that distinguishes these two phenomena is precisely what Sheldon would later remark on in his critique of Catholic miracles. While many may have heard of Garnet's straw, "the eyes of all the people" were unable to "behol[d] it."[27]

Garnet's *A Treatise of Equivocation*

The case made by the state had its own post-mortem trump card in the form of a discovered pamphlet on equivocation that Catholics had been secretly readying for the press. The authorship of *A Treatise of Equivocation* was not known at the time, but the text has now been attributed to Garnet.[28] Its preface and dedication to Southwell indicate that it was written with the intent to clarify and justify the remarks on equivocation Southwell had made at his trial. The effect of the text was opposite, however; especially given its discovery during the investigation of the Gunpowder Plot, it served only to harden public opinion against the English Jesuits and heighten suspicion of Catholic subjects.[29] As David Jardine has observed, the doctrine of equivocation called into question all that the public had heretofore seen and observed of the Catholic martyrs:

> The positive assertions of Catholic witnesses, and the solemn protestations of innocence by accused persons at their trials and on the scaffold, had raised doubts, even amongst Protestants, respecting the truth of the numerous charges of Roman Catholic plots and conspiracies in the latter years of Queen Elizabeth's reign; but doubts of this kind were converted into ready and willing belief by the exposure of this manual of contrivances for deception and justifications of falsehood. Sympathy for the supposed victims of religious persecution was exchanged for suspicion and dislike of the votaries of a system as inconsistent with morality as with civil government.[30]

Although the text was not attributed to Garnet until recently, equivocation had played an important role in his trial and execution, such that public knowledge of the treatise came to undermine his own bid for martyrdom by casting further suspicion on his honesty and innocence.

In its prosecution of Southwell, the government characterized equivocation as "a doctrine by the which all judgments, all giving of Testimonies should be perverted."[31] By way of defending his fellow Jesuit and the doctrine he had upheld, Garnet's *Treatise* aims to clearly define what is meant by the term "equivocation" and to distinguish it from the sin of lying. As Perez Zagorin reminds us, the doctrine defended by the English Jesuits was not their own invention but had a long history in rhetoric and ethics.[32] According to those models, Garnet situates mental reservation within a broader Aristotelian paradigm of "propositions." He defines equivocation as a "mixed proposition," an instance when an individual utters part of a statement aloud and reserves another part for private communication with God. The statement cannot be a lie if both its spoken and unspoken parts, taken together, constitute the truth. The relevant audience for such a proposition is not the hearer but God, to whom the truth is always due (10–11). Garnet supports this practice of equivocation by mental reservation through copiously argued sections of the treatise that trace the lawfulness of this behavior back to Christ. When Christ tells his apostles that he will not go up to the city to celebrate Passover and then goes (John 7:8) and that he does not know the day of judgment (Mark 13:32), these are instances of equivocation. In both cases, Garnet argues, Christ reserved a part of the proposition in his mind that rendered the statement true when taken in totality. The Christological justification for equivocation works as follows: without this reserved part, Christ's statements would be false; Christ cannot utter a falsehood; Christ's statements can only be made true by a mixed proposition, that is, by equivocation; therefore, equivocation must be lawful because it is practiced by Christ himself.[33]

One of the criticisms waged against equivocation at Southwell's trial was that it undermines communication and threatens human society. Garnet admits that its abuse could indeed have deleterious effects if it is not practiced prudently. "[I]t is very necessary that we applye here certaine fitte limitations," he writes, "and use that convenient moderation, without the which neyther God would be pleased, nor the lyncke and conjunction of humane societyes, eyther sivill or ecclesiasticall and spirituall, could be deuly mayntayned" (53–54). He insists that equivocation can be used only to preserve "the health of our bodye or sowle, pietye, charytye, just profitt or necessitye"; employing it under less dire circumstances is at least a venial sin, and perhaps even a mortal one (57). On the question of whether or not one may equivocate in matters of faith, Garnet is adamant. In some things, he says, one must always deal sincerely, "The first whereof is fayth; which although we may hyde ordinarily by permitting others to thincke that we are of a false religion, or by not shewinge ourselves what we are, except eyther some notable glory of God, or great profitt of our neighbour, may seeme to bynde us ther unto, yet may we never, no, not for to save our lyfe, or goods, or the whole worlde, eyther expressely make any shewe in worde or deede of a false religion, or geve any sufficient cause that probablye others may thincke so of us" (57–58). Garnet's advice works on several levels. One of the cornerstones of Christian belief is the imperative of confession: those who deny God will be denied by him in turn. It is therefore critical that Garnet clarify—for the benefit of both Catholics and their detractors—that equivocation does not interfere with this fundamental Christian precept. A priest's denial of his priesthood, he suggests, is not the same as denying his faith or Christ, the first allowable by equivocation and the second a mortal sin "dishonorable to God" (60). In clarifying this point, Garnet touches on elements of Catholic practice that are specifically relevant to English recusants, providing them religious guidance at the same time that he justifies their secrecy to a government that posits it as evidence of treason. He argues that it is not required that Catholics go about openly proclaiming their faith; rather, it is perfectly permissible to let others think what they will so long as one does not actively further misapprehension by participating in heretical religion. For Garnet, church papists who hold Catholic beliefs but attend the Anglican service to avoid harassment and fines are committing mortal sin. Priests who rely on disguises, aliases, and equivocation are not.

According to Garnet, equivocation is necessary not just to protect oneself or the Catholic cause but to avoid bringing harm to others. Yes, God expressly issued a commandment against lying. But other imperatives of Christian behavior impress themselves on these situations as well, and an individual's behavior must accordingly be dictated by a larger structure of moral living. "[T]here is injustice," Garnet says, "if we sweare to affirme that which, albeit it be trewe, yet cannot be revealed by me without injustice towards my neighboure" (88). Moreover, virtues like charity and justice enforce their own moral requirements, so that equivocating for one's personal benefit but to another's detriment is itself sinful.

The question of when one may or may not justly equivocate touches a nerve at the heart of the conflict between the Catholic church and the English government. Like Southwell before him, Garnet insists that a person is bound to answer with complete sincerity only "before a competent judge lawfully examininge" (62). In order for a lawful examination to take place, several prerequisites must be met: the judge must have rightful authority over the examinee; the judge must have rightful authority over the matter in question; and the judge must be executing a just law (68–69). Garnet writes, "even as the law whan it is unjust is no lawe, so a judge in the execution of an unjust law is no judge" (69). He continues, "In these cases, whan order of law is not observed, a man is not onley not bound to confesse any thinge of hym selfe, but he is also bound to confesse nothing at all; for it were to prejudice hym selfe without necessitye. And no man maye prejudice his owne fame, or goodes, or lyffe, without at the least a veniall synne, except he be bound thereunto by order of law" (70). This rule puts Catholics in a precarious position indeed, for if they fail to equivocate when circumstances require, they may inadvertently commit the sin of self-incrimination. Because Catholic doctrine does not acknowledge the supremacy of secular rule over ecclesiastical matters, the questioning of priests and other Catholics about any aspect of their religious life is necessarily viewed by Garnet as unjust. But the broad guidelines he lays out would have provided little in the way of practical direction, even if *A Treatise on Equivocation* had been published. No real parameters are described: priests and lay Catholics are left to determine for themselves when they are being questioned unjustly and are bound to equivocate versus when the examination is just and equivocation forbidden. Even the bull of excommunication against Elizabeth—a direct command from the pope outlining Catholics' obligations to their temporal leader—had failed to provide real clarity for Catholics, as priests' varying interpolations of papal prerogative demonstrate.

Garnet's discussion of oath-taking likewise relies on the general principle that an individual is not bound to deal sincerely when asked to swear in an unjust matter. Garnet works from the premise that "in every oath is understood a condition that I will do or say so farr as I may lawfully do or say, or else the oath is unjuste and indiscrete" (78). This premise leads him to conclude, "if I do take an oath to aunswere directly, yet whan they come to unjust questions, I am not bound to answere, although I thought not expressly of that condition when I sware" (78). It is perfectly lawful, he says, to answer not literally what the judge is asking but "to the remote intention of the lawe" (81). For example, if Catholic A understands that the judge's "remote intention" is to catch traitors, and he knows that his priest, Father B, is not a traitor, it is perfectly lawful to answer under sworn oath that he does not know Father B, as this answer more accurately responds to what the judge is trying to determine. By assuming the "remote intention" of either the oath itself or a specific question asked under oath and answering according to that intention, the individual can avoid the sin and crime of perjury. Through this stratagem, Garnet renders it possible even to swear under oath that the oath is taken without any equivocation. He describes how such a scenario would work: "And if they make hym sweare that he hath no private intention, or secreat meaning, lett hym sweare it also with that very same secrett understandinge, that he hath no such meaning to tell them. And with this generall meaning at the begynning whan he tooke the oath, lett hym not doubte but he shalbe safe from all perjury, although he answere trewly to nothinge, because in these cases he is bound to aunswere directlye to nothing" (104).[34] With Garnet's book as a guide, the Catholic subject would be armed against any oath or examination the government could devise.

It is no surprise that James and his ministers found this text disturbing. The doctrine of equivocation described in Garnet's *Treatise* highlights the philosophical impasse that separated Cecil's *Execution of Justice* and Allen's *Defense of English Catholics*. Catholic doctrine held that the monarch was not a legitimate ecclesiastical leader and that the state's investigation into Catholics' religious activities or associations fell solely under the jurisdiction of Rome. The state, conversely, viewed Catholic subjects' allegiance to the pope as a threatening political alliance and the affairs of English Catholics as fundamental to questions of national security. This essential difference produced an untenable legal atmosphere wherein subjects being questioned by secular judges did not regard themselves as bound to tell the truth under oath. By claiming that it is morally just to use mental reservation during trial and under oath, the doctrine of equivocation cast suspicion on all Catholic utterances. The effect of the doctrine was to subvert not only all of Catholics' protestations of political innocence and allegiance but also their typological martyr utterances, so that the very language and gestures that might inscribe them into martyrological legitimacy were suspected as mere shadows and half-truths, if not outright lies. In this way, Garnet's *Treatise* challenges his own claim to martyrdom, along with the claims of Southwell, Campion, and the other priests and Catholic laypeople put to death for treason. If swearing one's fidelity to the Crown could be equivocated, so could a statement of innocence. The precepts of equivocation cut both ways.

This is particularly true for post-Southwell polemics. Garnet's *Treatise* attempts to carve out an ethical response to the problems of lying, self-incrimination, and the incrimination of others. But equivocation had already been absorbed by the rhetoric of Southwell's trial and execution into a discourse of treason. It had come to stand as a very symptom—a semiotic code, even—of treason, which is why it worked as such an efficient polemical tool in the state's case against Garnet. Catholic justifications of equivocation like Garnet's *Treatise* operate as further signs of treason, strengthening the retrospective project of traitor-making in which government polemics were constantly engaged.

The Oath of Allegiance Controversy

In consequence of the Gunpowder Plot and the heightened anxiety about Catholic secrecy it engendered, James's government developed the Oath of Allegiance in 1606 in an effort to clearly delineate true subjects from those who presented a potential threat to the realm (see Appendix C). Any suspected recusants, along with members of the clergy and government, were required to swear according to the oath that they believed James to be their rightful king and that no papal injunction to the contrary could depose him or relieve his subjects from allegiance. Further, they were made to swear that they believed the papal prerogative to depose princes to be a "damnable doctrine" and "impious and Hereticall."[35] Those who swore the oath vowed never to take up arms against their king and to apprise the state of any treasonous conspiracies they may discover. Finally, they were required to state that they swore "according to the plaine and common sense and understanding of the same words, without any Æquivocation, or mentall evasion, or secret reservation whatsoever."[36]

For those who believed in it, the doctrine of equivocation provided an approach to the oath that would outwardly satisfy both king and pope, thus relieving the individual from charges of treason or heresy. Garnet's advice that Catholics might equivocate an oath itself—even if the oath required the swearer to forego all equivocation and mental reservation—suggested that Catholics might lawfully take James's oath if it was required of them. In this, Garnet's *Treatise* seemed to anticipate how secular authority would seek to counter the effects of equivocation. It is unclear how the Jacobean government expected the oath to work under these circumstances. Perhaps the state trusted that its effort to link treason and equivocation in the trials of Southwell and Garnet had been sufficiently successful to prevent large-scale equivocation of the oath.

Or perhaps James and his ministers foresaw precisely what did happen when English Catholics were confronted with the oath: it became a catalyst for conflict among Catholics. Michael Questier calls it "the most destructive anti-Romish act of state since the Elizabethan restoration" because of its power to divide the already-weakened community against itself in a "cataclysm of dissention and disobedience among English papists."[37] When Pope Clement VIII ordered the subordination of English secular priests to Jesuit leadership in 1598, the ensuing Appellant Controversy had exposed festering tension between disparate factions of English missionary priests.[38] The Oath of Allegiance renewed the differences between English priests, some arguing that Catholics could take it in good conscience and others warning it would be heresy to do so. Father George Blackwell, the papally appointed English Archpriest, wrote a treatise advising Catholics to take the oath,[39] but Pope Paul V issued instructions to the contrary, warning that "such an Oath cannot be taken without hurting of the

Catholique Faith and the Salvation of your Soules; seeing it conteines many things which are flat contrary to Faith and Salvation."[40] The Jesuit cardinal Robert Bellarmine likewise weighed in against taking it, and then James himself entered the controversy, defending the oath in response to Bellarmine and the pope.[41] Whether by design or by accident, the oath widened the gap between English Catholics and papal authority that the treason trials so effectively produced by forcing some Catholics to line up with the pope and against the king in the dangerous territory of treason and other Catholics to adopt the peculiar position of having rejected the admonitions of their spiritual leader in favor of allegiance to their temporal monarch.

In his defense of the oath, *Triplici nodo, triplex cuneus*,[42] James exploits this development to return the discussion to the basic question at the heart of these polemics: whether Catholics are wrongfully persecuted for religion or justly punished for political crime—in other words, whether they are martyrs or traitors. James reacts against the narrative of Catholic martyrdom posited by Bellarmine and the pope that positions him in the role of persecutor: their claims of martyrdom "detrac[t] as much unjustly and uncharitably from his Majestie our Soveraigne, in accounting of him thereby as a bloody persecutour."[43] Not unlike Lord Burghley before him, James makes rhetorical use of the martyr paradigm to advance his own argument. If the Catholic church is looking to make English papists into victims, they should look to the pope himself as the author of their suffering. By forbidding James's Catholic subjects from taking the oath, the pope becomes "the cause of the due punishment of many: which if it fall out to be, let the blood light upon the Popes head, who is the onely cause thereof."[44] James accuses church leadership of condemning the oath in order to make martyrs of English Catholics:

> And as for the vehement exhortation unto them to persevere in constancie, and to suffer Martyrdome and all tribulation for this cause; it requireth no other answere than onely this, That if the ground be good whereupon hee hath commaunded them to stand, then exhortation to constancie is necessarie: but if the ground be unjust and naught (and indeed it is, as I have in part already

proved) then this exhortation of his can worke no other effect, then to make him guilty of the blood of so many of his sheepe, whom hee doeth thus wilfully cast away; not onely to the needlesse losse of their lives, and ruine of their families, but even to the laying on of a perpetuall slander upon all Papists; as if no zealous Papist could be a trew subject to his Prince; and that the profession of that Religion, and the Temporall obedience to the Civill Magistrate, were two things repugnant and incompatible in themselves.[45]

In the trials of Campion and Southwell, the state effectively asserted and then reproduced the incompatibility of Catholic orthodoxy and obedience to the Crown. Here, James argues that it is the pope who forces this predicament by forbidding Catholics to demonstrate any modicum of secular allegiance. This argument further complicates the project of Catholic martyr-making by obscuring both the cause for which the victim suffers and the author of that suffering. Situating the pope in the role of persecutor, James overtly seeks to rupture the martyr paradigm that might persuade Catholics away from their "naturall duetie to their Soveraigne."[46]

The Polemics of Robert Persons

The disagreement among Catholics over the Oath of Allegiance was part of a broader controversy over the role of the Jesuits in the English mission. These chain-of-command quarrels were exacerbated by the debate over equivocation: the doctrine was professed and defended by Jesuits, but many secular priests complained that its effects were to increase popular hatred of Catholics and to encourage persecution. The controversy over equivocation presented an ongoing challenge to the legitimacy of the recusant cause and the Jesuit victims it claimed as its martyrs. Father Robert Persons (or Parsons, as he is sometimes called), the rector of the English College in Rome and a tireless apologist for English Catholics, wrote copiously to defend equivocation against both Appellant priests and Protestant detractors. His first discussion of the doctrine appeared in a 1602 tract aimed at the Appellants, *A Briefe Apologie, or Defence of the Catholike Ecclesiastical hierarchie, & subordination of England.* As its title suggests, the text primarily addresses itself to questions of church hierarchy raised by disaffected secular priests, but a handful of its nearly five hundred pages specifically argue for the lawfulness of equivocation. Persons chastises the Appellants for their attempts to "slaunder and calumniate every where the fathers of the Society."[47] He specifically takes issue with their efforts to besmirch the memory of Southwell through their open criticism of Southwell's defense of equivocation: "these good fellowes conspiring with the persecutors have sought to disgrace him ever synce for the same, and not only him but all his whole order, and namely those that are in England."[48] Persons's accusation points to the trend in both the popular and polemical rhetoric of the period of vilifying Southwell as an example of the insidious Jesuit order.

According to Persons himself, then, the anti-Jesuit faction within the Catholic church had taken up the project of revisiting and reinterpreting Southwell's death, using the doctrine of equivocation as a weapon in its campaign to challenge Southwell's martyrdom and inscribe his execution into a narrative of disgrace. Persons's book unintentionally shows how the compensatory strategy of equivocation had itself become a marker of treason, even to portions of the Catholic community. Far from providing the seed that would grow the Catholic church in England, equivocal martyr stories like Southwell's found themselves in such profound tension with the topoi of typological suffering that they could no longer produce uniform confidence among the members of the church.

Persons responded to this problem with an apology for equivocation titled *A Treatise tending to Mitigation towardes Catholicke-Subjectes in England* (1607). The text attempts to define the practice of equivocation and the parameters of its application for an audience of both Catholics and their detractors. More specifically, it tries to recover equivocation from the rhetoric of treason by positing it as exemplary moral behavior. Persons describes lying as a sin not of speech but of the heart or mind; there can be no spoken lie if the truth is held and acknowledged in the mind of the speaker. Rather than being "enunciative," lies are "internall actions and operations of the mind."[49]

One of the primary objections to equivocation made by Protestant opponents was that it denied the relevance of the hearer by situating the human utterance in a suprahistorical space shared only by the speaker and God. In addressing this concern, Persons falls back on Aristotelian descriptions of a proposition, claiming that "the definition of a proposition or enunciation nameth not the hearer," and he never fully engages the problem of how mental reservation erodes understanding between one human being and another (329). In fact, he goes so far as to make the claim that the purpose of mental reservation is not deception at all but merely the defense of oneself against capture, and that the speaker has no responsibility for the hearer's misunderstanding: "I [speak] a truth in it self according to my meaning, though he taking it otherwise is deceaved thereby, but without any fault of mine" (346).

Like Garnet, Persons justifies the practice of mental reservation only in cases of unlawful examination, which he defines in much the same terms. But here again Persons's argument creates more complications than it resolves. In attempting to further define what is meant by a judge who is "not lawful or competent," he describes "a lay Magistrate in a Catholicke countrey [who] would enquire of matters not belonging to his jurisdiction, as for example, sacred or secret" (342). While the basic circumstances of this hypothetical inquiry suggest a reference to the harassment of English Catholics, it is difficult to imagine that Persons, even for rhetorical purposes, would represent England as "a Catholicke countrey" under the current rule. His remarks specifically concerning priests shed little additional light on this problem: an instance of unlawful questioning, he says, would be when "a lay Judge should examine priests of Ecclesiasticall matters, who both by divine and humane law according to Catholicke Doctrine are exempted from lay mens jurisdiction" (415). Persons implies that the rules dictated by "Catholicke Doctrine" continue to be relevant in a country that has established laws to the contrary. In this way, he points again to the manner in which the doctrine of equivocation abstracts the Catholic speaker from the bounds of temporal law and deposits him or her under the superseding banner of religious doctrine. The defense of equivocation thus relies on the same assumptions as the claim to martyrdom: no matter what English law may dictate, the behavior of English Catholics ultimately belongs to the category of religion and can be judged only according to God and his divinely sanctioned church.

Persons insists on Christ as the model of equivocation and describes the doctrine as an exemplary response to life's moral dilemmas, suggesting that Protestants need not even trouble themselves with equivocating since they have no scruples about lying. In his criticism of anti-Catholic rhetoric, however, he attacks Protestant divines for their own use of equivocation by expanding the definition of the term to include a number of incidents he condemns. After arguing for more than three hundred pages that equivocation and lying are not the same thing, Persons accuses his adversaries of practicing "false, and synfull" equivocation, making them thereby "wilfull lyer[s]" (483, 510). The main object of his attack is the deceased Anglican bishop of Salisbury, John Jewel, whom he accuses of "wilfull falsification" and "slaunderous speech" (506). The incidents in which he accuses Jewel of having equivocated are largely theological points over which Catholics and Protestants disagree. The complex doctrinal disputes Persons raises in his criticism of Jewel bear little or no relationship to the test case he returns to repeatedly through the course of the book: whether or not a priest may deny his priesthood using equivocation. His use of equivocation as an aspersion to be cast back at his critics undermines the text's broader attempt to justify the doctrine, diluting the moral superiority of mental reservation. At the same time that Persons attempts to locate Catholic utterances in a transcendent religious space, he undermines his own categories by flattening the distinction between the exemplary practice of equivocation and antagonistic or dishonest speech acts.

Complicating matters further, Persons attempts to make the practice of mental reservation palatable to Protestant divines by situating it within a broader spectrum of equivocal propositions that even his adversaries have approved. He argues that verbal ambiguity—the use of words that have more than one meaning or that can signify different things in different contexts—is no less a form of equivocation than mental reservation, so the Protestant condonement of these practices should extend to mental reservation as well. In other words, the distinction between what detractors describe as "logical equivocation," or verbal ambiguity, and "jesuitical equivocation," or mental reservation, is erroneous; the two are morally equivalent. For him, any utterance that is not "plaine and literal" is an example of equivocation and the moral equal of mental reservation. This includes the use of hyperbole, metaphor, and "all Rhetoricall topoi, and figures" (318–19). By this logic, he argues that Christ's regular use of such devices is proof of their lawfulness. For example, Christ's warning to the Jews that he would destroy the "temple" and rebuild it in three days (John 2:19) when the temple he refers to is his own body forms an instance of equivocation as just and moral as the mental reservation defended by Southwell.[50]

The effect of this argument is not only to smooth out the differences between equivocation and morally neutral forms of metaphorical expression but to erode the very model of Catholic exemplarity that Persons sets up. Christ is no morally ambiguous figure; the consistent invocation of his utterances as paradigms for equivocation claims an inherent comparison between those like Christ who equivocate and those who are more concerned with the moral weight of temporal interactions. Protestants fall into the latter category, Persons suggests. Catholics, on the other hand, are ever aware of their duty to God and to his church. But by describing metaphor and the exemplary behavior of equivocation as one and the same, Persons undermines the claim to exemplarity altogether, making the notion of Catholic exemplarity itself a mere metaphor. In his effort to rescue equivocation from the categories of lies, sin, and treason, Persons strips it of its potential to denote integrity or moral superiority. There can be no exemplarity in a morally neutral space, and this is what Persons's defense of equivocation creates.

Persons's argument mirrors the way the Catholic defendant's relationship to religious orthodoxy is flattened by the mechanisms of the treason trial. Just as Campion sought to distance himself from the precepts of Catholic doctrine in order to demonstrate secular allegiance, Persons attempts to disarm the potentially alienating precepts of equivocation by de-emphasizing their moral gravity. In both circumstances, the defensive position must obscure difference to avoid condemnation, but it is this difference that would legitimize both Campion and the doctrine of equivocation as Catholic and exemplary. The function of the treason trial—and of the anti-Catholic, anti-Jesuit, antiequivocation rhetoric surrounding it—is to make difference a marker of crime so that it cannot operate as a marker of exemplarity. Without access to effective modes of demonstrating exemplarity, both equivocation and martyrdom become relegated to the status of metaphor.

Mason's *The New Art of Lying*

One of the Protestant divines who took up the task of responding to Persons was Henry Mason, whose book *The New Art of Lying* (1624) was derived from sermons on the topic of equivocation that he had delivered at Saint Andrew's Church in London. Mason's book does not make original contributions to the debate so much as it articulates several relevant popular opinions about equivocation and its proponents. As its title suggests, the book represents equivocation as a "deceitfull Arte" recently invented by Catholicism: "it may be noted that this Father [Persons] is as bold to alleadge Universality, Antiquity, and Consent for the proofe of this Art, as the rest are for the proofe of their Church."[51] He holds the Jesuits—specifically the English Jesuits—responsible for proliferating the insidious doctrine, stating that they "have chiefly polished it, and most boldly practiced it" (128–29). The result is a Catholic population that believes it can equivocate "for what end or reason soever" (2).

Mason astutely describes the perception of equivocation as a violation of the rules of human interaction. He reconnects equivocation to its essential nature as a communicative speech act to conclude that the doctrine makes no sense in practical application. Mason insists on equivocation as first and foremost an utterance, and utterances are governed by a social contract made "by appointment and agreement among men" (260). While Persons seeks to abstract the concepts of truth and lie from the realm of human communication, Mason insists that "Truth as it is here meant and Lying which is the contrary to it, are morall acts contained in the second Table of the Decalogue or Tenne Commandements: and therefore do include a respect to our Neighbours, nor can they be understood without reference and relation unto other men" (307). Through this assertion, Mason suggests that the concept of Christian morality is itself relational and that other human beings are part of that relationship—in other words, that God is not the only being in relation to whom moral behavior is defined. This supposition governs both morally virtuous and morally reprehensible behavior, as he explains: "both lying and truth morally taken, which hee calleth veracitie, do consist in relation and reference to others; so that no words uttered, without respect of signifying somewhat to some other by them, can be either the sinne of lying, or the vertue of true speaking" (310–11).

Mason's analysis of equivocation illustrates the fundamental rhetorical dispute between English Catholics and their government. Persons's problematic defense of equivocation relies on defining individual existence not in relation to temporal power but in relation first and foremost to God. In a variety of ways, the Catholic position suggests that human identity is fundamentally a metaphysical construct—that what is true and relevant about one's life is that which transpires above the mundane level of temporal events. Mason, on the other hand, insists on the moral relevance of those temporal events, arguing that they manifest an individual's virtue or vice.

Revising Southwell

According to Mason, equivocation taints Catholics' interactions at every level. Their oaths are worth nothing because even an oath can be equivocated: if they believe the oath to be unlawful, they may, "by an equivocall reservation, break the band of that Oath, before they take it" (173–74). Likewise, miracles claimed by the Catholic church, especially those claimed by Jesuits, can have no validity, since equivocators would certainly stoop "to fitten and faine and tell of glorious facts, and admirable wonders which were never done" (189). Neither can they be believed when they write in defense of their faith, when they testify in court, when they relate stories of Protestants who are disgraced for their beliefs or who recant, or "in matters of common life, and civil conversation" (337–46). "[T]herefore wise Christians beware of them," he warns, "and if we not be deceived, we must not beleeve either their words or oaths, in what businesse soever we have to doe with them" (336). *The New Art of Lying* articulates the increasingly popular belief that nothing Catholics do or say can be trusted. As Zagorin has observed, "In the years following the polemical exchanges between Persons and [Thomas] Morton, although anti-Romanist controversies in England continued, discussion centering upon equivocation and mental reservation gradually waned. That Catholics were prone to lying and dissimulation was taken for granted and became one of the common beliefs of popular Protestantism."[52]

Importantly, Mason suggests that the nefarious nature of equivocation is intimately connected with the larger problem of Catholic treason: "for as in matter of State, they have found out a mysterie; that a Clergieman of their church may move *Rebellion* against his *Prince,* and yet be no *Traytor*: so in Conferences with men, they have found a like mysterie; that any man of the Romane church, may speake, and say, and sweare whatsoever himselfe pleaseth, though it bee never so false, and yet be no Lyer" (21, italics original). In this syllogism, religion and equivocation function as two sides of the same Catholic defense, which seeks to redefine treason and perjury as innocence. What transpires "in Conferences with men" is a microcosmic representation of what happens "in matter of State": equivocation is treason on a smaller scale, a kind of "Rebellion" against the customs of civil society. Mason's anatomy of the relationship between equivocation and treason demonstrates how the admissions of equivocation by Southwell and Garnet come to function as damning evidence of treason, not only in their trials but in the narrative and polemical afterlife of those events.

More specifically, Mason connects equivocation to the treason of the Gunpowder Plot by rehearsing the relationship between the doctrine and Garnet's claim to immunity through the seal of confession. Mason writes that equivocation allows priests not only to conceal those whom they have reconciled to the church but also those who "have conspired against the life of the King, or have beene acquainted with a plot of blowing up the Parliament" (179). In his formulation, equivocation operates as the thread connecting the manifest crimes of the Gunpowder Plot back to the man who introduced it to English Catholics, Robert Southwell: "This use Southwell the Jesuit made of this Art. For, fearing to be detected, he instructed a Woman-Disciple of his, that if she should be examined, whether himselfe were or had bin in that house, she should upon her oath utterly deny it; and so she might safely do, using but the help of this art, though she had often seene him there; and knew him to be in the house. And to like purpose Tresham, of the Gun powder Traitors, upon examinations did confesse that F. Garnet was privy to the Treasons and had talked with him about it" (181–82).[53] Mason demonstrates how the victim's narrative continues to be revised and shaped years after his death. Southwell introduces equivocation at his trial; the doctrine emerges again to play a central role in the conviction of Henry Garnet; and thus the memory of Southwell is entailed in the Gunpowder Plot, though he was executed a decade earlier. In the retrospective project of traitor-making, the odium of equivocation associated with Southwell becomes translated into the vehicle for attempted regicide, just as the attempted regicide is invoked to construct the infamy of Southwell.

This translation is made possible because of the essential nature of equivocation: it is an act of silence—a refusal to utter the mind, a hole where language should be. Equivocation produces a cipher instead of a subject. The zero of equivocation is adapted into an equation in which *silence = treason*. Equivocation represents a very real threat to the management of the state by producing individuals who cannot be deciphered—literally, de-ciphered. The equivocal subject lays claim to a territory beyond law, as Stephen Mullaney has pointed out: "if amphibology seduces the traitor, it also presents authority with a considerable dilemma, and with it we move into a linguistic sphere the law cannot control."[54] But equivocation (or "amphibology," a synonymous term) also presents a representational problem for the subject who uses it, because the cipher of silence provides a blank slate on which the state writes its own meaning. In the trials of Southwell and Garnet, the state sets up elaborate rhetorical arguments to validate the interpretation of silence as treason. By the time we get to Mason's text, the nuances of that rhetoric have been ironed into a neat semiotic equation that effortlessly links Southwell to equivocation to Gunpowder.

This equation provides the state with a code for interpreting both past and future acts of equivocation, and Mason's text demonstrates how that code is deployed. Chapter 4 described how the resurrection of Christ provides Christians with a conclusive reading of his Passion, showing how the miracle of his rising from the dead operates to retrospectively ratify his claim of divinity. The miracle-event establishes the lens through which the earlier passion-event is interpreted, securing Christ's identity as the true God and the true martyr. In precisely this way, the deaths of Catholic victims continue to be retrospectively interpreted through the lens of later events. In the case of Southwell, however, the interpretive frame is established not by a great miracle of God's validation but by its opposite, a terrific crime. Through the semiotics of equivocation, the Gunpowder Plot comes to serve the same function as the Resurrection, providing Southwell's detractors with a concrete event by which his execution and equivocation are defined. Without an equally persuasive, equally public episode to retrospectively signal his sanctity, the rival discourse of Southwell's martyrdom founders.

The Gunpowder Plot successfully absorbs Southwell into a model of treason because the structural elements of that model are already in place. The structure of treason is initiated by the pope's bull of excommunication and the philosophical crisis it forces between secular and religious allegiance. It is fortified by the argument of the treason trial, which divides the defendant from the sources of religious and political legitimacy. It is demonstrated by the scene at the scaffold—by the assertion of treason and the record of crime made on the victim's body.

These are not the elements of a martyr's story. What's more, recusant life itself was already at odds with the paradigms of martyrdom. The secrecy, duplicity, and equivocation that Catholics relied on to evade the condemning charge of treason have no analogues in typological narratives of martyrdom, including those of Foxe. Catholic texts themselves cannot help exposing their inconsistencies with the martyrological model. In their effort to justify Catholic victims, stories of recusant persecution inevitably highlight the reasons why their subjects fail to achieve typological transcendence.

Gerard's *The Autobiography of a Hunted Priest*

One such story—the story with which this book began—is Father John Gerard's *The Autobiography of a Hunted Priest,* written in Latin in about 1609 after Gerard had escaped from the Tower, rejoined the mission, and finally returned to the safety of the Continent. Gerard's book is unique in many ways. Philip Caraman, the twentieth-century translator and editor of the text, describes it as "a private account of his adventures written for his fellow Jesuits and perhaps, in the first place, for the novices under his direction [at Louvain]."[55] It was not written for a public audience, so its narrative is not composed to edify the recusant population or to encourage schismatics to return to the church. It tells the unusual story of a priest who is imprisoned, tortured, and prepared for martyrdom but who lives to describe his experience. It provides fascinating insight into how the recusant community, both in prison and out, lived, communicated, and sustained itself in a hostile environment. And it vividly maps the problem faced by Counter-Reformation martyrology. At the same time that the *Autobiography* describes the persecution of faithful Catholics, it exposes the distance between the practical experience of recusancy and the typological imperatives of martyrdom.

Gerard joined the mission late in the year 1588. From then until his capture in the spring of 1594, he ministered to a number of wealthy Catholic families and their households, carrying out his public life under an alias and in the guise of a country gentleman.[56] Following his arrest, Gerard underwent rigorous interrogation about his Catholic associates, particularly Father Garnet, whom authorities were anxious to capture. He refused to provide them any information and was tortured by both the rack and manacles. He was eventually transferred to the Tower to await trial, and from there he managed to escape. With the help of Catholic friends on the outside, Gerard and a fellow prisoner climbed down a rope that they had strung from the top of the Tower wall to a safe landing place outside its perimeter. After recuperating from his ordeal, he resumed his missionary work. Gerard left England for refuge in Louvain in May 1606 when the fallout of the Gunpowder Plot rendered the ministry unproductive and unreasonably dangerous. There he wrote his fascinating *Autobiography*, and there he died in 1637.

Gerard's portrait of faith and suffering is consistent with several aspects of the Christian martyr paradigm; indeed, the institution of martyrdom organizes his understanding of his own suffering as well as that of his fellow Catholics. Once he is arrested and his identity as a Jesuit found out, Gerard fully expects he will be executed, and there is no evidence to suggest that any other outcome was in store for him. The topoi of martyrdom become a way for him to make meaning of his own persecution and to connect his experience to a larger narrative of Christian and Catholic suffering. This connection is a comfort to him. The physical pain of being bound after capture is quickly supplanted by a "great happiness that [he] had been allowed to suffer this much for Christ's sake, and [he] thanked our Lord for it as well as [he] could" (66). He describes his legs as "adorned" by his shackles and his suffering as a source of happiness and a gift from God (71). The days in prison before his torture begins are pleasant ones for Gerard despite his cramped and stinking quarters, because there he "enjoyed that peace of soul which the world does not and cannot give" (99). Although he believes himself unworthy of martyrdom, he looks forward to the tortures threatened by Topcliffe with hope, and he welcomes rumors of his impending trial as "good news" (70, 123).

The narratives of other martyrs, both primitive and contemporary, provide a template for Gerard's own experience. In considering the circumstances of his arrest, he wonders why it is that he and other Catholics are betrayed by their own, and the narrative of Christ's Passion illuminates his understanding. He reasons that Catholics are given up by other Catholics so that their suffering will imitate Christ's: "in order to make them more like the Master for whom they suffered, God allowed them to be betrayed by one of their own household, a man they all loved" (51). Through these parallels, God makes Gerard's suffering legible to him as typology, and in turn Gerard makes that typology legible to his audience. The deaths of priests Edmund Campion and Henry Walpole provide models for Gerard's behavior in captivity, and the fact that they once suffered at the same prison helps him to endure torture and confinement.[57] Following the example of Campion, he drops to his knees each time he is brought to the torture chamber and prays for God's help in bearing the pain.[58] The cell once occupied by Walpole becomes a kind of sanctuary for him, a place he begs his jailer to take him for prayer and meditation before he is interrogated. He writes, "It was a great comfort to me to find myself in a place sanctified by this great and holy martyr, and in the room where he had been tortured so many times—fourteen in all, as I have heard" (105). By following the examples of his contemporary Catholic sufferers, Gerard reinforces their roles as typological martyr figures.

Throughout his ministry in prison and at large,[59] Gerard's faith in the Jesuit teachings and in the doctrine of the Catholic church is strengthened by visible proofs of the spiritual efficacy of these institutions. And as in devotional martyrologies of the period, the efficacy of Catholic belief and practice is confirmed time and again in Gerard's story by miracles and wonders. However, this element is balanced in Gerard's text against the stark details of recusant life. Priests were at the mercy of their servants and confidantes, who could do a great deal of damage if they turned double-agent: they had access to information and could get rich by betraying Catholics and discovering their hiding places. "The defection of any of those we had to work with would have damaged and set back our cause more than anything else," Gerard writes; "if any one of them had chosen to betray us he would have worked havoc among Catholics" (74). Living conditions were so perilous for priests and their supporters that priests who died of natural causes had to be buried in sercret: "all priests who live in hiding on the mission are also buried in hiding" (87).[60] Priests had to be ready to hide at all times, and the circumstances under which they existed—tucked away in tiny holes between walls—were brutal. During a household search from which Gerard manages to escape, he is crouched in a hiding space for four days with nothing to eat (59–60).

Life after capture was far worse. Although Gerard often uses the topoi of happiness-in-suffering that are common to martyrological narrative, he also recounts the physical and psychological horrors of torture and imprisonment. He describes his first session in the manacles: "such a gripping pain came over me. It was worst in my chest and belly, my hands and arms. All the blood in my body seemed to rush up into my arms and hands and I thought that blood was oozing out from the ends of my fingers and the pores of my skin. But it was only a sensation caused by my flesh swelling above the irons holding them. The pain was so intense that I thought I could not possibly endure it" (109).[61] In this moment of terrific pain, Gerard experiences "an interior temptation" that can only be overcome by God's comfort and the knowledge that they can harm him no worse than killing him.

> The Lord saw my weakness with the eyes of His mercy and did not permit me to be tempted beyond my strength. With the temptation He sent me relief. Seeing my agony and the struggle going on in my mind, He gave me this most merciful thought: the utmost and worst they can do to you is to kill you, and you have often wanted to give your life for your Lord God. The Lord God sees all you are enduring—He can do all things. You are in God's keeping. With these thoughts, God in His infinite goodness and mercy gave me the grace of resignation, and, with a desire to die and a hope (I admit) that I would, I offered Him myself to do with me as He wished. From that moment the conflict in my soul ceased, and even the physical pain seemed much more bearable than before, though I am sure it must, in fact, have been greater with the growing strain and weariness of my body. (109–10)

Although Christ and martyrs like Walpole and Campion provide him with comfort through their modeling of suffering, Gerard is ultimately faced with his own horrors, and in that moment only the expectation of death can opiate his pain.

Gerard's use of martyrological formulations to order his experience of persecution, his complete faith in the institutions of Catholicism and the Jesuit order, and his gritty and ingenuous descriptions of recusant life both in and out of captivity posit an image of the Jesuit that is consistent with martyrological paradigms. In these elements of the text, Gerard emerges as a man of deep faith and tremendous sacrifice who manifests an earnest belief in the salvific efficacy of Catholic doctrine and who suffers hardship and horrific punishment for that belief. But this inspiring and sympathetic figure—this recognizable martyrological subject—is compromised by the practical matters of recusant life: disguises, aliases, hiding places, and a myriad other forms of duplicity. Gerard's *Autobiography of a Hunted Priest* exposes not only the faith and suffering of a prospective martyr but the schemes and contrivances of a potential traitor.

Gerard was arrested during the second year of Southwell's three-year captivity, and although Southwell's support of equivocation was not made public until his trial, his accusers knew of it before then. According to Christopher Devlin, "A sentence blurted out by Topcliffe at the trial reveals that Southwell in one of his examinations in prison had expounded to Sir Robert Cecil the theory and practice of 'equivocation.'"[62] Logically, Gerard came to be questioned about it too, on one occasion by the Attorney General, who asked him about the doctrine and then "began to disparage Father Southwell's character" (125). Gerard defended the doctrine with much the same argument presented by his fellow Jesuits. When it came to applying the doctrine, he was quite scrupulous, at least in his retrospective telling of events.[63] Under interrogation about his Catholic friends and maintainers, he often clarifies negative responses by adding that he "could and should" deny something "even if it were true" (57). This caveat, which equivocation does not require, signals to his examiners that he rejects the proceedings as binding and has no plans to cooperate. By doing this, he makes it impossible for his examiners to claim that he has misled them. However, he is not always so transparent. Initial questions about his identity produce an alias. When they reveal that they know who he is, however, Gerard changes his tack: "Realizing at once that the pursuivant had given me away, I said that I would be quite frank and give straight answers to all questions concerning myself, but added that I would say nothing which would involve others" (66). This is Gerard's general strategy: he carefully calculates when he will equivocate to spare himself or others harm. Asked whether or not he has reconciled people to the church, he decides to answer "forthrightly" because he knows he is "already compromised because of [his] priesthood" (95). When a suit of his is discovered at the home of a Catholic family who sheltered him and the authorities seek to entrap the family by having Gerard claim the suit, he "refuse[s] to admit" ownership (74). Doubtless Gerard's equivocations spared others the charge of treason, imprisonment, and even death; and they reveal a savvy and sophisticated strategist.

This aspect of Gerard's identity is supported by the book's fascinating revelations about his life as a secret priest. He adopts the persona of a "gentleman of moderate means," dressing the part and socializing with the upper classes. There is wisdom, he suggests, in keeping the lie as close to the truth as possible: "it was thus that I used to go about before I became a Jesuit, and I was therefore more at ease in these clothes than I would have been if I had assumed a role that was strange and unfamiliar to me" (17–18). As an accessory to his gentlemanly persona, Gerard shows an interest in pastimes like hunting, falconry, and cards, and takes evident pride in how well he carries off this charade. He reports converting one woman who does not know he is a priest. She has been so taken in by his gentleman-of-leisure persona that she is incredulous when his identity is revealed. "She was amazed," Gerard writes. "'How can he possibly be a priest?' she protested. 'Why, the man lives like a courtier. Haven't you watched him playing cards with my husband—and the way he plays, he must have been at the game for a long time. And he's been out hunting with my husband, and I've heard him myself talking about hunting and about hawking, and he never trips in his terms. No one could do that without being caught out unless he was thoroughly familiar with the sport'" (165). She is assured that "he's quite a different person when he drops the part he has been playing," and yet by reinforcing how convincing Gerard is in his native-born role, the episode demonstrates that the hunter and hawker is perhaps no more a part to be played than that of the Jesuit priest (166). The circumstances of the Catholic mission require that Gerard devote his life to playing both roles.

In prison Gerard is no longer occupied with concealing his identity, but neither is he an open book. Much of his duplicity while imprisoned is aimed at communicating with his fellow Catholics at large. As Caraman notes, "it was very important for friends of a prisoner to know, if possible, what answers he had made [under examination], both to take steps to ensure their own safety, if necessary, and to know how far to go in their own answers if they were caught and examined."[64]

This imperative leads to several incidents of coded speech, when Gerard utters something seemingly benign that is pregnant with significance for a select part of his audience, whose job it is to pass the coded message on. On one occasion he is questioned under torture about the location of Garnet's house. While being led back to his cell, he remarks—ostensibly to the warden but loudly enough for other prisoners to hear—that he is surprised that the commissioners continue to question him on this subject: "Surely they know it is a sin to betray an innocent man? I will never do it, even if I have to die" (111). Gerard then goes on to explain that he said this so that his fellow Catholics could not be duped into believing that he had made a confession under torture. Furthermore, he says, "I also wanted word to get round through these men that it was chiefly concerning Father Garnet that I had been questioned, so that he might get to hear and look to his own safety" (111). According to Caraman, "this ingeniously despatched message got through."[65]

Gerard's written messages are similarly coded. He bribes the warden to allow him to write letters to friends, but he knows that they could be intercepted before delivery and is careful not to disclose potentially damaging information. In order to communicate private business, he employs a method that others in the Catholic community apparently used as well.[66] He describes how he used the juice from lemons and oranges as invisible ink: when the paper is heated, the writing becomes legible. The choice of what kind of juice to use—lemon or orange—depends on the circumstances of the letter. Lemon juice writing fades to invisibility as the paper cools, but orange juice writing is permanently visible once it has been heated, thus signaling to the reader that the letter has been intercepted and read by the enemy. Gerard pays his warden to bring him oranges, and he fashions the dried peels into rosaries that he wraps up in paper and sends to his friends. On the paper, he writes words of spiritual encouragement in pencil and secret instructions in orange juice. He explains, "In the pencilled letter I confined myself to spiritual topics, but in the white spaces between the lines I gave detailed instructions to different friends of mine outside" (118). Gerard's letters thus become double texts, the "spiritual topics" operating as vehicles for other kinds of information. In a quite literal sense, the spiritual becomes intertwined with the secret in a duplicitous communication that requires the reader to read between the lines. Furthermore, the rosary acts as a means of carrying out this duplicity, functioning as a vehicle for thwarting secular authority. While Gerard does not disclose the substance of his secret writings, it is plain that the spiritual is being exploited to mask other content.

The celebration of Mass comes to play a similar function in Gerard's story. He desires to have Mass with a fellow Catholic prisoner, and after cajoling and bribing his warden to let him visit the man and arranging a clandestine delivery of the necessary paraphernalia, the two have their private service. When he returns to his own cell, Gerard begins to consider the position of the other man's cell on the perimeter of the Tower compound and the ease with which an escape from that spot could be managed. He sounds out the plan with Father Garnet through what must be more orange juice letters, and upon Garnet's approval he makes arrangements with helpers on the outside. When the scheduled night of the escape comes, he once again bribes the warden to let him visit his Catholic friend under the guise of spiritual conference. Once the warden has left them alone, they make their successful escape (128–36). While the Mass does not operate as a cover for clandestine business as overtly as the orange-peel rosaries, it is nonetheless the occasion from which the escape plan germinates. Further, the subsequent visits to the man's cell are largely focused, according to Gerard's narrative, on escape, and yet the warden is surely being deceived into believing the meetings are of a spiritual nature. Gerard's position as a priest and his desire to commune with his fellow Catholic are translated into vehicles for what is unquestionably a subversive, if not criminal, act.

Moreover, Gerard's claim to political innocence is compromised from the opening of the narrative, where he relates the story of his coming into England. The time when he received orders to join the English mission coincided with the launching of the Spanish Armada. "[I]t was just the time that the Spanish Fleet had set sail and was approaching England—the illustrious Cardinal Allen, for a number of reasons connected with the Catholic cause, petitioned to have me sent to England" (6). The "number of reasons" are elided, but it is difficult to imagine that Gerard was ignorant of them. In fact, the wreck of the Spanish fleet while Gerard is en route from Rome to France to catch his ship for England results in a change of his orders. Persons informs him that his presence in England is no longer immediately necessary: "The situation, he said, had changed a great deal since we had left Rome, but the work we had in hand was God's undertaking, we were free either to go ahead with the enterprise or stay back until things in England had quietened down" (8). The connection between his transfer to England and Spain's attempt at invasion betray Gerard's awareness of the relationship between the two events, suggesting that he understood what his role would be on the occasion of Spanish success.

The Unmartyred Martyr

What Gerard's text ultimately suggests is that the Jesuit priest—and, more broadly, the recusant Catholic under his guidance—cannot adequately be described by the terms "martyr" or "traitor." Gerard's relationship to institutions of temporal and spiritual legitimacy exceeds the boundaries of both categories. There is no evidence in his *Autobiography* that Gerard ever meddled in specific acts of treason; on the contrary, he issued a written public condemnation of the Gunpowder Plot, denying any knowledge of it under the seal of confession or otherwise (203–4). At the same time, Gerard emerges from the *Autobiography* as a master of disguise, a crafty strategist who makes no step without careful calculation and who is exceptionally adept at manipulating his environment.

In *Domination and the Arts of Resistance*, James C. Scott argues that "there is a third realm of subordinate group politics that lies strategically between" open rebellion and submission: "This is a politics of disguise and anonymity that takes place in public view but is designed to have a double meaning or to shield the identity of the actors."[67] Scott identifies this form of dissidence with the trickster figure, whose artful maneuvering "celebrate[s] the cunning wiles and vengeful spirit of the weak as they triumph over the strong." He calls the discourse of this mode of resistance "the hidden transcript," the dissenting voice embedded in the texts, appearances, and activities of the oppressed.[68] Although Scott's notion of trickster dissidence aptly describes the double texts, disguises, and secret workings of a figure like Gerard, it does not describe the conventional Christian martyr figure. As Daniel Boyarin observes, the Judeo-Christian tradition gradually resolved questions about ideal modes of resistance during the early centuries after Christ: "The debate between tricksterism and martyrdom as the most honored and most valuable response to oppression was in the air as a living and active cross-confessional issue at the time that the talmudic literature was being composed."[69] Boyarin demonstrates that orthodox Christianity increasingly defined itself against rabbinic Judaism through a preference for open rebellion—for martyrdom. So although Gerard may be a compelling figure of shrewd and wily resistance against an oppressive Protestant regime, these very features of his dissidence mark him out as incoherent with Christianity's definition of the martyr.

Gerard's *Autobiography* illustrates the crisis faced by Counter-Reformation martyrology: the topoi of typological martyrdom are inadequate to encompass what is entailed in the recusant Catholic experience. Conventional martyrological structures cannot accommodate ambiguous figures like Gerard, his dubious mission to England, and the strategies on which he relies for survival. Through its engagement with the forces of law and the accusations of crime, the English Catholic community is driven out of martyrology's behavioral and narrative structures and into a discourse of cunning, duplicity, and disguise from which the traditional topoi of Christian martyrology can provide no easy asylum.

It is no accident that the final text in this book's study of Counter-Reformation martyrology is in fact not a martyrology at all but the narrative of an individual who escaped and survived. John Gerard's *Autobiography* illustrates both the complex nature of the English Catholic subject during this period of persecution and the failure of traditional martyr typology. The study of Counter-Reformation martyrology is the study of a form in distress—a form that can no longer successfully be reproduced according to conventional modes. Rather than demonstrating the continuity of martyrological structures, as texts like *The Golden Legend* and Foxe's *Acts and Monuments* do, Counter-Reformation martyrology rehearses their diffusion and fracture. As a consequence, the uniform, typologically consistent set of transcendent martyr figures we find in earlier martyrology are succeeded by a roll call of diverse and problematic individuals: Campion, the martyr-traitor; Clitherow, the martyr-suicide; Southwell, the martyr-equivocator; Garnet, the martyr-plotter; and Gerard, the unmartyred martyr. The mere plurality of subject positions represented by Catholic victims, not to mention the deeply problematic nature of those specific positions, challenges the production of martyr discourse, which depends on the legible recapitulation of uniform structures.

The splintering of Catholic victims from the behavioral and narrative sources of martyrological legitimacy produces the diversity of martyr figures found in texts of the period. Because the reproduction of martyrdom is the reproduction of legible, exemplary difference, the erosion of exemplarity and the emergence of martyrological diversity are ultimately markers of generic crisis. Just as the exemplary status of equivocation is flattened into metaphor by Persons's compensatory discourse, martyrdom too becomes a metaphorical category—a mode of describing the subjective experience of Catholic suffering while bracketing matters that are structurally and paradigmatically incoherent. As the next chapter's study of *Eikon Basilike* suggests, the further development of the martyr from a typologically and religiously defined figure into an abstract metaphor of interior experience ensures the survival of the discourse beyond the Counter-Reformation.

Chapter 6

Beyond Typology

King Charles and the Martyrdom of Conscience

I may (without vanity) turn the reproach of My sufferings,

as to the world's censure, into the honour of a kind of Martyrdom,

as to the testimony of My own Conscience.

—King Charles I, *Eikon Basilike*

The semiotic rupture between discrete deaths and religious typology in Counter-Reformation martyr texts marks a defining development in English martyr discourse. It is a moment that opens up irreconcilable discrepancies between the executions of English Catholic victims and the literary typology that attempts to organize and inscribe their experience. Because England would never again return to systematic heresy inquisitions, the generic fracture that surfaces in Counter-Reformation martyrology represents a constitutive break between pre- and post-Elizabethan constructions of martyrdom.

We know from the continued vitality of the term "martyr" that the cleaving of historical event from the conventions of literary typology did not initiate an end to the discourse. A figure with enormous historical, imaginative, and institutional significance, the martyr is not easily given up. But if the martyr story no longer describes typological persecution, what does it describe? How does martyr discourse adapt to accommodate new forms of witness and suffering? This final chapter addresses these questions by turning to one of the most popular texts of the seventeenth century, *Eikon Basilike: The Pourtraicture of His Sacred Majestie in His Solitudes and Sufferings,* and to John Milton's painstaking response, *Eikonoklastes.* Published within a week of King Charles I's beheading at Whitehall in January 1649, *Eikon Basilike* ("Royal Portrait") elaborates Charles's scaffold-speech claim to be "the Martyr of the People" by representing the king in his personal meditations leading up to death.[1] Turning inward to locate the sacred within the regal conscience, the text traces the emergence of a new kind of martyr, one both enabled and necessitated by the formal fissures in Counter-Reformation martyrology. Milton's response, commissioned by the Commonwealth and published nine months later, rejects Charles's claims to martyrdom by resolutely insisting on the record of Caroline rule. Even as they mark new developments in martyrological discourse, these two texts—whose histories are themselves tellingly dialogic— rehearse the widening disparity between the form's organizing imperatives: to represent the events of history and to construct the textual locus of history's subversion and transcendence.

Typological Echoes

Elizabeth Skerpan has called *Eikon Basilike* "the most popular and influential tract of the English Revolution."[2] In the year of Charles's death, the "King's Book" went through thirty-five editions in England and another twenty-five on the Continent.[3] Publishers added poetry and illustrations, versified and set to music Charles's prayers, and subtly "democratized" the text with each iteration.[4] In their introduction to the most recent edition (2006), Jim Daems and Holly Faith Nelson observe that *Eikon Basilike* derives its power from the manipulation of "a curious hybrid of genres: political memoir, *apologia,* spiritual autobiography, martyrology, hagiography, meditation, and Psalter."[5] Positing itself as royally authored, it constructs for public gaze the private conscience and meditations of the king.[6] Each of its twenty-eight first-person chapters is comprised of Charles's commentary on an aspect of the controversy with Parliament followed by a prayer.[7]

Though largely unconventional in its construction of Charles as martyr, *Eikon Basilike* does include some familiar martyrological topoi, such as the confrontation between victim and persecutor. Because Charles, as king, would naturally occupy the role of persecutor in the paradigms of Christian martyrology, his inversion of that role depends first on his claim of powerlessness. Strategically stripping himself of military strength, Charles claims, "They knew My chiefest Arms left Me, were those only, which the Ancient Christians were wont to use against their Persecutors, Prayers and Tears. These may serve a good man's turn, if not to Conquer as a Soldier, yet to suffer as a Martyr" (88). Identifying his plight with that of the "Ancient Christians," Charles claims the weakened position of the victim who has neither the means nor the desire to "Conquer" but is furnished only with spiritual "Arms." Those who doom him to death are likewise extracted from contemporary power politics to become conventional martyrological villains, bloodthirsty "Murderers" whose "malice" can only be "satiate[d]" by his "sufferings" (204, 177).

The analogue between Charles and the martyrs of the early church is augmented by a number of other typologically resonant echoes. Charles describes himself being "tried in the furnace of afflictions" and undergoing a "fiery trial [to] consume the dross," metaphors of purification that are staples of martyrological literature (128, 177). These metaphors, along with his description of himself as tortured on the rack by "sacrilegious Cruelty," invoke the horrific physical suffering central to the Christian martyr tradition in order to make Charles's painless imprisonment and death legible as martyrdom. Also central to this characterization of Charles is his invocation of conventional Christian virtues in the face of his sufferings: he writes, "Yet I thank God I can not only with patience bear this, as other indignities, but with Charity forgive them" (160). In addition to naming the virtues of patience and charity, the text strategically emphasizes Charles's "indignities" above the dignities of kingship that he likewise invokes throughout the text. In his claim to victimization and martyrdom, Charles characterizes himself as "desolate and afflicted," as in his supplication to God: "do not despise the weakness of my prayers" (176, 174).[8] From this position of lowliness, "deprived of [God's] temporal blessings," Charles hopes to achieve the highest level of spiritual elevation: "yet I may be happy to enjoy the comfort of thy mercies, which often raise the greatest Sufferers to be the most glorious Saints" (69). The hope expressed here not only constructs a future of canonization for Charles but announces a valuation of spiritual above earthly comfort, a commonplace of Christian piety.

Caroline Christology

Like the Protestant and Counter-Reformation martyrology that precedes it, *Eikon Basilike* creates both behavioral and narrative parallels between its subject and Christ. In keeping with the paradigms of pious suffering that reach back to Saint Stephen, the apostle and proto-martyr, Charles consciously seeks to construct his suffering as an *imitatio Christi,* reminding himself not to "forget to imitate My crucified Redeemer" (183). He describes his suffering as a narrative that shares essential (and telling) structural components with the story of Christ's Passion: "My Enemies (being more solemnly cruel) will, it may be, seek to add (as those did, who Crucified Christ) the mockery of Justice, to the cruelty of Malice: That I may be destroyed, as with greater pomp and artifice, so with less pity, it will be but a necessary policy to make My death appear as an act of Justice, done by Subjects upon their Sovereign" (197). Here Charles uses key conventional features of the Passion story, especially "the mockery of Justice," to organize the events and persons of his own experience, thereby situating the especially problematic issue of his trial and conviction for high treason into a familiar narrative in which both his suffering and sovereignty are iterations of Christ's. This narrative in place, his antagonists become legible as Christ's chief persecutors, Judas and Pontius Pilate, "wash-[ing] their own hands of that innocent blood, whereof they are now most evidently guilty" (197).

Importantly, however, Charles's claim to a typological likeness between his suffering and Christ's makes significant departures from martyrological convention in which the victim generally aspires no higher than these narrative and behavioral echoes. Charles sees his death functioning as a redemptive transaction that replicates Christ's sacrifice. He writes, "Yea, I could be content (at least by my silence) to take upon me so great a guilt before men, If by that I might allay the malice of my Enemies, and redeem my People from this miserable War" (87). In this illuminating passage, Charles announces himself as the scapegoat for England's sins—the silent, passive sacrificial victim who willingly accepts the burden of "guilt" for the redemption of his subjects. In a longer passage later in the text, Charles elaborates the details of this transactive death: "But O let the blood of Me, though their King, yet a sinner, be washed with the Blood of My Innocent and peace-making Redeemer, for in that thy Justice will find not only a temporary expiation, but an eternal plenary satisfaction; both for my sins, and the sins of my People; whom I beseech thee still own for thine, and when thy wrath is appeased by my Death, O Remember thy great mercies toward them, and forgive them! O my Father, for they know not what they do" (87–88). In this prayer, the redemptive roles of Christ and Charles are complexly interlayered, forming a palimpsest of sacrificial blood that communicates both the primacy of Christ's offering and its indistinction from Charles's. Charles first prays for expiation from sin through the purifying sacrifice of Christ's death. The prayer then seamlessly slips into a second death, Charles's own—figured, like Christ's, as a sacrificial offering to "appease" God's wrath and avert punishment from England. Through this slippage, Charles becomes a second "peace-making Redeemer" whose death provides God with the "plenary satisfaction" required. By the final sentence, Charles himself is speaking from the cross: the distinction between his redemptive death and Christ's has been erased.

Charles's representation of the redemptive power of his own death precisely articulates René Girard's "theory of sacrificial substitution."[9] According to Girard, sacrifice is a response to the uncontained violence that ultimately threatens total societal annihilation. The sacrificial victim is offered in place of the community to contain and divert violence onto one individual rather than allowing it to spread like a contagion to all. In Charles's narrative, the threat of violence comes from God's wrath, which demands appeasement by blood. Charles offers himself as a "plenary satisfaction"—a sacrificial surrogate—to fulfill God's desire for vengeance. He envisions that, having satisfied his wrath, God will then offer "great mercies" and forgiveness to the people of England. In this way, Charles's death becomes a means of saving his people.

Girard also helps us understand why Charles can function as an appropriate sacrificial surrogate. For sacrifice to work, the arbitrary act of substitution must be erased, and the relationship between the original object of violence and the surrogate must be naturalized and reinforced. "Without [an] awareness [of that relationship]," Girard writes, "no substitution can take place and the sacrifice loses all efficacy."[10] But while the logic of sacrifice depends on the surrogate's likeness to the original object of violence, the surrogate must also be distinct enough to act as a terminus of violence. There must be no confusion about who the victim is to be, and the victim's social identity (or species) must render it impossible for the sacrifice to initiate acts of reciprocal violence. For Girard, appropriate victims include animals that are part of the domestic economy, "prisoners of war, slaves, small children, unmarried adolescents, and the handicapped . . . [and] the king himself."[11] In Girard's formulation, the king is an apt sacrificial victim because he is both of the people and above the people: he resembles the original objects of violence, the populace, sufficiently enough to surrogate them, but because he has no social equal, his death cannot initiate cycles of reciprocal vengeance. He can therefore function successfully as a terminal object of violence, which is, according to both Girard's and Charles's formulations, the purpose of sacrifice.

Charles's positioning of himself as a sacrificial surrogate works as a key component of *Eikon Basilike*'s argument that he is not a traitor but an anointed king, counteracting his associations with Catholics and foreigners by reinforcing his likeness to his people. It positions him as an Englishman who is not merely without treason but a shining example of patriotism—an Englishman willing to give his life for the expiation of his nation's sin and suffering. Moreover, it confirms his exceptionality and, thereby, his kingship, for who but a true king would be willing to give so much? And whose death but a king's could successfully divert the wrath of God from the destruction of an entire nation? Surely no heinous traitor's carcass would suffice. Christ's crucifixion provides just such a model of this logic: God's ire must be spent on a sufficient victim if the whole of mankind is to be redeemed at the crucifixion. Only a man who is himself divine can complete the sacrificial transaction. At the same time, Christ's nature as human is essential to the logic of sacrificial substitution: he must be us and stand in for us if he is to divert violence away from us.

In the conflation of his sacrifice with Christ's, Charles thus does more than posit himself as a pious and even exemplary sufferer, as earlier martyrology had done. He exploits the power of Christ's singular example to express his unique existential status as both Englishman and king. Further, he reconstitutes his opprobrious death as evidence of not only his monarchy but the monarchy. As Girard tells us, "Because the victim is sacred, it is criminal to kill him—but the victim is sacred only because he is to be killed."[12] Charles's claim to Christological, sacrificial status is therefore also a claim to the sacredness of his person and of the institution he represents. In turn, that claim works to desacralize the budding commonwealth that put him to death, instead criminalizing their actions. Rather than being eroded by a treason execution, Charles's sacredness is confirmed and even constituted by his death.

Charles's invocation of a Christological model demonstrates the terrific flexibility and complexity of that model. Christian martyrdom is largely a project of *imitatio Christi*—a narrative and behavioral repetition of Christ's actions as a mode of constructing and communicating the meaning of death. The model offered by Christ is static—fixed by the gospel narratives—and this is the principal reason the genre of martyrology appears so formulaic on its surface. However, what it means to imitate Christ is not at all fixed. On the contrary, the genre's discrete engagements with the imperatives of *imitatio Christi* are highly responsive to historical circumstance. Marian martyrs, keen to demonstrate Protestantism's biblical authority, imitate Christ by passively accepting death and repeating his words on the cross. Harassed by discriminatory law, Counter-Reformation martyrs seek shelter and legitimacy through the example of Christ's ambiguity, evidence of his—and their—persecuted circumstances. Charles, the king who would be martyr, invokes Christ as the exemplar of the human-divine scapegoat. The genre's specific deployment of *imitatio Christi* demonstrates how the construction of martyrdom is at once rigidly formulaic and subtly responsive, exposing both the persistence of representational structures and the development of the form over time. Charles's engagement with the Christological model reveals the depth and nuance of that typology and its sensitivity to the specific imperatives of his historical moment.

The Davidic Charles

In addition to *imitatio Christi*, one of the most persistent traditional modes of behavioral and narrative martyr construction is typological identification between the victim and biblical and patristic figures of righteous suffering. While *Eikon Basilike* occasionally claims Charles as a type of Job or Abel, it does not invoke the more common New Testament models, Saint Stephen and the apostles, nor the martyrs of the early church. Rather, through explicit allusions and through a far-reaching engagement with the Book of Psalms, *Eikon Basilike* posits a typological symmetry between Charles and an unconventional martyr model, King David. Allusions to Psalms and to the history of David comprise more than a quarter of the total biblical references in *Eikon Basilike*.[13] As Lydia Whitehead has demonstrated, praying the Psalms—especially the Miserere, Psalm 51—was standard procedure for Foxe's martyrs as an expression of penitence in preparation for death.[14] However, David does not function as a comprehensive martyr analogue in either the Catholic or Protestant traditions. Charles's complex appropriation of the Davidic voice demonstrates several key ways *Eikon Basilike* modifies martyrological paradigms to accommodate and justify the figure of Charles.

The analogue between Charles and David, the consummate Old Testament figure of pious penitence, is announced by the frontispiece of the text, which figures Charles in royal attire spurning the crown of state to take up the crown of Christ's Passion (Figure. 6.1). Hannibal Hamlin compares this engraving by William Marshall to the title page Marshall designed for a popular devotional work by Lewis Bayly, *The Practice of Pietie* (7th edition, 1616). Tracing individual iconographic elements of both engravings, Hamlin concludes that both allude to

Figure 6.1. Frontispiece. John Gauden, *Eikon Basilike* (London, 1649).
Reproduced by permission of The Huntington Library, San Marino, California.
RB 121950.

David: "The popularity of Bayly's book suggests that not only was the
image on its title page the model for Marshall's later image of Charles,
but that the later image was intended to recall the former, reinforcing for the reader the general resemblance of Charles to David with a
specific visual allusion."[15] According to Kevin Sharpe, the frontispiece
and its subsequent copies and variations—central to the iconography
of Charles—were sold on their own and reproduced in other polemical literature.[16]

The allusion to David was not lost on either *Eikon Basilike*'s supporters or its detractors. Milton complains that the book is "model'd into the form of a privat Psalter" and that Charles "use[s] presumptuously the words and protestations of *David*, without the spirit and conscience of *David*."[17] Another response to *Eikon Basilike*, titled *The Life and Reigne of King Charls, Or the Pseudo-Martyr discovered* (1651), complains that Charles is "depicted in imitation of *David* in his ejaculations to Heaven . . . the better to stir up the People and vain beholders to pity him."[18] The "industry of extracts, copies, and imitations" described by Sharpe[19] include the *Psalterium Carolinum* (1657), in which John Wilson, Doctor of Music at Oxford, "Rendered in Verse" Charles's prayers and "Set [them] to Musick for 3 Voices, and an Organ, or Theorbo."[20] The devotional popularity of psalters and *Eikon Basilike*'s mimicry of the genre suggest that the book imagines itself as another "private Psalter," offering the meditations of the pious king as a model for shaping the individual's relationship to God.[21]

The text's particular strategies for incorporating Psalms have significant implications for the representation of Charles. The prayer that concludes the chapter titled "Upon the listing, and raising Armies against the KING" is comprised of a string of psalmic borrowings in which Charles ventriloquizes the righteous Davidic voice and subject position: he is the godly king, the "servant" of the Lord who is "upright in heart" but beset by "bloody and deceitful men" (87).[22] Like most of Charles's allusions to specific psalms, these appear in the italicized prayer that follows the roman-face chapter in which the king turns from the reader to directly address God.[23] Within the prayers, however, there are no indications of quotation or allusion, no explicit assignation of Charles's words to the authors of sacred text. Daems and Nelson observe that "by italicizing the concluding section as a whole, the entire prayer—a composite of the biblical and kingly word—appears biblical in origin"; this functions to "identify the words of Charles I with the Word."[24] With no textual indication that Charles is speaking from scripture and assimilating Psalms as his own, the text erases the signs of biblical quotation, so that the words of the Bible seem to flow spontaneously from his mouth. This effect is central to the broader argument of the text, suggesting that scripture is Charles's innate language. Charles speaks like David because he is another David. When he addresses himself to God in prayer, righteousness logically structures that prayer as sacred text.

This Davidic ventriloquization figures Charles in important ways. First, it functions to articulate his unique status as a divinely anointed king by connecting him not merely to a pious figure with whom other would-be martyrs may identify but with the greatest of all biblical monarchs. In so doing, *Eikon Basilike* subtly, persistently makes an argument in defense of the sacred institution of monarchy and in denunciation of the regicide.

Second, because the Book of Psalms was such a foundational element of Christian devotion, these allusions function to link Charles's interior experience with that of his readers. Einar Bjorvand writes: "One of the exegetical traditions that helped to give to the psalms a special place in the generation of religious identities is closely linked to the use of the psalms in private devotion. It is the tradition which sees David (the supposed author of all the psalms) as everyman. He is our representative, like us a sinner in need of grace, lending us a voice whether for supplication or complaint, in contrition and praise."[25] As another David, Charles too is an everyman whose interior relationship to God is voiced through a language he shares with the broader community of English believers.[26] This works as another critical counterargument to the antiroyalist campaign, which sought to posit Charles as a traitor to his people, one whose sympathies were foreign rather than domestic.

Third, as a Davidic figure, Charles becomes an analogue of the pious penitent, especially in the passage in which he invokes Psalm 51. Hamlin identifies Psalm 51 as "the preeminent psalm of penitence. It is the middle psalm, and the most important, of the seven Penitential Psalms (6, 32, 38, 51, 102, 130, 143)," those in which David laments his adultery with Bathsheba and the *de facto* murder of her husband.[27] Charles's adapted version of Psalm 51 appears at the conclusion of the book's second chapter, in which he expresses his regret for consenting to the execution of the Earl of Strafford. This moment—the only one in *Eikon Basilike* in which Charles admits wrongdoing—reveals the text's complicated and equivocal appropriation of the Davidic figure.[28]

King David functions as the model of penitence because despite the fact that he is a mighty king whose actions can be punished by no one but God, he prostrates himself in abject sorrow and responsibility for his actions:

> For I know my transgressions:
>> and my sin is ever before me.
> Against thee, thee only, have I sinned,
>> and done this evil in thy sight,
>> that thou mightest be justified when thou speakest,
>> and be clear when thou judgest.
> Behold, I was shapen in iniquity,
>> and in sin did my mother conceive me. (Psalm 51:3–4)

In its adaptation of these verses, however, *Eikon Basilike* creates a subtle loophole for Charles. Charles declares guilt for signing Strafford's death warrant but claims that his motives were pure—that he "was persuaded by shedding one man's blood to prevent after-troubles" (57). Those who urged Strafford's death emerge as the more guilty parties for demanding an action that put Charles at odds with his own faultless conscience. Hamlin elaborates:

> The near quotation of verses 3, 14, 4, and 7 of Psalm 51 aligns Charles with David as a divinely appointed and favored king, sinful but repentant, to be left to the judgment of God rather than men. Or at least, since he had already been judged and executed by men, to be mourned as a martyr to godless regicides. There is some deviousness in this strategy, visible first in the clause added to Ps. 51:4, "for Thou sawest the contradiction between my heart and my hand." This evasion of responsibility is entirely in contradiction to the pervasive emphasis in Psalm 51 on the *corruption* of the heart and everything else human.[29]

As Hamlin goes on to point out, this strategy itself obfuscates another, broader evasion. It was not for his abandonment of Strafford that Charles was condemned and executed for treason, nor was his assent to Strafford's death popularly criticized.[30] Charles's equivocal confession of this dubious sin functions to deflect graver questions of guilt. In this way, *Eikon Basilike* demonstrates a careful and selective deployment of Davidic typology. Charles fulfills the model of regal, Davidic penitence without condemning himself for Davidic transgression.

The Interior Witness

The ordeals that comprise early church martyrology turn on the victims' refusal to perform acts contrary to Christian law, namely sacrificing to pagan idols. The confrontation between victim and persecutor that ensues is thus fundamentally religious in nature, providing the victim an opportunity to perform his or her commitment to the Christian faith through confession and death. The Marian heresy trials that set the terms of conflict in Foxe's *Acts and Monuments* initiate this same opportunity, structuring the confrontation between killer and killed as explicitly religious in nature. By contrast, Queen Elizabeth's recourse to the treason trial as the legal apparatus for managing Catholic dissidence changed the terms of the conflict in ways that impede the occasion to witness. Bereft of the circumstances that had previously produced the acts of witnessing central to a martyr story, figures like Campion, Southwell, Garnet, and Gerard were caught in a transitional moment in which martyrological discourse had not yet developed viable adaptive strategies or alternative modes of construction. Counter-Reformation martyrology demonstrates that when the opportunity for religious confession is compromised, the narrative production of the martyr figure—historically defined by that very confession—is likewise significantly impaired.

Given the degree to which acts of religious witnessing are foundational to successful iterations of Christian martyrdom, how can a king executed for treason hope to inscribe himself into the genre of martyrology? *Eikon Basilike* makes only a nominal attempt to replicate the crucial structural component of religious confession and persecution. In chapter 17, "Of the differences between the KING and the two Houses, in point of Church-Government," Charles defends episcopacy against the pressure favoring decentralized, presbyterian church organization. More precisely, he defends his defense of episcopacy, invoking scriptural support for the bishopric and referring his opinion to the apostolic model of the primitive church. Charles argues that the power of the bishops is descended from "divine right"; those who seek other forms of church government are therefore "perverse Disputers, proud Usurpers, against true Episcopacy: who, if they be not Traitors and Boasters, yet they seem very covetous, heady, high-minded; inordinate and fierce, lovers of themselves, having much of the form, little of the power of godliness" (138). This argument sets the promoters of presbyterian church government not merely against Charles but against God, such that their desire to end episcopacy "is no less sin, than Sacrilege; or a robbery of GOD" (143). Further, as the defender of divinely established church hierarchy, Charles suffers in defense of the faith against those who threaten it. This conflict sets up the terms of martyrdom, which the text then witnesses through imagery of Charles as the faithful victim tortured by irreligious persecutors: "Yet upon this Rack chiefly have I been held so long, by some men's ambitious Covetousness, and sacrilegious Cruelty; torturing (with Me) both Church and State, in Civil dissentions" (144). In the prayer at the end of the chapter, Charles claims martyrdom more explicitly by declaring, "Thou, O Lord, seest how much I have suffered with, and for thy Church" (146).

In chapter 19, "Upon the various events of the War; Victories, and Defeats," Charles's discussion of martyrdom invokes similar paradigms but also reveals these paradigms to be in radical flux. Charles seeks to contradict the claim made by "some parasitic Preachers [who] have dared to call those Martyrs, who died fighting against Me, the Laws, their Oaths, and the Religion Established" (151). The fact that the term "martyr" has been used to describe soldiers enlisted against Charles suggests an expansion of the martyr discourse to incorporate deaths that are not explicitly related to individual faith or acts of religious witnessing. In response, Charles rehearses a version of the Augustine martyrological argument, *non poena sed causa* ("the cause, not the death"): "But sober Christians know, That glorious Title [of martyr], can with Truth be applied only to those, who sincerely preferred God's Truth, and their duty in all these particulars before their lives, and all that was dear to them in this world. . . . The destruction of their bodies being sanctified, as a means to save their Souls. Their wounds, and temporal ruin serving as a gracious opportunity for their eternal health and happiness" (151). While the basic argument here—that it is the cause, not the death, that sanctifies the wounds and the wounded—is conventional, in Charles's case it is both unconventionally applied and unconventionally conceived. Traditionally, *non poena sed causa* is invoked by confessionally motivated polemicists to dispute alternative theological claims—to argue that martyrdom cannot be constructed from the defense of heretical beliefs. Interestingly, Charles does not argue that the soldiers' deaths are not religious, which would effectively contradict the diluted, broadly inclusive notion of martyrdom that would justify them. Rather, Charles avoids this issue altogether by invoking *non poena sed causa*. In so doing, however, he makes a subtle but crucial adjustment in the central act that defines martyrdom. Instead of professing God's truth—the essential act of Christian martyrdom—the martyr defined by *Eikon Basilike* merely "prefer[s] God's Truth." The shift from profession to preference marks a significant development in the very concept of martyrdom from an exchange that takes place in social space to one that is negotiated in the heart and mind of the believer. Both acts require the suffering, but the cause that makes the martyr shifts in Charles's definition from the exterior, visible action of professing to the interior, invisible action of preferring.

In *Eikon Basilike,* the conscience becomes the site where that preference is articulated. The final sentence of chapter 17 reads, "And in this integrity both of My Judgement and Conscience, I hope God will preserve Me." The prayer that follows opens with, "For Thou, O Lord, knowst my uprightness, and tenderness, as thou hast set me to be a Defender of the Faith, and a Protector of thy Church, so suffer me not by any violence, to be overborne against my Conscience" (145). Both sentences situate Charles's conscience—not the church or any point of faith—as the sacred institution under attack. It is the "integrity" of Charles's "Judgement and Conscience" that must be preserved. Lacking the grounds to claim an explicitly religious persecution, *Eikon*

Basilike situates the sacred not in the conventional loci of transcendent authority—the Bible and the teachings of the church—but in the individual conscience. *Eikon Basilike* reconstitutes the category of the sacred within the conscience, then implicitly argues that dying for the sacred—not in defense of religious tenets—is what makes a martyrdom. In this way, the text marks an important shift in the martyrological genre, a moment of transition from a narrowly religious discourse to a broadly conscientious discourse.

The King's Conscience

Charles's defense of his conscience unto death functions as his principal act of martyrdom, as in the claim that his death is "a kind of Martyrdom, as to the testimony of My own Conscience" (188). While *Eikon Basilike* positions him as a Christ figure whose death is necessary to the preservation of the kingdom, even more consistently the text emphasizes Charles's unwillingness to act against his conscience. In several places, he prioritizes the demands of conscience over those of England: "the best rule of policy is to prefer . . . the peace of My Conscience before the preservation of My Kingdoms" (55); "I know no resolutions more worthy a Christian King, than to prefer His Conscience before His Kingdoms" (72); "I should not so much weaken my outward state of a King; as wound that inward quiet of my Conscience, which ought to be, is, and ever shall be (by God's grace) dearer to me than my Kingdoms" (94).

Charles's preference for a clean conscience over political peace replicates a familiar martyrological formulation in which the victim rebuffs wordly trappings in preference of spiritual reward. The family, whose demands the Christian is otherwise bound to honor (especially in the case of parents) constitutes a form of interference—a kind of spiritual static—that presents a potential conflict of obligations. Charles's narrative is structured in similar terms, setting up a tension between "the peace of [his] Conscience" and "the preservation of [his] Kingdoms" that mirrors the martyr's conventional conflict between duty to God and family. Positioned between his obligations as England's patriarch and his obligations to God, Charles defends a righteous path in contradiction to the obligations impressed by his kingdom. This is the choice announced by the frontispiece, in which Charles spurns the royal crown under foot, embraces the crown of thorns, and looks hopefully toward the crown of heavenly glory. The visibility of this conventional martyrological topos, however, must not shift our attention away from the unconventional nature of Charles's "prefer[ence]"—to return to his word for describing the martyr's defining act. Unlike conventional martyrs, who spurn their families to witness to points of theology or doctrine, Charles spurns his kingdom to witness to his own conscience.

To understand the implications of this substitution of individual conscience in the discourse of religious doctrine, we must understand how the conscience functions in Caroline metaphysics and political philosophy. In a dense passage in the prayer that concludes chapter 11, Charles articulates the relationship between God, human understanding, and the conscience: "O thou first and eternal Reason, whose wisdom is fortified with omnipotency, furnish thy Servant, first with clear discoveries of Truth, Reason, and Justice, in My Understanding: then so confirm My will and resolution to adhere to them, that no terrors, injuries, or oppressions of my Enemies may ever enforce me against those rules, which thou by them hast planted in My Conscience" (100). Human understanding operates as a surrogate of divine Reason, "first and eternal," and provides us with "clear discoveries" or "rules" to guide decision making. These are "planted" in the conscience by the work of "Truth, Reason, and Justice." Charles's explication of these metaphysical relations indicates both the divine origins of conscience's judgments and the crucial role played by the individual—by our "understanding."[31]

These relations are echoed in mainstream Protestant casuistry of the period. In *A Discourse of Conscience*, William Perkins, a contemporary of Charles, maps the medial place of conscience between human and divine: "conscience is of a divine nature, and is a thing placed of God in the middest betweene him and man, as an arbitratour to give sentence & to pronounce either with man or against man unto God."[32] Conscience is both "a little God"—the voice of the divine within the human—and an aspect of the individual, for "every particular man hath his owne particular conscience."[33] Indeed, as is suggested by Perkins's *Discourse of Conscience,* by his lengthier *Whole Treatise of Cases of the Conscience,* and by the countless other serpentine works of seventeenth-century casuistical divinity, solving matters of conscience is not as simple as reading the direct word of God.[34] Rather, conscience functions as an interpreter between the word of God and the unique individual, whose specific circumstances form one of the primary documents of conscience's evaluative work. Thus when Charles refers to the imperatives of his conscience, he is gesturing not just to the sacred, inviolable "little God" within but to a sacred, inviolable element of the self. Indeed, the sacredness of the conscience is confirmed by the fact that it is a sin to act against it.[35]

Charles's existential position as divinely anointed king constellates a particular set of relations between God, himself, his conscience, and his kingdom. Sharpe writes,

> The conscience, Charles told Alexander Henderson, was God's "vicegerent"; and as God's vicegerent on earth, the king's duty was to be the conscience of his people. . . . The king's conscience then was never in theory at odds with his practice of government; it was the essence of his kingship. "To look to my own conscience," Charles put it, was "the faithful discharge of my trust as a king." Those who advised Charles to compromise his conscience on certain matters so as to preserve his throne sought to separate what he saw as inviolably married: his conscience and his regality. . . . In compromising his conscience, the king surrendered, along with his regality, his trust, his honour, his very humanity. Matters of conscience could not be negotiated or treated, because the conscience was "more dear" than life.[36]

According to Sharpe, Charles's conscience functions as "vicegerent" over not only himself but his kingdoms, such that the conscience of the king operates as the conscience of the kingdom. Because Charles's political philosophy is grounded in an explicitly religious ethics—one that posits conscience as the divinely informed foundation of just kingship—his deferral to conscience necessarily constellates the regal self, the conscience, and the institution of monarchy as sacred by virtue of their declension from the divine.

Whereas traditional constructions of martyrdom hinge on the defense of faith to sacralize death, *Eikon Basilike*'s construction of martyrdom constitutes the sacred in territory merely contiguous to the divine: in kingship, conscience, and the self. In this way, the text reifies the individual as a locus of sacred authority—as a generator of individual truths and commandments whose denial constitutes sin. The cause that constructs death as martyrdom becomes relocated from a fundamentally doctrinal or theological discourse to a discourse of individual conscience. Additionally, the death itself plays a pivotal role in sacralizing that conscience, as Girard's precept reminds us: "Because the victim is sacred, it is criminal to kill him—but the victim is sacred only because he is to be killed."[37] Charles's claim that he dies in defense of his conscience situates conscience within the sacralizing relations between victim and violence that Girard describes. The sacredness of Charles's conscience is affirmed by the fact that it must be violently subdued. The construction of a causal connection between the violence done to Charles and the integrity of Charles's conscience is thus one of the central projects of *Eikon Basilike*.

The Problem of Disclosure

In addition to radically revising the basic terms of the martyr's cause, the discourse of conscience reintroduces the problems of transparency and disclosure that proved so troubling for Counter-Reformation martyrology. As chapters 3, 4, and 5 have shown, the introduction of the treason charge as the principal mode of managing Catholic dissidence short-circuited opportunities for defendants to perform the acts of religious witnessing central to both the rehearsal of legible martyrdom and the construction of martyrological texts. This was further complicated by the secretive practices of the Catholic mission, especially the doctrine of equivocation, which provided interior hiding spaces that obscured the individual from public view. Charles's referral throughout *Eikon Basilike* to the truth and dictates of his conscience raises this same set of potential problems. The conscience, like

Desdemona's honor, is an invisible "essence that's not seen."[38] Unlike a set of religious doctrines or affiliations, both of which can be articulated under interrogation, the text of conscience is the self speaking to itself within the hidden recesses of the self. How can this text produce a legible document of martyrdom?

Christian casuistry's terms for describing the operations of conscience indicate a symmetry with martyrological discourse; at the same time they introduce a particular set of challenges for martyr construction. Just as the martyr's declarations bear external witness to his or her interior faith, "the conscience also bears witness" to the self and of the self (Romans 2:15); it is "the testimony of our conscience" that tells us whether we have acted justly (2 Corinthians 1:12). Perkins's anatomy of the conscience relies heavily on these Pauline notions of witnessing, testimony, and declaration, also central to acts of martyrdom. According to Perkins, the primary function of conscience is to "bear[e] witnes of our secret thoughts" and "discover all" to ourselves.[39]

However, Perkins's discussion of witnessing also suggests why conscience is not an ideal text from which to construct martyrdom. Perkins stresses the closed nature of this text, which can be read only by the individual and God.

> *Scire*, to know, is of one man alone by himselfe: and *conscire* is, when two at the least knowe some one secret thing; either of them knowing it together with the other. Therefore the name συνείδησις, or *conscientia*, Conscience, is that thing that combines two togither, and makes them partners in the knowledge of one and the same secret. Now man and man, or man and Angel cannot be combined; because they cannot know the secret of any man unlesse it be revealed to them: it remains therefore that this combination is onely betweene man and God. God knows perfectly all the doings of man, though they be never so hid and concealed: and man by a gift given him of God; knowes togither with God, the same things of himselfe: and this gift is named Conscience.[40]

Perkins's explication of the term "*conscientia*" articulates the "secret" nature of what conscience knows. That which is "hid and concealed" from angels and other humans is a knowledge shared between the individual and God. While Perkins goes on to say that conscience "discover[s] all" and "may beare witnes even of thoughts," he repeatedly emphasizes the interiority and hiddenness of this witness and discovery. What conscience does, "it doth inwardly & secretly whithin the heart." Given the limitations of what other humans or even angels can know, conscience functions in Perkins's formulation as proof of the very existence of God: "And to whom is [conscience] a witnesse? to men or Angels? that cannot be, for they cannot heare the voice of conscience, that cannot receive consciences testimonie, nay they cannot see what is in the heart of man. It remaines therefore that there is a spirituall substance, most wise, most holy, most mightie, that sees all things, to whom conscience beares a record, & that is God himself."[41] Maintaining conscience's essential function as "witnesse," "voice," "testimony," and "record," Perkins elaborates a closed discursive circle in which God is the only being outside the self who can "heare," "receive," and "see" it.

If conscience is the new locus of the sacred—the text worth dying for—the secret nature of that text presents complications for constructing martyrdom. Conscience is invisible and illegible to all outside the self. But martyrdom cannot be achieved by a cipher, as Counter-Reformation martyrology demonstrates. The construction of martyrdom depends on the exteriorization and legibility—the public "witnesse" and "testimony"—of the heart of the victim, particularly in circumstances when an alternative text of the heart is being asserted, as in the injunction to "behold the heart of a traitor." Thus, while conscience's role as witness maps it easily into the paradigms of martyrological discourse, its inaccessibility poses inherent challenges to the legible reproduction of martyrdom.

Eikon Basilike brings anxiety about this illegibility to the surface while developing a number of strategies for making Charles's conscience known to his readers. Charles expresses awareness of equivocation's power to undermine claims about the interior contents of conscience. Addressing his decision to pass the Bill for the Triennial Parliaments, he writes, "yet I need no secret distinctions or evasions before God. Nor had I any reservations in My own Soul, when I passed it" (67). Later he takes care to remark that his prayers "[go] not out of feigned lips" (178). In contrast to the equivocator, who takes shelter in a privileged, private discursive space shared only with God, *Eikon Basilike* seeks to disclose the contents of that space by denying any discrepancy between what escapes Charles's lips and what resides in Charles's soul. Charles is not just concerned about being perceived as an evasive or dishonest text, however; he also recognizes the potential problem of being altogether unreadable—of being an indecipherable, ambiguous signifier. He prays, "Suffer not my silence to betray mine innocence," expressing concern about precisely the kind of interpretive conundrum produced by a figure like Margaret Clitherow, whose reluctance to disclose her motives led to semiotic and discursive ambiguity (129). Charles's prayer invokes the signifying potential of passive, silent suffering in the context of a project— *Eikon Basilike*—in which he is insistently and strategically voicing himself.

If the primary problem posed by conscience is the closedness of its discursive space, then the construction of martyrdom upon the defense of conscience depends on opening that space to public view—on creating an audience outside of Charles and God. This is one of the principal functions of the prayers in *Eikon Basilike*: they create the impression of inwardness being exteriorized—of the private dialogue between Charles and God disclosed for others to see. The text at once emphasizes the inaccessible nature of the human heart and seeks to make that heart available to the reader. Charles begins his prayer at the end of chapter 3 with, "But thou, O Lord, art my witness in heaven, and in my Heart," and addresses God as "Thou that seest not as man seeth, but lookest beyond all popular appearances, searching the heart, and trying the reins, and bringing to light the hidden things of darkness" (59).[42] These moments emphasize the privacy and inaccessibility of the contents of conscience at the same time that they discover the conscience in confessional dialogue with God. Indeed, the text's insistence on the secrecy of conscience is one of the key ways *Eikon Basilike* constructs the legitimacy of its own disclosures: our access to the private place of Charles's conscience is access to the truth of his character and kingship precisely because it is private. As Charles prays, we "witness" with God "the hidden things" within Charles's heart.

Charles's very capacity to pray functions rhetorically to construct the truth of the heart that prays: "Nor am I without that Integrity, and Peace before God, as with humble confidence to address My Prayer to Him" (86). Here what is visible "before God" is fully exteriorized by the action (and subsequent publication) of his prayer, such that praying itself operates as a proof text of the king's "Integrity" and "Peace." The invocation of God's punishment likewise works to ratify the conscience exposed by the text. Charles prays to God that if he has been the occasion of the wars, "let thy hand be against me, and my Father's house. O Lord, thou seest I have enemies enough of men; as I need not, so should I not dare thus to imprecate thy curse on me and mine, if my Conscience did not witness my integrity, which thou O Lord knowst right well" (108). By inviting divine judgment on Charles's actions and inviting the reader into this weighty transaction between Charles and his Maker, the prayer situates Charles in a confessional crucible designed to enforce truth. The conscience that witnesses to Charles's integrity is exposed to the reader, who shares, through the text, what the "Lord knowst right well." Through this mechanism, the reader is brought into the secret discourse between Charles, his conscience, and God.

By representing Charles in this intimate moment of conversation with God, who sees all things, the text enlists God as witness to his utterance. This positioning of God as witness is one element of *Eikon Basilike*'s systematic invitation to the reader to share what "God knows." This phrase is repeated throughout the text, in one place appearing four times within four paragraphs (66–67). It often introduces abstract direct objects — "God knows" Charles's "motives," "design," "intent" — that are not explicitly disclosed by his actions (58). Thus in referring to what "God knows," the text positions its audience as witnesses of the inward content usually reserved for God's all-seeing eye. Like the text's concern about the coherence of the soul and lips, this invitation to share the privileged knowledge of God contravenes the impulses of equivocation. Rather than claiming shelter in the private discursive space mapped by equivocation, *Eikon Basilike* seeks — at least rhetorically — to open that space to the reader's gaze.[43]

The Domesticated King

The other significant element of the text's argument for transparency is its invitation of the reader into Charles's private, domestic life. The chapter titled "Upon the Queen's departure, and absence out of England" moves beyond Charles's and Henrietta Maria's political roles to reveal an intimate marital bond. Within the chapter itself, Charles never refers to Henrietta Maria as "the Queen" but only as his "Wife." The effect of this is to deemphasize her public identity in favor of a domestic, marital, and romantic identity. This, in turn, posits Charles as a husband rather than merely as a king. He expresses his attachment to her in unabashedly romantic language, declaring, "I am content to be tossed, weather-beaten, and shipwrecked, so as she may be in safe Harbour. This comfort I shall enjoy by her safety in the midst of my Personal dangers, that I can perish but half, if she be preserved" (74). Charles declares his confidence in the love that his wife has for him as a man, not as king—a love that remains steadfast despite his downfallen state: "Her sympathy with Me in My afflictions, will make her virtues shine with greater lustre, as stars in the darkest nights; and assure the envious world, that she loves Me, not My fortunes" (75).[44] The effect of these moments is to pull back the curtain of Charles's regal identity to expose the private and faithful figure behind.

While these personal disclosures are deployed strategically in *Eikon Basilike,* the book likewise suggests Charles's desire to maintain when and how his person is revealed. He expresses deep offense at Parliament's publication of the letters between himself and the queen that were captured at the Battle of Naseby. Charles calls this publication, a book titled *The King's Cabinet Opened,* an "odious divulging" and declares it "wholly barbarous" to imagine that every person does not deserve privacy, "nor is there any thing more inhuman than to expose [his papers] to public view" (159). At the same time that he complains of Parliament's "malicious intentions," he declares his desire that his subjects know his inmost person: "I am content so much of My heart (which I study to approve to God's omniscience) should be discovered to the world, without any of those dresses, or popular captations, which some men use in their Speeches, and Expresses; I wish My Subjects had yet a clearer sight into My most retired thoughts" (159-60). Even though Charles claims that all the letters disclose is "My constancy to My Wife, the Laws, and Religion," his objections register a significant distinction between the kind of private disclosure he makes in his chapter on the queen's departure and Parliament's campaign to discredit him—"to have rendered [him] as a Vile Person, not fit to be trusted or considered, under any Notion of Majesty" (160, 162).

Joad Raymond's discussion of the publication of Charles's private correspondence uses the word "expose" to describe the effect of *The King's Cabinet Opened.* The word is not unlike "discover," which Charles himself uses in reference to his desire to reveal himself to his people. But "expose" implies that the agency of disclosure has been shifted away from Charles to his detractors. Charles expresses the desire for full disclosure throughout *Eikon Basilike,* but his objection to being exposed by *The King's Cabinet Opened* indicates how carefully managed the text's discoveries are and how important it is that Charles maintain agency over the act of revelation. In other words, the text's transparency is conditional. Having lost control of his public image through the publication of his letters, Charles uses the discursive space of *Eikon Basilike* to defend and reconstitute himself.

As it turned out, even the exposures wrought by *The King's Cabinet Opened* came to work to Charles's benefit. While Charles's detractors insisted that the letters exposed a man unfit to rule—especially given his intimacy with the queen, who "though she be of the weaker sexe, borne an Alien, bred up in a contrary Religion, yet nothing great or small is transacted without her privity & consent"—royalists were appalled by the "unprecedented" and unseemly invasion of the king's privacy.[45] The result, Raymond notes, was that the scandal "backfired" by rendering human and vulnerable a king who had historically "sought to enhance the mystery and majesty of kingship by distance and inaccessibility."[46] Sharpe writes: "This was no longer the monarch mysteriously distant from his subjects, but a man, a husband, flawed but human, with whom other mortals could empathize."[47] This humanity and vulnerability, iterated throughout the prayers and reflections of *Eikon Basilike,* formed the foundations of the cult of Charles's royal martyrdom.

Milton Responds

The rhetorical power of *Eikon Basilike* resides in what Lana Cable has called "the triumph of style over substance."[48] Its historical claims are secondary to its emotional appeal—to its construction of a sympathetic figure beset by enemies who seek to divide him from his conscience and from his queen. It was the book's emotional resonance with which Milton had mainly to contend in responding to the claims of *Eikon Basilike*. Commissioned by the new commonwealth as a response to this troubling representation of Charles, Milton's *Eikonoklastes* (October 1649) methodically retraces the events discussed by *Eikon Basilike*, answering each of the book's chapters with one of its own. Milton urges his audience to attend to the cold, hard facts of Charles's reign and not to be manipulated by *Eikon Basilike*'s affective cues. As Thomas N. Corns observes, "Milton's text works to kill emotion."[49] While the aim of *Eikon Basilike* is to unfold the king's vulnerable, pious, and conscientious inner person through a series of self-referential gestures, the project of *Eikonoklastes*, or "Idol-breaker," is to argue that the subject of those reflexive gestures is not the unvarnished, unselfconscious Charles whom "God knows" and "God sees" but, rather, a set of discursive manipulations. There is nothing transparent in *Eikon Basilike*, Milton argues, apart from its manifest sophistry. The strategy of *Eikonoklastes* is to train the reader's eye on the Charles constructed by the events of his reign rather than on the slippery figure outlined by *Eikon Basilike*.

In contradiction to *Eikon Basilike*'s impulse to conflate Charles's regal and personal identities, Milton insists on their strict separation. Charles's domestic disclosures may have a humanizing effect, but Milton argues the inappropriateness of this information and enlists it to weaken the figure of the dead king. "[W]hat concernes it us," he asks, "to hear a Husband divulge his Houshold privacies, extolling to others the vertues of his Wife; an infirmity not seldom incident to those who have least cause[?]" (419). For Milton, this disclosure is evidence of neither the king's nor the queen's particular virtue but of an unseemly intrusion of the private into the public sphere. For similar reasons and with characteristic edge, Milton likewise attacks Charles's closing address, "To the Prince of Whales": "What the King wrote to his Son, as a Father, concerns not us; what he wrote to him, as a King of *England,* concerns not him; God and the Parlament having now otherwise dispos'd of *England*" (568).

The intimacy between Charles and Henrietta Maria disclosed by both *Eikon Basilike* and *The King's Cabinet Opened* serves as an entry point for *Eikonoklastes*'s attack on Charles's fitness for kingship, specifically his masculinity. Rather than be guided by Parliament, "the great Counsel of his Kingdom," Charles is governed by "one Woman" whom Milton declares the king's "Regent" (421, 526). Milton laments the "great mischeif and dishonour hath befall'n to Nations under the Government of effeminate and Uxorious Magistrates"; a king under such domestic influence, "govern'd and overswaid at home under a Feminine usurpation, cannot but be farr short of spirit and autority without dores, to govern a whole Nation" (421). Indeed, he claims, Charles's *"constancy to his wife* is set in place before Laws and Religion" (541). This line of argument is consistent with the broader misogynist strain of *Eikonoklastes,* which systematically represents the Caroline court as debauched and ineffectual under of the influence of women and unmanly men. Milton doubts whether "there were any Males among" the "dissolute rabble of all his Courtiers . . . , both hees and shees" (455). He cites feminine influence as both a symptom and cause of national ills—"the certain sign of a dissolute, degenerat, and pusillanimous Common-wealth" (370).

Charles's domestic disclosures likewise provide an opening for the anti-Catholic theme that animates *Eikonoklastes.* Milton claims that "it is op'nly known that [the queen's] Religion wrought more upon him, then his Religion upon her, and his op'n favouring of Papists, and his hatred of them call'd Puritans, made most men suspect she had quite perverted him" (422). The association between Charles and "perver[se]" Catholicism operates as a device for discrediting not just the king but the King's Book, which Milton likewise tarnishes with Catholic sensibilities. He translates its title as "The King's Image; and by the Shrine he dresses out for him, certainly, would have the people come and worship him," for the book encourages the "inconstant, irrational, and Image-doting rabble" toward "a civil kinde of Idolatry"

(343, 601, 343). In an effort to taint them with Catholic practice, Milton uses the word "rosary" to describe Charles's prayers, a foundational element of *Eikon Basilike*'s rhetorical design (364). By associating Charles and *Eikon Basilike* with the beliefs and practices of Catholicism, Milton posits the reader who is sympathetic to *Eikon Basilike* as prey to the text's dangerous, idolatrous manipulations.

Milton on Conscience

For Milton, the influence of femininity and Catholicism on Charles's domestic life and on his role as a Protestant king points to an egregious weakness in Charles's kingship: his habitual conflation of public and private identities. This complaint also underwrites *Eikonoklastes*'s emphatic critique of Charles's conscientious discourse. Apart from disclosing Charles's misgivings about Strafford and his reluctance to disenfranchise the bishops, *Eikon Basilike* is generally vague on what Charles's conscience bids him do. He prefers the peace of his conscience to the preservation of his kingdoms, but the text is seldom explicit about how and why these conflict. Rather, it treats the imperatives of conscience, whatever they be, as themselves sacred and inviolable. Casuistical texts like Perkins's *Discourse of Conscience* implicitly support this position by warning that it is a sin to act against one's conscience. However, Perkins also writes at length about how conscience can be led astray, and he declares that following the dictates of an erroneous conscience is a sin.[50] It is this aspect of casuistical discourse that underlies Milton's reply. Charles's claims of conscience are no justification for his behavior, Milton argues, because "he hath given over to delusion; [his] very mind and conscience is defil'd" (368). Charles's is an "ill edifi'd" and "self-will'd conscience . . . especially in the deniall of that which Law and his regal Office by Oath bids him to grant to his Parlament, and whole Kingdom rightfully demanding" (418). The peace of conscience Charles seeks above his kingdom's preservation is "the flattering peace of an erroneous and obdurat conscience" (434–35). According to Milton, even the passages of *Eikon Basilike* that appear to represent genuine interior conflict are misleading, such as Charles's misgivings over Strafford's death. Charles does not repent having given an innocent man over to execution but having "given up to just punishment so stout a Champion of his designes, who might have bin so usefull to him in his following civil Broiles. It was a worldly repentance not a conscientious" (373). By Milton's account, Charles not only relies on the guidance of a bad conscience but manipulates the discourses of conscience and repentance to cover nefarious intent.

Even more infuriating for Milton are the political hierarchies implied by Charles's conscientious claims, because they articulate precisely what is intolerable about Charles's form of monarchical rule. Milton refers the reader to Charles's coronation oath, in which the king "was never sworn to his own particular conscience and reason, but to our conditions as a free people; which requir'd him to give us such Laws as our selves shall choose" (519). The claims of Charles's individual conscience, central to the sacralizing claims of *Eikon Basilike,* have no place in questions of national politics, Milton complains: "And thus the welfare, the safety, and within a little, the unanimous demand of three populous Nations to have attended still on the singularity of one mans opinionated conscience; if men had always bin so tame and spiritless; and had not unexpectedly found the grace to understand, that if his conscience were so narrow and peculiar to it self, it was not fitt his Authority should be so ample and Universall over others. For certainly a privat conscience sorts not with a public Calling; but declares that Person rather meant by nature for a privat fortune" (368–69). While *Eikon Basilike* seeks to justify Charles—and monarchy more generally—by publicly disclosing the interior of the king, Milton argues the fundamental inappropriateness of precisely that move, insisting on the separation between the king's public and private identities. For Milton, Charles's referral of political questions to his "privat conscience" in itself demonstrates his unfitness for "a public Calling." Indeed, Charles's desire to rule the country by "the privat and overweening Reason of one obstinat Man" marks him as "an Instrument of Tyranny" and England "by consequence no Common-wealth, nor free; but a multitude of Vassalls in the Possession and domaine of one absolute Lord" (416, 373, 458).[51]

Milton contests not only Charles's claims to the righteousness of his conscience but the topoi of transparency by which that conscience is disclosed to the reader. He disputes the text's basic claim to be "The Portraiture of His Sacred Majestie in His Solitudes and Sufferings," arguing that, on the contrary, *Eikon Basilike* is a piece of royalist propaganda that shamelessly enlists the topoi of pious meditation to manipulate a gullible public. It is "the cunning drift of a factious and defeated Party" intended for "the promoting of thir own future designes" (338). Anticipating the diction and phonic effects *Paradise Lost* would employ, Milton posits Charles as a Satanic figure full of "suttle dissimulation"—the master manipulator who "presents [his actions] speciously and fraudulently to impose upon the simple Reader; and seeks by smooth and supple words . . . to make som beneficial use or other ev'n of his worst miscarriages" (376–77).[52] Invoking the language of anti-Catholic polemic to link Charles with the reviled figure of the Jesuit priest, Milton describes the King's Book as a "[f]abric" of "equivocal repentences," of "shifts and evasions"—a text of "Jesuitical slight" in which Charles "seemes not one, but double" (350, 373, 545, 526, 371). Indeed, he suggests, *Eikon Basilike* exceeds these models of "craft and affectation" by finding yet "a newer method of Antichristian fraud" (482, 510).

"A Peece of Poetrie"

Beyond the factual misrepresentations that Milton claims, *Eikonoklastes* takes particular issue with Charles's engagement with sacred text. In its systematic ventriloquism of Psalms, *Eikon Basilike* posits sacred text as a transparent medium for exposing the heart of the king, suggesting that because it represents dialogue between a soul and God, it is inherently sincere. Milton responds with a version of a line Shakespeare's Antonio speaks to Shylock, "The devil can cite Scripture for his purpose"[53]: "It is not hard for any man, who hath a Bible in his hands, to borrow good words and holy sayings in abundance; but to make them his own, is a work of grace onely from above. He borrows heer many penitential Verses out of *Davids* Psalmes. So did many among those Israelites, who had revolted from the true worship of God, *invent to themselves instruments of music like David*, and probably Psalmes also like his, and yet the Profet *Amos* complaines heavily against them" (553–54). In Milton's analogy, Charles's psalms function not to disclose but to obscure: they are "borrow[ed]" for the purpose of dishonest self-"invent[ion]." This kind of "Psalmistry," as he calls it, is evidence of corruption rather than piety, for "the deepest policy of a Tyrant hath bin ever to counterfet Religious" (360–61). Milton counts *Eikon Basilike* as merely another "salable peece of English Divinity, that the Shops value," like the "lip-work of every Prelatical Liturgist, clapt together, and quilted out of Scripture phrase" (360).

The term "lip-work" articulates what Milton sees as a crucial discrepancy between the Davidic heart and the Caroline text. In answer to *Eikon Basilike*'s strategic deployment of Psalms to expose Charles's interior conscientious sincerity, Milton argues that Charles "use[s] presumptuously the words and protestations of *David*, without the spirit and conscience of *David*" (381–82). The text manifests a basic incongruity between words and deeds, he complains: the king is "transported with the vain ostentation of imitating *Davids* language, not his life" (555). As Achsah Guibbory observes, Milton thus sees Charles's prayers as "'counterfet' in two senses: the piety is mere pretence, and the words, stolen from others, are passed off as the real thing."[54] More broadly, Milton seeks to undermine *Eikon Basilike*'s basic rhetorical assumption that the discourse of prayer constructs the individual in naked conversation with God. Representing Charles at prayer does not guarantee the sincerity of the prayer, Milton insists. On the contrary, Charles "abuses the words of *David*, and dissembles grossly eev'n to the very face of God" (555). The fact that Charles's prayers were "writt'n to be divulg'd" makes them even more suspect than that which is "pray'd in secret" (601). When Milton himself invokes Psalms in the closing moments of *Eikonoklastes*, it is this disconnect between heart and tongue that he cites: the Israelites "*flatter[ed] [God] with thir mouth, and ly'd to him with thir tongues; for thir heart was not right with him*" (600).[55] For Charles, as for the Israelites, prayer is merely "the outward work of Devotion" that does not necessarily represent the interior heart (362).

Thus in Milton's reading, *Eikon Basilike* misappropriates the language of prayer into a form of equivocation. For Milton, Charles's prayer is a discursive disguise, a hiding hole much like those used by the Jesuits: it may look like a respectable country manor from the outside, but its interior spaces harbor secret truths and hypocrisies. This concern with Charles's prayers as "equivocal repentences" and "lip-work" articulates a broader suspicion of linguistic construction that emerges as a central theme of *Eikonoklastes* (373). One of the primary ways this suspicion is expressed is through Milton's criticism of *Eikon Basilike* as a literary object—one that at times comes "almost to Sonnetting" (421). Milton attacks the text's sundry poetic flourishes, arguing their inappropriateness to political subjects: "The Simily wherewith he begins I was about to have found fault with, as in a garb somewhat more Poetical then for a Statist: but meeting with many straines of like dress in other of his Essaies, and hearing him reported a more diligent reader of Poets, then of Politicians, I begun to think that the whole Book might perhaps be intended a peece of Poetrie. The words are good, the fiction smooth and cleanly; there wanted only Rime, and that, they say, is bestow'd upon it lately" (406). Milton's suggestion that *Eikon Basilike* is "a peece of Poetrie" rather than the work of a "Statist" uses "poetry" as a pejorative term, a sarcastic insult to a text that clearly imagines itself more objective. In his preface to *Paradise Lost,* Milton would later note "vulgar readers[']" desire for rhyme; for Milton, the addition of this "modern bondage"[56] in adaptations like the *Psalterium Carolinum* merely increases *Eikon Basilike*'s already built-in appeal to what *Eikonoklastes* disdainfully calls the "miserable, credulous, deluded thing that creature is, which is call'd the Vulgar" (426). And *Eikon Basilike* isn't just poetry, Milton argues; it's bad poetry. In the tone of cultural and aesthetic superiority that pervades *Eikonoklastes,* he belittles Charles's nature similes—his sunshine, owls, bats, and birds—and the king's poetlike bid for immortality. "Poets indeed use to vapor much after this manner," Milton writes. "But to bad Kings, who without cause expect future glory from thir actions, it happ'ns as to bad Poets; who sit and starve themselves with a delusive hope to win immortality by thir bad lines" (502).

The text's literariness thus functions for Milton as evidence of its generic bastardization: its audience is beneath serious, political conversation; its own content is more literary than political; and its "Scolastic flourishes [are] beneath the decencie of a King" (372). Labeling the book "poetry" categorizes its revelations as artificial and therefore suspect as historical record, as the passage above suggests. It is a "fiction" whose ideas are decorated in literary "garb" and "dress." Like the claim of Charles's "lip-work" and "outward work of Devotion," the text's literary language undermines its transparency and confessional credibility, instead functioning as obfuscatory clothing—as another hiding place for the truth about Charles. Milton extends this critique beyond the text to Charles's reign itself when he describes Charles as "he who acted over us so stately and so tragically," as though the king were a player in a drama or "Masking Scene," as he calls the frontispiece (364, 342).[57] The nature of kingship is inherently theatrical, Milton observes, as "Princes of all other men, have not more change of Rayment in thir Wardrobes, then variety of Shifts and *palliations* in thir solemn actings and pretences to the People" (577). In Milton's critique, Charles's "ill-acted regality" is itself a fiction—and a poor one at that, for he only "weakly . . . plaid the King" (355, 408).

Milton extends the analogy between *Eikon Basilike*'s "Stage-work" and its shows of pious kingship in a passage that compares Charles to Shakespeare's Richard III (530). Like *Eikon Basilike*, *Richard III* is the "Tragedie" of "a deep dissembler, not of his affections onely, but of Religion" (362). Glancing at Charles's possession of a Second Folio during his imprisonment, Milton describes Shakespeare as an author "whom wee well know was the Closet Companion of these his solitudes," an author

> who introduces the Person of *Richard* the third, speaking in as high a strain of pietie, and mortification, as is utterd in any passage of this Book; and sometimes to the same sense and purpose with some words in this place, *I intended,* saith he, *not onely to oblige my Friends but mine enemies.* The like saith *Richard, Act 2, Scen.* 1,
>
> > *I doe not know that Englishman alive.*
> > *With whom my soule is any jott at odds,*
> > *More then the Infant that is borne to night;*
> > *I thank my God for my humilitie.* (361; italics original,
> > indicating quotation)

In place of the model of the sacred King David, this passage links Charles with England's homegrown villain-king, "the worst of Kings"—a "Tyrant" speaking "pious words" (361–62). Milton suggests the literariness of Charles's prayers by locating the "sacred" original in Shakespeare rather than the Bible: it was Shakespeare's *Richard III* that was Charles's "Closet Companion" during the "Solitudes and Sufferings" that *Eikon Basilike* describes.[58] In Milton's argument, the King's Book presents an ever-receding horizon of truth. It is a fiction within a fiction copied from the work of a poet.

The accusation of copying is itself a key component of Milton's complaint. For Milton, Charles's borrowings are "no holy theft" but shameless "*Plaigiarie*" that has "unhallow'd, and unchrist'nd the very duty of Prayer it self" (547, 362). Milton links mimesis with inauthenticity, arguing that Charles's prayers demonstrate surface rather than depth, language rather than action. "It is no new, or unwonted thing," he writes, "for bad men to claime as much part in God as his best servants; to usurp and imitate thir words, and appropriate to themselves those properties which belong onely to the good and righteous" (528). "Words," in the case of Charles and other such "bad men," do not reflect interior "properties" but act as mere imitation. Milton is particularly apoplectic about a borrowing from Sir Philip Sidney's *Arcadia* that appears in Charles's "Prayer in time of Captivity" at the end of the book—"*Pammela's* Praier, stol'n out of Sir *Philip*" (547).[59] He expresses horror that Charles bequeathed this prayer to his bishop before his execution, "a pretious peece of mockery . . . not more secretly then shamefully purloind," "a Prayer stol'n word for word from the mouth of a Heathen fiction praying to a heathen God; & that no serious Book, but the vain amatorious Poem of Sr *Philip Sidneys Arcadia*" (364, 362). Like the claim that Charles ventriloquizes Richard III, the echo of Sidney's Pamela constructs a series of referents whose object is fundamentally fictitious. For Milton, Charles's prayers expose a series of troubling fabrications, "like a rott'n building newly trimm'd over" (377). The very king of the King's Book is a lie, and *Eikon Basilike* finally points to nothing authentic but this fact.

Milton's charges of plagiarism are particularly interesting in the context of martyrological discourse. As earlier chapters have suggested, the mimetic rehearsal of martyr language and action is what makes an individual legible as a martyr. Rather than a marker of inauthenticity, imitation functions as the genre's principal strategy for martyr construction and authentication. By refusing to grant mimetic privileges to Charles, Milton implicitly denies the text's claims as martyrology, instead critiquing it according to alternative discursive terms. As Steven N. Zwicker puts it, "Milton understood that to combat the book and its legacy he would need to deny its capacity as literature and its imaginative authority; but in a more complex and what must have been for Milton more difficult move, he aimed altogether to deny the authority of the aesthetic within political discourse."[60] Declining to read Charles's imitation on martyrology's terms, Milton instead reads it as evidence of plagiarism and fraud. Charles is a mere simulacrum, "say-[ing] over what our Saviour said" (447).

"Farr Differing Deeds"

In *Eikonoklastes,* it is action rather than language that witnesses to what is authentically Charles. Milton treats Charles's poetic language as the place where lies happen, and it is therefore "No marvel though [Charles] knit contradictions as close as words can lye together" (372–73). The work of *Eikonoklastes* is to locate some form of truth that is outside rhetorical representation, that precedes retrospection, and that is not subject to linguistic manipulation. Charles's inward-looking gesture of prayer, intended to expose him as nakedly as if the reader shared God's omniscience, is inverted in *Eikonoklastes,* which turns the reader's attention outward to the stage of Charles's public conduct. To that end, Milton plods through the events of Charles's reign to contrast Charles's constructions of himself—his "fair spok'n words"—with an alternative document of the king—his "farr differing deeds, manifest and visible" (346–47). While *Eikon Basilike* claims to disclose the inner workings of Charles's heart and mind, *Eikonoklastes* disputes the accessibility and relevance of this interior text, arguing instead that "What hee thought we know not; but that hee ever took the contrary way wee saw" (356). *Eikonoklastes* seeks to call the reader's attention away from the "Sorcery" and "charm" of Charles's language, by which the reader is "fatally stupifi'd and bewitch'd" (601, 347). In place of the "truth and sinceritie which [Charles] praies may be alwaies found in those his Declarations to the people" Milton asserts the events of Charles's reign, the "actions [that] whill bear eternal witness" to the kind of king Charles was, constituting "a surer evidence then what we hear now too late in words" (469, 356). Whereas "meer words" are equivocal and ambiguous, Milton insists on the document of "clear Actions" and "evident reasons" (497). Action "shews us plainly"; action "declar[es]"; action "demonstrat[es]"; "action g[i]ve[s] it out beyond all supposition"; "action . . . bear[s] eternal witness" (375, 372, 447, 403, 469).

In the process of directing the reader's attention outward to the external and visible world of action, Milton contests Charles's abstract claims to virtue, emotion, and conscientious dilemma, insisting instead on a concrete world of bodies and events.

> [Charles] complaines, *That civil Warr must be the fruits of his seventeen yeares raigning with such a measure of Justice, Peace, Plenty, and Religion, as all Nations either admir'd or envi'd.* For the Justice we had, let the Counsel-Table, Starr-Chamber, High Comission speak the praise of it. . . . Who can number the extortions, the oppressions, the public robberies, and rapines, committed on the Subject both by Sea and Land, under various pretences? (435)
>
> Not to speake of those many whippings, Pillories, and other corporal inflictions wherwith his raign also before this Warr was not unbloodie; some have dy'd in Prison under cruel restraint, others in Banishment, whose lives were shortn'd through the rigour of that persecution wherwith so many yeares he infested the true Church. (439)

Against Charles's abstract claim of "Justice, Peace, Plenty, and Religion," Milton asserts a vivid and unruly history grounded in the practical relations between subject and subject and between subject and king. In this way, *Eikonoklastes* seeks to deny Charles the shelter of abstract language and to force him into an arena of debate that is ruled by the visible. He accuses Charles of habitually manipulating language to obscure history—of conveniently renaming the past according to his fancy, "it being so easie for him, and so frequent, to call his obstinacy, Reason, and other men's reason, Faction" (356). Milton contrasts the contents of Charles's "variable and fleeting conscience"—the central subject of *Eikon Basilike*—with what "his own ensuing actions declar'd," asserting what "is op'nly known" and in "the op'n view of man" as precedent over the abstract, interior world constructed by Charles's text (371–72, 422).

In casting suspicion on Charles's devotional and conscientious discourses and in directing the reader elsewhere to discover Charles, *Eikonoklastes* insists on a stable locus of meaning that is not constructed by poetic language or subjective judgment. While *Eikon Basilike* is radically subjective—taking subjectivity *as* its subject, in fact—*Eikonoklastes* posits itself as an objective, dispassionate, historically accurate account of Charles's monarchy. Because martyrdom is fundamentally a retrospective construction that depends on mimicry and typological legibility, Milton's suspicion of the potentially deforming power of language and literature operates as a kind of generic confrontation with the formal claims made by *Eikon Basilike. Eikonoklastes* denies Charles's martyrdom not merely by offering an alternative narrative but by constructing an alternative discourse of the past—by claiming through its own formal commitments that *Eikon Basilike* is a contaminated generic hybrid. *Eikonoklastes* thus constitutes a generic confrontation with the King's Book in its insistence that the structures of Charles's bastardized martyrology simply do not pertain.

A Dialogic Legacy

The dialogue between *Eikon Basilike* and *Eikonoklastes* illustrates both the development of martyrological discourse beyond conventional typological models and the representational limitations produced by these very adaptations. Without an explicitly religious conflict to die for, Charles must construct something else. His turn to the interior dictates of conscience extracts the project of martyr-making from the historical domain that Milton wants to insist upon. For Counter-Reformation martyrology, faultlines surface at the site where typological formulas meet ambiguous events. Reconstituting the site of martyrological truth, *Eikon Basilike* adopts a radical subjectivity, circumventing representational incoherence by divorcing the martyr from history. The conventional martyrological contest between victim and persecutor once legible at the surface of historical event becomes not only internalized but metaphorized. Unbounded by theological conflict, doctrinal dispute, or even historical record, martyrdom becomes for Charles a powerful figurative language for articulating an ambiguously drawn conscientious struggle.

Milton objects to precisely this project of metaphorization. In the argument of *Eikonoklastes*, *Eikon Basilike* becomes generically defined by its literary qualities, especially its use of poetics and quotation to obscure the discrepancy between the events of Charles's reign and Charles's aestheticized representation of himself. Milton's project is to interrogate the connection between tenor and vehicle implicit in Charles's martyr metaphor, suggesting that the simulacrum collapses under objective scrutiny. Milton would draw our attention to the domain of action—the domain of event—which he suggests can be apprehended directly and without the slippery mediation of literary constructs that leave the reader "fatally stupifi'd and bewitch'd" (347). While *Eikon Basilike* looks to the interior conscience of the king to "discover" his martyrdom, *Eikonoklastes* insists that this gesture is purely rhetorical—that all that we need to read about the reign of King Charles I is written in the annals of history.

The Restoration brought with it a feast day for the "Martyr King,"[61] and by Milton's own admission, *Eikon Basilike* was wildly successful at inculcating its version of Charles's reign, even converting some detractors.[62] For more than three hundred years, however, *Eikon Basilike* has been inextricably bound up with its inimical Miltonic twin, surviving as a text of critical interest in some measure because Milton responded to it. While on the one hand *Eikon Basilike* appears to have solved the problems of fractured martyr construction that Counter-Reformation texts could not smooth over, on the other, its dialogue with *Eikonoklastes* encodes an ever-present countertext to Charles's claims and rhetorical strategies. *Eikonoklastes* testifies to a discursive glitch at the heart of *Eikon Basilike*—a glitch generated not by confessional or political difference but by the demands of the martyrological form. In its construction of a martyrdom for Charles, *Eikon Basilike* addresses only one of the two constitutive elements of traditional martyrological discourse, presenting an aestheticized representation of transcendence without narrating the contextualizing events of persecution. Summarized by the stylized, typologically vivid, but entirely ahistorical scene of its frontispiece, this figurative impulse is the central feature of Charles's martyrology.

Although *Eikonoklastes* did not persuade the English people against sacralizing their dead king, it nonetheless continues to haunt the King's Book. The persistence of *Eikonoklastes* illustrates the price of Charles's inward-looking, tenuously metaphorized martyrdom, which dislocates intention from action and disengages the figure of the martyr from the historical circumstances that conventionally generate martyrdom. Charles is celebrated as a martyr to this day, but what these two texts demonstrate is that martyrdom is no longer what it once was. Though conventionally a figure located at the intersection of history, religious typology, and literary form, the martyr of *Eikon Basilike* is an abstract representation of conscientious conflict, a religious metaphor for nonreligious conflict, abjection, and transcendence.

Postscript

Ten years after September 11, 2001, the world continues to
observe with reverence the memory of the victims whose martyrdom
will be a symbol of freedom, justice and true peace against all those
who defy God's greatest gift of life.

—Archbishop Hovnan Derderian

Father Mychal Judge was the first officially documented fatality of the terrorist attacks of September 11, 2001. By Archbishop Derderian's account, Judge was a martyr—unlike Father John Gerard, with whose story this book began.[1] Judge was a Franciscan friar and a chaplain with the New York City Fire Department who was killed at Ground Zero when the south tower of the World Trade Center fell. In the aftermath of his death, the public learned that Judge was gay, although celibate; his gay identity is a central topic of the 2006 documentary *Saint of 9/11*, a filmic hagiography celebrating Judge's service to marginalized populations of New York City, especially his dedication to gay Catholics and AIDS patients.[2] Ignored by the Roman Catholic Church, whose condemnation of homosexuality Judge disregarded in his ministry, he was canonized by the Orthodox Catholic Church of America in 2002. An Orthodox parish in Lexington, Kentucky, which

describes itself as "alternative, collaborative, and progressive," has taken
him for their patron, naming their congregation St. Mychal the Martyr
Parish.[3] The sanctuary features an image of Judge wearing Franciscan
robes and encircled by a nimbus. He holds his right hand up in bene-
diction and carries an FDNY helmet in his left.[4]

What makes Judge a martyr? Is it his priesthood? His homosexuality? His affiliation with the fire department? His death in a terrorist
attack? His death in this particular terrorist attack? The terrorists' Is-
lamic beliefs? These are questions that the biography of Judge published by St. Mychal the Martyr Parish does not fully answer. The
parish website states: "The word martyr comes from the Greek word
for witness. Mychal Judge was a true martyr who died bearing witness
to God's mercy and beneficence, after a long life living the same way. . . .
The word martyr has been twisted out of shape in the 21st century as
religious extremists throughout the world try to impose their version of
God's will. This joyful Franciscan friar from New York can remind us of
the stuff of which martyrs are really made and challenge us to witness
to God's compassion, however mad our world may seem."[5] This explanation of Judge's martyrdom is at once intensely aware of and altogether indifferent to the historicity of the term and to the formal
and circumstantial conventions that govern martyr-making. On the
one hand, by invoking the Greek etymology of the term "martyr," the
passage acknowledges the necessary continuity between old and new
martyrs and the need to situate Judge legibly in relation to traditional
representations. The distinction made between its own claims and the
contemporary construction of martyrdom that the passage rejects depends on the logic of tradition: the martyr is an inherited figure whose
identity hinges on his or her coherence with originary constructs. The
parish biography suggests, thereby, that innovation and misappropri-
ation result in illegitimate claims to martyrdom.

On the other hand, a number of significant elisions must occur in
order to make Judge fit the conventional martyr-making discourse the
parish website invokes. The notion of witnessing is signally abstracted
from the Christian tradition of active, explicitly religious persecution
and summoned broadly to describe an individual who did not die for
the faith per se—the sine qua non of conventional martyrdom—but

instead while performing his professional, albeit religious, duties. Moreover, when the events of history—both the history of the martyr figure and the history of Judge's death—are generalized into the notion of "bearing witness to God's mercy and beneficence," the passage forecloses the questions of agency, doctrine, and circumstance that organize traditional martyr narratives. In order to define Judge in contrast to the "religious extremists throughout the world" whose martyrdoms it dismisses, the martyrology deployed by St. Mychal the Martyr Parish must cancel the history of Christian extremism and the emphatic claims about God's will that underlie it. The deaths described by the stable martyrological past to which the passage gestures are themselves nothing if not examples of religion *in extremis,* as narratives ranging from the Maccabees martyrs and Saint Laurence to John Hooper, Margaret Clitherow, Robert Southwell, and Christ himself attest. Martyrs are definitionally "religious extremists," and yet the passage claims Judge's martyrdom in contrast to this model of religiosity. To make its claim, the parish biography must cancel the history of Christian martyrdom, the very history it invokes to celebrate Judge.

What is left of martyrdom, thus constructed, is an inward-turning gesture bereft of earlier martyrology's capacity to reveal or define. Claiming that Judge shows us "the stuff of which martyrs are really made," the passage demonstrates the ambiguity of the martyr in postmodern discourse. The martyr has become a figure who can only be defined through reference to "stuff," the aporia to which the text finally turns to locate the internal, invisible, indescribable essence of Judge's martyrdom. This aporia—this vague reference to a materialized notion of moral character—renders martyrdom an inchoate category that can be invoked, as it has been, to describe nearly every subject position represented in the September 11 terrorist attacks: the terrorists, the workers going about their everyday business in the World Trade Center, those who leapt from the burning towers, the firefighters and rescue workers who perished in the aftermath. Indeed, this aporia defines "martyr" in its current usage, rendering the term "martyrdom" incapable of describing historical events. Instead, as Archbishop Derderian's comments on the tenth anniversary of September 11 attest, martyrdom has become a "symbol" that indiscriminately encompasses any or all of "the victims."[6] It is a signifier without a referent, form without history.

In its construction of the martyr figure, the website of St. Mychal the Martyr Parish constitutes a natural development from the martyrological model represented by King Charles's *Eikon Basilike*. While Charles's martyrdom would likely have been illegible as such to the audience of *The Golden Legend, Eikon Basilike*'s mode of constructing martyrological conflict has far more in common with the reverence of Father Judge than with medieval stories of pagan emperors boiling Christians in oil. An illustration of the discourse in transition, *Eikon Basilike* models how the concept of martyrdom is adapted to an increasingly secular post-Reformation West in which judicial punishment is the domain of the state rather than the church. As doctrinal and theological inquisitions move further into a distant past, the kind of metaphorization we see in Charles's text becomes the genre's dominant mode, making martyrdom's rhetorical power available to a broad range of secular and political discourses. What is familiar—what is early modern—in the construction of Charles is thus precisely the discursive development that organizes our own postmodern engagements with the concept of martyrdom. This development turns martyrological content into ineffable, essentialized "stuff." As the formal energy of generic convention becomes diluted by metaphorization, the discourse can evolve to accommodate entirely passive victims who only roughly represent the political, ideological, or religious positions once constitutive of martyrdom. Whereas the stories in Eusebius and *The Golden Legend* describe a flattened, alien world inhabited by two-dimensional literary types, *Eikon Basilike*'s post-typological representation of martyrdom is a clear precursor to the martyrological appropriations of September 11.

In its transition from a typological repetition that locates the sacred outside the self—in church doctrine, biblical paradigms, and patristic models—toward a conscientious discourse that sacralizes the interior dictates of a pious conscience, the genre of martyrology maps a set of developments coherent with other aspects of a nascent modernity: the appeal for freedom of conscience, the call for religious toleration, the humanist valuation of individual dignity, and the emerging notions of a secular morality. To simply situate these developments within a well-worn liberal humanist teleology, however, is to miss what is most provocative about them. Reading the genre as a narrative of progress from antiquated toward enlightened habits of thought overlooks the significant discursive compromise of precisely these developments. In its abstraction of martyrdom from traditional associations with doctrinal and faith-based conflict, the discourse turns so entirely inward that it can render the world outside—the political, cultural, and religious context of suffering—only figuratively. The notion of martyrdom functions in the discourses about September 11 to reconstitute the victims of the terrorist attacks into resonant symbols of national piety—or, more specifically in the case of Judge, gay American progressive Catholic piety.[7] The horror of that morning in the burning building disappears into the organizing topoi of meaningful sacrifice. These topoi have lost their traditional symbolic purchase over historical data, which the claim to martyrdom now ultimately works to efface. Once a discourse that transcendentalized history, the martyr story can no longer articulate the refined elements of individual belief or the particular politics of conflict.

Given the vague, lacunate "stuff" of current martyr discourse, it is tempting to take Milton's claim that *Eikon Basilike* is a debased "peece of Poetrie" as a canny summation of the gradual dehistoricization that *The English Martyr from Reformation to Revolution* has traced. In many ways, Milton sums up this dehistoricization: the discourse of martyrdom that emerges from the regicide is disabled of the capacity to communicate anything precise about historical events, leading to a category that is evacuated of all but figurative meaning. At the same time, taking Milton's formulation as conclusive overlooks one of the foundational principles of the martyrological genre. In maligning the literary qualities of the King's Book, *Eikonoklastes* represents the aesthetic as a contaminant—an adulterating "garb" that delegitimizes claims to martyrdom. But the function of martyr literature has always been to reorganize sites of horror into sites of beauty—to reconstitute dismembered, burned, and opened bodies into closed and perfected hermeneutic systems. What Milton's critique fails to admit is the constitutive role of the poetic in all martyrology, a form whose core animating impetus is the aestheticization of atrocity. Although this book observes a gradual shift in the degree to which this impetus toward aestheticization shapes the discourse, the aesthetic necessarily comes at some expense to the contours of historiography. The martyr claims made by *Eikon Basilike* and by St. Mychal the Martyr Parish therefore represent not a bastardization but an evolution of the genre according to one of its own native imperatives. In the afterlives of the martyr, we discover a tension that has always resided at the heart of the form: between historical record and typological resonance, between human suffering and human storytelling.

Appendix A. The Bull of Excommunication Issued against Elizabeth by Pope Pius V

The following translation of *Regnans in Excelsis* is from Thomas Barlow's *Brutum Fulmen* (1681, pages 1–6), which reproduces the original Latin in parallel.

Pius Bishop, Servant to God's Servants, for a perpetual memorial of the matter.

He that reigneth on high, to whom is given all Power in Heaven & in Earth, committed one Holy, Catholick and Apostolick Church (out of which there is no Salvation) to one alone upon Earth, namely, to *Peter* the Prince of the Apostles, and to *Peter*'s Successor the Bishop of *Rome*, to be governed in fulness of Power. Him alone he made Prince over all People, and all Kingdoms, to pluck up, destroy, scatter, consume, plant and build, that he may contain the faithful that are knit together with the band of Charity, in the Unity of the Spirit, and present them spotless, and unblameable to their Saviour.

§. 1.   In discharge of which Function, we which are by God's goodness called to the Government of the aforesaid Church, do spare no pains, labouring with all earnestness, that Unity, and the Catholick Religion (which the Author thereof hath for the trial of his Children's Faith, and for our amendment, suffered to be punished with so great Afflictions) might be preserved uncorrupt: But the number of the ungodly hath gotten such power, there is now no place left in the whole World, which they have not assayed to corrupt with their most wicked

Doctrines: Amongst others, *Elizabeth*, the pretended Queen of *England*, a Slave of Wickedness, lending thereunto her helping hand, with whom, as in a Sanctuary, the most pernicious of all men have found a Refuge. This very Woman having seized on the Kingdom, and monstrously usurping the place of Supream Head of the Church in all *England*, and the chief Authority and Jurisdiction thereof, hath again brought back the said Kingdom into miserable destruction, which was then newly reduced to the Catholick Faith and good Fruits.

§. 2.   For having by strong hand inhibited the exercise of the true Religion, which Mary lawful Queen of famous memory, had by the help of this See restored, after it had been formerly overthrown by Henry the Eighth, a Revolter therefrom; and following and embracing the Errors of Hereticks, she hath removed the Royal Council consisting of the English Nobility, and filled it with obscure men, being Heretics, oppressed the Embracers of the Catholick Faith, placed impious Preachers, Ministers of Iniquity, abolished the Sacrifice of the Mass, Prayers, Fastings, Choice of Meats, Unmarried Life, and the Catholick Rites and Ceremonies. Commanded Books to be read in the whole Realm containing manifest Heresie; and impious Mysteries and Institutions, by her self entertained, and observed according to the Prescript of *Calvin*, to be likewise observed by her Subjects; presumed to throw Bishops, Parsons of Churches, and other Catholick Priests, out of the Churches and Benefices; and to bestow them and other Church Livings upon Hereticks, and to determine of Church Causes, prohibited the Prelates, Clergy, and People to acknowledge the Church of *Rome*, or obey the Precepts and Canonical Sanctions thereof, compelled most of them to condescend to her wicked Laws, and to abjure the Authority and Obedience of the Bishop of *Rome*, and to acknowledge her to be sole Lady in Temporal and Spiritual matters, and this by Oath; imposed Penalties and Punishments upon those which obeyed not, and exacted them of those which persevered in the Unity of the Faith, and their Obedience aforesaid, cast the Catholick Prelates and Rectors of Churches in Prison, where many of them, being spent with long languishing and sorrow, miserably ended their lives. All which things, seeing they are manifest and notorious to all Nations, and by the gravest

Testimony of very many so substantially proved, that there is no place at all left for Excuse, Defence, or Evasion.

§. 3.   We seeing that impieties and wicked actions are multiplied one upon another; and moreover, that the persecution of the faithful, and affliction for Religion, groweth every day heavier and heavier, through the Instigation and Means of the said *Elizabeth*; because we understand her Mind to be so hardned and indurate, that she hath not only contemned the godly Requests and Admonitions of Catholick Princes, concerning her healing and conversion, but also hath not so much as permitted the Nuncios of this See, to cross the Seas into *England*; are strained of necessity to betake our selves to the Weapons of Justice against her, not being able to mitigate our sorrow, that we are drawn to take punishment upon one, to whose Ancestors the whole State of Christendom hath been so much bounden. Being therefore supported with his Authority, whose pleasure it was to place Us (though unable for so great a burthen) in this Supream Throne of Justice, we do out of the fulness of our Apostolick power, declare the aforesaid *Elizabeth*, being an Heretick, and a favourer of Hereticks, and her Adherents in the matters aforesaid, to have incurred the sentence of Anathema, and to be cut off from the Unity of the Body of Christ.

§. 4.   And moreover, we do declare Her to be deprived of her pretended Title to the Kingdom aforesaid, and to all Dominion, Dignity, and Priviledge whatsoever.

§. 5.   And also the Nobility, Subjects, and People of the said Kingdom, and all others, which have in any sort sworn unto her, to be for ever absolved from any such Oath, and all manner of Duty, of Dominion, Allegiance, and Obedience; As we also do by Authority of these Presents absolve them, and do deprive the same *Elizabeth* of her pretended Title to the Kingdom, & all other things abovesaid. And we do Command and Interdict all and every the Noblemen, Subjects, People, and others aforesaid, that they presume not to obey her, or her Monitions, Mandates, and Laws: And those which shall do the contrary, We do innodate with the like Sentence of Anathema.

§. 6.   And because it were a matter of too much difficulty, to convey these Presents to all places wheresoever it shall be needful; our will is, that the Copies thereof, under a publick Notaries hand, and sealed with the Seal of an Ecclesiastical Prelate, or of his Court, shall carry altogether the same Credit with all People, Judicial and Extrajudicial, as these Presents should do, if they were exhibited or shewed. Given at *Rome,* at St. *Peters,* in the Year of the Incarnation of our Lord, 1570. the Fifth of the Calends of *May,* and of our Popedom the Fifth year.

Appendix B. The Six Questions for Interrogating Catholic Priests and Recusants

These questions appear in William Allen's *A Briefe Historie of the Glorious Martyrdom of XII Reverend Priests* and *A True, Sincere, and Modest Defense of English Catholics.* They also appear in *A particular declaration or testimony,* which may have been Allen's source and is the source of the text reproduced here. The last of the six questions came to be known as the "Bloody Question."

1.   Whether the Bull of Pius quintus against the Queenes Majestie, be a lawfull sentence, and ought to be obeyed by the subjects of England?

2.   Whether the Queenes Majestie be a lawfull Queene, and ought to be obeyed by the subjects of England, notwithstanding the Bul of Pius quintus, or any other Bul or sentence that the Pope hath pronounced, or may pronounce against her Majestie?

3.   Whether the Pope have or had power to authorize the Earles of Northumberlande and Westmerland, and other her Majesties subjectes, to rebell or take armes against her Majestie, or to authorize Doctour Saunders, or others, to invade Irelande, or any other her dominions, and to beare armes against her, and whether they did therein lawfully or no?

4. Whether the Pope have power to discharge any of her highnes subjects, or the subjects of any Christian prince from their allegiance or othe of obedience to her Majestie, or to their prince for any cause?

5. Whether the said Doctour Saunders, in his booke of the visible monarchie of the Church, and Doctour Bristowe, in his booke of Motives (writing in allowance, commendation, & confirmation of the saide Bul of Pius Quintus) have therein taught, testified, or mainteined a truth or a falsehood?

6. If the Pope doe by his Bull of sentence pronounce her Majestie to be deprived, and no lawful Queene, and her subjects to be discharged of their allegiance and obedience unto her: & after, the Pope or any other by his appointment and authoritie, doe invade this Realme, which part woulde you take, or which part ought a good subject of England to take?

Appendix C. The Oath of Allegiance

The oath appears in King James I's published defense of it against papal objections, *Triplici nodo, triplex cuneus* (1606).

I doe trewly and sincerely acknowledge, professe, testifie and declare in my conscience before God and the world, That our Soveraigne Lord King James, is lawfull King of this Realme, and of all other his Majesties Dominions and Countreyes: And that the Pope neither of himselfe, nor by any authority of the Church or Sea of Rome, or by any other meanes with any other, hath any power or authoritie to depose the king, or to dispose any of his Majesties Kingdomes or Dominions, or to authorize any forreigne Prince to invade or annoy him or his countreys, or to discharge any of his subjects of their Allegiance and obedience to his majestie, or to give Licence or leave to any of them to beare Armes, raise tumults, or to offer any violence or hurt to his majesties Royall Person, State or Government, or to any of his Majesties subjects within his Majesties Dominions. Also I doe sweare from my heart, that notwithstanding any declaration or sentence of Excommunication, or deprivation made or granted, or to be made or granted, by the Pope or his successors, or by any Authoritie derived, or pretended to be derived from him or his Sea, against the said king, his heires or successors, or any absolution of the said subjects from their obedience; I will beare faith and trew allegiance to his Majestie, his heires and successors, and him and them will defend to the uttermost of my power, against all conspiracies and attempts whatsoever, which shalbe made against his or their Persons, their Crowne and dignitie, by reason or colour of any such sentence, or declaration, or otherwise, and will doe my best endevour to disclose and make knowne unto his Majestie, his heires and successors, all Treasons and traiterous conspiracies, which I shall know or heare of, to be against him or any of them. And I doe further sweare, That I doe from my heart abhorre, detest and abjure as impious and Hereticall, this damnable doctrine and position, That Princes which be excommunicated or deprived by the Pope, may be deposed or murthered by their Subjects or any other whatsoever. And I doe beleeve, and in conscience am resolved, that neither the Pope, nor any person whatsoever hath power to absolve me of this Oath, or any part therof; which I acknowledge by good and full authoritie to bee lawfully ministered unto mee, and doe renounce all Pardons and Dispensations to the contrarie. And all these things I doe plainely and sincerely acknowledge and sweare, according to these expresse words by mee spoken, and according to the plaine and common sense and understanding of the same words, without any Equivocation, or mentall evasion, or secret reservation whatsoever. And I do make this Recognition and acknowledgment heartily, willingly, and trewly, upon the trew faith of a Christian. So helpe me God.

Appendix D. Conversations between Father Henry Garnet and Father Edward Oldcorne

The following is a transcription of the manuscript accounts written by two men stationed to eavesdrop on four clandestine conversations that took place in late February and early March, 1606, between Henry Garnet and Edward Oldcorne (referred to here by his alias, Hall) while they were imprisoned in the Tower of London in connection with the Gunpowder Plot. The manuscripts can be found in *State Papers Domestic of James I (1603–1610),* volumes 18 and 19, documents 18.111, 18.117, 18.122, and 19.7.

February 23, 1606 (18.111)

A   So soone as they came to speake togeather, they seemed to confess them selves one to the other, First Hall and then Garnet which was short, with a prayer in Lattin before they did confess to each other. and binding their handes on their brestes Garnet confessed that he had had a great suspision of one, (whose name I could noo here), but said he found it but a mere suspition and that he hath bin subject muche to that kind of Frailty.

B   Said Garnet I had forgott to tell you, I had a note from Rockwood, you know him, and he telleth me that Greenway is gon over, I am very glad of that. And I had an other from Mr. Garrat that he meaneth to goe over to Father persons and therefore I hope if he be not yet taken he is escayped, but it seemeth he hathe bin put to great plauges. I thinck Mistress Ann is in the Towne, if she be I have writ a note that my keeper may repair to her nerehand and convey me anie thing unto her which will let us here from all our friendes

C   I gave him an Angle [Angel] yesterday because I will be before hand with him, and he tooke it very well, with great thankes, and now and then at meales I make very muche of him, and give him a cupp of sack and send his wiff an other, and that he taketh very kindly, so I hope we shall have all well, you should doe well now and then to give him a shilling and some times send his wiff some what, he did see me write to Mr. Rockwood. but I will give him noe more moni yet.

D   I must needes confess White Webbs that wee mett there, but I will answere it thus, that I was there but knew nothing of the matter.

E   They prest me to take an oathe as by your preisthood for triffles, but they said my [illegible] was nothing I might be pardoned of [illegible].

F   Then Hall said something more softly to Garnet, and answerd Good Lord how did they know that. It is noe matter. [In margin: This I did not well here onely I heard Garnetes answere.]

G   Perhaps they will press me with certaine prayers that I made against the time of the Parliment for the good success of that business, which indeed is true. But I may answere that well, For I will say It is true that I did doubt that at this next parlament there would be more sevear lawes made against the catholicques, and therefore I made these prayers, And that will answere it well enoughe.

H   Mr. Attornie tould me very friendly that he would make the best construccion to the king of my examinacions to doe me good, and used me very kindly.

J   But Sir William Waad will some times skarse speake to me, and yet some times he will sitt downe as he passeth thorrow my chamber and use me with very good worde, but when he falleth into speache, of Jesuits, Lord how he inveyeth at them, and speaketh the straingliest that can be, And he tould me that wee were the lewedest people, and then would protest against us, and saith that we are all of opinion that Catholick Religion must be maintained under one Monarchy, and whoe is that Monarche but the King of Spaine: Nay he tould me that he knew a gentlewoman that had a child by a Jesuite and that I know her well enoughe, and in these bitter tearmes did he tell me that he could dyrectli charge me with divers severall treasons, confest by sundry persons that were witnesses in the Queenes time.

K   For my sending into Spaine before the Queenes deathe I need not deny it But I care not for those thinges, he knoweth I have my pardon for that time and therefore he will not urdge them to doe me hurt.

L   If I can satisfy the kings will in this matter it will be well, but I thinck it not convenient to deny that wee were at Whit[e] Webbs, they doe so much insist upon that place, since I came out of Essex I was there two times and so I may say I was there, but they press me to be there in October last which I will by noe meanes confess, but I will tell them I was not there since Bartholmewtide nither will I tell [4–6 illegible words (paper damaged)] the servantes there, for they may then examine and perhaps torture some of them, and make them yield to some confession, But if they aske me of the servantes, I will tel them, they never came up to me where I was.

M   But I was afraid when they spake to me of Sir Edmund Baynam that I should be asked somewhat of the letter my Lord Montague did write and send by him, but I hope they will not, yet perhaps hereafter they will.

N   And in truith I am well perswaded that I shall write my self out of this matter, and for anie former busines I care not.

Harke you harke you, Mr [illegible] whilst I shutt the dore make a hauking and a spitting.

February 25, 1606 (18.117)

Interlocutions between Garnett and Hall the Jesuit in prison over-heard by 2 worthy Gentlemen that were in insidiis.

Sir William told me I was indicted. I marvel whether it were before the Proclamation or since. If before, it will be the worse for Mr. Abington; if since, it is no good hurt to him.

Garnet said, he was charged with some advice he should give in Queen Elizabeth's time of the blowing up of the Parliament House with Gunpowder. Indeed (said he to Hall) I told them at that time it was lawful, but wished them to do their best to save as many as they could that were innocents. (His words we concieved, tended to this purpose.)

They pressed me with a Question what Noblemen I knew that have written any Letters to Rome and by whom? Hall, I see they will justify my Lord Mountegle of all this matter. I said nothing of him, neither will I ever confess him. Then Garnett mentioned my Lord of

Northumberland, my Lord of Rutland and one more (whom we heard not well) but to what effect they were named we could not hear by occasion of a Cock crowing under the window of the room and the cackling of a Hen at the very same instant.

Saith Garnett, there is one special thing of which I doubted they would have taken an exact account of me; sc[ilicet] of the causes of my coming to Cawton which indeed would have bred a great suspicion of the matter. I will write to day or to-morrow (to whom we could not hear) to let them know that I am resolved to do my Lord no hurt.

Garnett used some words to this effect; (I hope they have yet no knowledge of the great Lord.) But it was not well heard by either of us.

I will need take knowledge that you were with me at White Webbs. Then he told Hall of a Lease that was shewed him for taking of White Webbs and other words to that effect. You did not confess that we came together to Mrs. Abington's for you know what we resolved upon. Then they seemed to think that they had failed in their several confessions toe their meeting and about their Horses; and Garnett seemed to be very sorry that Hall held not better concurrence. But now they contrived how to answer that point with more concurrence; so, as if Garnett or Hall had misnamed one the other instead of a third person, whom they have now resolved upon. Garnett said "they went away unsatisfied, and therefore we must expect at the next time either to go to the Rack or to pass quietly with the rest." But said he, they pressed me with so many trifles and circumstances that I was troubled to make answer; and I told them if they would demand any thing concerning myself I was ready to deal plainly, but to accuse any other that were innocent it might be some matter of conscience to me, and I told them that none could be judge of my conscience but myself. Mr. Attorney was about to write, but when he had written three lines he gave it over and seemed to be angry, saying, I had lost my credit for he had undertaken for me to the King.

Then they conferred how to get more money, and Garnett said that he had a friend to whom he would send his keeper.

Garnett said he was charged about certain prayers to be said for the success of this business at the beginning of the Parliament, to which he answered that if they would shew him any such praier he would confess if they were done by him; which was refused to be done: They then prest me whether if it could be proved that I made such praier I would yield myself privy to all the rest? Indeed upon Allhallows day we used those praiers, and then I did repeat to them two Latin Verses; which both praiers and Verses Garnett did now rehearse to Hall, confessing that he made them both.

Garnett said they mentioned the Letters sent into Spain; but I answered that those Letters were of no other matter but to have pensions.

Garnett said something to Hall of a gentlewoman that if he were charged with her he would excuse her conversing with him; but how we could not well hear.

Garnett said he was asked of Robert Chambers and said somewhat of James or Johnson who he heard was upon the Rack for three hours at which he marvelled for said he Fawkes was but half an hour and yet they won him to confession.

They spake of Strange who they heard should be hanged then Garnett said upon what point do they touch him Hall as well as we could hear named something he had done against Sir Robert Cecil but the rest we heard not.

Garnett bid Hall take his shovel and make a noise amongst the coales whilst he might shut the door.

He did observe that from the beginning to the ending of all the conferrence neither of them named God or recommended their cause or themselves to God but applied themselves wholly to the matter.

Edward Forsett

J. Locherson

February 27, 1606 (18.122)

Garnet how now how doe you, is all well, said Garnet, And so they proceeded to the rehearsal of the examination yesterday taken, and then Hall (whoe spake moste at this time) seemed to relate to Garnet the pointes of his confession, which we could not well heare more then when wee heard Garnettes likeing or dislike thereof And where he liked, he said noe more butt well well, that was well;

I thinck said Garnet they have [illegible] don with examining of me, and truly I hope they will not bring me to anie Araignment.

Then it seemed unto us that Hall tould Garnet how he answered the matter of White Webbs; which Garnet said it was well, but said he for the other matter of our meeting on the way, it were better to leave it in a contradiccion as it was, lest perhaps the poore Fellow shall be tortured for the cleering of that pointe.

Said Garnet, I was asked of some noble men but I answered it well enoughe I thinck,

Garnet said he was asked againe about the prayer which he was charged to have made, and he did name the prayer by a spetiall name to Hall, therby putting Hall in rememberance thereof, but said he I shall avoyd that well enoughe.

He spake of witnesses to be produced unto him Face to Face, but to what end, we did not here him declare,

Garnet said that Mr. Attornie did raile against the Pope, and that all the Jesuites should rew for it, then Garnet desired that the whole, should not be charged with the Faultes of some particullar men nay said Mr. Attornie they doe all look to be made saintes for suche their practizes, and toald me that my name would be putt into the callender of Saintes. Then Garnet said, that if the Pope and their generalles should apoint them to anie accion wherein the pope may thinck to deserve to be a Sainte in heaven: therein I may hope for suche cause to be a Saint in the Callender.

In deed I was prest againe with Cawton which I most Feared, questioning with me of my times of coming thither, the place at suche a time, and the compainie, whereunto we did not heare anie report of Garnetes answere.

Garnet mencioned a place where they had said Mass on a Sonday, but his wordes that followed wee could not heare.

Then Garnet said that Mr. Attornie asked him if he were not at the christening of a child at White Webbs, and that Sir William Waad said Gibebingly, he was surely at the christening if he were not at the getting of it, then said Garnet it were not fitt to use those wordes to him at that time in this place of Justice, then said Mr. Attornie to him again, whie said he you knowe it well enough it was Mrs Brookesbyes child it had a shaven crowne.

Garnet made mencion of one Mrs Jeninges whoe onely wee heard named,

Then Garnet bid Hall hould up his mouth heer

Garnet said they lett him see James, but saith he he went but along by me

Then Hall haveing said some what to Garnet, which wee could not heare, Garnet tould him that he had answered them that there was divers that knew him whome he knew not.

Then said Garnet well I will leave you now. Then Garnet retorned to Hall againe and asked him, what he had given the keeper in all, Halles answere wee could not here, well well we will remember him well enoughe saith Garnet, and so I tould him, Garnet was often going from Hall.

Well said Garnet if they examine me anie more I will urge them to bring prooffe against me for said he, they speake of three or Fower witnesses.

Then Hall said some what.

Well said Garnet leave now wee shall have occacion to come to-geather often enoughe, and so he bid Hall shake the great Fyer shovell amongst the coles.

Wee againe observed that neither at their first meeting, nor at parting, nor in anie part of their conferrence they used noe one word of God-liness or Religion, or recomending themselves or their cause to God, but all hathe bin how to continue safe answeres and to concurr in so muche as may concern those matters they are examined of.

Edward Forsett

J. Locherson

March 2, 1606 (19.7)

A   Harke you is all well said Garnet, let us goe to confession first if you will.

B   Then began Hall to make his confession whiche we could not here well, but Garnet did often interupt him and said well well;

C   And then Garnet confest himself to Hall which was uttered very muche more softlier than he used to whisper in theis interloqucions, and but short, and confest that because he had drunck extraordinarily he was fane to goe twoe nighte to bedd betimes.

D   Upon speeches by Hall of one he saw yesterday (as wee gessed) Garnet tould him that he was assured that Litle John would not confess anie thing of importance of him.

E   Hall tould Garnet (as we gess by Garnetes repeticion thereof) that he should gaine noe favor,

F   Garnet used some speeches to Hall of the Jesuits and said that can not be, I am chauncellor and said it might proceed of the mallice of the priestes.

G   Garnet asked Hall what was said by him of White Webbs. Halles answere we could not here.

H   Garnet made great hast away for he said he that receavied a letter from him.

I   Garnet tould Hall that if it be not knowne that Mr. Abington was acquainted with him being in his howse, he would doe well enoughe.

And so Garnet broke of in hast for the reading or writeing of a letter, and spake to Hall to make a noise with the shovell.

Edward Forsett
J. Locherson

Notes

Introduction

1. Gerard, *Autobiography of a Hunted Priest*, 109.
2. Allen, *XII Reverend Priests*, 7.
3. Rather than making either particularized or random use of "Jesus" and "Christ," this book uses "Christ" throughout both for internal consistency and for consistency with terms such as "*imitatio Christi*," "Christological," and "Corpus Christi."
4. Martyrdom has been the topic of several recent monographs: Coffey, *Persecution and Toleration*; Covington, *Trail of Martyrdom*; Dillon, *Construction of Martyrdom*; Knott, *Discourses of Martyrdom*; Monta, *Martyrdom and Literature*; and Gregory, *Salvation at Stake*.
5. S. Cohen maps the history of these developments in a seminal essay on historical formalism, "Between Form and Culture." For an insightful articulation of the philosophical, theoretical, and methodological underpinnings of the turn to religion, see Jackson and Marotti, "Turn to Religion."
6. Jameson, *Political Unconscious*, ix.
7. Much of this work appears in two important essay collections: S. Cohen, *Historical Formalism*, and Rasmussen, *Renaissance Literature*. See also the introduction in B. Robinson, *Islam*; Group Phi, "Doing Genre"; Levinson, "What Is New Formalism?"; and the special journal issues *Representations* 104 (2008) and *Modern Language Quarterly* 67, no. 1 (2006).
8. S. Cohen, *Historical Formalism*, 3.
9. Bruster, "Composite Text," 44.
10. S. Cohen, *Historical Formalism*, 32.
11. Recent monographs that pursue sustained historical formalist projects are devoted principally to drama and include Hutson, *Invention of Suspicion*; Manley, *Literature and Culture*; Robinson, *Islam*; and Zucker, *Places of Wit*. M. Murray's *Poetics of Conversion* studies religious verse.
12. Gregory, *Salvation at Stake*, 1, 11. Another study in this vein is Covington's *Trail of Martyrdom*.

13. Lupton, *Afterlives of the Saints*, 38.

14. Fuchs, "Forms of Engagement," 4.

15. Although confessionally focused, this body of criticism has greatly expanded our understanding of early modern Catholic and Protestant culture and includes Coffey, *Persecution and Toleration*; Corthell et al., eds., *Catholic Culture*; Dillon, *Constructions of Martyrdom*; Dolan, *Whores of Babylon*; Highley and King, eds., *Foxe and His World*; Loades, ed., *Foxe and the English Reformation*; Marotti, *Religious Ideology* and Marotti, ed., *Catholicism and Anti-Catholicism*; Shell, *Catholicism, Controversy* and *Oral Culture and Catholicism*; and Tuttino, *Law and Conscience*.

16. Monta, *Martyrdom and Literature*, 75.

17. S. Cohen, *Historical Formalism*, 15.

18. Monta, *Martyrdom and Literature*, 29.

Chapter 1. Medieval Models

1. The epigraph from Augustine is quoted in Jacobus, *Golden Legend*, 1.107. All English translations of *The Golden Legend* are from this edition. Subsequent citations will be parenthetical.

2. See William Granger Ryan's introduction in Jacobus, *Golden Legend*, xiii.

3. Reames, *Legenda Aurea*, 4–5.

4. Ibid.

5. Ryan's introduction in Jacobus, *Golden Legend*, xiv; Reames, *Legenda Aurea*, ch. 5–6.

6. Coogan, *Annotated Apocrypha*, 2 Maccabees 6:24, 27–28.

7. Ibid., 2 Maccabees 6:30.

8. Ibid., 2 Maccabees 7.

9. According to Jacobus, Old Testament saints other than the Maccabees martyrs are celebrated by the Eastern church, but the Western church "does not celebrate feasts of saints of the Old Testament, on the ground that they descended into hell" (2.33).

10. Talmudic scholars have challenged the historical validity of the distinction between Judaism and Christianity as it has been applied to beliefs held in the first few centuries and to early martyrology. Glen W. Bowerstock, *Martyrdom and Rome*, argues that the Maccabees narrative is more reflective of Christian than of Jewish concerns: "the two stories in the books of the Maccabees have nothing to do either with the authentic history of the Maccabees

or with the lost original text that recounted it"; rather, he argues, they "have everything to do with the aspirations and literature of the early Christians" (12–13). Responding to Bowerstock, Daniel Boyarin erodes these categories yet further: "Indeed, for the first-century (or even second-century) milieu in which 4 Maccabees was produced, the whole distinction [between Hellenistic Judaism and Christianity] could make no sense whatever, any more than the question of whether James or Peter was a Jew or a Christian could" (*Dying for God*, 115). For a full analysis of Maccabees, see van Henten, *Maccabean Martyrs*.

11. In some cases, the analogues between Maccabees and later martyr legends are particularly close, as in Jacobus's legend "Seven Brothers, Sons of Saint Felicity," the tale of seven young men whose martyrdom in about 110 c.e. is essentially a repetition of the story of the Maccabees brothers (1.364–65).

12. Ryan's English translation of *The Golden Legend* makes very liberal use of exclamation points, especially in the exchanges between martyrs and their persecutors. This exuberance grows distracting at moments and lends a bitter spitefulness to these confrontations that is not always evident in the Latin.

13. The five fires are, first, "Gehenna, the fire of hell; the second, the fire of material flame; the third, the fire of carnal concupiscence; the fourth, that of grasping greed; the fifth, that of raging madness [of the persecutor]" (2.72). Jacobus discusses each of these individually, then describes the "three refrigerants within himself as well as three fires in his heart, by which he moderated all external fire by cooling it, and surpassed it with the greater heat of his ardor" (2.73). The three refrigerants are "the longing for the kingdom of heaven," "meditation on the divine law," and "purity of conscience" (2.73).

14. According to Jacobus, the feast of Saint Laurence is the only martyr's feast that includes a vigil; the only martyr's or confessor's feast, other than the martyr Stephen's and the confessor Martin's, that includes an octave; and the only feast, other than Saint Paul's, that includes the repetition of the antiphons (2.74).

15. Lampe, "Martyrdom and Inspiration," 132.

16. Eusebius, *Ecclesiastical History*. See especially Book VIII.

17. A rare exception is found in the story of Saint Catherine, who confronts Emperor Maxentius because he is forcing Christians to sacrifice to idols. In their fear of death, many succumb (2.334).

18. Lampe, "Martyrdom and Inspiration," 118. On concerns about martyrdom and suicide in the Middle Ages, see A. Murray, *Suicide in the Middle Ages*, vol. 2, ch. 3.

19. Reames notes that "one of the central virtues celebrated in the *Legenda* . . . is transcendence of the earthly code of values that labels life preferable to death, health to suffering, sensory pleasure to insensibility, and so on" (*Legenda Aurea*, 161).

20. This hierarchy is part of a larger one Jacobus outlines in his section on the feast of All Saints in which he ranks martyrs second behind apostles in the highest degree of precedence among saints, followed by confessors and then virgins (2.275).

21. White, *Tudor Books*, 38.

22. Eusebius, 2.277–79.

23. Quoted in Jacobus, *Golden Legend*, 1.107. Ryan translates the word "play" from the original Latin "*ludus.*" This word is central to V. A. Kolve's seminal study of Corpus Christi drama, a drama that identifies itself as "*ludus.*" Kolve writes, "it is this word *ludus*, in its English equivalents 'play' and 'game,' that becomes the ubiquitous generic term for the vernacular drama" (*Play Called Corpus Christi*, 12). For an English reader of the Latin *Legenda Aurea*, Vincent's reference to "*ludus*" could therefore suggest that he and his fellow Christian sufferers regard their torture as at once of play, game, and theatre.

24. Quoted in Jacobus, *Golden Legend*, 1.107.

25. Ibid., 2.71.

26. See John 12:24–25 and Matthew 17:20.

27. For an intriguing but problematic discussion of milky wounds, see ch. 6 of Heffernan, *Sacred Biography*. Heffernan suggests that the milk is symbolic of female saints' identification with the Virgin Mary and that through martyrdom they achieve the dual figuration of Christ's bride and mother (283). Other than the woman's virginity, however, there is nothing in these moments to identify the saint with Mary. Sanok's suggestion that the milk flowing from the martyr's severed breasts "highlights the saint's spiritual maternity" seems more accurate ("Legends of Good Women," 166).

28. Brown, *Cult of the Saints*, 80.

29. Jacobus's rendering of Christina's legend is particularly sparse and compressed, which makes the pattern of attempted torture followed by miraculous delivery more dominant that it is in other versions such as Bokenham's *Legendys* and the *South English Legendary*, where the martyr prays piously for God's deliverance at regular intervals. This compression alters the overall feel of the legend: instead of constant defiance, we also observe, through the saint's supplication, a sense of human fear and humility.

30. White, *Tudor Books*, 42.

31. Ibid.

32. The *South English Legendary* places even greater emphasis on the fact of Sebastian's miraculous preservation from arrows by including a Christian woman who comes to bury him and finds him alive and his body "hol & sond wiþout wonde" (p. 18, line 68). She takes him to her house, where he recovers completely before confronting Diocletian.

33. Many scholars have considered the motif of attempted rape in virgin martyr narratives, including Constantinou, *Female Corporeal Performances*; Gravdal, *Ravishing Maidens*; Heffernan, *Sacred Biography*, 277-81; Innes-Parker, "Sexual Violence"; Salih, "Performing Virginity"; and Saunders, *Rape and Ravishment*, 120–51. For a full study of virgin martyrs, variations among legends, and the cultural appropriation of these legends across the Middle Ages, see Winstead, *Virgin Martyrs*. Although few surviving manuscripts of *The Golden Legend* are illuminated, Easton's study of one such manuscript discovers that the illuminations heighten the sexual prurience of the virgin martyr stories ("Pain, Torture, and Death").

34. Marshall makes a related point about the simultaneous fetishization and devaluation of the body in Foxe's *Acts and Monuments*: "Words and bodies interact in complex, multifaceted ways in the *Acts and Monuments*. While Foxe's martyrs demonstrate their transcendence of the flesh by enduring its torturous destruction, theirs is no dualistic logic of body and soul. If the body were completely devalued, as martyrs and mystics sometimes claim, its loss could not occasion martyrdom" (*Shattering of the Self*, 91). The same is true for the loss of virginity, which is at once obsessively defended and meaningless in the economy of earthly values that *The Golden Legend* everywhere articulates.

35. Jacobus silently quotes from Ambrose.

36. Reames writes, "Evidence of miracles has ordinarily been considered no less indispensable in the dossier of a saint than evidence of virtuous conduct; the two reinforce each other, helping to guarantee that the declaration of sanctity came from God, not just from fallible human opinion" (*Legenda Aurea*, 65).

37. Brown, *Cult of the Saints*, ch. 5. Heffernan touches on this point as well: "The miracle stories in the narratives of the saint's life, aside from their importance as agents in the drama of the tale, serve to authenticate the genuineness of an individual's sanctity. Moreover, the miracle, standing as it does outside the normative round of experience, paradoxically becomes the *topos* which is the most accurate location of the dwelling place of the holy in this world, that is the saint" (*Sacred Biography*, 128).

38. Heffernan, *Sacred Biography*, 196.

39. "It is probably under the influence of this emphasis on Christian martyrdom as participation in the suffering and death of Jesus that the word

μάρτυς and its cognates tend in the second century to lose the sense of 'witness,' at least as their primary meaning, and a distinction comes to be drawn between the martyr who literally dies with Christ and the confessor who witnesses to him before persecutors but does not actually suffer the death penalty" (Lampe, "Martyrdom and Inspiration," 120).

40. Ibid., 129.

41. Lampe, 129–30, quoting Mark 13:11.

42. Acts 1:8.

43. Acts 4:8–13.

44. White observes that "There is the wonder of the way in which the suddenly manifest wisdom of the simple and the unlearned confounds the wisdom of the wise—naturally, one of the most popular manifestations of the power of God" (*Tudor Books,* 47).

45. In the legend of Cecilia, it is her husband, Valerian, who reads from the book (not to be confused with the bishop Valerian in the legend of Saint Vincent).

46. The disjunction between Agnes's age and her speaking ability is emphasized in Bokenham's *Legendys* by the inclusion of several additional instances in which the martyr enters into argument with her persecutors (110–29). On the question of whether virgin martyrs' speech represents victimization or agency, see R. Mills, "Can the Virgin Martyr Speak?" 187–213.

47. See, for example, Eusebius's narration of the martyr Blandina, who withstands countless tortures, continuing throughout to defend her faith and the morality of the Christian community by simply repeating, "I am a Christian woman and nothing wicked happens among us" (*Ecclesiastical History,* 1.415).

48. Situating *The Golden Legend* within the church's contemporary problems with heresy and apostasy, Reames argues that the persecutors' punishments were meant to communicate to the audience what would be in store for them if they strayed from the church's teachings (*Legenda Aurea,* 131–33).

49. Alford suggests another aspect of this cosmic significance in his discussion of the typological relationship that stories of saints' lives often draw between the events they describe and Old Testament stories of good versus evil, remarking that the world described by saints' lives is "peopled with biblical heroes and villains" ("Scriptural Self," 4).

50. Scarry, *Body in Pain,* ch. 1. See also Oliver, "Sacred and (Sub)-Human Pain."

51. The commonly agreed-upon range of dates for each cycle is as follows: York, 1463 to 1561; Wakefield, late fifteenth century to early sixteenth century; Chester, 1422 to 1575; and N-Town, c. 1500. The first three cycles are

named according to the towns in which they were performed. The N-Town cycle is from the East Midlands, but its specific origin is unknown. Its name derives from a reference in the cycle's banns to their appearance "In N-town," a place left unnamed, possibly indicating traveling performances. See The Proclamation, line 527, in *N-Town Play*.

52. Travis, "Semiotics of Christ's Body," 71.

53. See Scourging, line 13, in *Towneley Plays*. The conventions for referring to this cycle of plays has shifted from "Towneley" (the name of an eighteenth-century owner of the manuscript) to "Wakefield," producing a discrepancy between the title of the Early English Text Society (EETS) edition and the term used in current criticism. This chapter uses "Wakefield" throughout. For more on the singularity of Wakefield's Pilate, see Williams, *Characterization of Pilate*, and Kolve's commentary on Williams in *Play Called Corpus Christi*, 232–36.

54. Kolve, *Play Called Corpus Christi*, 221–22.

55. See the Towneley Buffeting, where the *tortores* sue to Annas and Caiaphas to condemn Christ, and the Crucifixion, where Caiaphas and Annas are absent altogether.

56. Bevington, *Medieval Drama*, 536–37.

57. Towneley Buffeting, line 417.

58. Christ's encounter with Herod appears in Luke 23:7–12.

59. N-Town Trial Before Annas and Cayphas (play 29), lines 29–36. According to Spector's commentary in the EETS edition of the play, Woolf suggests that "the depiction of Herod as a persecutor of Christians seems to derive from hagiography" (507). See Woolf, *English Mystery Plays*, 250. Wakefield's Pilate similarly expresses an anachronistic enjoyment of persecuting Christians (Scourging, lines 46–48).

60. Christ Before Annas and Caiaphas, lines 43–44, in *York Plays*.

61. Ibid., line 271. "With his flagrant lies he flouts our laws." Modern English translations of York are based on Beadle's glossary in the EETS edition and on the glosses in Beadle and King, *York Mystery Plays*.

62. Ibid., lines 387–88. "Say [to Pilate that] this lad with his lying has our laws destroyed; and say that this same day he must be slain."

63. Trial, lines 132–3, in *Chester Mystery Cycle*. "To condemn him we are keen, lest he us all destroy." Modern English translations of Chester are based on the glossary in Lumiansky's and Mills's EETS edition and on Mills's modern spelling edition.

64. Towneley Buffeting, lines 133–34. "He would gladly bring down our laws with his voice." Modern English translations are based on the glos-

sary in Stevens and Cawley's EETS edition of the Towneley plays and on glosses in Bevington's *Medieval Drama.*

65. Ibid., lines 172–73. "If he reigns any longer, our laws will be miscarried."

66. N-Town Conspiracy (play 26), stage direction between lines 164 and 165.

67. Ibid., lines 180, 220, 315. "Our laws he destroys daily with his deeds"; "If he proceeds, he will destroy our laws"; "Jesus has nearly destroyed our laws." Modern English translations of N-Town are based on the glossary in Spector's EETS edition and on glosses in Bevington's *Medieval Drama.*

68. See especially N-Town Last Supper (play 27), lines 78–88.

69. N-Town Betrayal (play 28), lines 131–32, 272.

70. Chester Trial, lines 189, 198–200. The phrases translate, "dumb and deaf as a doted doe" and "to clothe men who are crazy or mad, as now he makes himself, as well seems by his face."

71. York Christ before Herod, lines 335–56.

72. Ibid., line 351. "Fonned" means "foolish."

73. Ibid., lines 2,505–6; lines 281–82.

74. Beadle and King, *York Mystery Plays,* 175.

75. Davidson, "Realism of the York Realist," 271.

76. See, for example, York Christ before Annas and Caiaphas, line 324; and N-Town Last Supper (play 27), line 309.

77. Beadle and King, *York Mystery Plays,* 155.

78. Bevington, *Medieval Drama,* 477. E. Cohen coins the term "philopassianism" to describe the development of Christianity's attitudes toward edifying pain across the late Middle Ages ("Towards a History of European Physical Sensibility," 58–62).

79. Kolve, *Play Called Corpus Christi,* 175.

80. Beadle and King, *York Mystery Plays,* 155.

81. *Northern Passion,* line 1,180 (Cambridge MS) or 1,742 (Oxford MS). The search for the rood tree leads into a lengthy discourse on the history of the cross.

82. York Crucifixio Christi, line 147; N-Town Crucifixion (play 32), line 68.

83. Towneley Crucifixion, line 525. "Blo" means "blue."

84. See Matthew 26–27, Mark 14–15, Luke 22–23, and John 18–19.

85. York Christ before Annas and Caiaphas, lines 293–95; "Sir, you say it yourself, and truly I say that I shall go to my father that I come from and dwell with him worthily in bliss forever."

86. Ibid., line 308.

87. See Towneley Buffeting, line 201, and N-Town Trial Before Pilate (play 30), lines 225–28.

88. On the function and representation of cruelty in medieval literature and culture, see Baraz, *Medieval Cruelty,* and Enders, *Medieval Theater of Cruelty.*

89. N-Town Last Supper (play 27), lines 351–52.

90. Sponsler, *Drama and Resistance,* 152. Sponsler's chapter "Violated Bodies" shows how Christ is forced into a feminized or infantilized role by his torturers.

91. Towneley Buffeting lines 276–77: "Unless I give him a blow, my heart will burst."

92. Ibid., lines 279–80, 289. "Thrust out both his eyes in a row" and "strike off his head."

93. Towneley Scourging, lines 176–78. Bevington translates: "Let me strike with my rusty weapon, so that the blood will run down" (*Medieval Drama,* 558).

94. York Christ Before Pilate 2, lines 350, 357. "I am eager in this matter"; "I am eager to pay him [with blows]."

95. Kolve, *Play Called Corpus Christi,* 178.

96. Travis, "Semiotics of Christ's Body," 71.

97. For a sociological study of the erotics of captor-captive violence, see W. S. Wooden and Parker, *Men Behind Bars,* 13–14.

98. Sponsler, *Drama and Resistance,* 149.

99. For mocking games in the gospel passions, see Matthew 26:65–68 and 27:27–31, Luke 19:63–65 and 23:11–12, and John 19:1–3.

100. Kolve, *Play Called Corpus Christi,* 181.

101. See Towneley Buffeting, lines 1–2 and 619–21, and Scourging, lines 70–78.

102. Chester Trial, lines 98-99. The word "beshitt" appears only in the Harley 2124 MS of the cycle. Other manuscripts have either "Though he store stryke" or "Though he sore stricke." A similar phrase is repeated in the Chester Passion, line 67, where Harley has "shyte" and other manuscripts have varying forms of "stryke."

103. Chester Passion, line 149.

104. York Christ before Pilate 2, lines 408–19.

105. York Mortificacio Christi, lines 40–104.

106. Towneley Scourging, lines 196–247.

107. E. Cohen points out a basic representational discrepancy that lies at the heart of this chapter's comparison—a discrepancy between Christianity's

constitution of divine suffering and of the resilience of its later martyrs: "A religion that had accomplished such a major revolution regarding the human body, that had deliberately made its God into a suffering man, could hardly be expected to create its heroes in an impassible, super-human mold. And yet that is precisely what Christianity did. Early Christian martyrs displayed a number of supernatural characteristics, all connected with their extraordinary ability to withstand pain" ("Towards a History of European Physical Sensibility," 54). For fuller studies of late-medieval formulations of Christological and martyrological pain, see E. Cohen, *Modulated Scream*, ch. 7 and 8, and Perkins, *Suffering Self*, ch. 3, 4, and 8.

108. N-Town Last Supper (play 27), lines 91–92.

109. Kolve, *Play Called Corpus Christi*, 200.

110. Roston, *Biblical Drama*, 17.

111. N-Town Last Supper (play 27), lines 369–72. "And as we have eaten the paschal lamb that was used for a sacrifice in the old law, so the new lamb that shall be consecrated by me shall be used for a most precious sacrifice."

112. Ibid., lines 445–46.

113. Beckwith, *Christ's Body*, 60.

114. York Crucifixio Christi, lines 193–94.

115. Beadle and King, *York Mystery Plays*, 211–12.

116. Beckwith, *Signifying God*, 66.

117. In contrast to Beckwith, Ross sees the dramatized crucifixion not as itself sacramental but as preparation for sacraments such as the Eucharist and Confession that might be motivated by one's viewing of the plays (*Grief of God*, 68).

Chapter 2. New Actors in an Old Drama

1. Persons, *Treatise*, and Harpsfield, *Dialogi Sex*. Although he is generally referred to as "Robert Persons," *Treatise* is published under the alternate spelling of his name, "Parsons." Following convention, "Persons" is used throughout the book. Harpsfield's book was published under the pseudonym "Alan Cope." In his thorough discussion of Foxe's detractors, Mozley writes that Persons's book "remains the *locus classicus* for the anti-Foxean case" (*Foxe and His Book*, 227). For a general overview of Foxe's critics and defenders, also see W. W. Wooden, *John Foxe*, especially 105–12. Sullivan, "Oppressed by the Force," discusses Persons's argument in detail.

2. English translations of Foxe's Latin preface are from the editorial apparatus of *Unabridged Acts and Monuments Online*. *Ad Doctum Lectorem* was printed in the 1563 edition of *Acts and Monuments*, excised in the 1570 and 1576 editions, and restored in the 1583 edition. Even before Foxe's much-anticipated 1563 edition was published, critics had begun to refer to it pejoratively as "Foxe's Golden Legend." *Ad Doctum Lectorem* rejects this comparison and, as Mozley has put it, "shows us how truly Foxe foresaw the storms of anger that would burst upon him, and indeed were even already beginning to burst" (*Foxe and His Book*, 132). Mozley's discussion of the four original editions suggests that Foxe excised the preface in 1570 and 1576, under pressure to delete the many Latin passages of 1563 and in an effort to keep the text at a manageable length. By 1583, Foxe's supporters had encouraged him to include all of this original matter in the newest edition; thus, along with *Ad Doctum Lectorem*, the 1583 edition also revives the 1563 Latin prayer to Christ, *Eucharisticon*. See Mozley, *Foxe and His Book*, ch. 5. Unless otherwise indicated, all material cited from *Acts and Monuments* appears alike in the first four editions overseen by Foxe (1563, 1570, 1576, and 1583). Spelling and punctuation follow the 1583 edition. Subsequent citations from Foxe will be parenthetical.

3. *Unabridged Acts and Monuments Online*.

4. Greenblatt, *Norton Anthology*, 631–32.

5. Haller, *Elect Nation*. For the argument against Haller, see Bauckham, *Tudor Apocalypse*; Collinson, "Foxe and National Consciousness"; Firth, *Apocalyptic Tradition*; and Olsen, *Foxe and the Elizabethan Church*.

6. On the relationship between *Acts and Monuments* and Eusebius's *Ecclesiastical History*, see W. W. Wooden, *John Foxe*, 20–26, 52–53; White, *Tudor Books*, 12–13, 169–70; and Olsen, *John Foxe and the Elizabethan Church*, 22–24.

7. Collinson is an exception. In "Foxe and National Consciousness," he demonstrates the difficulty of discerning the original author of much of Foxe's martyr material and resorts to referring to the author of *Acts and Monuments* as "Foxe," in quotes. There is indeed an identity problem in Foxe, one that is difficult to manage gracefully when writing about the text.

8. Hogarde, *Displaying of the Protestantes*, folios 49, 43. Cited in Knott, *Discourses of Martyrdom*, 15.

9. The first English edition of Eusebius was *The Auncient Ecclesiasticall Histories of the First Six Hundred Yeares after Christ*, translated by Meredith Hanmer, 1577.

10. Knott, *Discourses of Martyrdom*, 82.

11. Jacobus, *Golden Legend,* 2.66 and 2.322.

12. Eusebius, *Ecclesiastical History,* 1.423. Foxe's much expanded edition of 1570 featured a history of the early church martyrs in which he included a version of this passage from Eusebius (p. 71 in the 1570 edition, p. 47 in the 1576 and 1583 editions).

13. W. W. Wooden has observed that "the history Foxe wrote is also a Protestant martyrology, with closer ties to the Catholic tradition of hagiography than its author would admit," but the implications of this statement do not appear to substantively shape his reading of the text (*John Foxe,* 41).

14. Mueller, "Pain, Persecution," 172–73.

15. Ibid., 175.

16. See Jacobus, *Golden Legend,* 1.142.

17. Ibid., 2.67.

18. Ibid., 1.107.

19. Mueller, "Pain, Persecution," 171.

20. Boyarin makes a similar claim about the erroneous distinction between Jewish and Christian modes of representing martyrdom: "We must think of circulating and recirculating motifs, themes, and religious ideas in the making of martyrdom, a recirculation between Christians and Jews that allows for no simple litany of origins and influence" (*Dying for God,* 118).

21. The *Oxford English Dictionary* suggests several relevant sixteenth-century meanings for the word "monument," most of them concurrent with modern usage. Specifically, it identifies Foxe's use of the word in his title as denoting a commemorative written document.

22. Knott, "Foxe and the Joy of Suffering," 732–74.

23. Betteridge, "Truth and History," 148.

24. W. W. Wooden, *John Foxe,* 55.

25. Propp, *Morphology of the Folktale,* 21.

26. Other critics have suggested similar three-part structures for Foxe's martyr narratives. Mueller identifies the three segments as trial, confirmation of impasse, and execution ("Pain, Persecution," 162). W. W. Wooden suggests inciting conflict, arrest, and imprisonment/torture as one segment, trial as the second, and execution as the third (*John Foxe,* 60–61).

27. Bourdieu, *Logic of Practice,* 54.

28. Montrose, "Professing the Renaissance," 20.

29. Bourdieu, *Logic of Practice,* 55.

30. This passage is from Foxe's history of the first ten persecutions of the early church, which does not appear until the 1570 edition.

31. Jacobus, *Golden Legend,* 1.61.

32. Freeman, "Fate, Faction, and Fiction."

33. Walsham, *Providence,* 230.

34. Several of these incidents betray the flexibility and interchangeability of the terms "miracle," "marvel," and "providence" that Walsham describes. For example, Foxe refers to the incident when John Wycliffe is nearly prevented from coming to trial by a providential earthquake as a "great miracle of gods divine admonition or warning" (436). "[B]y the Providence of Almighty God," John Philpot's hidden account of his trial is "mervaylously reserved from the sight and hand of hys enemies" (1,830). And the printing press, which Foxe figures as God's instrument to preserve his people from the tyranny of the Latin Bible and mass, is called a "divine and miraculous invention" (707). Foxe's discussion of the printing press does not appear until 1570.

35. Mozley suggests that Foxe's accounts of punished persecutors exhibit greater credulity and less restraint than any other aspect of his narratives (*Foxe and His Book,* 163–64). It is precisely this position that Freeman challenges in "Fate, Faction, and Fiction," demonstrating that this material was some of the most thoroughly researched and revised in the book.

36. Jacobus, *Golden Legend,* 2.318–23 (Cecilia), 2.63–74 (Laurence), 1.242 (Dacian), 2.23 (Lucretius).

37. Eusebius, *Ecclesiastical History,* 2.353; Jacobus, *Golden Legend,* 1.354, 1.273, 2.323.

38. This statement applies to the accounts from John Huss (d. 1415) forward. Foxe's relation of the ten persecutions of the early church includes several spectacular or objective miracles he repeats from his patristic sources, though often with open dissent.

39. For a rhetorical analysis of Foxe's execution accounts, see White, *Tudor Books,* 159–62.

40. See Palmer, "Histories of Violence." Palmer observes that Foxe uses dialogue to suggest that the martyrs are speaking directly through the text and that the text is unmediated by him, a strategy aided by the "techniques of printed performance," which allow dialogue to be set off from the body of Foxe's text (89).

41. Foxe does not appear to know Badby's name in the 1563 edition. The woodcut is included, and the 1563 narrative clearly points to Badby in its reference to Prince Henry's attendance at his execution (the gallant on horseback). But the 1563 narrative is very brief and does not contain this direct reference to the woodcut (see p. 172 in the 1563 edition). Foxe apparently gathered more information about the martyr's identity and his execution for the second edition. It is also worth noting that the banderole in the

1563 woodcut is more clearly a supplication for relief from physical pain. It reads, "Lord Jesus Christ help me" instead of "Mercy Lord Jesus Christ, mercy." This difference corresponds to changes in the narrative between the 1563 and later editions.

42. Some critics have described the use of illustrations in *Acts and Monuments* as problematic because their pictorial representations of sanctity refer to an earlier tradition of religious iconography, one that Calvinism brought under suspicion. In an article tracing the history of the Protestant illustrative tradition, Pettegree accounts for this seeming discrepancy by situating *Acts and Monuments* at a singular moment in history "when the English printing industry had attained the maturity to take on such a project, but before the iconophobia of continental Calvinism had yet made its influence felt" ("Illustrating the Book," 35).

43. On the repetition of woodcuts, see Aston and Ingram, "Iconography."

44. Luke 9:26.

45. Romans 10:10.

46. Revelation 21:8.

47. Ridley is also careful to warn his readers not to remain in England as a way of inviting violence on themselves, because this may not be God's will. He recommends that Protestants leave England instead of staying to give themselves to death, contending that there is no shame in flight. He warns that Christians "must beware of presumption, and rashnesse in suche thinges" and must be called to martyrdom, which comes "without thyne owne presumptuous provocation" (1,781). "To dye in Christes cause is an high honour," Ridley explains, "to the whiche no man certaynly shall or can aspire, but to whom God vouchsafeth that dignitie: for no man is allowed to presume for to take unto hym selfe any office of honour, but he which is thereunto called of God" (1,784). Protestant divines like Ridley and Cranmer seem sensitive to the potential charge that their martyrdom is in fact a kind of self-willed suicide, an issue that will arise for the Catholic martyrs studied in chapter 4. Byman ("Suicide and Alienation") has argued that many of Foxe's martyrs are driven not by a desire to serve God through confession and martyrdom but to flee melancholia and religious despair. His discussion of the martyr Julius Palmer is thorough and convincing, but his other evidence is thin and relies a great deal on oversimplified psychoanalysis of characters only vaguely sketched in Foxe's text.

48. Breitenberg, "Flesh Made Word," 404.

49. Fairfield, "John Bale," esp. 149–51. For general discussions of the influence of Bale on Foxe's conception of history, see Christianson, *Reformers and Babylon*, ch. 1, esp. 14–22; and Levy, *Tudor Historical Thought*.

50. Paul Christianson writes: "Even before Henry VIII and his parliament removed the pope's jurisdiction from England, exiles like Robert Barnes, John Frith, and William Tyndale had proclaimed apocalyptic explanations for the Reformation. These early Reformers had enunciated individual elements of what became the English Protestant apocalyptic tradition. . . . Shortly after the break with Rome it appeared that a Protestant perspective had arrived as official policy. As part of the anti-papal campaign of 1536, for example, Archbishop Cranmer preached a sermon at St. Paul's Cross in which he identified the contemporary pope as antichrist and derided the authority of the emperor" (*Reformers and Babylon*, 13). For a full discussion of the figure of Antichrist in early modern religious discourse, see Lake and Questier, *Anti-Christ's Lewd Hat*, esp. sections 1 and 2.

51. Maozim is a false god mentioned in Daniel 11:38–39.

52. For example, chapter 1 noted that the characters of Annas and Caiaphas in the N-Town passion play are dressed in red robes signifying their affiliation with Jewish law (see p. 40).

53. Matthew 7:15.

54. This sentence appears in the 1563 edition, p. 130.

55. The graphic woodcut of Bonner whipping a Protestant man in his garden has been the subject of much critical interest. For an especially original treatment arguing that the woodcut depicts Bonner as a sexual predator, see Burks, "Polemical Potency." Burks notes that although the woodcut remained, some of the more peripheral stories of Bonner's cruelty were excised from the 1570 edition along with several scathing poems about the bishop. "[T]he decision," Burks explains, "may be an indication that Foxe grew uncomfortable with the scurrilous and titillating elements of this section of the first edition" (274, n. 30).

56. W. W. Wooden identifies this as an instance of Foxe's use of "paralipsis, the rhetorical figure in which the speaker effectively tells what he pretends to pass over" (*John Foxe*, 54).

57. This preface was printed only in the 1563 edition of *Acts and Monuments*, p. B4v.

58. Collinson, "Foxe and National Consciousness," 29. In another article, Collinson suggests that many of the individuals memorialized by Foxe maintained radical religious doctrines far from orthodox Protestantism. See the section titled "Truth and Legend" in Collinson, *Elizabethan Essays*.

59. On Foxe's management of the potential disruption to traditional gender hierarchies represented by female martyrs' assertive speech acts, see Peters, *Patterns of Piety*, ch. 11, and Macek, "Emergence of a Feminine Spirituality."

60. See Robinson, "Doctors, Silly Poor Women," for a discussion of the tension between these dismissive descriptions of women and the scriptural authority granted them in Foxe's text.

61. Along with Robinson, Levin describes women in Foxe as self-consciously co-opting these commonplaces to manipulate their male counter-parts. In particular, they both cite the incident in which Queen Catherine Parr escapes investigation for heresy by telling Henry that she is just a "silly woman" who looks for his guidance in all things (Levin, "Women in the Book of Martyrs," 198–99; Robinson, "Doctors, Silly Poor Women," 246–47). J. King draws similar conclusions about Anne Askew ("Fiction and Fact," 17).

62. The *Oxford English Dictionary* does not suggest that the words "silly" and "seely" are alternative spellings of the same word, but the two words share the suggestion of foolishness, helplessness, and simplicity. In addition to these definitions, "seely" can mean "spiritually blessed." The context of Ridley's remark points to his use of it to denote simplicity or innocence.

63. On the Pauline martial model, see Knott, *Discourses of Martyrdom*, 29.

64. Breitenberg remarks: "Without control over the visible operations performed on their own bodies, the martyrs seized their invisible and thus inviolable souls as the basis for a symbolics of power. In this fashion, Protestants could wrest from their Catholic tormentors the ability to direct the meaning of the execution in order to enlist the moment of death as supreme evidence of the 'truth' of their beliefs" ("Flesh Made Word," 402).

65. The quotation from Oldcastle appears on p. 563 of the 1583 edition. Foxe's remarks appear on p. 313 of the 1563 edition.

66. Knott, *Discourses of Martyrdom*, 73. His second chapter describes the "conflict of styles, the plainness and simplicity of the Protestant martyrs versus the formality and ceremonialism of the spokesmen of the church" as keys to Foxe's larger argument about the fundamental spiritual differences between Protestant and Catholic and the moral foundation of each, but Knott also points out the inherent theatricality of the Marian martyrs' management of their trials and deaths.

67. This quotation is from a letter written by Marsh that Foxe did not include in 1563. Several other letters of Marsh's appear beginning in 1570, suggesting that Foxe acquired them between editions.

68. Romans 9:36.

69. Breitenberg, "Flesh Made Word," 399–400.

70. Knott, *Discourses of Martyrdom*, 27–30. See especially Matthew 24:9 and 5:10, Romans 9:36, 2 Timothy 3:12, and Revelation 2:10.

71. Stephen's martyrdom is related in Acts 7.

72. Luke 23:45 and Acts 7:60.

73. See 1 Peter 1:7 and Wisdom 3:6–8.

74. Eusebius, *Ecclesiastical History,* 1.353. Foxe quotes this incident from Eusebius in his relation of the ten persecutions of the early church (p. 43 in the 1583 edition). This material does not appear in the 1563 edition.

75. Zollinger, "The Booke, the Leafe," 113–14.

76. The second chapter of Knott's *Discourses of Martyrdom* is devoted to the letters of the Marian martyrs, especially Bradford. He situates these writings within the tradition of the Pauline epistles, observing that they self-consciously model themselves on Paul (89–90).

77. In her discussion of martyr interpretation, Susannah Brietz Monta emphasizes the self-assurance of the victim's religious truth, particularly the Protestant martyr's inward-looking search for evidence of election. See Monta, *Martyrdom and Literature,* ch. 1.

78. The 1563 edition has a less detailed account of Flower's martyrdom that does not report his prayer at the stake: "To his burnyng lyttell wood was brought. Wherupon for the lack of fagottes there not sufficient to bourne him, they were fayne to stryke him downe into the fire, (and whiche was pitifull to beholde) he beyng there layde uppon the grounde, his nether part was covered with fire, whyle his upper part lyeng without the fire, his tongue dydde move in his head" (1,139).

79. Barthes, "Reality Effect." Marshall interprets this aspect of the text according to Lacan's notion of "the Real," or "those aspects of existence that escape symbolic articulation altogether" (*Shattering of the Self,* 98). She concludes that Foxe "sought to shatter readers by bringing them up against the Real in extreme form and did so by way of motivating their embrace of the protective identity of Christian faith" (99).

80. This passage does not appear until 1570. The 1563 account of Bilney's burning is shorter and less detailed.

81. Most of Foxe's material on the German, French, and Italian martyrs did not appear until the 1570 edition.

82. Pettegree suggests that those who supplied Foxe with narratives may also have had a hand in shaping the victim's identity as a Christian martyr by describing the scene of execution through familiar martyrological language: "These witnesses, too, might have been equally aware of the martyr paradigms echoed in these modern events, as indeed would the victims themselves. Did they perhaps consciously conform, themselves, to the way of dying indicated by this tradition; or did witnesses come to understand the events they had observed within the 'correct' ritual of interrogation and passion—in which case

their depositions for Foxe might have reflected this understanding alongside their own recollections?" ("Haemstede and Foxe," 293–94).

83. Rubin, "Choosing Death," 153.

84. Foucault, *Discipline and Punish,* ch. 1 and 2. Höfele suggests the subversive power of these execution scenes by linking them to the disruptive potential of theatre ("Stages of Martyrdom").

85. Monta suggests that the effort to controvert Lewes's martyrdom succeeded in producing a recantation from a woman who had been an advisor of hers, Agnes Glover (*Martyrdom and Literature,* 39–40).

Chapter 3. Secular Law and Catholic Dissidence

1. For a discussion of these and other reasons why straightforward religious persecution may have best been avoided, see Allen, *Defense of English Catholics,* xxxi–iii.

2. Earl, "Typology and Iconographic Style," 21, 18.

3. Barlow, *Brutum Fulmen,* 6. Barlow's text includes the original Latin and a parallel English translation of Pius V's bull of excommunication *Regnans in Excelsis* (1–6). For a fuller discussion of the excommunication, see Tutino, *Law and Conscience,* ch. 1.

4. "An Act whereby certain offences be made treasons" in Elton, *Tudor Constitution,* 73–77.

5. "Declaring Jesuits and Non-Returning Seminarians Traitors" in Hughes and Larkin, *Tudor Royal Proclamations,* 489–501; and "An Act for provision to be made for the surety of the Queen's most royal person" in Elton, *Tudor Constitution,* 77–80.

6. "Establishing Commissions Against Seminary Priests and Jesuits" and "Specifying Questions to be Asked of Seminary Priests" in Hughes and Larkin, *Tudor Royal Proclamations,* 86–95.

7. James VI and I, *Triplici nodo,* 11, 12. See Tuttino, *Law and Conscience,* ch. 5.

8. "Campion's Challenge" was published in a document that refuted it (Hanmer, *Great Bragge and Challenge*). On the various responses to "Campion's Challenge" and his Latin treatise in defense of his faith, *Decem Rationes,* see Milward, *Elizabethan Age,* 54–59. Kilroy, *Edmund Campion,* situates Campion's writings within the broader context of underground Catholic communications.

9. On Anthony Munday's relationship to the Anti-Catholic campaign, see Hamilton, *Anthony Munday.*

10. Howell, *State Trials*, 1,052–53. Subsequent references will be parenthetical.

11. Corthell, "Secrecy of Man," 274.

12. The place name designated by the blank is excluded in the trial transcript. The prosecutor's catalog of Campion's attire comes from a description of him that was circulated to aid his capture.

13. An account of the priests' answers to the six questions can be found in a pamphlet titled *A particular declaration or testimony, of the undutiful and traitorous affection borne against her Majestie.* This short text was published by Christopher Barker, the queen's printer, and is therefore presumed to be an officially sanctioned document. Because *A particular declaration* appears in its entirety in *State Trials* (immediately following the account of Campion's trial), page numbers from this text refer to the *State Trials* version.

14. Because Pope Pius V died less than two years after he issued the bull of excommunication against Elizabeth, there was some question among Catholics about whether or not it was still officially in effect. Six subsequent popes would hold office by the time Elizabeth died in 1603, and none cared to weigh in on the issue with either a renewal or retraction of the bull. However, Pope Paul V, who was elected in 1605, made a statement warning English Catholics not to take James's Oath of Allegiance. In it, he advised them that the contents of the oath—especially the rejection of the pope's power to depose and excommunicate—were heretical and that the oath could not be taken without imperiling one's salvation. This decree indicates that although the papacy issued no official position on Elizabeth after Pius V's bull, the question of papal prerogative that was central to trials like Campion's remained a consistent point of Catholic orthodoxy.

15. Imprisoned Catholics routinely expressed their desire for martyrdom, and Campion was no exception. Marotti writes: "When Campion had entered England, he did so with no reluctance, as he said to the authorities, to 'enjoy your Tyburn.' Like other militant Jesuits, he thought of himself as a martyr in the making" (*Religious Ideology*, 91).

16. Lupton, *Citizen-Saints*, 13.

17. Coffey suggests that the practice of executing religious dissenters for heresy had come to be associated with Roman Catholicism and was therefore regarded warily by a broad range of early modern English theologians, including King James I, who told Parliament that "it is a sure rule in Divinitie, that God never loves to plant his Church by violence and bloodshed" (quoted in Coffey, *Persecution and Toleration*, 27).

18. Alfield, *A true reporte*, A2v. Subsequent references will be parenthetical.

19. The text was published anonymously, but Alfield has long been considered its author. Subsequent references will be parenthetical.

20. Lemon, *Treason by Words*, 2–4.

21. See Kingdon's introduction in Burghley, *Execution of Justice*, xxxvi–xxxvii.

22. Allen, *XII Reverend Priests*, 2. Subsequent references will be parenthetical.

23. Although Allen's claims are technically correct, they do not take into account how the Catholic church's own medieval heresy trials had sometimes been carried out. The crime of heresy was essentially a crime of thought or belief to which no outward act had to be attached in order for the sentence of death to be passed. But as Henry Ansgar Kelly has pointed out, in order for heresy to be lawfully prosecuted, the individual would have had to manifest heresy in some way, most likely by speaking it to another. Only through establishing *fama publica* (public declaration) of heresy could someone be justly brought to trial; it was not lawful to bring an individual in for questioning in the hopes of revealing secret heretical belief that was previously undisclosed, though this did happen. Kelly cites Joan of Arc as one such case: "Many of the questions put to Joan concerned points of theology that she clearly had not considered previously. That is to say, even if her responses could have been considered sinfully heretical, they would not have been past sins, which could have been confessed and absolved in the sacrament of penance, but rather fresh sins committed on the spot, recorded and considered as public crimes, subject to public abjuration and punishment" ("Inquisitorial Due Process," 423). This explanation of Joan's prosecution suggests that—legally or not—the Catholic church had engaged in practices similar to those condemned by Allen.

24. Foxe, *Acts and Monuments*, 1,535, 1,037.

25. "[H]e surrendered himself to death and was counted among the wicked" (Isaiah 53:12).

26. The addendum addressing Campion's torture is titled *A Declaration of the Favorable Dealing of Her Majesty's Commissioners* and appears in all editions of *The Execution of Justice* after 1584.

27. See Kingdon's introduction in Burghley, *Execution of Justice*, xvii. For publication history, see Milward, *Elizabethan Age*, 68–69.

28. Burghley, *Execution of Justice*, 37, 14-15. Subsequent references will be parenthetical.

29. See Psalm 58:3–4.

30. Mark 14:61–64. See also Matthew 26:63–66.

31. Luke 23:2.

32. Luke 23:5, 14.

33. John 19:12.

34. N-Town Conspiracy (play 26), lines 309-12. "Mekyl" means "much."

35. Allen, *Defense of English Catholics*, 59. Subsequent references will be parenthetical.

36. Allen specifically addresses Foxe's story of the Guernsey martyrs, repeating some of Nicholas Harpsfield's claims against the woman executed in Guernsey whose child, born while she was at the stake, was thrown back into the fire (104).

37. The link between martyrdom and suicide will be discussed at greater length in chapter 4.

38. *Plures efficimur quotiens metimur a uobis; semen est sanguis Christianorum.* Tertullian, *Apologiticus*, 144.

Chapter 4. "The Finger of God Is Heere"

1. For fuller biographical accounts of Mush and Clitherow than those provided in Mush's martyrology, see Cross, "Elizabethan Martyrologist," and Longley, *Saint Margaret Clitherow*.

2. Mush, *Life and Martyrdom*, 413. Subsequent references will be parenthetical. Three women—Clitherow, Margaret Ward, and the Countess of Salisbury—were executed under Elizabethan anti-Catholic policy, though many more were imprisoned. See Dillon, *Construction of Martyrdom*, 284–85.

3. On Mush's biography and authorship, see Dillon, *Construction of Martyrdom*, ch. 6. From her study of extant manuscripts, Dillon concludes that Mush was not the text's only author. However, she explains, "The title page of some of the manuscripts attributes total authorship to John Mush" and as a matter of convenience, she refers to him as the author of the text throughout her chapter (280). This chapter's discussion of the Clitherow narrative follows Dillon's example. On the history of the manuscript, see Longley, *Saint Margaret Clitherow*, Appendix A.

4. The text became literally hagiographic when Clitherow was canonized by Pope Paul VI in 1970.

5. Dillon argues that this representation of Clitherow's life provides a model of Catholic living under Elizabethan law, a model that "urg[es] recusancy as a form of martyrdom" (*Construction of Martyrdom*, 278). According to Lake and Questier, the text's claim to absolute recusancy as the only mode of pious Elizabethan Catholicism should be contextualized within local and national tensions among Catholics over what was demanded of them in such

a time, an argument they pursue broadly in "Margaret Clitherow," 54–67, and in compelling, persuasive detail in *The Trials of Margaret Clitherow*. Tensions around the matter of recusancy would later develop into the Appellant Controversy, which will be addressed briefly in chapter 5. The title of another martyrology, Thomas Worthington's *Relation of Sixtene Martyrs: Glorified in England in Twelve Monethes. With a Declaration. That English Catholiques Suffer for the Catholique Religion. and That the Seminarie Priests agree with the Jesuites. In answer to Our Adversaries calumniations, touching these two points,* suggests the role martyrology could play in intrafaith disputes like the Appellant Controversy. Mush would become a moderate voice for church papism as his career developed and would side in print with the Appellants, suggesting the instability of opinions on the correct approach to questions of recusancy.

6. Marotti, "Alienating Catholics," and Lake and Questier, "Margaret Clitherow," suggest that Clitherow's recusancy and her intimate, obedient relationship with Mush would have been perceived by her community as a challenge to her husband's authority and an affront to proper domestic hierarchy.

7. Dillon notes that Thomas More argued that "faithfulness to the law of God has to take precedence over that of a man-made legislation, and that one's conscience must be the final judge" (*Construction of Martyrdom*, 294). She suggests that Clitherow's martyrdom is modeled after More in this point and in the silence she adopts (295). More refused to take an oath declaring Mary Tudor's illegitimacy and declined to explain his refusal. For a contemporary account of More's life and death, see Roper, *Life of Sir Thomas More*.

8. Blackstone writes that "the statute of Edward I. directs such persons 'as will not put themselves upon inquests of felonies before the judges at the suit of the King, to be put into hard and strong prison (*soient mys en la prisone forte et dure*), as those which refuse to be at the common law of the land.' And, immediately after this statute, the form of the judgment appears in Fleta and Britton to have been only a very strait confinement in prison, with hardly any degree of sustenance; but no weight is directed to be laid upon the body, so as to hasten the death of the miserable sufferer. . . . It also clearly appears, by a record of 31 Edw. III., that the prisoner might then possibly subsist for forty days under this lingering punishment. I should therefore imagine that the practice of loading him with weights, or, as it is usually called, *pressing him to death*, was gradually introduced between 31 Edw. III. and 8 Hen. IV., at which last period it appears in our books" (*Commentaries*, 328).

9. If Clitherow had been pregnant, her execution would have been delayed until she gave birth, but she refused to either confirm or deny pregnancy, testifying, "I can neither say that I am nor that I am not, having been deceived

heretofore in this, and therefore I cannot directly answer you, but of the two I rather think that I am than otherwise" (421). She told Mush that she did not want a stay of execution, "for it was the heaviest cross that ever came to her, that she feared she should escape death" (420). The women sent to examine her on this matter concluded that "she was with child as far as they could perceive or gather by her own words" (419). Lake and Questier address the court's decision to ignore this information ("Margaret Clitherow," 78–79).

10. For Mush's borrowings from John Bale's narrative of Anne Askew, Roper's *Life of Sir Thomas More,* and elements of the cult of St. Margaret, see Dillon, *Construction of Martyrdom,* 295–310. On the gendered dimensions of Mush's appropriation of Askew, consult Matchinske, *Writing, Gender, and State,* ch. 2, and Peters, *Patterns of Piety,* ch. 11.

11. Dillon, *Construction of Martyrdom,* 294–95.

12. Donne, *Biathanatos,* 66. This book was written in about 1608 but not published until 1647.

13. Donne, *Pseudo-Martyr,* 31.

14. Allen, *Defense of English Catholics,* 115.

15. "Yorkshire Recusant's Relation," 99.

16. "Ancient Editor's Notebook," 52.

17. Monta, *Martyrdom and Literature,* 68.

18. Dillon, *Construction of Martyrdom,* 294.

19. Pollen, *Acts of the English Martyrs,* 98–126.

20. Holtby, "Persecution in the North," 118–213.

21. Ibid., 227–29.

22. Wilson, *English Martyrologe,* 8v. The quotation appears in the "Advertisment of the Author to the Catholicke Reader." Apart from the calendar, the other prefatory address is titled "To the Catholicks of England, Scotland, and Ireland."

23. Wilson, *English Martyrologe,* 66, 127, 133, 135, 29. Wilson classifies Henry VI as a martyr because he "was wrongfully deposed by King Edward the 4.& cast into the tower of London, where a little after he was most barbarously slayne by Richard Duke of Glocester" (134).

24. Gennings, *Life and Death,* 99. Subsequent references will be parenthetical. For a brief publication history, see Shell, *Shakespeare and Religion,* 94. Shell's "'Lives' of Edmund Gennings" discusses other manuscript and print biographies of Gennings. According to Shell, the 1614 edition appears to be based on an earlier, lost biography from 1602 or 1603 and was likely written in concert with John Wilson. In his critique of the Gennings biography in *Survey of Miracles* (discussed toward the end of this chapter), Richard

Sheldon disparagingly suggests Wilson as a likely author: "I should have reputed the same, the worke of some childish *Punie,* or ignorant *Wilson*" (323; also quoted in Shell, "'Lives' of Edmund Gennings," 216). An abridged and anonymous edition of the life of Gennings was published during the Popish Plot era of the late 1680s or early 1690s.

25. Shell notes that this verse preface may not have been written by John Gennings ("'Lives' of Edmund Gennings," 217).

26. Sheldon, *Survey of Miracles,* 323. Subsequent references will be parenthetical. Sheldon's discussion of Gennings appears in an "Addition" to the main text of the lengthy *Survey,* the body of which is a refutation of another Catholic work: a defense of Catholic miracles by Jesuit John Floyd, *Purgatories Triumph* (1613). On the polemical exchange over miracles, see Milward, *Jacobean Age,* 159–65.

27. Gennings, *Life and Death of Mr. Edmund Geninges,* 86.

28. Monta, *Martyrdom and Literature,* 72.

29. Dudley, "Conferring with the Dead," 291.

30. Ibid., 280. Dudley quotes from Scarry, *Body in Pain,* 14, 193, 14.

31. Monta argues that Protestants' erroneous beliefs make them incapable of reading the Gennings miracles as such and that Gennings's martyrology works didactically, "attempt[ing] to model for those of a different religion what their responses ought to be" (*Martyrdom and Literature,* 73). On the contrary, however, the Gennings text imagines a Catholic audience.

Chapter 5. "This Deceitfull Arte"

1. Allen, *XII Reverend Priests,* 7.

2. Marotti's "Alienating Catholics" describes the relationship between the fear of Jesuits and the prejudice against foreign influence. Lake, "Anti-Popery," discusses more general sources of anti-Catholic sentiment.

3. Janelle reports that when Elizabeth read some of his poems, probably either *Saint Peter's Complaint* or *Mary Magdalen's Tears,* she was moved to sympathy and felt grief for his death (*Robert Southwell,* 86). Janelle's source for this claim is the biography of Southwell by his contemporary, Diego de Yepes. On the relationship between Southwell's martyrdom and poetry, see Monta, *Martyrdom and Literature,* ch. 5.

4. Based on documents from the later indictment of Anne's father, Richard Bellamy, Devlin and Janelle each report that Topcliffe either seduced or raped the young woman while she was under his arrest and that she was

transformed by his influence from a respectable Catholic girl into a desperate, licentious turncoat. In order either to rid himself of the now-pregnant woman or to affect his own financial gain, Topcliffe arranged a marriage between Anne and his servant, Nicholas Jones, the son of a weaver. His hope that her family would bestow a large dowry on the bride was never realized. See Devlin, *Life of Robert Southwell*, 275, and Janelle, *Robert Southwell*, 62.

5. Torture by manacles was intended to inflict greater pain but less visible damage than torture by rack, which had been used on earlier Catholic prisoners such as Campion. Drawing from modern medical research, Devlin explains why this form of torture was so extraordinarily painful and how dangerously close to death it could bring its victims. According to his medical sources, the manacles produced a physiological effect much like that of crucifixion (*Robert Southwell*, 285–86).

6. Pollen, *Unpublished Documents*, 335. The contemporary manuscript account of Southwell's trial that Pollen includes in his collection was written by Thomas Leake, a priest living in London at the time of Southwell's trial and execution.

7. Ibid., 334.

8. Ibid., 335.

9. Caraman argues that "the government played some part in engineering [the Plot] for its own ends" (*Henry Garnet*, 322). Caraman is joined by a number of historians who have suggested that the Gunpowder Plot was essentially concocted by the government to create an occasion for entrapping Catholics and Jesuits. A general sketch of this theory appears in Dutton, *Ben Jonson*, 18–22.

10. Howell, *State Trials*, 243. On Cecil's role in Gunpowder Plot polemics, see Nowak, "Propaganda and the Pulpit," and Dutton, *Ben Jonson*.

11. Garnet eventually wrote two statements disclosing his knowledge of the plot that were printed in the nineteenth century. See Gardiner, "Two Declarations." The most thorough contemporary accounts written by Catholics are those of Jesuits John Gerard and Oswald Tesimond. Tesimond's narrative was written in rather poor Italian, left unfinished, and never published. The twentieth-century editor and translator of Tesimond's narrative, Francis Edwards, states that Gerard's and Tesimond's narratives derive from a common Latin source and are therefore similar on many counts. See Gerard, *Narrative*, and Edwards, *Narrative of Tesimond*. Caraman's book *Henry Garnet* incorporates material from Gerard's account as well as public records and letters into a biography of Garnet, which discusses his involvement in the plot. While Caraman's study relies on a wide range of primary documents, it is a decidedly

pro-Catholic, pro-Jesuit text (Caraman was himself a Jesuit), and his conclusions often seem to be ideologically rather than historiographically inspired. A more balanced but less detailed account of the plot appears in Fraser, *Faith and Treason.*

12. Caraman, *Henry Garnet,* 332–34. Caraman bases his summary of this letter on the manuscript at Stonyhurst. The letter itself has never been published.

13. He is referring to the Watson Plot of 1603. See Caraman, *Henry Garnet,* 323, 334.

14. Caraman reports that Hinlip had been outfitted with more than a dozen secret hiding places devised by Nicholas Owen, or "Little John," the Jesuits' faithful servant who had a knack for developing and building ingenious crannies in which priests and Catholic contraband could be hidden if a house were searched. For a biography of Nicholas Owen, consult Waugh, *Blessed Nicholas Owen.* A fuller discussion of priest holes can be found in Hodgetts, *Secret Hiding Places;* Squiers, *Secret Hiding Places;* and Yates, "Parasitic Geographies" and *Error, Misuse, Failure.*

15. The owner of Hinlip Hall, Thomas Habington, was arrested in this siege and spent six years in the Tower before being released. Nicholas Owen was also taken. According to Gerard's *Narrative of the Gunpowder Plot,* Owen was tortured to death in the Tower, having spoken nothing that would incriminate his friends. Gerard claims that Owen suffered from an abdominal condition that should have exempted him from being tortured. He was racked and manacled repeatedly, however, and his abdomen split open, causing his bowels to spill out (188). Based on Gerard's account, Caraman writes that "he lingered in unspeakable agony until the next morning, 2 March. To cover their crime, the Council gave out in London that he had taken his own life" (*Henry Garnet,* 366). It is unclear what Gerard's source for this story was. Owen's twentieth-century biographer, Margaret Waugh, writes that "Little John, lame, ingenious, silent, died as secretly as he had lived" (*Blessed Nicholas Owen,* 23).

16. Gerard, *Narrative of the Gunpowder Plot,* 170. Gerard claims that Garnet was then tortured to extract from him the identity of this "one" and that, after his torture, Garnet disclosed the conversation in which Tesimond had told him the details of the plot. According to Tesimond's narrative, Gerard was not tortured but, rather, made this statement when threatened with torture (Edwards, *Narrative of Tesimond,* 188–92). Caraman disputes Gerard's narrative on this point and correctly asserts that the eavesdroppers' notes make no mention of this remark to Oldcorne, nor does the transcript of Garnet's trial.

See Caraman, *Henry Garnet,* 373–75. These "interlocutions," as eavesdroppers Edward Forset and J. Lockerton labeled them, have never been printed. The manuscript notes are *State Papers Domestic of James I,* documents 18.111, 18.117, 18.122, and 19.7. They are transcribed here as Appendix D.

17. *State Papers Domestic,* 18.122.

18. Howell, *State Trials,* 211. The version of the proceedings against Garnet in *State Trials* is taken from the official account, *A True and Perfect Relation,* published by the king's printer. Because the seventeenth-century text is unpaginated, *State Trials* is cited throughout. Subsequent references will be parenthetical.

19. In his written statement about his knowledge of the plot, Garnet described Tesimond's confession as somewhat unusual "because it was too tedious to relate so long a discourse in confession kneeling, if I would take it as in confession, walking, and after take his confession kneeling either then or any other time, he would tell me" (Gardiner, "Two Declarations," 514). The prosecution used this as evidence that it was not a true confession and therefore not bound by the seal of confession that Garnet claimed as his reason for concealing the plot.

20. This is not the only problem with Garnet's defense. Because Catesby did not tell Tesimond of the plot under the seal of confession, Tesimond was bound by common law to disclose the plot to the authorities. Instead, he told Garnet about it, whose advice as his confessor and Superior should have been that Tesimond must turn Catesby in.

21. This is *A True and Perfect Relation of the whole proceedings against the late most barbarous traitors, Garnet a Jesuite, and his Confederates.* See note 18 above.

22. In this official account, the administrators of Garnet's execution refer to a document describing four points of treason that they claim he has signed in assent. The points are: "1. That Greenway [a.k.a. Tesimond] told him of this [Catesby's plan], not as a fault, but as a thing which he had intelligence of, and told it him by way of consultation. 2. That Catesby and Greenway came together to him to be resolved. 3. That Mr. Tesimond and he had conference of the particulars of the Powder Treason in Essex long after. 4. Greenway had asked him who should be the Protector [after the successful coup]? but Garnet said, That was to be referred till the blow was past" (*State Trials,* 356). Garnet's assent to these points would mean that he colluded in the plot far beyond what his written narrative of the plot admitted.

23. Gerard, *Narrative,* 289–94. Subsequent references will be parenthetical.

24. This document was never mentioned in Garnet's trial and never published after his death, a fact that would seem to support Garnet's claim that it was a fiction. It is possible that Garnet signed such a confession in the weeks between his trial and execution, but this would not explain why such an important piece of evidence was never published. In the official version of the execution, the document is referenced but not exhibited and does not appear to have been at hand.

25. Howell, *State Trials*, 356. See also Gerard, *Narrative of the Gunpowder Plot*, 292.

26. See Monta, *Martyrdom and Literature*, 69–70. See also Walsham, *Providence*, in which she discusses the polemical response to Garnet's straw in England and abroad and writes that it "caused considerable consternation at the highest political levels" (243).

27. Sheldon, *Survey of Miracles*, 333.

28. On Garnet's authorship, see Allison, "Writings of Henry Garnet."

29. On the origin of the text, see Jardine's preface in Garnet, *Treatise of Equivocation*. Subsequent references will be parenthetical.

30. Preface to Garnet's *Treatise of Equivocation*, xix–xx. *A Treatise of Equivocation* never appeared in print. Jardine's nineteenth-century edition is based on the original manuscript now at the Bodleian Library at the University of Oxford.

31. Pollen, *Unpublished Documents Relating to the English Martyrs*, 335.

32. Zagorin's *Ways of Lying* outlines the rhetorical, theological, and casuistical background of the doctrine of equivocation as it was described and defended by the Jesuits.

33. Zagorin's study of equivocation traces these particular biblical examples through sixteenth-century Catholic casuistry, particularly that of Dr. Navarrus (Martín de Azpilcueta), the sixteenth-century canonist and theologian whose works were used in the training of English Jesuits (*Ways of Lying*, ch. 8 and 9).

34. The manuscript of *A Treatise of Equivocation* has occasional editorial notes in Garnet's hand; he was apparently readying the text for press. In reference to this passage, Jardine remarks that Garnet inserted the words "in their understanding" between "answere" and "trewly" but then crossed them out. The text uses words like "sincerely" and "truly" throughout to denote those utterances made without any equivocation, and such adjectives tend to undermine Garnet's claim that equivocation is not a form of falsehood. His indecisiveness about this passage seems to suggest that he was aware of this delicate distinction and was wrestling with how best to handle it.

35. James, *Triplici nodo*, 12. The text of *Triplici nodo*, James's defense of the Oath of Allegiance, includes within it Pope Paul V's 1606 command that English Catholics refuse the oath. The oath itself is transcribed in full within this papal brief.

36. Ibid., 12–13.

37. Questier, "Loyalty, Religion, and State Power," 318, 313. It is Questier's compelling thesis that this dissent was the designed purpose of the oath.

38. Unlike priests such as Jesuits, Franciscans, or Dominicans, secular priests are those who are not affiliated with a specific order. On the Appellant Controversy, see Questier, *Catholicism and Community*, ch. 8; Holmes, *Resistance and Compromise*; and Law, *Historical Sketch*.

39. Blackwell, *Mr. George Blackwel*.

40. Quoted in James, *Triplici nodo*, 13. Pope Paul V issued two breves condemning the oath, the first in September 1606, and the second in August 1607.

41. For a bibliography of the controversy, see Milward, *Jacobean Age*, 89–93. Lemon provides a brief summary of contemporary debates about the oath and scholarly responses to it (*Treason by Words*, 108–11).

42. The complete title of this work is *Triplici nodo, triplex cuneus. Or an Apologie for the Oath of Allegiance. Against the two Breves of Pope Paulus Quintus, and the late Letter of Cardinall Bellarmine to G. Blackwel the Arch-priest*. A note in Sommerville's edition of King James's political writings explains "*Triplici nodo, triplex cuneus*" to mean "A triple wedge for a triple knot (in wood); the two breves of Paul V and the letter of Bellarmine to Blackwell are the triple knot; James' replies are the triple wedge which destroys the knot" (*King James VI and I*, 284, n. 497).

43. James, *Triplici nodo*, 59.

44. Ibid., 21.

45. Ibid., 28.

46. Ibid., 3.

47. Persons, *Briefe Apologie*, 201v.

48. Ibid., 203r.

49. Persons, *Treatise Tending to Mitigation*, 329. Subsequent references will be parenthetical.

50. Ibid., ch. 9. By way of justifying mental reservation, Persons offers a number of examples from the New Testament of what he categorizes as equivocation. Nearly all are instances of metaphorical speech.

51. Mason, *New Art of Lying*, 20, 75. Subsequent references will be parenthetical.

52. Zagorin, *Ways of Lying*, 212.

53. According to Caraman's account, however, none of the conspirators ever implicated Garnet in the plot.

54. Mullaney, *Place of the Stage*, 121.

55. Gerard, *Autobiography*, xvii. Subsequent references will be parenthetical.

56. In the introduction to his translation of Gerard, Caraman describes the importance of the upper classes to the maintenance of priests and the support of the English mission (Gerard, *Autobiography*, xviii).

57. Walpole was a Jesuit who had been executed in 1595 after being imprisoned and severely tortured in the Tower.

58. Caraman says that Garnet's account of Campion describes this same behavior. According to Garnet, Campion "used to fall down at the rackehowse dore upon both knees to commend himself to God's mercie and to crave His grace of patience in his paines." Caraman concludes that "the reading of this passage can certainly be taken as part of J. G.'s [Gerard's] preparation for his own ordeal, so that Campion's behaviour had by now established a ritual among all the martyrs" (Caraman's footnote in Gerard, *Autobiography*, 108).

59. Before being moved to the Tower, Gerard spends several months imprisoned first in the Counter in the Poultry and then in the Clink, where he gains a remarkable amount of freedom and is able to minister to fellow Catholics in prison and out. He writes of his time in the Clink, "by after a few months we had, by God's grace, everything so arranged that I was able to perform there all the tasks of a Jesuit priest, and provided only I could have stayed on in this prison, I should never have wanted my liberty again in England" (*Autobiography*, 78).

60. Caraman notes that some of these priests were even buried inside houses because it was too dangerous to bring out the corpse of a man who was not accounted for (Caraman's footnote in Gerard, *Autobiography*, 87).

61. Christopher Devlin's medically informed explanation of why the manacles were so painful and dangerous describes this passage from Gerard as evidence of the physiological effects at work (*Robert Southwell*, 285).

62. Ibid., 300.

63. Gerard wrote *The Autobiography of a Hunted Priest* more than ten years after the events he describes, and by the time he set down his story the Gunpowder Plot and its fallout were past. It is clear from studying Persons's texts that priests' opinions about how the doctrine should be deployed were somewhat unstable, so it is difficult to know how much Gerard may or may not have revised the account of his answers under interrogation to accord with later developments in his opinion of equivocation.

64. See Caraman's footnote in Gerard, *Autobiography,* 56.

65. Ibid., 111.

66. On the private circulation of relics, books, and other objects among the recusant Catholic community, see Myers, "Gerard's Object Lessons."

67. Scott, *Domination and the Arts of Resistance,* 19.

68. Ibid., 19.

69. Boyarin, *Dying for God,* 55–56.

Chapter 6. Beyond Typology

1. Knott, "'Suffering for Truths Sake,'" asserts that in Charles's claim to be a "Martyr of the People" and in the martyr figure outlined in *Eikon Basilike,* "Charles sought to associate himself with the tradition of Protestant martyrs popularized by Foxe" (161). This claim reflects trends in the study of martyrology that draw broad associations between Foxe's representation of martyrdom and subsequent Protestant figures. By contrast, this chapter demonstrates that there is not much about *Eikon Basilike*'s representation of martyrdom that is Foxean or explicitly marked by Protestant belief.

2. Skerpan, "Rhetorical Genres and the *Eikon Basilike,*" 123.

3. Daems and Nelson, *Eikon Basilike,* 14. For a complete bibliography of editions, see Madan, *New Bibliography.* Zwicker, *Lines of Authority,* traces the publication and popularity of both *Eikon Basilike* and *Eikonoklastes.*

4. Skerpan Wheeler, "*Eikon Basilike* and the Rhetoric of Self-Representation," 123. Skerpan Wheeler observes that "There is no single, unified, 'official' version of the text" (123). See also Lacey, "Elegies."

5. Daems and Nelson, *Eikon Basilike,* 23, italics original. Subsequent citations will be parenthetical.

6. Scholars agree that *Eikon Basilike* is, to a significant degree, the work of Dr. John Gauden, Dean of Bocking during Charles's reign, although we know that Charles was engaged in some kind of composition during his imprisonment. For the sake of simplicity, this chapter refers to Charles throughout as the voice of the text, though we might usefully think of him more as the speaker of the book than as its author. On the question of authorship, consult Knachel, *Eikon Basilike,* xxii–xxxii; Daems and Nelson, *Eikon Basilike,* 16–21; Madan, *New Bibliography,* 126–63; and Trevor-Roper, "*Eikon Basilike,*" 211–20.

7. The chapter headings are the only element of the book in the third person. In all editions of *Eikon Basilike* surveyed, the prayers are set off from the main body of the chapters with italics. The italics are eliminated here for readability.

8. Raymond describes the development of representations of Charles during the period of his imprisonment, noting that "[i]ncreasingly, Charles became presented as a lonely victim" ("Popular Representations," 60).

9. Girard, *Violence and the Sacred*, 5.

10. Ibid., 5.

11. Ibid., 12.

12. Ibid., 1.

13. Corns, *Uncloistered Virtue*, 88. On the figure of David in Charles's closing address, "To The Prince of Whales," see Skerpan Wheeler, "*Eikon Basilike* and the Rhetoric of Self-Representation," 126–29.

14. Whitehead, "*A Poena Et Culpa*."

15. Hamlin, *Psalm Culture*, 194–95.

16. Sharpe, "'Image Doting Rabble,'" 35.

17. Milton, *Eikonoklastes*, 360, 381–82. Subsequent citations will be parenthetical; all italics are original.

18. *Pseudo-Martyr Discovered*, 178–79. Cited in Daems and Nelson, *Eikon Basilike*, 28.

19. Sharpe, "'Image Doting Rabble,'" 33.

20. Wilson, *Psalterium Carolinum*, title page.

21. On the popularity and variety of psalters, see Hamlin, *Psalm Culture*, ch. 1 and 2.

22. See Psalms 7:10 and 55:24. Footnotes in Daems and Nelson, *Eikon Basilike*, indicate all references to Psalms, as well as those to Isaiah, Deuteronomy, and Hebrews that appear in this prayer.

23. This use of roman and italic type is a feature of all 1649 English editions of *Eikon Basilike*.

24. Daems and Nelson, *Eikon Basilike*, 26.

25. Bjorvand, "Religious Self-Fashioning," 43.

26. Skerpan Wheeler discusses several of the text's strategies for creating sympathy between Charles and ordinary English readers ("*Eikon Basilike* and the Rhetoric of Self-Representation").

27. Hamlin, *Psalm Culture*, 173.

28. In chapter 19 of *Eikon Basilike*, Charles states, "I am guilty in this War of nothing, but this, That I gave such advantages to some men, by confirming their power, which they knew not to use with that modesty, and gratitude, which became their Loyalty and My confidence" (153). This is characteristic of Charles's approach to guilt and blame throughout: he essentially declares himself innocent by claiming that his only error was in trusting people who turned out to be untrustworthy. In other words, it is they, not he, who are guilty.

29. Hamlin, *Psalm Culture*, 193.

30. Corns suggests even more strongly that Charles's abandonment of Strafford met with approval: "With a perverse genius, *Eikon Basilike* offers as his sin one of the very few actions Charles performed in 1640 which secured the support of his parliamentary opponents" (*Uncloistered Virtue*, 89).

31. In "Writings of James VI and I" and "Writings of Charles I," Sharpe outlines the notions of conscience Charles inherited from James, a number of which are articulated in the book James addressed to the future king (first Henry, then Charles), *Basilicon Doron*.

32. Perkins, *Discourse of Conscience*, 6.

33. Ibid., 9, 6. James uses the phrase "little God" to describe the role of the king in James I, *Basilicon Doron*, 12. This anticipates Charles's belief that the conscience rules the king just as the king rules the kingdom.

34. See Perkins, *Cases of Conscience*. For a discussion of the range and popularity of casuistical literature in the seventeenth century, consult Slights, *Casuistical Tradition*, esp. ch. 1 and 2, and Nowak, "Witness of the Times."

35. Perkins, *Discourse of Conscience*, 3. In accordance with casuists both Catholic and Protestant, Perkins also maintains that it is a sin to act with a doubting conscience (41).

36. Sharpe, "Writings of Charles I," 653.

37. Girard, *Violence and the Sacred*, 1.

38. Shakespeare, *Othello*, 4.1.19.

39. Perkins, *Discourse of Conscience*, 7, 8.

40. Ibid., 7.

41. Ibid., 7–8.

42. This final phrase is a paraphrase of 1 Corinthians 4:5.

43. Gallagher discusses Queen Elizabeth's deferral to conscience in the case of Mary, Queen of Scots, providing an illuminating contrast to Charles's treatment of conscience. He writes: "The official record of Elizabeth's words and actions during the critical period when the conscience of the queen was most susceptible to public judgment—both before and after the sentencing and execution of her cousin—provided ample evidence that any attempt to read, to scrutinize and judge, her conscience was destined to be frustrated by what appeared to be the inherent *aporia* of such an act. Elizabeth conveyed the message that to read the monarch's conscience was, by definition, to misread it; and, by misreading it, to affirm what the queen herself had not explicitly set up as a claim that might be disputed or subjected to critical interrogation: the inviolability of the monarch's conscience. In other words, Elizabeth tailored the deconstructive operation of the discourse of conscience in order to disable an implicit assault on a fundamental principle behind her divinely sanctioned, sovereign power" (*Medusa's Gaze*, 58). Thus while Elizabeth con-

structs power from the unknowable mystery of her regal conscience, insisting that any attempts to read it must encounter an ever-receding horizon, Charles seeks precisely the opposite: he wants to translate the illegible content of conscience into the text of *Eikon Basilike,* thereby ratifying both the institution and the person of the king.

44. Sharpe discusses the importance of the royal marriage in the representation of Charles and the monarchy during the early years of his reign ("'So Hard a Text,'" 387–89).

45. *The Kings Cabinet Opened,* 43 (quoted in Raymond, "Popular Representations," 58); Raymond, "Popular Representations," 59.

46. Raymond, "Popular Representations," 60, 53. See also Sharpe, "'So Hard a Text,'" 390–91.

47. Sharpe, "'So Hard a Text,'" 391.

48. Cable, "Milton's Iconoclastic Truth," 138.

49. Corns, *Uncloistered Virtue,* 205.

50. Thomas writes, "The process by which Protestant theologians shifted from maintaining that it was sinful to follow an erroneous conscience to upholding the view that all that mattered was the sincerity of intention has yet to be fully documented. Yet this transition, it has been rightly said, was the origin of the modern, more secular, belief that, whatever we do, we retain our moral integrity so long as we obey our consciences" ("Cases of Conscience," 52).

51. Zaller connects the representation of Charles as a tyrant—both in Milton's text and in the discourse of his condemnation—to the figure of the pope and to iconographic and dramatic traditions of tyranny: "The tyrant was familiar in the classical protype of Tiburius and Nero; as a stage figure, who had strutted before provincial audiences for centuries in the mystery and miracle plays; as a persecutor of the faithful, depicted in countless sermons as an Ahab or a Nebuchadnezzar" ("Breaking the Vessels," 768). See also Zaller's "Figure of the Tyrant."

52. On the relationship between Milton's characterization of Charles and the Satan of *Paradise Lost* and *Paradise Regained,* see Bennett, "God, Satan, and King Charles" and Hughes, "Milton's *Eikon Basilike.*"

53. Shakespeare, *Merchant of Venice,* 1.3.93.

54. Guibbory, "Charles's Prayers," 287.

55. Psalm 78:36–37. Like many texts of the period, *Eikonoklastes* italicizes passages from scripture.

56. Milton, *Paradise Lost,* 2.

57. Not all editions of *Eikon Basilike* agree at this passage. Some read "trampl'd" instead of "acted."

58. Milton is not the first author to insinuate the generic incompatibility of martyrology and the works of Shakespeare. In a poem prefacing *The Life and Death of Mr. Edmund Geninges Priest,* John Gennings draws a comparison between the efficacious content of his book and the poetic, courtly entertainment provided by a work like *King Lear.* See Shell, *Shakespeare and Religion,* 94–100; Shell, "'Lives' of Edmund Gennings," 217–18; and Brownlow, "Jesuit Allusion."

59. See Daems and Nelson, *Eikon Basilike,* 205.

60. Zwicker, *Lines of Authority,* 39.

61. At the Restoration, January 30 was declared a feast day in honor of Charles the Martyr. Regarding the celebration of the feast day and representations of Charles after the Restoration, see Knoppers, "Reviving the Martyr King"; Lacey, *Cult of King Charles*; Potter, "Royal Martyr"; and Raymond, "Popular Representations," 65–66.

62. In his preface to *Eikonoklastes,* Milton complains that because of the King's Book, "they who before hated [Charles] for his high misgoverment, nay fought against him with display'd banners in the field, now applaud him and extoll him for the wisest and most religious Prince that liv'd" (345).

Postscript

1. The epigraph from Derderian comes from an address to an interfaith gathering of religious leaders and community members in Los Angeles on September 10, 2011, commemorating the tenth anniversary of the September 11 attacks. Derderian is primate of the Western Diocese of the Armenian Church and chair of the Los Angeles Council of Religious Leaders. See "Religious Leaders Honor Memory of 9/11 Victims."

2. *Saint of 9/11* is directed by Glenn Holsten and narrated by Sir Ian McKellen. Holsten's film was instrumental in establishing Judge's identity as a "gay saint." On Judge's gay iconicity, see Burke, "Gay Catholic Icon."

3. St. Mychal the Martyr Parish, "Mission Statement."

4. St. Mychal the Martyr Parish, introductory statement.

5. The parish website borrows this passage from the website of the Orthodox Church of America. See Orthodox-Catholic Church of America, "St. Mychal Judge."

6. See epigraph for the full quotation.

7. On the problematic construction of national piety from the events of September 11, see Simpson, *Culture of Commemoration.*

Works Cited

Alfield, Thomas. *A true reporte of the death & martyrdome of M. Campion Jesuite and preiste, & M. Sherwin, & M. Bryan preistes, at Tiborne the first of December 1581.* 1582.

Alford, John A. "The Scriptural Self." In *The Bible in the Middle Ages: Its Influence on Literature and Art,* edited by Bernard S. Levy, 1–21. Binghamton: Medieval and Renaissance Texts and Studies, 1992.

Allen, William. *A Briefe Historie of the Glorious Martyrdom of XII Reverend Priests, executed within these twelvemonthes for confession and defence of the Catholike faith. But under the false pretence of Treason.* 1582.

———. *A True, Sincere, and Modest Defense of English Catholics.* In *The Execution of Justice in England and A True, Sincere, and Modest Defense of English Catholics,* edited by Robert M. Kingdon. Ithaca: Cornell University Press, 1965.

Allison, Anthony F. "The Writings of Father Henry Garnet S.J. (1555–1606)." In *A Catalogue of Catholic Books in English Printed Abroad or Secretly in England, 1558–1640. Biographical Studies* 1, no. 1. London: Arundel, 1951. This journal is now called *Recusant History.*

An Ancient Editor's Note Book. In *The Catholics of York Under Elizabeth,* edited by John Morris, 2–59. London: Burns and Oates, 1891.

Aston, Margaret, and Elizabeth Ingram. "The Iconography of *Acts and Monuments.*" In *John Foxe and the English Reformation,* edited by David Loades, 66–142. Aldershot: Ashgate, 1994.

Baraz, Daniel. *Medieval Cruelty: Changing Perceptions, Late Antiquity to the Early Modern Period.* Ithaca: Cornell University Press, 2003.

Barlow, Thomas. *Brutum Fulmen: Or, the Bull of Pope Pius V. Concerning the Damnation, Excommunication, and Deposition of Q. Elizabeth.* London, 1681.

Barthes, Roland. "The Reality Effect." In *The Rustle of Language,* translated by Richard Howard, 141–48. New York: Hill and Wang, 1987.

Bauckham, Richard. *Tudor Apocalypse.* Oxford: Sutton Courtenay, 1978.

Beadle, Richard, and Pamela M. King, eds. *York Mystery Plays: A Selection in Modern Spelling.* New York: Oxford University Press, 1984.

Beckwith, Sarah. *Christ's Body: Identity, Culture and Society in Late Medieval Writings.* New York: Routledge, 1993.

———. *Signifying God: Social Relation and Symbolic Act in the York Corpus Christi Plays.* Chicago: University of Chicago Press, 2001.

Bennett, Joan S. "God, Satan, and King Charles: Milton's Royal Portraits." *PMLA* 92, no. 3 (1977): 441–57.

Betteridge, Thomas. "Truth and History in Foxe's *Acts and Monuments.*" In *John Foxe and His World,* edited by Christopher Highley and John N. King, 145–59. Burlington: Ashgate, 2002.

Bevington, David. *Medieval Drama.* Boston: Houghton Mifflin, 1975.

Bjorvand, Einar. "Religious Self-Fashioning and *The Book of Psalms.*" In *Self-Fashioning and Metamorphosis in Early Modern English Literature,* edited by Olav Lausund and Stein Haugom Olsen, 34–44. Oslo: Novus, 2003.

Blackstone, William. *Commentaries on the Laws of England.* Vol. 4. Edited by Joseph Chitty. London, 1826.

Blackwell, George. *Mr. George Blackwel, (Made by Pope Clement 8. Arch-Priest of England) his Answeres upon sundry his Examinations: Together, with his Approbation and taking of the Oath of Allegeance: And his Letter written to his Assistants, and brethren, mooving them not onely to take the said Oath, but to advise All Romish Catholikes so to doe.* London, 1607.

Bokenham, Osbern. *Legendys of Hooly Wummen.* Edited by Mary S. Serjeant-son. Early English Text Society OS 206. London: Oxford University Press, 1938.

Bourdieu, Pierre. *The Logic of Practice.* Translated by Richard Nice. Stanford: Stanford University Press, 1990.

Bowerstock, Glen W. *Martyrdom and Rome.* Cambridge: Cambridge University Press, 1995.

Boyarin, Daniel. *Dying for God: Martyrdom and the Making of Christianity and Judaism.* Stanford: Stanford University Press, 1999.

Breitenberg, Mark. "The Flesh Made Word: Foxe's *Acts and Monuments.*" *Renaissance and Reformation* 25, no. 4 (1989): 381–407.

Brown, Peter. *The Cult of the Saints: Its Rise and Function in Latin Christianity.* Chicago: University of Chicago Press, 1981.

Brownlow, Frank W. "A Jesuit Allusion to *King Lear.*" *Recusant History* 28, no. 3 (2007): 416–23.

Bruster, Douglas. "Shakespeare and the Composite Text." In *Renaissance Literature and Its Formal Engagements,* edited by Mark David Rasmussen, 43–66. New York: Palgrave, 2002.

Burghley, William Cecil. *The Execution of Justice in England.* In *The Execution of Justice in England and A True, Sincere, and Modest Defense of English Catholics,* edited by Robert M. Kingdon. Ithaca: Cornell University Press, 1965.

Burke, Daniel. "Gay Catholic Icon Rev. Mychal Judge." *Huffington Post,* September 22, 2011, http://www.huffingtonpost.com/2011/08/25/gay -catholic_n_937205.html.

Burks, Deborah. "Polemical Potency: The Witness of Word and Woodcut." In *John Foxe and His World,* edited by Christopher Highley and John N. King, 263–76. Burlington: Ashgate, 2002.

Byman, Seymour. "Suicide and Alienation: Martyrdom in Tudor England." *Psychoanalytic Review* 61, no. 3 (1974): 355–73.

Cable, Lana. "Milton's Iconoclastic Truth." In *Politics, Poetics, and Hermeneutics in Milton's Prose,* edited by David Loewenstein and James Grantham Turner, 135–52. Cambridge: Cambridge University Press, 1990.

Caraman, Philip. *Henry Garnet, 1555–1606, and the Gunpowder Plot.* London: Longmans, 1964.

The Chester Mystery Cycle. Edited by R. M. Lumiansky and David Mills. Early English Text Society SS 3, 9. New York: Oxford University Press, 1974.

Christianson, Paul. *Reformers and Babylon: English Apocalyptic Visions from the Reformation to the Eve of the Civil War.* Toronto: University of Toronto Press, 1978.

Coffey, John. *Persecution and Toleration in Protestant England 1558–1689.* New York: Longman, 2000.

Cohen, Esther. *The Modulated Scream: Pain in Late Medieval Culture.* Chicago: University of Chicago Press, 2010.

———. "Towards a History of European Physical Sensibility: Pain in the Later Middle Ages." *Science in Context* 8, no. 1 (1995): 47–74.

Cohen, Stephen. "Between Form and Culture: New Historicism and the Promise of a Historical Formalism." In *Renaissance Literature and Its Formal Engagements,* edited by Mark David Rasmussen, 17–41. New York: Palgrave, 2002.

———, ed. *Shakespeare and Historical Formalism.* Aldershot: Ashgate, 2007.

Collinson, Patrick. *Elizabethan Essays.* London: Hambledon, 1994.

———. "John Foxe and National Consciousness." In *John Foxe and His World,* edited by Christopher Highley and John N. King, 10–36. Burlington: Ashgate, 2002.

Constantinou, Stavroula. *Female Corporeal Performances: Reading the Body in Byzantine Passsions and Lives of Holy Women.* Stockholm: Elanders Gotab, 2005.

Coogan, Michael D., ed. *The New Oxford Annotated Apocrypha.* 3rd ed. Oxford: Oxford University Press, 2001.

Corns, Thomas N. *Uncloistered Virtue: English Political Literature, 1640–1660.* Oxford: Oxford University Press, 1992.

Corthell, Ronald J. "'The Secrecy of Man': Recusant Discourse and the Elizabethan Subject." *English Literary Renaissance* 19, no. 3 (1989): 272–90.

Corthell, Ronald, Frances E. Dolan, Christopher Highley, and Arthur F. Marotti, eds. *Catholic Culture in Early Modern England.* Notre Dame: University of Notre Dame Press, 2007.

Covington, Sarah. *The Trail of Martyrdom: Persecution and Resistance in Sixteenth-Century England.* Notre Dame: University of Notre Dame Press, 2003.

Cross, Claire. "An Elizabethan Martyrologist and His Martyr: John Mush and Margaret Clitherow." In *Martyrs and Martyrologies,* edited by Diana Wood, 271–82. Studies in Church History 30. Oxford: Blackwell for the Ecclesiastical History Society, 1993.

The Croxton Play of the Sacrament. In *Non-Cycle Plays and Fragments,* edited by Norman Davis. Early English Text Society SS 1. New York: Oxford University Press, 1970.

Daems, Jim, and Holly Faith Nelson, eds. *Eikon Basilike with Selections from Eikonoklastes.* Ontario: Broadview, 2006.

Davidson, Clifford. "The Realism of the York Realist and the York Passion." *Speculum* 50 (1975): 270–83.

Devlin, Christopher. *The Life of Robert Southwell, Poet and Martyr.* New York: Longmans, 1956.

Dillon, Anne. *The Construction of Martyrdom in the English Catholic Community, 1535–1603.* Burlington: Ashgate, 2002.

Dolan, Frances E. *Whores of Babylon: Catholicism, Gender, and Seventeenth-Century Print Culture.* Notre Dame: University of Notre Dame Press, 2001.

Donne, John. *Biathanatos.* In *Selected Prose,* edited by Neil Rhodes, 61–85. New York: Penguin, 1987.

———. *Pseudo-Martyr.* Edited by Anthony Raspa. Montreal: McGill-Queen's University Press, 1993.

Dudley, Scott. "Conferring with the Dead: Necrophilia and Nostalgia in the Seventeenth Century." *English Literary History* 66, no. 2 (1999): 277–94.

Dutton, Richard. *Ben Jonson, Volpone, and the Gunpowder Plot.* Cambridge: Cambridge University Press, 2008.

Earl, James. "Typology and Iconographic Style in Early Medieval Hagiography." *Studies in the Literary Imagination* 8, no. 1 (1975): 15–46.

Easton, Martha. "Pain, Torture and Death in the Huntington Library *Legenda Aurea.*" In *Gender and Holiness: Men, Women, and Saints in Late Medieval Europe,* edited by Samantha J. E. Riches and Sarah Salih, 49–64. New York: Routledge, 2002.

Edwards, Francis, ed. *The Gunpowder Plot: The Narrative of Oswald Tesimond Alias Greenway.* London: Folio Society, 1973.

Elton, G. R., ed. *The Tudor Constitution: Documents and Commentary.* Cambridge: Cambridge University Press, 1965.

Enders, Jody. *The Medieval Theater of Cruelty: Rhetoric, Memory, Violence.* Ithaca: Cornell University Press, 1999.

Eusebius. *The Auncient Ecclesiasticall Histories of the First Six Hundred Yeares after Christ.* Translated by Meredith Hanmer. London, 1577.

Eusebius. *The Ecclesiastical History.* Translated by Kirsopp Lake (vol. 1) and J. E. L. Oulton and H. J. Lawlor (vol. 2). New York: Putnam's Sons, 1926–32.

Fairfield, Leslie P. "John Bale and the Development of Protestant Hagiography in England." *Journal of Ecclesiastical History* 24, no. 2 (1973): 145–60.

Firth, Katharine R. *The Apocalyptic Tradition in Reformation Britain, 1530–1645.* New York: Oxford University Press, 1979.

Floyd, John. *Purgatories Triumph Over Hell.* London, 1913.

Foucault, Michel. *Discipline and Punish: The Birth of the Prison.* Translated by Alan Sheridan. New York: Vintage, 1977.

Foxe, John. *Actes and Monuments.* London, 1583.

Fraser, Antonia. *Faith and Treason: The Story of the Gunpowder Plot.* New York: Doubleday, 1996.

Freeman, Thomas S. "Fate, Faction, and Fiction in Foxe's *Book of Martyrs.*" *The Historical Journal* 43, no. 3 (2000): 601–23.

Fuchs, Barbara. "Forms of Engagement." *Modern Language Quarterly* 67, no. 1 (2006): 1–6.

Gallagher, Lowell. *Medusa's Gaze: Casuistry and Conscience in the Renaissance.* Stanford: Stanford University Press, 1991.

Gardiner, S. R. "Two Declarations of Garnet Relating to the Gunpowder Plot." *English Historical Review* 3 (1888): 510–19.

Garnet, Henry. *A Treatise of Equivocation.* Edited by David Jardine. London: Longmans, 1851.

Gennings, John. *The Life and Death of Mr. Edmund Geninges Priest.* 1614.

Gerard, John. *The Autobiography of a Hunted Priest.* Translated by Philip Caraman. New York: Pellegrini & Cudahy, 1952.

———. *Narrative of the Gunpowder Plot.* In *The Conditions of Catholics Under James I,* edited by John Morris. London: Longmans, 1871.

Girard, René. *Violence and the Sacred.* Translated by Patrick Gregory. Baltimore: Johns Hopkins University Press, 1979.

Gravdal, Kathryn. *Ravishing Maidens: Writing Rape in Medieval French Literature and Law.* Philadelphia: University of Pennsylvania Press, 1991.

Greenblatt, Stephen, ed. *The Norton Anthology of English Literature.* 8th ed. Vol. B. New York: Norton, 2006.

Gregory, Brad S. *Salvation at Stake: Christian Martyrdom in Early Modern Europe.* Cambridge: Harvard University Press, 1999.

Group Phi. "Doing Genre." In *New Formalisms and Literary Theory,* edited by Verena Theil and Linda Treddenick. New York: Palgrave, forthcoming 2012.

Guibbory, Ashsah. "Charles's Prayers, Idolatrous Images, and True Creation in Milton's *Eikonoklastes.*" In *Of Poetry and Politics: New Essays on Milton and His World,* edited by P. G. Stanwood, 283–94. Binghamton: Medieval and Renaissance Texts and Studies, 1995.

Haller, William. *The Elect Nation: The Meaning and Relevance of Foxe's Book of Martyrs.* New York: Harper & Row, 1963.

Hamilton, Donna B. *Anthony Munday and the Catholics, 1560–1633.* Aldershot: Ashgate, 2005.

Hamlin, Hannibal. *Psalm Culture and Early Modern English Literature.* Cambridge: Cambridge University Press, 2004.

Hanmer, Meredith. *The great bragge and challenge of M. Champion a Jesuite, commonlye called Edmunde Campion, latelye arrived in Englande, contayninge nyne articles here severallye laide downe, directed by him to the Lordes of the Counsail, confuted & aunswered by Meredith Hanmer, M. of Art, and Student in Divinitie.* London, 1581.

Harpsfield, Nicholas. *Dialogi Sex.* Antwerp, 1566.

Heffernan, Thomas J. *Sacred Biography: Saints and Their Biographers in the Middle Ages.* New York: Oxford University Press, 1988.

Highley, Christopher, and John N. King, eds. *John Foxe and His World.* Burlington: Ashgate, 2002.

Hodgetts, Michael. *Secret Hiding Places.* Dublin: Veritas, 1989.

Höfele, Andreas. "Stages of Martyrdom: John Foxe's *Actes and Monuments.*" In *Performances of the Sacred in Late Medieval and Early Modern England,* edited by Susanne Rupp and Tobias Döring, 81–94. New York: Rodopi, 2005.

Hogarde, Miles. *The Displaying of the Protestantes.* London, 1556.

Holmes, Peter. *Resistance and Compromise: The Political Thought of the Elizabethan Catholics.* New York: Cambridge University Press, 1982.

Holtby, Richard. "On the Persecution in the North." In *The Catholics of York Under Elizabeth,* edited by John Morris, 103–219. London: Burns and Oates, 1891.

Howell, T. B., ed. *Cobbett's Complete Collection of State Trials.* Vol. 1. London, 1816.

Hughes, Merritt Y. "Milton's *Eikon Basilike.*" In *Calm of Mind: Contemporary Essays on* Paradise Regained *and* Samson Agonistes *in Honor of John S. Diekhoff,* edited by Joseph Anthony Wittreich, 1–24. Cleveland: Press of Case Western Reserve University, 1971.

Hughes, Paul L., and James F. Larkin, eds. *Tudor Royal Proclamations 1588–1603.* New Haven: Yale University Press, 1969.

Hutson, Lorna. *The Invention of Suspicion: Law and Mimesis in Shakespeare and Renaissance Drama.* Oxford: Oxford University Press, 2007.

Innes-Parker, Catherine. "Sexual Violence and the Female Reader: Symbolic 'Rape' in the Saints' Lives of the Katherine Group." *Women's Studies* 24 (1995): 205–17.

Jackson, Ken, and Arthur F. Marotti. "The Turn to Religion in Early Modern English Studies." *Criticism* 46, no. 1 (2004): 167–90.

Jacobus de Voragine. *Legenda Aurea.* Osnabruck: O. Zeller, 1969.

———. *The Golden Legend: Readings on the Saints.* Translated by William Granger Ryan. 2 vols. Princeton: Princeton University Press, 1993.

James I. *Basilicon Doron.* In *Political Works of James I,* edited by Charles Howard McIlwain, 3–52. Cambridge: Harvard University Press, 1918.

———. *Triplici Nodo, triplex cuneus. Or an Apologie for the Oath of Allegiance. Against the two Breves of Pope Paulus Quintus, and the late Letter of Cardinall Bellarmine to G. Blackwel the Arch-priest.* London, 1607.

Jameson, Fredric. *The Political Unconscious: Narrative as a Socially Symbolic Act.* Ithaca: Cornell University Press, 1981.

Janelle, Pierre. *Robert Southwell, the Writer: A Study in Religious Inspiration.* London: Sheed and Ward, 1935.

Kelly, Henry Ansgar. "Inquisitorial Due Process and the Status of Secret Crimes." In *Proceedings of the Eighth International Congress of Medieval Canon Law,* edited by Stanley Chodorow, 407–27. Citta del Vaticano: Biblioteca Apostolica Vaticana, 1992.

Kilroy, Gerard. *Edmund Campion: Memory and Transcription.* Aldershot: Ashgate, 2005.

King, John N. "Fiction and Fact in Foxe's *Book of Martyrs.*" In *John Foxe and the English Reformation,* edited by David Loades, 12–35. Burlington: Ashgate, 1997.

The Kings Cabinet opened. London, 1645.

Knachel, Philip, ed. *Eikon Basilike: The Portraiture of His Sacred Majesty in His Solitudes and Sufferings.* Ithaca: Cornell University Press for the Folger Shakespeare Library, 1966.

Knoppers, Laura L. "Reviving the Martyr King: Charles I as Jacobite Icon." In *The Royal Image: Representations of Charles I,* edited by Thomas N. Corns, 263–87. Cambridge: Cambridge University Press, 1999.

Knott, John R. *Discourses of Martyrdom in English Literature, 1563–1694.* Cambridge: Cambridge University Press, 1993.

———. "John Foxe and the Joy of Suffering." *Sixteenth Century Journal* 27, no. 3 (1996): 721–34.

Knott, John R., Jr. "'Suffering for Truths Sake': Milton and Martyrdom." In *Politics, Poetics, and Hermeneutics in Milton's Prose,* edited by David Loewenstein and James Grantham Turner, 153–70. Cambridge: Cambridge University Press, 1966.

Kolve, V. A. *The Play Called Corpus Christi.* Stanford: Stanford University Press, 1966.

Lacey, Andrew. *The Cult of King Charles the Martyr.* Rochester: Boydell, 2003.

———. "Elegies and Commemorative Verse in Honour of Charles the Martyr, 1649–60." In *The Regicides and the Execution of Charles I,* edited by Jason Peacey, 225–46. New York: Palgrave, 2001.

Lake, Peter. "Anti-Popery: The Structure of a Prejudice." In *Conflict in Early Stuart England: Studies in Religion and Politics, 1603–1642,* edited by Richard Cust and Ann Hughes, 72–106. New York: Longman, 1989.

Lake, Peter, and Michael Questier. *The Antichrist's Lewd Hat: Protestants, Papists and Players in Post-Reformation England.* New Haven: Yale University Press, 2002.

———. "Margaret Clitherow, Catholic Nonconformity, Martyrology and the Politics of Religious Change in Elizabethan England." *Past and Present* 185 (2004): 43–90.

———. *The Trials of Margaret Clitherow: Persecution, Martyrdom, and the Politics of Sanctity in Elizabethan England.* London: Continuum, 2011.

Lampe, G. W. H. "Martyrdom and Inspiration." In *Suffering and Martyrdom in the New Testament: Studies Presented to G. M. Styler,* edited by William Horbury and Brian McNeil, 118–35. Cambridge: Cambridge University Press, 1981.

Law, Thomas. *A Historical Sketch of the Conflicts between Jesuits and Seculars in the Reign of Queen Elizabeth.* London, 1889.

Lemon, Rebecca. *Treason by Words: Literature, Law, and Rebellion in Shakespeare's England.* Ithaca: Cornell University Press, 2006.

Levin, Carole. "Women in *The Book of Martyrs* as Models of Behavior in Tudor England." *International Journal of Women's Studies* 4, no. 2 (1981): 196–207.

Levinson, Marjorie. "What Is New Formalism?" *PMLA* 122, no. 2 (2007): 558–69.

Levy, F. J. *Tudor Historical Thought.* San Marino: Huntington Library, 1967.

The life and reigne of king Charls or, the pseudo-martyr discovered. London, 1651.

Loades, David, ed. *John Foxe and the English Reformation.* Brookfield: Scolar Press, 1997.

Longley, Katharine M. *Saint Margaret Clitherow.* Wheathampstead: Anthony Clarke, 1986.

Lupton, Julia Reinhard. *Afterlives of the Saints: Hagiography, Typology, and Renaissance Literature.* Stanford: Stanford University Press, 1996.

———. *Citizen-Saints: Shakespeare and Political Theology.* Chicago: University of Chicago Press, 2005.

Macek, Ellen. "The Emergence of a Feminine Spirituality in the *Book of Martyrs.*" *Sixteenth Century Journal* 19, no. 1 (1988): 63–80.

Madan, Francis F. *A New Bibliography of the Eikon Basilike of King Charles the First.* Oxford: Oxford University Press, 1950.

Manley, Lawrence. *Literature and Culture in Early Modern London.* Cambridge: Cambridge University Press, 2005.

Marotti, Arthur F. "Alienating Catholics in Early Modern England: Recusant Women, Jesuits, and Ideological Fantasies." In *Catholicism and Anti-Catholicism in Early Modern England,* edited by Arthur F. Marotti, 1–34. New York: St. Martin's, 1999.

———. *Religious Ideology and Cultural Fantasy: Catholic and Anti-Catholic Discourses in Early Modern England.* Notre Dame: University of Notre Dame Press, 2005.

Marshall, Cynthia. *The Shattering of the Self: Violence, Subjectivity, and Early Modern Texts.* Baltimore: Johns Hopkins University Press, 2002.

Mason, Henry. *The New Art of Lying, Covered by Jesuites under the Vaile of Equivocation.* London, 1624.

Matchinske, Megan. *Writing, Gender, and State in Early Modern England.* Cambridge: Cambridge University Press, 1998.

Mills, David, ed. *The Chester Mystery Cycle: A New Edition with Modernised Spelling.* East Lansing: Colleagues Press, 1992.

Mills, Robert. "Can the Virgin Martyr Speak?" *Medieval Virginities,* edited by Anke Bernau, Ruth Evans, and Sarah Salih, 187–213. Cardiff: University of Wales Press, 2003.

Milton, John. *Eikonoklastes.* In *Complete Prose Works of John Milton,* Vol. 3, edited by Merritt Y. Hughes, 335–601. New Haven: Yale University Press, 1962.

———. *Paradise Lost.* Edited by Gordon Teskey. New York: Norton, 2005.

Milward, Peter. *Religious Controversies of the Elizabethan Age: A Survey of Printed Sources.* London: Scholar, 1977.

———. *Religious Controversies of the Jacobean Age: A Survey of Printed Sources.* Lincoln: University of Nebraska Press, 1978.

Monta, Susannah Brietz. *Martyrdom and Literature in Early Modern England.* Cambridge: Cambridge University Press, 2005.

Montrose, Louis. "Professing the Renaissance: The Poetics and Politics of Culture." In *The New Historicism,* edited by H. Aram Veeser and Stanley Fish, 15–36. New York: Routledge, 1989.

Mozley, J. F. *John Foxe and His Book.* New York: Macmillan, 1940.

Mueller, Janel. "Pain, Persecution, and the Construction of Selfhood in Foxe's *Acts and Monuments.*" In *Religion and Culture in Renaissance England,* edited by Claire McEachern and Debora Shuger, 161–87. Cambridge: Cambridge University Press, 1997.

Mullaney, Stephen. *The Place of the Stage: License, Play, and Power in Renaissance England.* Chicago: University of Chicago Press, 1988.

Murray, Arthur. *Suicide in the Middle Ages.* 2 vols. Oxford: Oxford University Press, 2000.

Murray, Molly. *The Poetics of Conversion in Early Modern English Literature: Verse and Change from Donne to Dryden.* Cambridge: Cambridge University Press, 2009.

Mush, John. *A True Report of the Life and Martyrdom of Mrs. Margaret Clitherow.* In *The Catholics of York Under Elizabeth,* edited by John Morris, 331–440. London: Burns and Oates, 1891.

Myers, Anne M. "Father John Gerard's Object Lessons: Relics and Devotional Objects in *Autobiography of a Hunted Priest.*" In *Catholic Culture in Early Modern England,* edited by Ronald Corthell, Frances E. Dolan, Christopher Highley, and Arthur F. Marotti, 216–35. Notre Dame: University of Notre Dame Press, 2007.

The Northern Passion. Early English Text Society OS 183. Edited by Wilhelm Heuser and Frances A. Foster. London: Oxford University Press, 1930.

Nowak, Thomas S. "Propaganda and the Pulpit: Robert Cecil, William Barlow and the Essex and Gunpowder Plots." In *The Witness of Times: Manifestations of Ideology in Seventeenth Century England,* edited by Katherine Z. Keller and Gerald J. Schiffhorst, 34–52. Pittsburgh: Duquesne University Press, 1993.

The N-Town Play. Edited by Stephen Spector. Early English Text Society SS 11, 12. Oxford: Oxford University Press, 1991.

Oliver, Sophie. "Sacred and (Sub)Human Pain: Witnessing Bodies in Early Modern Hagiography and Contemporary Spectatorship of Atrocity." In *Promoting and Producing Evil,* edited by Nancy Billias, 111–30. Amsterdam: Rodopi, 2011.

Olsen, V. Norskov. *John Foxe and the Elizabethan Church.* Berkeley: University of California Press, 1973.

The Orthodox-Catholic Church of America. "St. Mychal Judge." http://www.orthodoxcatholicchurch.org/saints.html.

Palmer, Daryl W. "Histories of Violence and the Writer's Hand: Foxe's *Actes and Monuments* and Shakespeare's *Titus Andronicus.*" In *Reading and Writing in Shakespeare,* edited by David M. Bergeron, 82–115. Newark: University of Delaware Press, 1996.

Parsons, Robert. *A treatise of three conversions of England from Paganisme to Christian Religion.* 1603.

A particular declaration or testimony, of the undutifull and traiterous affection borne against her Majestie by Edmond Campion Jesuite, and other condemned priestes. London, 1582.

Perkins, Judith. *The Suffering Self: Pain and Narrative Representation in the Early Christian Era.* New York: Routledge, 1995.

Perkins, William. *The Discourse of Conscience.* In *William Perkins 1558–1602,* edited by Thomas F. Merrill. The Hague: De Graff, 1966.

———. *The Whole Treatise of the Cases of Conscience.* In *William Perkins 1558–1602,* edited by Thomas F. Merrill. The Hague: De Graff, 1966.

Persons, Robert. *A Briefe Apologie, or Defence of the Catholike Ecclesiastical Hierarchie, & Subordination of England.* 1602.

———. *A Treatise Tending to Mitigation Towardes Catholicke-Subjectes in England.* 1607.

Peters, Christine. *Patterns of Piety: Women, Gender, and Religion in Late Medieval and Reformation England.* Cambridge: Cambridge University Press, 2003.

Pettegree, Andrew. "Haemstede and Foxe." In *John Foxe and the English Reformation,* edited by David Loades, 278–94. Burlington: Ashgate, 1997.

———. "Illustrating the Book: A Protestant Dilemma." In *John Foxe and His World,* edited by Christopher Highley and John N. King, 133–44. Burlington: Ashgate, 2002.

Pollen, John Hungerford, ed. *Acts of the English Martyrs Hitherto Unpublished.* London: Burns and Oates, 1891.

————, ed. *Unpublished Documents Relating to the English Martyrs.* London: Catholic Record Society, 1908.

Potter, Lois. "The Royal Martyr in the Restoration." In *The Royal Image: Representations of Charles I,* edited by Thomas N. Corns, 240–62. Cambridge: Cambridge University Press, 1999.

Propp, Vladimir. *Morphology of the Folktale.* Translated by Laurence Scott. 2nd ed. Austin: University of Texas Press, 1968.

Questier, Michael C. *Catholicism and Community in Early Modern England: Politics, Aristocratic Patronage and Religion, c. 1550–1640.* Cambridge: Cambridge University Press, 2006.

————. "Loyalty, Religion, and State Power in Early Modern England: English Romanism and the Jacobean Oath of Allegiance." *Historical Journal* 40, no. 2 (1997): 311–29.

Rasmussen, Mark David, ed. *Renaissance Literature and Its Formal Engagements.* New York: Palgrave, 2002.

Raymond, Joad. "Popular Representations of Charles I." In *The Royal Image: Representations of Charles I,* edited by Thomas N. Corns, 47–73. Cambridge: Cambridge University Press, 1999.

Reames, Sherry. *The Legenda Aurea: A Reexamination of Its Paradoxical History.* Madison: University of Wisconsin Press, 1985.

Robinson, Benedict S. *Islam and Early Modern English Literature.* New York: Palgrave, 2007.

Robinson, Marsha S. "Doctors, Silly Poor Women, and Rebel Whores: The Gendering of Conscience in Foxe's *Acts and Monuments.*" In *John Foxe and His World,* edited by Christopher Highley and John N. King, 235–48. Burlington: Ashgate, 2002.

Roper, William. *The Life of Sir Thomas More.* In *Two Early Tudor Lives,* edited by Richard S. Sylvester and Davis P. Harding, 195–254. New Haven: Yale University Press, 1962.

Ross, Ellen M. *The Grief of God: Images of the Suffering Jesus in Late Medieval England.* New York: Oxford University Press, 1997.

Roston, Murray. *Biblical Drama in England from the Middle Ages to the Present Day.* Evanston: Northwestern University Press, 1968.

Rubin, Miri. "Choosing Death? Experiences of Martyrdom in Late Medieval Europe." In *Martyrs and Martyrologies,* edited by Diana Wood, 153–83. Studies in Church History 30. Oxford: Blackwell for the Ecclesiastical History Society, 1993.

Saint of 9/11. Directed by Glenn Holsten. IFC Films, 2006.

Salih, Sarah. "Performing Virginity: Sex and Violence in the Katherine Group." In *Constructions of Widowhood and Virginity in the Middle Ages,* edited by Cindy Carlson and Angela Jane Weisl, 95–112. New York: St. Martin's, 1999.

Sanok, Catherine. "Legends of Good Women: Hagiography and Women's Intervention in Late Medieval Literature." PhD dissertation, University of California, Los Angeles, 2000.

Saunders, Corinne. *Rape and Ravishment in the Literature of Medieval England.* Cambridge: Brewer, 2001.

Scarry, Elaine. *The Body in Pain: The Making and Unmaking of the World.* New York: Oxford University Press, 1985.

Scott, James C. *Domination and the Arts of Resistance: Hidden Transcripts.* New Haven: Yale University Press, 1990.

Shakespeare, William. *The Merchant of Venice.* Edited by John Russell Brown. 2nd ed. London: Arden Shakespeare, 1964.

———. *Othello.* Edited by A. J. Honigman. 3rd ed. London: Arden Shakespeare, 1996.

Sharpe, Kevin. "'An Image Doting Rabble': The Failure of Republican Culture in Seventeenth-Century England." In *Refiguring Revolutions: Aesthetics and Politics from the English Revolution to the Romantic Revolution,* edited by Kevin Sharpe and Steven N. Zwicker, 25–56. Berkeley: University of California Press, 1998.

———. "Private Conscience and Public Duty in the Writings of Charles I." *The Historical Journal* 40, no. 3 (1997): 643–65.

———. "Private Conscience and Public Duty in the Writings of James VI and I." In *Public Duty and Private Conscience in Seventeenth-Century England,* edited by John Morrill, Paul Slack, and Daniel Woolf, 77–100. Oxford: Clarendon, 1993.

———. "'So Hard a Text'? Images of Charles I, 1612–1700." *The Historical Journal* 43, no. 2 (2000): 383–405.

Sheldon, Richard. *A Survey of the Miracles of the Church of Rome, Proving Them to Be Antichristian.* London, 1616.

Shell, Alison. *Catholicism, Controversy, and the English Literary Imagination.* Cambridge: Cambridge University Press, 1999.

———. *Oral Culture and Catholicism in Early Modern England.* Cambridge: Cambridge University Press, 2009.

———. "The Seventeenth-Century 'Lives' of Edmund Gennings (1566–91)." *Recusant History* 30, no. 2 (2010): 213–28.

———. *Shakespeare and Religion.* Arden Critical Companions. London: Methuen, 2010.

Simpson, David. *9/11: The Culture of Commemoration.* Chicago: University of Chicago Press, 2006.

Skerpan, Elizabeth. "Rhetorical Genres and the *Eikon Basilike*." *Explorations in Renaissance Culture* 2 (1985): 99–111.

Skerpan Wheeler, Elizabeth. "*Eikon Basilike* and the Rhetoric of Self-Representation." In *The Royal Image: Representations of Charles I,* edited by Thomas N. Corns, 122–40. Cambridge: Cambridge University Press, 1999.

Slights, Camille Wells. *The Casuistical Tradition in Shakespeare, Donne, Herbert, and Milton.* Princeton: Princeton University Press, 1981.

Sommerville, Johann P. *King James VI and I: Political Writings.* Cambridge: Cambridge University Press, 1994.

The South English Legendary. Edited by Charlottte D'Evelyn and Anna J. Mill. Early English Text Society OS 235, 236, 244. London: Oxford University Press, 1956–1959.

Sponsler, Claire. *Drama and Resistance: Bodies, Goods, and Theatricality in Late Medieval England.* Minneapolis: University of Minnesota Press, 1997.

Squiers, Granville. *Secret Hiding Places: Origins, Histories and Descriptions of English Secret Hiding-Places Used by Priests, Cavaliers, Jacobites & Smugglers.* London: S. Paul, 1933.

St. Mychal the Martyr Parish. "Mission Statement." http://stmychalthemartyr.org/stmms.html.

———. Introductory statement. http://stmychalthemartyr.org/index.html.

State Papers Domestic of James I, 1603–1610. Vols. 18 and 19. British National Archives, Kew.

Sullivan, Ceri. "'Oppressed by the Force of Truth': Robert Persons Edits John Foxe." In *John Foxe: An Historical Perspective,* edited by David Loades, 154–66. Aldershot: Ashgate, 1999.

Tertullian. *Apoligeticus.* Translated by Alex Souter. Cambridge: Cambridge University Press, 1917.

Thomas, Keith. "Cases of Conscience in Seventeenth-Century England." In *Public Duty and Private Conscience in Seventeenth-Century England,* edited by John Morrill, Paul Slack, and Daniel Woolf, 29–56. Oxford: Clarendon, 1993.

The Towneley Plays. Edited by Martin Stevens and A. C. Cawley. Early English Text Society SS 13, 14. Oxford: Oxford University Press, 1994.

Travis, Peter W. "The Semiotics of Christ's Body in the English Cycles." In *Approaches to Teaching Medieval English Drama,* edited by Richard K. Emmerson, 67–78. New York: Modern Language Association, 1990.

Trevor-Roper, H. R. "*Eikon Basilike*: The Problem of the King's Book." In *Historical Essays.* London: Macmillan, 1957.

A True and perfect relation of the whole proceedings against the late most barbarous traitors, Garnet a Iesuite, and his confederats. London, 1606.

Tutino, Stefania. *Law and Conscience: Catholicism in Early Modern England, 1570–1625.* Burlington: Ashgate, 2007.

The Unabridged Acts and Monuments Online (1583 edition). Sheffield: HRI Online Publications, 2011, http//www.johnfoxe.org. Includes editorial commentary and additional information.

van Henten, Jan Willem. *The Maccabean Martyrs as Saviors of the Jewish People: A Study of 2 and 4 Maccabees.* Leiden: Brill, 1997.

Walsham, Alexandra. *Providence in Early Modern England.* Oxford: Oxford University Press, 1999.

Waugh, Margaret. *Blessed Nicholas Owen: Jesuit Brother and Maker of Hiding-Holes.* London: Office of the Vice-Postulation, 1961.

Western Diocese of the Armenian Church, Divan of the Diocese. "Religious Leaders Honor Memory of 9/11 Victims." *Western Diocese of the Armenian Church News,* September 16, 2011, http://www.armenianchurchwd.com/news/religious-leaders-honor-memory-of-9-11-victims/.

White, Helen C. *Tudor Books of Saints and Martyrs.* Madison: University of Wisconsin Press, 1963.

Whitehead, Lydia. "*A Poena Et Culpa*: Penitence, Confidence, and the *Miserere* in Foxe's *Acts and Monuments.*" *Renaissance Studies* 4, no. 3 (1990): 287–99.

Williams, Arnold. *The Characterization of Pilate in the Towneley Plays.* East Lansing: Michigan State College, 1950.

Wilson, John. *The English Martyrologe.* 1608.

———. *Psalterium Carolinum: The Devotions of his Sacred Majestie in his Solitudes and Sufferings, Rendered in Verse.* London, 1657.

Winstead, Karen. *Virgin Martyrs: Legends of Sainthood in Late Medieval England.* Ithaca: Cornell University Press, 1997.

Wooden, Warren W. *John Foxe.* Boston: Twayne, 1983.

Wooden, Wayne S., and Jay Parker. *Men Behind Bars: Sexual Exploitation in Prison.* New York: Plenum, 1982.

Woolf, Rosemary. *The English Mystery Plays.* London: Routledge, 1972.

Worthington, Thomas. *A Relation of Sixtene Martyrs: Glorified in England in Twelve Monethes. With a Declaration. That English Catholiques Suffer for the Catholique Religion. and That the Seminarie Priests agree with the Jesuites. In answer to Our Adversaries calumniations, touching these two points.* Douai, 1601.

Yates, Julian. *Error, Misuse, Failure: Object Lessons from the English Renaissance.* Minneapolis: University of Minnesota Press, 2003.

————. "Parasitic Geographies: Manifesting Catholic Identity in Early Modern England." In *Catholicism and Anti-Catholicism in Early Modern English Texts*, edited by Arthur F. Marotti, 35–62. New York: St. Martin's, 1999.

The York Plays. Edited by Richard Beadle. Early English Text Society SS 23, 24. New York: Oxford University Press, 2009.

"A Yorkshire Recusant's Relation." In *The Catholics of York Under Elizabeth*, edited by John Morris, 61–102. London: Burns and Oates, 1891.

Zagorin, Perez. *Ways of Lying: Dissimulation, Persecution, and Conformity in Early Modern Europe.* Cambridge: Harvard University Press, 1990.

Zaller, Robert. "Breaking the Vessels: The Desacralization of Monarchy in Early Modern England." *Sixteenth Century Journal* 29, no. 3 (1998): 757–78.

————. "The Figure of the Tyrant in English Revolutionary Thought." *Journal of the History of Ideas* 54, no. 4 (1993): 585–610.

Zollinger, Cynthia Wittman. "'The Booke, the Leafe, Yea and the Very Sentence': Sixteenth-Century Literacy in Text and Context." In *John Foxe and His World*, edited by Christopher Highley and John N. King, 102–16. Burlington: Ashgate, 2002.

Zucker, Adam. *The Places of Wit in Early Modern English Comedy.* Cambridge: Cambridge University Press, 2011.

Zwicker, Steven N. *Lines of Authority: Politics and English Literary Culture, 1649–1689.* Ithaca: Cornell University Press, 1993.

Index

Page numbers in italics indicate illustrations.

Alice Dailey
is associate professor of English at Villanova University.